S0-FBW-729

GREENBERG'S PRICE GUIDE

to LIONEL TRAINS: 1901-1942

by

Robert Pauli
Henry Edmunds
Roland LaVoie
James Sattler
Robert Friedman
and Bruce C. Greenberg

Edited by Roland LaVoie,

With the assistance of Philip Smith
and Bruce Greenberg

Photographs by:
Roger Bartelt and
by courtesy of Frank Hare, Iron Horse Publications
and Tom McComas of TM Productions

Greenberg Publishing Company
Sykesville, MD 21784
301 795-7447

Third Edition

Manufactured in the United States of America

Greenberg Publishing Company offers the world's largest selection of Lionel, American Flyer and other toy train publications as well as a selection of books on model and prototype railroading. To receive our current catalogue, send a stamped, self-addressed envelope marked "catalogue."

Greenberg Publishing Company sponsors the world's largest public model railroad shows. The shows feature extravagant operating model railroads for N, H0, 0, Standard and 1 Gauges as well as a huge marketplace for buying and selling nearly all model railroad equipment. The shows feature, as well, a large selection of doll house miniatures.

Shows are currently offered in New York, Philadelphia, Pittsburgh, Baltimore, and Washington, D.C. To receive our current show listing, please send a self-addressed stamped envelope marked "Train Show Schedule."

ISBN: 89778-502-9

Library of Congress Number: 82-082325

TABLE OF CONTENTS

ACKNOWLEDGEMENTS

The purpose of this book is to provide a comprehensive collector's guide with current prices for Lionel locomotives, rolling stock and accessories in 0, 0-27, Standard, 2-7/8 and 00 Gauges manufactured between 1901 and 1942. A listing of Lionel catalogues and instruction manuals is also included.

The research and writing of many talented and generous people have contributed to this book. **Reverend Robert Pauli** conducted research on 0 Gauge freight cars and dramatically increased our knowledge about these pieces. His effort was the largest and most comprehensive ever undertaken in Lionel prewar freight cars. His findings have laid the foundation for a new research field. **Henry Edmunds** and **Roland LaVoie** studied 10 and 100 Series Lionel freight cars and provided us with new insights into Lionel's development. **George Koff's** collection was the key resource for the study of Standard and 0 freight cars. George was a gracious host and helped **Robert Pauli, Henry Edmunds** and **Roland LaVoie** to conduct their lengthly studies of freight car variations. **Roger Bartelt,** staff photographer, took many of the clear and interesting black and white photos for this book,(more of which will appear in future editions). He also helped generate many of the concepts and causal analyses to explain Lionel's development. Roger's ideas were crucial in the writing of the introductory chapter: Four Factors in Understanding Lionel.

Dr. Robert Friedman wrote the comprehensive report on 00 Lionel and provided intriguing photographs as well. **James Sattler**, whose 2-7/8 Gauge chapter provided the single most important contribution to the previous edition, carried his analysis of 2-7/8 further and incorporated new findings into the existing chapter.

Roger Arcara's masterful linking of the toy trains with their prototypes added realism and authenticity to the world of Lionel toys. **William Meyers,** the Secretary of the Lionel Operating Train Society (L.O.T.S.) graciously permitted us to use his article about the Hell Gate Bridge. This article originally appeared in the L.O.T.S. journal.

Charlie Phillips and **Hank Degano** provided very helpful market information. **A.G. Thomson** read and made helpful comments on a substantial part of the text.

Dave Ely's and Dave Christianson's analytic framework for classifying four wheel freight cars was an important contribution. **Dave Ely** also made very substantial contributions to the 10 and 100 series freight listings.

Lou Redman's definitive article on the development of the 700 and 150 series locomotives not only shed light on the particular pieces under study but illuminated the broader questions of how change and development occured. **Lou** and **Ken Sherer's** study of motors aided the research in this volume and provided the basis for future study.

Lou Bohn made extensive additions to our paper listings and provided important new information about the Lionel Directions pamphlets. Lou made many comments throughout the text and was particularly helpful describing lithographed freight cars. **Warren Blackmar** made a number of additions to the lithographed cars and assisted with pricing. **Richard Sullens** most cordially permitted us to visit and record his fine collection of early Lionel.

Frank Hare, publisher of **TOY TRAIN TREASURY Volumes I and II,** gave valuable support and counsel and made available his magnificent color plates. **Tom McComas** and **James Tuohy** permitted us to use their fine color plates from **LIONEL: A COLLECTOR'S GUIDE AND HISTORY Volume I and III.**

Woody Hoffman provided detailed reports on many new prewar varieties and market price information. Photos of **LaRue Shempp's** magnificent collection are shown in a number of color plates. **Birk Leip** made a number of suggestions to improve literary style. **Al Weaver** provided us with an enormously useful collection of prewar color slides which helped confirm existing variations and add new ones. **Joe Kotil** provided an extensive listing of new variations.

The following people also assisted in this book: **M. Diamond, Ken Markley, George Brewer, H.M. Exter, Ed Kriedemaker, John Trowill Jr., C. Adair Roberts, Chris Rohlfing, Donald McErlean, Richard S. Hann, Everett Murray, David Clayton, Richard Clement, Jerry Williams, Pat and Trip Riley, J.B. Cunningham, Ed Prendeville, William Miles, Irving Bernstein, Bob Peca, John B. Gilmer, Ronald Griesbeck, LaRue Shempp, Emil Vatter, Peter Miller, Michael D. Foster, J.L. MacDonald, Gilbert Carlin, Terry Lemieux, W. Mark Anderson III, Robert Bowes, Eric Hundertmark, Richard Merrill, J.A. Grams, Nelson Brueck!, Jack McLaren, W.M. Read, R.K. Fincham, Bill Schuppner, and Bob Cirrillo.**

A book of this magnitude makes enormous physical and psychological demands on the editor. **Roland LaVoie**, the final editor, performed magnificently. I have never seen an editor work so ably under such demanding time constraints. I appreciate his great efforts.

FOREWORD

The train values in this book are based on prices obtained at predominately East Coast train meets during the summer of 1983 and from private transactions reported by our panel of reviewers. East Coast meets are our primary data source since the greatest dollar volume of transactions occur there.

As we indicated, prices in this book were derived from large train shows. If you have trains to sell and you sell them to a person planning to resell them at another train show, you will NOT obtain the prices reported in this book. Rather you may expect to achieve about 50 percent of these prices. Basically for your items to be of interest to such a buyer, he must buy them for considerably less than the prices listed here.

For each item we provide three conditions. Good, Excellent and Restored. The Train Collectors Association defines these conditions as:
GOOD - Scratches, small dents, dirty
EXCELLENT - Minute scratches or nicks, no dents or rust

In the toy train field there is a great deal of concern with exterior appearance and less concern with operation. If operation is important to you, you should ask the seller whether the train runs. If the seller indicates that he does not know whether the equipment operates, you should test it. Most train meets have test track provided for that purpose.

In this book we do not show a value for Very Good. Generally, Very Good items are valued between those listed as Good and Excellent. We have not listed Mint since these items are extremely rare, and market values are difficult to establish. We have included the term "Restored" since such items are becoming an increasingly important part of the market. Restorations differ in quality. The values quoted are for professionally restored items.

We define RESTORED as: Professionally refinished to a color that very closely approximates the original finish. All trim and ornament are present and in like-new condition. The finish appears in like-new condition.

We have had a number of inquiries as to whether or not a particular piece is a "good value". This book will help you to answer that question and will sensitize you to factors affecting that value. But, there is NO substitute for experience in the marketplace.

WE STRONGLY RECOMMEND THAT NOVICES DO NOT MAKE MAJOR PURCHASES WITHOUT THE ASSISTANCE OF FRIENDS WHO HAVE EXPERIENCE IN BUYING AND SELLING TRAINS.

If you are at a train meet and do not know who to ask about a train's value, look for the people running the meet and discuss with them your goal of getting assistance. Usually they can refer you to an experienced collector who will be willing to examine the piece and offer his opinion.

The **Prewar Price Guide** involved the collaboration of many people who generously gave their time and efforts. Only through such cooperative ventures can studies of this kind be carried out - it is impossible for one person to put together what the factory and the market dispersed to the four corners of the country (or more properly to the nooks and crannies of our basements and attics). I can only express my very deep appreciation to my fellow enthusiasts for their willingness to share their information and knowledge with me. This work is not finished; fortunately, there is always more to be learned. If you discóver items that are omitted or errors, please tell me about them on the form provided so that the correct or additional information may be incorporated into the book's next revision.

Bruce C. Greenberg

INTRODUCTION

FOUR VITAL CONCEPTS IN UNDERSTANDING LIONEL TOY TRAINS

This book is the result of many enthusiasts sharing their knowledge. This commitment to scholarship has enabled us to make great progress in our documentation of Lionel production since our first publications in 1976. Despite a multitude of discoveries, we still have much to learn. To assume that this book is an absolutely complete document would be sheer folly.

Due to the diligence and scholarship of enthusiasts like Bob Pauli, Henry Edmunds and Roland LaVoie - and many others like them - we have identified hundreds of new varieties for this edition. However, we do not know the relative scarcity of most of these new varieties. You, our readers, would be of great assistance if you would compare your collections with the descriptions in this book and report to us concerning which variations you have. We will then compile this information and provide relative frequency counts for our next edition.

Since we are in the knowledge generation business, we are trying to learn what the Lionel factory produced on a year-to-year basis. Our problems have been compounded because the dust of 17 to 82 years of history has settled upon the facts. The workers who could enlighten us have, for the most part, gone to their final rewards, leaving only their magnificent trains as testimony to their craftsmanship and skill. If there is one major difference between prewar and postwar research, it is the lack of personal reports for the factory's production in the early years.

However, if direct testimony is lacking, many indirect clues exist which allow us to draw reasonable inferences based upon evidence. One major data source is the annual consumer catalogue. Through these catalogues, Lionel provided reasonably reliable reports about its items. Many times, the sets are found with the exact components in the exact colors shown in the catalogues. However, other items clearly shown in the catalogue have never been found. Although we have not confirmed an item's existence, we still cannot assume it was not made. Any item pictured in the catalogue signifies that, at the very least, a pre-production mock-up was made. These mock-ups might have been a previous production run hand-painted with the new design, or even a wood and/or plastic model of the proposed piece. This practice persists even today.

In the text, we generally report major catalogued items which we believe never reached production. We do this because people often have the catalogues and wonder if an item they have seen catalogued was actually made. We also do this expecting that, on occasion, a previously unreported item will be found and the finder will let us know that we were apparently in error in listing the item as not manufactured. This has happened more than once!

Although the consumer catalogues have been the major research tool for model train historians, other "paper" produced by the factory can be as important or more important than the consumer catalogue. Factory wholesale price sheets often contain corrections to the consumer catalogue and report that an item was not made, although catalogued (or, conversely, made although uncatalogued). Two cases in point are the 1916 catalogue insert and the 1946 catalogue insert 30 years later. These sheets retain their importance even today in the Fundimensions era. For example, as recently as 1980, the Fundimensions Catalogue showed a Texas and Pacific diesel freight set which was never produced - as the factory wholesale sheets have confirmed.

This book examines in considerable detail many Lionel pieces. However, there are relationships between these pieces which are not explicit in our descriptions. This in unfortunate, since Lionel trains compose a "system" (to use the contemporary jargon) of interrelated and interdependent units which "interface" in definite patterns. Unlike most toys, model trains form a complex interdependent system. Not only must the track fit together tightly to carry the current, it must also hold its shape within certain tolerances so that a train runs easily. The locomotive wheels and middle rail pickups require spacing, or "gauge", within certain physical limits. The middle rail pickup must press against the center rail with a predetermined tension. The cars of the train need couplers which match in both height and type; they must also have weight relationships so that cars can be placed at different locations in the train, without undue stress causing derailment.

The systematic aspects of model railroading are potentially delightful; the railroad can grow and become more complex, and its parts will work together. Yet these aspects are also a potential nightmare for a designer or a manufacturer. Relatively small changes in some component could have unforeseen consequences which cause operating difficulties or - even worse - the end of operation.

Besides the systematic nature of Lionel's production, Lionel's technology must be given closer examination. Lionel, of course, always claimed to be a leader in toy train technology - not without good reason. But there is a broader question which must be addressed, especially in relation to the technology used by Lionel's competitors. Was Joshua Lionel Cowen, in the last analysis, like the ancient Greeks, a true innovator and pioneer of toy train technology? Or was Cowen more like the ancient Romans - one of the great synthesizers and adapters of technology pioneered by others? Although this question is very difficult to answer (evidence for both sides abounds), the attempt should be made. When we understand the nature of Lionel's technology, we will begin to understand why one path was chosen over another. For instance, we may come to a better understanding concerning Lionel's abandonment of 00 Gauge trains after World War II.

We must also recognize that Lionel trains were made and sold in competitive markets. The relationship between Lionel's products and those of its competitors is crucial to understanding the Lionel phenomenon itself, and the descriptive mode of our book gives short shrift to that concept. What marketing strategies worked - or failed? Was Joshua Lionel Cowen's advertising skill the crucial element in making Lionel the preeminent maker of toy trains in the prewar era, rather than the innate quality of the trains themselves? Joshua Lionel Cowen was, after all, the prototype of the American entrepreneur in a time when the entrepreneurial spirit was unchecked by government regulation. What elements enabled Lionel to succeed where Ives did not?

The competitive nature of Lionel's market leads to one final element which must be discussed: the relationship of Lionel to its time and its place within American society. Like all other businesses, Lionel was a product of its time - and that society is far removed from us now. Significantly, Lionel's beginnings pre-date Henry Ford's mass production ideas. Additionally, the catalogue prices can cause amazement unless they are seen as part of the whole. Six dollars for a fine locomotive looks irresistible unless one remembers that in these times, other prices were just as mind-boggling. In Theodore Roosevelt's time, 1907, a good dress shirt would sell for 25 cents, and the nickel beer was a reality. One might also buy a real brass bed for about fourteen dollars, and if a man wanted to jollify his family, he could lay out $4.50 for bonded Kentucky bourbon - a gallon of it! Even in the Thirties, when Lionel was selling its Blue Comet for about $75, the same amount could purchase a decent-running used car. Lionel trains were, in reality, very expensive. Lionel's famous advertising statements that "control of a Lionel train today by a boy means control of his life as an adult", or that Lionel trains were the "best way for a father to know his son", may seem preposterous to us now - yet Lionel successfully "sold" these ideas for decades. The nearly complete absence of women from the world of Lionel is another hallmark of a vanished era.

These four elements - the systematic nature of model railroading, the technology, the marketplace, and the historical era - are crucial to an understanding of Lionel production before World War II. In the introductory chapters to the various production areas, we will attempt to tie together some of these elements.

In fact, an examination of all these elements leads to a theme and a thesis for the entire book: Lionel was a very well-organized company which made consistent products for a given year. In other words, the characteristics of a particular item always went together - wheels, couplers, brakewheels, underframe lettering, etc. When people see variations of these characteristics, they may assume that all is confusion. Any confusion comes from inadequate data collection and analysis, not from the trains themselves. As this book clearly illustrates, the changes had definite patterns. Lionel consistently used the same elements together for a time and then changed the set to improve the design, save money or enhance the item's appearance.

The pattern is there. It is up to us to find it!

THE EARLY YEARS OF LIONEL: 1901-1905

It is easy to romanticize in our minds the moment when Joshua Lionel Cowen first hit upon the idea of the miniature electric train. One can visualize him standing before a static, lifeless window display and, with his fertile imagination, contemplating how motion would attract potential customers. Eureka! The muse of inspiration strikes! "I'll produce an electric car which will carry the goods around the window!" Cowen remarks. A "Fabulous Career" ensues.

If only the truth were that simple! The Lionel researcher could then assume, safely, that Cowen built the toy train industry almost single-handedly, and everyone else feebly copied his ideas - much to his displeasure. Unfortunately, the facts get in the way of such an idealized, uncluttered scenario. The truth even confirms to some extent that Joshua Lionel Cowen was ignorant of a thriving toy train industry in those days, much less the inventor of a new toy industry. Despite this, two points are quite clear: Cowen did make a high-quality product, and he was clearly the most innovative marketer of toy trains in the world. His entrepreneurial reputation best rests upon those two elements rather than his work as a pioneer of the industry. This is not meant to belittle Cowen's numerous technical innovations. Rather, it is an attempt at perspective. One of the more fascinating speculations for the Lionel historian would be whether Cowen would have proceeded differently had he known more about his competition in the early years. The answer is, of course, forever denied to us.

The toy train industry was very well established by 1901, when Cowen supposedly stood before that store window. Most of the toy train pioneers were of German origin. The Marklin Company had been manufacturing trains since the 1850's, not too long after the first real German railroad was built between Nuremberg and Furth in December of 1835. The Bing and Carette companies, also in Germany, were well established and had very extensive lines. In fact, the Bing line for 1902 included locomotives which were powered by clockwork or live steam in different gauges. Significantly, Bing also offered two electrically powered sets! Bing completed its line with the production of many different buildings and trackside accessories.

The German companies, although they were the most advanced, did not have the American market to themselves. The Ives Company had been producing toy trains in America since 1868. In 1902, Ives offered mechanical locomotives in two gauges as well as trackside buildings, although Ives did not produce live steam models at this time. In addition, the Carlisle and Finch Company, makers of electrical apparatus, had been offering trains and trolleys beginning in 1896. The Voltamp Company began its train production somewhat later, but it too offered excellent trains and trolleys during these years.

As this analysis indicates, the European toy manufacturers were much further advanced in the production of toy trains than were their American counterparts; their lines were far more extensive. As a result, the dominant American toy train producer of the time, Ives, did what any good competitor would do - it copied its competition. The Carlisle and Finch Company - and, ultimately, Lionel - appeared to be far less influenced by European competition.

Electricity was the new wonder of the age throughout the world; it represented the equivalent of today's computer and "high-tech" revolutions for the society of 1900. For example, one of the biggest attractions of the Paris Exposition of 1900 was the huge Palace of Electricity, with lighted fountains and thousands of multicolored lights to beckon the visitor. In the American world of toy trains, Carlisle and Finch achieved a major American innovation with its trolley of 1896. This relatively small trolley was made of lightweight material. It ran on strip track, which was composed of ties named after British "sleepers" and thin continuous metal strips placed within slots in the ties.

It was with this strip track that Lionel launched its modest toy train line in 1901. With such a track system, Lionel was already behind the times. Sectional track, which was far more reliable and easy to handle, had been introduced in Europe well before 1900 and apparently was introduced to America by Ives in 1901. It is important to emphasize Lionel's use of strip track, because this type of track system had major shortcomings.

Among the problems inherent to a strip track system was a

resistance of the metal strips to being put back in a straight line after being formed into a curve. In addition, connections between the strips were not reliable, whether there were overlapping connections or some sort of metal fastener. Moreover, the track had to be fastened to a hard surface in order to be used successfully. Worse than any of these problems, however, was the fact that the contact surface between track and wheel was extremely small, making for rather haphazard connections and transfer of track power to the motor. This is especially noteworthy when strip track is compared to the surface area of the tubular track which replaced it and the T-rail track which is the standard track for scale model railroads.

The foundation of Lionel in New York City was a stroke of good fortune because there was probably a larger market for electrical goods there than in any other turn-of-the-century American city. Soon after Thomas Edison built the first public power distribution system in lower Manhattan, the nation's first such system, New York became a center for the manufacture and sale of electrical devices.

With such a ready market for that new and not fully understood marvel, electricity, we need to consider Lionel's earliest marketing concepts as compared with those of Bing, Marklin, Ives, and Carlisle and Finch. It appears from a review of the recently discovered 1902 catalogue, as well as the catalogues for the 1903-1906 period, that Cowen's original and primary marketing concept was to produce goods for sale and use by "mechanical institutions for demonstrating purposes, as they give a thorough insight into the workings of the electric cars now so universally used" and that the original concept was expanded in 1902 and later: (1) to meet previously unanticipated demand "from the students and their friends for duplicate outfits"; (2) to attempt to create a new market consisting of retailers for "Window Display" purposes; and (3) to attempt to create a second new market for "Holiday Gifts" and "toys".

The covers of the 1902 and 1903 catalogues boldly announce "MINIATURE ELECTRIC CARS WITH FULL ACCESSORIES FOR WINDOW DISPLAY AND HOLIDAY GIFTS". Cowen obviously wanted to pitch his products to the retailers of New York and other rapidly growing American cities. The idea was to have the retailer put the track and the operating equipment in the window to attract the attention of passersby by loading the cars with small items of merchandise. It is, therefore, understandable that Cowen's first product was not an engine or trolley, but rather an open, motorized gondola. Such a product would serve the original marketing objective of "demonstrating" while also accomodating a "Window Display".

The new toy aspect of Cowen's "goods" is emphasized on page 5 of the 1902 catalogue where, in reference to the No. 200 hard wood "ELECTRIC EXPRESS" open gondola car, it is stated: "As a toy it will afford the user much greater pleasure than the trolley car, as it may be loaded and unloaded." It is unclear from the 1902 catalogue whether the "Holiday Gifts" aspect referred to making gifts of Cowen's "goods" themselves or to the displaying of small "Holiday Gifts" in the open cars.

For some unknown reason, but probably due to the greater demand for the goods as "toys", the emphasis was reversed on the covers of the 1904 and 1905 catalogues from "Window Display" and "Holiday Gifts" to "MINIATURE ELECTRIC CARS, MOTORS, Etc. for Holiday Presents and Window Display". The implication of the word change from "Gifts" to "Presents" is that the "goods" themselves would be "Presents" rather than vehicles for the display of "Holiday Gifts".

Interestingly, the words "train" and "trains" do not appear in any Lionel catalogue before 1909 (other than in passing in the description of the No. 100 electric locomotive which was introduced in 1903 as a "faithful reproduction of the 1,800 horse power electric locomotives used by the B. & O. R. R. for hauling trains through the tunnels of Baltimore"). In the 1909 catalogue, the cover announced for the first time "LIONEL Miniature Electric Trains and New Departure Battery Motors". Thus, it would appear that Cowen did not originally intend to compete with the established manufacturers of toy "trains" at all, but rather got into that business by a process of evolution. It appears that it was only after the demand for Cowen's "goods" as "toys" manifested itself that he correctly perceived that people were more interested in the gondola itself than in whatever small "Holiday Gifts" it may have carried in a "Window Display". This is not the only instance of a product differing from its original marketing concept. A few years later, a young printer's apprentice solved a serious printing problem with a new device. It seems that color printing blurred in the extreme summer humidity of New York City. The apprentice's device drew moisture out of the air and thus prevented the print from blurring. As a by-product, print shops became the most comfortable places in the city. The apprentice's name was Willis Carier, and he had invented air conditioning. By the time Cowen introduced Standard Gauge in 1906, something similar had occurred to his original marketing concept. His trains had become sophisticated, attractive playthings.

One of the ongoing themes in Lionel's history is the changing of Lionel's roster to match innovation within the real transportation world. Did Joshua Lionel Cowen actually see an electrically operated gondola to serve as a model for his miniature version? There is strong evidence that he did indeed observe a prototype. Research into the early records of American trolley and traction systems has been extensively documented by trolley enthusiasts. This research has shown that some trolley systems of the period were built with power from a cable in the street rather than from overhead wires. The system built by New York's Metropolitan Street Railway Company along Third Avenue in 1894 was such a system. Cowen almost certainly was able to observe this system, which eventually became the Third Avenue Line.

It is one of the intriguing stories of American traction that the traction companies not only moved people in large numbers, but also served as urban freight transit networks. This being the case, we are certain that work cars once existed which carried equipment and goods along transit lines. Recently, an underground electric railway for just such transportation has been unearthed in Chicago after being forgotten for many years. Cowen almost certainly observed the freight gondolas used by these transit companies; such cars could have given him the model for his window display gondola. There is further evidence in a later 2-7/8" gauge car known as the "jail car" because of the bars on its windows. This is a very fine model of the baggage cars used to transport goods in the early 1900's.

Lionel's second powered unit was a trolley; this obviously reflected the society of the turn of the century, when trolley lines were growing rapidly and innovation in trolley design was commonplace. The trolleys of the time, only recently freed from the horses which first drew them, were becoming larger, faster, and more comfortable. It made sense for Lionel to imitate the real world.

Of course, Lionel, as a beginning manufacturer, had a very

small plant and only a few employees. Therefore, it made good sense for Lionel to mate its drive train with a body from another manufacturer. Very fortunately for Lionel, the Morton E. Converse Company made a trolley of approximately the correct proportions to fit the Lionel drive train. The Converse trolley body was big - 16-1/2" long by 5" wide - and it was handsomely decorated. Most of the trolley bodies made by Converse for Lionel were painted quite differently from those used by Converse itself, although at least two original specimens of Converse "pull toys" trolleys are known to exist in paint colors identical to those supplied to Lionel. How many of these trolley bodies did Lionel use? We probably will never know for sure, although one of the dreams of the Lionel historian is to stumble over a carton of Converse records in some dingy book store or second-hand shop of lower Manhattan including correspondence between Lionel and Converse.

Historians have asked why Lionel chose such an odd gauge for its 1901-1905 production. Why did Lionel space its rails 2-7/8" apart, when toy train gauges of 0, 1, 2, and 3 had already been established by toy train makers? Was Joshua Lionel Cowen's idea to differentiate his product so that it could not be used by other systems? Or, was Cowen simply ignorant of the current practices of the toy train industry? (If so, such ignorance certainly did not last very long!) Was it just a coincidence that the then readily-available Converse trolley bodies happened to fit well on the previously determined 2-7/8" gauge system? Or was the decision to adopt the 2-7/8" gauge system dictated in whole or in part by the size of the Converse trolley bodies? Until the very earliest Lionel production can be satisfactorily documented, it will not be known for certain what all of the motivating reasons were for Cowen's decision to go with a 2-7/8" gauge system as opposed to one of the existing gauges.

LIONEL'S PREWAR TECHNOLOGY: PROBLEMS BEGET SOLUTIONS BEGET PROBLEMS . . .

"LIONEL ALWAYS LEADS", trumpeted the Lionel catalogues from the firm's earliest days. One might append the words . . . "IN WHAT?" to the statement, however. Did Lionel's greatest strengths lie in the firm's technological innovation? Or, was the admitted marketing genius of Joshua Lionel Cowen the real reason for Lionel's dominance over its competition? It would be very foolish to make a choice. Yet, Lionel was not nearly as innovative a firm as it claimed to be, although the Lionel Corporation did come up with some ingenious mechanisms over the years, such as the whistle and the non-derailing turnout.

It wasn't so much that an individual element of a Lionel product was truly innovative. The real technical genius of Lionel came about because the parts fit together into a systematic whole as well. In addition, Lionel very early committed itself to quality of the product - and hang the expense if necessary. That quality of manufacturing was trumpeted ceaselessly - and sometimes a little unfairly. In the 1923 catalogue (indeed, in much earlier ones), Lionel would show a picture of a competitor's car (usually the cheapest Ives car) twisted beyond recognition. In the same catalogue, on page 5, there appeared two pictures of tracks being tested by weight support. The competitor's track has snapped under a 20-pound weight, while Lionel's track is unscathed by a 110-pound weight. Look closely, because there are two misleading elements to these pictures. In the first place, Lionel's Standard Gauge track is being compared to the competitor's 027 style track - obviously much smaller and more lightly built track. Additionally, the 20-pound weight is fastened to the competitor's track with a piece of wire at one small point of the rail. The 110-pound weight is hanging from a much larger leather strap which distributes the pull over the rail much more evenly. To say the least, Lionel is playing with a stacked deck!

Such one-sided comparisons tend to obscure the real quality of much of Lionel's production, and that is too bad, because Lionel did establish technical leadership as well as marketing genius. Before World War I, the German firms of Marklin and Bing pioneered nearly every basic element of toy train railroading, and Lionel was a follower rather than a leader. The war with Germany gave Lionel a chance to overcome this early lead, and Lionel was able to establish a technical dominance it never relinquished. The only real challenge to Lionel after World War I came from the Ives Company, and it was the fate of that organization to be led by old-fashioned leadership which was slow to take up marketing challenges. Ives and the later American Flyer were no match for Lionel in the Twenties.

During the Twenties, Lionel's technical dominance rested largely upon the systemic quality of its trains rather than any single innovation. That was to change dramatically during the Thirties. Lionel had introduced remote control switches in 1926, for example, but these were not made non-derailing until 1931. Lionel's "Chugger", a relatively crude imitation of the sound of a steam engine, came out in 1933. Lionel's whistle, a truly ingenious device which worked from a spurt of DC current, appeared in 1935. The first automatic uncoupler appeared in 1938.

Technical innovation in model railroading sometimes causes mechanical and electrical problems because of the complexity and interdependence of a model railroad. A change to one part of a locomotive or a car can cause unanticipated problems elsewhere. A less charitable way of stating this fact is to say that Lionel's engineers were so smart that they sometimes outsmarted themselves. Nowhere was this more true than in the checkered history of Lionel's 0 Gauge automatic coupler systems.

At the onset of 0 Gauge trains by Lionel in 1914 (possibly as early as 1913), Lionel offered two series of 0 Gauge cars. The premium cars of the 820 freight series came with two four-wheel trucks, while the lower-priced 800 series freight cars had only four wheels. Unfortunately, the frames of these cars stood at different heights atop the rails, with the 820 cars being quite a bit higher. As long as Lionel continued to use its simple hook couplers, these height differentials did not matter very much because the hook couplers have half an inch of vertical play. There is enough stretch within this system to compensate for the height differences between the two series of cars.

In 1924, however, Lionel introduced a new degree of complexity - and confusion - when it brought the latch coupler to the 0 Gauge cars. This coupler, which had been used on Standard Gauge cars a year earlier, makes a horizontal connection rather than a vertical connection. The play or stretch is along the horizontal dimension rather than the vertical. (This reflects where the play actually exists in prototype equipment). Since both lines of freight cars were continued, Lionel now had four lines of moderately incompatible 0 Gauge cars - low and high hooks, low and high latches!

To solve at least part of the problem, Lionel made transitional latch couplers known as combination couplers. These couplers had a slotted tab which would accept the earlier hook couplers. After a few years, Lionel only made regular latch couplers (we are not sure when the combination coupler was dropped). Lionel did make attempts to steer customers to compatible equipment, as can be seen on page 31 of the 1924 catalogue, but these problems must have turned the hair of many salesmen prematurely gray. (Grandmom, you say you want a tank car for Billy's train set? Do his cars have four or eight wheels? Do they have this little hook or this little latch? You don't remember? Help!)

One of the greatest innovations in Lionel's history was the introduction of remote-control electrically-operated couplers in 1938. Although Lionel had advertised that its older latch couplers were automatic, they were extremely difficult to couple by backing the train into a car. (The similar Ives couplers were, ironically, much more likely to work in this fashion). The new mechanism would permit the operator to uncouple a car at the touch of a button.

This mechanism used a box coupler with a lip on the leading lower edge of the box which caught the pin of the adjacent coupler. The initial mechanism consisted of an electromagnet with a cone-shaped core end which, when energized, attracted the bottom back flap of the box coupler towards the core. This would lift the front edge of the box coupler and permit the pin of the adjacent cars to slip out. Lionel had been using a non-automatic version of this box coupler since 1935. This improvement on the latch coupler provided secure attachment, yet ease of unlatching and a more realistic appearance.

So far, so good. However, Lionel's engineers had short memories which would embarrass the company severely. The power for the 1938 automatic couplers electromagnet came from a metal shoe on one side of the truck. This was essentially a resurrection of the sliding shoe pickups from the early Standard Gauge motors of 1906-1923. In 1923, Lionel "improved" its switches. However, as the sliding shoe touched the outside rail of the switch, it shorted out. Lionel solved that problem by adding a piece of fiber to the rail surfaces. Lionel's engineers forgot about this when they reintroduced the sliding shoe for the uncoupling mechanism in 1938. The pickup shoe contacted a center rail when going through the curved section of the switch. Therefore, the electromagnet was energized and the cars uncoupled.

Lionel's red-faced engineers changed the pickup shoe in 1939. The new shoe had only a small rivet head for electrical contact; the rivet head was encased within a plastic shoe. Although the small contact area was prone to oxidation, which would prevent current from reaching the electromagnet, this redesigned shoe was successful enough to last into the postwar era. It became the energizing device for many of Lionel's postwar operating cars after its use on couplers was discontinued after 1948.

Many more changes were made to these coupler mechanisms. In 1938, Lionel produced two automatic coupler types, each with a different shape to its electromagnet. Larger trucks of the 2800 Series had large cylindrically-shaped electromagnets. The differentiation might be a simple matter of proper size for the truck. On the other hand, differences in the magnetic flux might be involved. We invite reader comments. In 1939, a rod was inserted through an electromagnet on the truck. When the coil was activated, the rod was pulled away from the car center towards the car end. The rod then pushed against a plate connected to the box lid, which then tilted and released its opposing coupler pin. This solenoid mechanism was very reliable; it continued into the postwar knuckle coupler.

Ironically, Lionel still had not solved the problem of coupler heights! As if the complexity and costs for all the design changes were not enough to crinkle an accountant's cost sheets, Lionel's 0 Gauge cars still came in two heights. Since the box coupler was a modification of the latch coupler, there still was little vertical play. Consequently, Lionel had to produce two different box coupler mechanisms!

Even today, Lionel's engineers can outsmart themselves by failing to anticipate operating problems. When Fundimensions introduced its Geep diesels in 1970, it put hollow-roller power pickups on the power trucks. Such pickups had worked well for inexpensive late Lionel 027 production, but the Fundimensions people forgot that these engines often stalled when crossing switches. As howls of protest began to reach the factory, Fundimensions hurriedly installed sprung solid-roller assemblies on the trailing trucks until it produced a solid-roller pickup for the power truck.

For all the headaches and problems caused by an individual component, it must be remembered that these were only momentary lapses of an individual component within a model railroading system which always worked well. It was not an accident that Lionel's commitment to quality in the prewar years meant prompt attention to design problems and a constant search for improvement. Perhaps Lionel was never the innovator it claimed to be. Yet the fact remains that no other American firm ever developed a toy railroading system with the dependability and durability of those developed by the Lionel Corporation.

MAKING THE TRAINS MOVE: LIONEL'S ELECTRICAL POWER AND REVERSING SYSTEMS

Like many young men of his age and society, Joshua Lionel Cowen was an inveterate experimenter and tinkerer. In his later years, he was fond of pointing out that one of his earliest experiments went wrong and "blew up his parents' kitchen". He was also reported to have rewired a friend's apartment so that the light switch would turn on the toaster instead. It really does not matter whether these stories are true or not. What they do point out is the insatiable curiosity of an inventive mind.

We do know that Cowen's curiosity settled upon electricity very early. He patented a "photographer's flash light apparatus" which used a small dry cell battery to set off a charge of magnesium powder. In speaking of these early years, Cowen said that he sold off this patent to a man who used it as the foundation for the Ever-Ready Flash Light Company, but evidence for this tale is lacking. He also patented an electric fan motor which, while not very effective for a fan, was the basis for Cowen's "New Departure" motors used in his earliest trains.

Once Cowen settled upon the idea of a moving window display for merchants, he realized that he would need a reliable low voltage power supply. While the contemporary practice of the toy train market was usually to use wet cell batteries as a low-voltage source of direct current, Lionel offered two different sources of battery power in its 1902 catalogue, dry cell batteries and "OUR PLUNGE BATTERY" which was to be charged "with electric sand, which may be purchased at any electric supply house." A third power source was portrayed and described as "the proper way to operate our cars when utilizing direct electric current." This sinister-looking collection of two glass jars, lead plates and wires called for filling the jars with water and adding "a sufficient amount of sulphuric acid". The bold warning was given to "NEVER ADD WATER TO THE ACID IN ANY EVENT, BUT POUR THE ACID ON TOP OF THE WATER". The apparatus was to wired to a 110-volt direct current source and called for a 32-candle-power incandescent bulb to be used "or, if a higher speed is desired, a lamp of greater candle-power should be employed". The price of the jars and plates was a whopping 50 cents.

Sulphuric acid is a hideous substance to handle even for an experienced chemist, let alone an unskilled retailer of dry goods. In its concentrated form, it will eat through almost any substance rapidly, and when it touches skin it absorbs the water in the tissues, leaving horribly charred burns. This was not the stuff of a child's toy, to say the least! The 1903 and later catalogues contain the much safer and saner suggestion that "We have found it advisable when making up outfits complete with battery, to supply four dry cells, which work satisfactorily when used intermittently for from ten to fifteen hours. . . ." Such dry cell battery systems, with individual batteries about the size of a mortar shell, were well established by the time Standard Gauge trains made their appearance in 1906.

Cowen realized the danger of wet cells and the limitations of dry cells and in his 1906 catalogue offered a light bulb and shunt mounted on a base to reduce the high voltage DC house current to low voltage. Unfortunately, this use of a light bulb as a resistor to reduce 110 volts of DC current to 15 volts DC was rife with hazard. There would still be a 110 volt potential in the track. If the "hot" line went to the bulb first, and the ground side of the circuit were hooked directly to the track, any child touching a ground (say, a radiator) and the track would conduct only a 15 volt DC flow. But heaven help that child if the wires were mistakenly reversed! A lethal electric shock would result.

Add to these hazardous power methods the fact that some toy trains were powered by live steam, and one might readily observe that there was much left to chance in these toys, to say the least! Lack of electrical safety apparently was caused by the "buyer beware" mentality of business in those years. What a difference from today this is! The Consumer Products Safety Commission will not even let Fundimensions make an AC transformer with an output of more than 100 watts - let alone resurrect the 275 watt ZW of postwar days. Had Cowen been foolish enough to distribute a wet cell system today, he would be serving a lengthy prison term!

By the early teens, however, Lionel had scrapped its earliest systems for power in favor of dry cell batteries with rheostats to control current. Since the electrical distribution systems in most American cities used alternating current, Lionel soon offered relatively safe AC transformers without rheostats - except in some sections of its own home base, New York, which continued to use batteries and rheostats because the main current remained DC for quite some time. These two power systems made the operation of toy trains relatively safe for children.

The early Lionel transformers worked, as all transformers do, by induction. They consisted of a primary and a secondary coil with three to five taps taken from the secondary. The combination of these taps and the return terminal gave a range of fixed voltages. Lionel's designers wired the secondary taps to the brass caps on the transformer's external face. Another set of taps was taken from the secondary coil and connected to various fixed terminal posts.

This method produced highly reliable voltage sequences. However, as the controller moved from one brass cap to the next, there was a momentary current interruption. As long as the locomotives were reversed by a hand lever on the locomotive itself, these momentary lapses were no problem, since the engine would merely glide for a split second. Clearly, this situation would no longer suffice when Lionel introduced its pendulum-type reversing switch unit in 1926. Any current interruption while the operator changed voltage taps would result in the immediate reversing of the locomotive with a two-position reversing unit. This, of course, would cause derailments, crashes, and generally unstable operation.

Curiously, Lionel chose not to redesign the tranformer itself so that voltage would change consistently. Instead, Lionel redesigned the No. 88 Battery Rheostat and created the No. 81 Controlling Rheostat, which first appeared without a number on page 17 of the 1926 catalog and with a number the next year. Because the AC current flow is heavier than the DC current from batteries, the coil for the No. 81 Rheostat was protected by a metal cover which was insulated from the resistance wire by a piece of asbestos. The No. 88 rheostat had no such cover.

The use of a separate rheostat had one negative effect upon the Lionel line of trains: Lionel was very slow to modernize its transformers. In fact, the brass button type of transformer persisted until 1938, long after American Flyer and other train makers introduced a continuous voltage dial-type transformer. In this AC tranformer, still used today, the controller slides continuously across the secondary coil, tapping infinitely variable voltage throughout the transformer's voltage range. However, all of Lionel's transformers from 1926 to 1938 required the use of a separate rheostat if the locomotive had a sequence reversing switch.

The combination of the transformer, the rheostat and the reversing unit formed a system which Lionel called its "Electric Control System". The key element to this system was the pendulum reversing unit, which allowed the operator to change the direction of the locomotive without manually throwing a switch on the locomotive itself. According to the 1926 Lionel catalogue, this reversing unit was only offered with Standard Gauge trains. However, by the next year Lionel had reengineered the unit to fit the smaller spaces of 0 Gauge equipment. In subsequent years, Lionel began to use Ives' drum reverse unit, and the system then was called "Distant Control".

The introduction of the pendulum reverse unit led to some curious anomalies in Lionel's roster of locomotives. The 254 locomotive is sometimes found with both pendulum reverse units and hand reverse units - on the same locomotive! In fact, the 1927 catalogue takes advantage of promoting this feature. On page 10, the catalogue states that "Another desirable feature of the Lionel Electrically-Controlled Locomotives is the fact that they can also be reversed by hand, and the controlling unit may be disconnected by moving another small lever." (We would welcome a wiring diagram of this arrangement from our electrically-oriented readers.) It is almost as if Lionel did not trust its own invention!

Not surprisingly, Lionel claimed that its pendulum reversing unit was superior to that of Ives, which predated Lionel's unit. "The construction throughout is dependable and must not be confused with so-called 'Automatic Reversing Locomotives' ", claimed the catalogue. Was Lionel's unit in fact more reliable? Since nearly 60 years have passed, this question is difficult to answer. However, there is one piece of circumstantial evidence that Lionel's claim of superiority for its pendulum reversing unit was not well founded. The Ives reversing unit operated by a rotating drum and pawl arrangement quite similar to the more modern E-unit reversing switch. After Lionel acquired sole control of the Ives Company in 1930, the pendulum reversing unit persisted. Three years elapsed before a re-engineered Ives drum unit was introduced. This unit has been used in Lionel production ever since, even to the present day! Only in the last few years has a fully electronic reversing switch begun to replace the pawl-and-drum design solenoid switch. Amazingly, many operators still prefer the old design to the electronic unit! Perhaps tradition dictates this, because E-unit "buzz" is a sound so closely associated with Lionel production after all these years.

In 1927, Lionel made another interesting comparison between its pendulum unit and the Ives drum unit. The Lionel pendulum unit's coil is only momentarily energized to cause sequence reversing. However, like the famous E-unit, the Ives reversing mechanism's coil is continuously energized as long as power is present in the track. Lionel was quick to point out that its unit operated ". . . without using extra current, with the result that Lionel locomotives are the only ones made that will operate as perfectly on direct current as on alternating current, dry cells or storage batteries." This claim meant that the extra current draw of the Ives unit was a serious disadvantage when the locomotive was run on dry or wet cell batteries. Was the claim true? Perhaps. However, as the use of electricity rapidly spread throughout the country, especially with the massive electrification programs of the Thirties, fewer and fewer people ran their trains from batteries. Therefore, the question rapidly became academic.

Whatever flaws they may have had, Lionel's power delivery systems from 1906 onward offered reliable, safe control of the operation of Lionel trains. Without the properly controlled use of that wonderful power source, electricity, Joshua Lionel Cowen's idea for the best toy trains in history would have remained a pipe dream. Lionel's transformers, rheostats, and reversing units made a gigantic contribution to the ultimate success of the Lionel Corporation. Today, in the eighties, the efficient control of power for these trains is with us still.

Brass Beauties: 7 and 54

Chapter I

STANDARD GAUGE LOCOMOTIVES

Standard Gauge was introduced in 1906 and replaced two-rail, 2-7/8" Gauge. According to Lionel catalogues, Standard Gauge was last offered in 1940. However, the factory continued to market Standard Gauge until 1942.

Standard Gauge can be divided into two periods - an Early Period from 1906 to 1923 and the Classic Period from 1923 to 1940. Early Period locomotives include the 5, 51, 6, 7, 1910, 1911, 53, 33, 34, 38, 42 and 54. Classic Period equipment includes the 8, 10, 318, 380, 402, 408, 9, 381, 384, 390, 385, 392, 400 and 1835. Early Period equipment usually appears in drab colors with rubber-stamped lettering. Classic Period equipment is characterized by bright colors, extensive use of copper and brass trim and brass and nickel plates.

Coupler types, as described below, are very useful in dating Standard Gauge equipment, especially where the equipment was manufactured over an extended time period:

1906-1914	Short and long straight hooks
1910-1918	Short and long crinkle hooks
1914-1925	Hook with ears
1924-1928	Combination latch (Latch with a slot for a hook coupler)
1925-1942	Latch

As far as can be determined, Standard Gauge equipment was not produced with manual or automatic box couplers.

Other design changes useful in dating equipment are: name changes, headlights, wheels and motor construction. For example, in 1918, Lionel changed its name from the Lionel Manufacturing Company to Lionel Corporation and the identification plates on its locomotives also changed.

The earliest headlights were pedestal-type; these were followed by strap headlights in the late teens and by cast headlights in the mid-twenties.

The earliest Standard Gauge equipment has cast-iron wheels with thin rims. These were followed by thick-rim iron wheels. In the early 1920's, die-cast wheels with bright steel rims replaced the iron wheels. Unfortunately, die cast wheels were subject to deterioration. In the mid or late 1930's, a new die-cast wheel was introduced with black tires replacing the bright metal tires. The wheels with black tires have resisted deterioration.

Motor construction is also a key to determine manufacturing dates. Lionel introduced the Super Motor in 1923, with large gears on one side of the motor. The gears prevented engines from passing easily through switches. Consequently, in 1925, the gearing was changed and the small gear Super Motor was introduced. Later, probably in 1927, the Bild-A-Loco motor was introduced for certain models. The Bild-A-Loco motor featured do-it-yourself construction with only a screwdriver. Slots were provided for axle bushings which were already mounted on axles. The last Standard Gauge motor featured black anodized sides.

The earliest Lionel headlights were the pedestal type. Lionel introduced the pedestal headlight by 1909 (it might have been introduced in 1907-1908 but we lack data for these years). In the late teens, Lionel introduced the strap headlight which was simpler and less expensive to manufacture.

Strap headlight

Celluloid insert headlight. Note tab for on/off switch.

In 1923, Lionel introduced the celluloid insert headlight with an off/on switch. This headlight was an elaboration of the strap headlight with side windows and a switch. It appeared in the top of the line 402 and 380, and the 0 Gauge 256.

Cast headlight with red and green painted panels on sides of light

In 1928, Lionel announced the die-case headlight with its red and green panels (1928 catalogue, page 6). The catalogue also shows for the first time an 0 Gauge motor with the fiber headlight connection that supplies power to the die-cast headlight (1928 catalogue, page 4). On page 7, thye catalogue indicated that the die-cast headlight was patented June 12, 1926.

Early Standard Steam

5(A)

5(G)

6(C)

6(E)

7 Thin Rim

7 Thick Rim

5 Special

51

Gd Exc Rst

5 Steam, 0-4-0, 1906-26, sheet steel, Russian iron boiler, soldered, black cab and red window trim and pilot, nickel plated trim, rubber-stamped in gold "N.Y.C. and H.R.R.R.", or less frequently "PENNSYLVANIA" or "B. and O.R.R.", with wooden dome, stack, pilot beam and boiler front, 11-1/2".

(A) 5 Early: Thin rim drivers, short crinkle hook coupler, large coal bunker, split frame, dummy slide-on headlight, lettered "N.Y.C. & H.R.R." (note absence of third R), 1906-1910, no tender, Sattler Collection **300 600 300**

(B) 5 Special with black and red trim, slope-back coal tender with one 10 series solid 3-rivet truck, lettered "PENNSYLVANIA", 1906-09 **900 1500 700**

(C) Same as (B) but lettered "N.Y.C. & H.R.R.R." **800 1200 650**

(D) Same as (B) but lettered "B.& O.R.R." **900 1500 650**

(E) 5 Special, same as (C), but tender has open, 3-rivet truck, 1907-09. Engine has slide-on headlight, 1908-09 **800 1200 600**

(F) 5 Special, same as (A), but with 8-wheel slope-back tender with two 100-series trucks, 1910-11, renumbered 51 in 1912 catalogue **700 1000 600**

(G) 5 Late, similar to (A), but thick rim drivers, long crinkle hook coupler, large coal bunker, solid frame, pedestal headlight, terminal on coal bunker to illuminate passenger cars, lettered "PENNSYLVANIA", 1911, no tender, two holes in boiler under sand dome directly under handrails, apparently intended for second set of handrail stanchions, but never installed, Sattler Collection **300 500 300**

51 5 Late with 8-wheel double truck tender, first catalogued in 1912 but previously called 5 Special, with single-rivet, open truck and strap headlight, 1912-23 **350 750 350**

6 Steam, 4-4-0, 1906-23, sheet steel, Russian iron boilers, soldered body, black cab with red window trim and red pilot, nickel plated trim, including two boiler bands. Gold rubber-stamped with various road names under cab window and on tender sides, black rectangular tender with red trim. Some tenders apparently were lettered "B.& M.R.R." See illustration of 6(C). Reader comments invited. Sattler observation.

(A) Early 6: Thin rim, cast-iron pilot wheels, dummy headlight, split frame **800 1000 700**

(B) Later 6: Thin rim wheels, cast-iron pilot wheels, operating slide-on headlight (1908-09). Pedestal headlight, 1910-11, large bell, solid frame. Gold rubber-stamped "PENNSYLVANIA" in sans-serif lettering on cab **800 1000 700**

(C) Same as (B) but lettered "N.Y.C. & H.R.R.R." in sans-serif block lettering **700 900 675**

(D) Same as (B) but lettered "B.& O.R.R." in sans-serif block lettering **800 1000 700**

(E) Latest 6: 1912-23, thick rim wheels, die-cast pilot wheels, steel strap headlight, 1918-23, pedestal headlight, 1912-1917, solid frame, regular hook couplers, small bell. Gold rubber-stamped on cab beneath window "N.Y.C. & H.R.R.R." in sans-serif block lettering. Tender is gold rubber-stamped "N Y C & H R R R" and "4351". Rubber-stamped lettering differs in size and thickness. **450 900 450**

6 Special: Steam, 4-4-0, 1908-09, early 6 loco and tender constructed from heavy sheet brass and nickeled brass. Nickeled tender has either open or closed three-rivet trucks. No lettering on loco or tender sides although shown lettered in catalogue. Engine boiler is brass while cab is nickel. Red pilot, driver spokes, pilot wheels, and tender stripes. A Special is indistinguishable from an Early 7. **1000 1500 1000**

7* Steam, 4-4-0, 1910-23, early models same as 6 Special with/without binding post inside cab, pilot wheels cast-iron to 1920, then die-cast

(A) Brass engine, thin rimmed wheels, 1910-11, with red spokes, red solid pilot wheels, large nickel bell 1908-14, nickel tender with single red bead line, tender with two open, 3-rivet trucks with red solid wheels **1700 2800 1700**

(B) Brass boiler, nickel cab, thick rims, red painted spokes and pilot wheels, small nickel bell 1912-23. Brass tender with unpainted wheels, no red bead line **1400 2300 1400**

(C) Same as(B) but engine(excluding light, bell, stack and dome) completely brass. Cab window outlined in red. Tender has double red bead trim, 2 open and spring embossed trucks with solid red painted wheels. Nickel sides on tender **1400 2300 1400**

(D) Brass boiler, nickel cab, thick rims, red painted spokes, pilot wheels and pilot. Brass tender with nickel painted outside and red interior, red wheels, red trim line along bottom edge, straight shank hook couplers **1400 2300 1400**

8 Electric, 0-4-0, 1925-32, New York Central prototype, smallest of late series Standard Gauge electrics, 11", combination latch or latch couplers, hand reversing. Two headlights, either cast or steel strap, small pantograph and whistle.

Note strap headlight and combination latch couplers. The ventilator inserts are unpainted brass and are part of the same sheet which forms the windows and number plates. Bartelt photograph

(A) Maroon with brass windows, ventilators and plates, strap headlights, large gear Super motor, combination latch couplers. Came with 35 and 36 passenger cars or 100 series freight cars, 1925-26. Price for loco only **75 135 75**

(B) Olive green with brass windows, ventilators and plates, cast headlights, latch couplers **60 125 75**

(C) Mojave with brass windows, ventilators and plates, latch couplers **80 145 75**

Note cast headlights and regular latch couplers and hand reverse at pantograph end. Bartelt photograph. The ventilator insert is painted brass and part of the same brass sheet which forms the windows and number plates.

(D) Red with cream windows and ventilators, brass name and number plates with black lettering, cream stripe, cast headlights, latch couplers, brass whistle and pantograph **60 125 70**

(E) Dark olive green with brass windows, ventilators and plates, strap headlights **60 125 75**

(F) Red with brass windows, ventilators and plates **60 125 75**

(G) Peacock with orange windows and ventilators and brass plates **100 175 95**

(H) Peacock, marked "Macy Special" **NRS**

---

*NOTE: A number of reproduction 7s have been made. Extreme caution is required in purchasing what is purported to be an original 7. It is highly recommended that a 7 known to be an original be compared against any prospective purchase. Many reproductions are not marked in any way. One reproduction that is carefully marked was manufactured by McCoy Manufacturing Co. It is the 7 (R) McCoy Manufacturing Co., a 1962 reproduction. Various components are stamped "M" or "McCoy". It is almost an exact duplicate of a late 7 with red spoked drivers, pilot and pilot wheels and tender wheels. A serial number is stamped inside the boiler. It came with an original No. 33 motor.

The Early Electrics

1912 Special — 1910 — 1912

34 — 33 EARLY (D) — 33 LATE (A) — 33 LATE (C)

53 EARLY — 53 LATER (A) — 53 LATEST

38 (A) — 38 (B) — 38 — 50 (D)

54 (A) — 42 (A) — 42 (E)

8E Electric, 0-4-0, similar to 8 but pendulum reversing unit, possibly with drum-type reversing unit

(A) Mojave with brass windows, ventilators and plates, red lettering, die-cast headlights, brass pantograph, nickel whistle, latch couplers **80 160 75**

(B) Red with brass windows, ventilators and plates **70 140 70**

(C) Red with cream windows, stripes and ventilators and brass plates **70 140 70**

(D) Peacock with orange windows and ventilators and brass plates, orange stripe **100 200 95**

(E) Pea green, cream stripe, red lettering. Macy special but not so marked **150 300 95**

(F) Olive green with brass windows, ventilators, and plates with block lettering **70 140 70**

9* Electric, 0-4-0, 1929 NYC prototype. Motor held to frame by four machine screws rather than latches used in other 9's, dark green, hand reversing knob, 14-1/2" **600 1200 650**

9E* Electric, 0-4-0, 1928-30, NYC, 14-1/2"

(A) Motor fastened with 2 quick release levers, wiring does not require disconnection with motor removal, orange **500 1000 600**

(B) Same as (A) but motor fastened with 4 machine screws, wires require disconnection with motor removal. Gray paint on headlight, Ely observation **500 1000 600**

(C) 2-4-2, two-tone green, low clerestory roof, pony trucks, motor fastened with 2 quick release levers, wiring does not require disconnection for motor removal. Catalogued 1931-33 with Stephen Girard passenger car set: 424, 425, 426; (Price for loco only) **500 1000 600**

9 Electric, 2-4-2, two-tone green, low roof tabbed in, brass trim, red wheels, "WRL" stamped into frame, "LIONEL" plates

(A) Two-tone green, brass trim, red wheels **— 175 —**

(B) Gunmetal, nickel trim, black wheels **— 175 —**

(C) 0-4-0, orange, high roof tabbed in, brass trim, red wheels, "WRL" stamped into frame, "LIONEL" plates **— 175 —**

(D) 0-4-0, same as (C) but dark green **— 175 —**

(E) Same as (C), reversing lever under roof, but gunmetal, plate reads "No. 9E BILD-A-LOCO. LIONEL LINES". Catalogued 1934-35 with 309, 310, 312 in rare two-tone green. (Price for loco only) **500 1000 600**

(F) 2-4-2 with E-unit slot, gunmetal, higher roof and pony trucks, motor fastened with 4 machine screws, lettered "LIONEL LINES, 9E". Catalogued 1934-35 with 309, 310, 312 in rare two-tone green. (Price for loco only) **500 1000 600**

9U Electric, 0-4-0, 1928-29, NYC, higher roof, motor fastened by quick release lever, orange. Came as kit with adapters for converting to 3-speed reversible motors, 8 sections of curved track, loco is lettered "9U"

(A) 9U with motor adapter and original box **700 1500 700**

(B) 9U without motor adapter and box **600 1200 600**

(C) Same as 9U (A), but assembled, without motor adapter and weighted frame, lettered "9U" **700 1500 700**

10 Electric, 0-4-0, 1925-29, Chicago, Milwaukee, St. Paul & Pacific Olympian prototype, (as with 380 and 381), hand reversing (lever). Early versions with large gear Super motor, combination latch couplers, strap headlights. Later, small gear Super motor, latch couplers, cast headlights. Combinations of these characteristics possible. One pantograph and one whistle, 11-1/2", Bowers comment

(A) Mojave with brass inserts, black lettering, strap headlights, combination latch couplers, nickel pantograph and whistle, Ely comment **75 160 95**

(B) Gray, brass inserts, black lettering, cast headlights, combination latch couplers, nickel pantograph and whistle **75 160 95**

(C) Peacock with brass inserts, red lettering, cast headlights, latch coupler **75 160 95**

(D) Peacock, brass inserts, black lettering, cast headlights, latch coupler, brass pantograph and whistle **75 160 95**

(E) Red, marked "Macy Special" **NRS**

(F) Same as (B), but red lettering and dark green frame, Ely Collection **NRS**

10E Electric, 0-4-0, 1926-30, similar to 10 above, but with E-unit reversing, usually with pendulum type mechanism, with "10E" on plates

(A) Peacock, black frame, brass inserts, red lettering, cast headlights, latch coupler **75 165 95**

(B) Peacock, dark green frame, Bild-A-Loco motor (Not Super motor), cast headlights and red lettering, orange stripe, Ely observation **125 300 125**

(C) State brown with dark green frame, Bild-A-Loco motor, cream stripe, red lettering, brass pantograph and whistle **150 475 125**

(D) Gray, black frame, latch couplers **75 165 95**

(E) Red with cream stripe,cast headlights, brass pantograph and whistle, black lettering **75 165 95**

(F) Same as (B), but no orange stripe, Ely Collection **NRS**

(G) Light olive green, black frame, red lettering, nickel trim, strap headlight and latch couplers, Ely Collection **NRS**

33 Early: electric, 0-6-0, 1913, NYC S-type, was "1910" with U-frame, nickel bell, gold vents, red window outline, 6-spoke wheels and cowcatcher, gold rubber-stamped letters/numbers, 10-3/8"

(A) "NEW YORK CENTRAL LINES" in oval, dark olive green **75 600 250**

(B) Same as (A), but in black **300 700 250**

(C) "PENN R.R." in black block letters **400 675 275**

(D) Similar to (A), but block lettering, no oval **275 600 250**

33 Later: electric, 0-4-0, 1913-24, NYC, round cab, with U-frame (1913-16) or straight frame (1916-24), nickel bell, gold vents, red window outline, 6-spoke wheels and cowcatcher, cast-iron wheels (1913-16) or die-cast wheels (1916-24), in 1916 added hand reversing and in 1924 a Super motor. Came in sets with 100 series freight cars and 35 and 36 series passenger cars, 10-3/8"

(A) Dark olive green, "NEW YORK CENTRAL LINES" in oval **60 125 65**

(B) Black, "C & O" **250 450 175**

(C) Black, "NEW YORK CENTRAL LINES" in oval **60 125 65**

(D) Gray **75 150 65**

(E) Maroon **125 250 100**

(F) Dark green **75 150 65**

(G) Red **175 375 125**

(H) Red with cream stripe **175 375 125**

(I) Peacock **125 375 100**

(J) Same as (A) but with Super motor, 1924 **100 225 75**

(K) Gray with Super motor **75 150 65**

(L) Midnight blue body, made especially for Montgomery Ward in 1912 as part of set with 35 and 36 passenger cars, extremely rare, Ely observation **NRS**

34 Electric, 0-6-0, 1912, NYC prototype, same as 33 0-6-0 in dark olive green with dark red outlined windows. Rubber-stamped "NEW YORK CENTRAL LINES" in gold block letters. Only the center axle is geared. Sliding shoe pickup, non-movable door, crinkle hook couplers, fillister head screws hold pilot to frame. One pedestal headlight, large gold painted stanchions support handrails atop hood. One nickeled bell. Probably included terminal for lighting passenger cars, 10-3/8" long, came as part of set with 35 and 36 passenger cars, very rare, Baeurie Collection **450 600 400**

34 Electric, 0-4-0, 1913, similar to 34 above, with U-frame, die-cast wheels, dark olive green, 10-3/8" **175 400 175**

38 Electric, 0-4-0, 1913, NYC prototype, slightly larger than 33, four thick rimmed drivers and side rods, rubber-stamped "NEW YORK CENTRAL LINES" in oval or block letters, 11-1/8"

(A) Black **70 175 65**

(B) Gray **80 140 65**

(C) Maroon **125 300 70**

(D) Brown **200 350 65**

(E) Red **300 650 65**

(F) Mojave **125 290 65**

(G) Dark green **175 200 65**

(H) Pea Green **200 500 70**

(I) Olive green **100 200 65**

(J) Peacock **250 500 65**

(K) Red with cream trim **250 500 70**

(L) Light olive green **NRS**

---

*Excellent reproductions of the 9 have been made by Williams Electric Trains, 1973-77.

Early Standard Sets

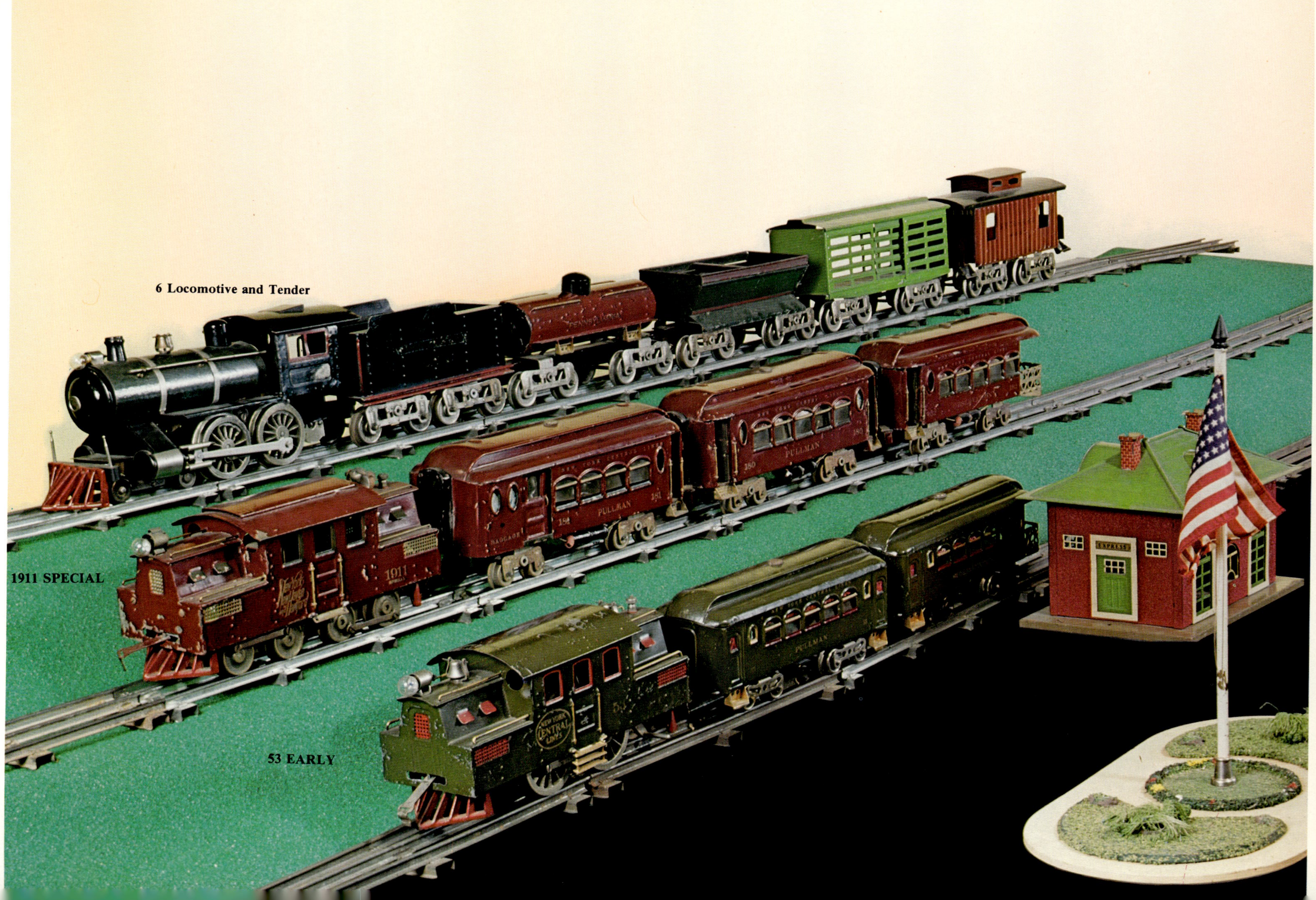

6 Locomotive and Tender

1911 SPECIAL

53 EARLY

42 Electric, 0-4-4-0, 1912 NYC prototype, square hood (same as 1912 loco), dark green only, rare, rubber-stamped "NEW YORK CENTRAL LINES" in oval or in block letters, 15-1/2" **800 1200 750**

42 Electric, 0-4-4-0, 1913-23, the epitome of Early Lionel electrics, a NYC prototype, round hood with NYC in the oval or in block letters. Early versions had a single motor (1913-21) and dummy second motor, three tread steps (1913-18), sliding doors and a coupler pocket soldered to the loco's outside end. Later versions have one-piece step and no sliding door; the coupler pocket was soldered to the inside of the body. In 1921, the 42 gained another motor and two switches, one for AC and DC operation, and one for hand reverse, 15-1/2" - 16"

(A) Black **200 450 200**
(B) Maroon **425 725 250**
(C) Dark gray **200 450 200**
(D) Dark green **200 450 200**
(E) Mojave **300 575 200**
(F) Peacock **425 725 250**
(G) Gray **200 450 200**
(H) Olive green **300 525 200**
(I) Dark olive green **200 450 200**

50 Electric, 0-4-0, 1924, NYC S-prototype, round hood body, same as 38, red window trim and pilots, red trim along body base, 4 brass ventilator screens, 2 steel strap headlights, gold painted handrails, nickel bell and whistle, gold rubber-stamped "NEW YORK CENTRAL LINES" in oval, hand reversing, three-hole step

(A) Dark green, Lionel standard motor with only one geared wheel, same as 38, hook, couplers, side rods **80 150 90**
(B) Same as (A) but dark gray **80 150 90**
(C) Same as (A) but maroon **90 200 90**
(D) Dark green, red trim along body base, Lionel early Super motor with large gears, no side rods, combination latch-hook couplers **80 150 90**
(E) Same as (D) but mojave **80 200 90**
(F) Same as (D) but dark gray **80 150 90**

51 See 5(H)

53 Early: electric, 0-4-4-0, 1912-14, NYC prototype, square hood with eight "flap"-type ventilators and four gold painted ventilator grills, gold rubber-stamped "NEW YORK CENTRAL LINES" in oval in either block or script lettering, one pedestal headlight, two large bells, auxiliary lighting post, long red painted pilots, long crinkle hook couplers, side rods, three-tread brass steps,roof with later monitor section, 12" **800 1700 750**

53 Later: electric, 0-4-0, NYC prototype, square hood, rubber-stamped "NEW YORK CENTRAL LINES" in oval in gold letters, 12-1/4". See 53 (EARLY) and 53 (LATEST) for other variations

(A) Maroon with pedestal headlight, two small bells, short, crinkle hook couplers, reversing switch, long low pilot, split frame, fixed cab doors **450 800 450**
(B) Mojave **450 800 450**
(C) Dark olive green **450 800 450**

53 Latest: electric, 0-4-0, 1920-21, NYC prototype, similar to a 38, with gold rubber-stamped "NEW YORK CENTRAL LINES" in oval, gold painted ventilators and handrails, strap headlight, bell and lighting post for cars, red pilot, side rods, gold painted three-hole steps, 11-1/8". See 53 (EARLY) and 53 (LATER) for other variations **200 400 200**

54 Early: electric, 0-4-4-0, 1912, the top of the line show piece in brass, NYC prototype, square hood with eight "flap"-type ventilators and four red painted ventilator grills located near ends on sides, no lettering on body sides although shown in catalogue, red painted pilots and wheels. Single motor with dummy motor, sliding doors, thick rim drivers, side rods. Two large nickeled bells, one pedestal or slide-on headlight and auxiliary lighting post. Reversing switch, 15-1/2" **2500 3500 2500**

NOTE: Reproduction 54s have been made and extreme caution is required in purchasing an original piece. Square cab Early 42s have been brass-plated and may be misrepresented as 54s. Expert advice is needed in purchasing an original. Also note that a Late 1912 is, in some cases, indistinguishable from an Early 54. Usually the 1912s can be distinguished by their thin rims, but it is believed that some 1912s came with thick rims

54 Late: electric, 0-4-4-0, 1913-23, the top of the line show piece in brass, NYC prototype, round hood without any lettering, red painted pilots, ventilators and wheel spokes

(A) Single motor with dummy motor, sliding doors, pedestal headlight, two bells, auxiliary lighting post, long straight hook couplers, thick rim wheels **1650 2600 1700**
(B) Two motors, fixed doors, strap headlights, two small nickeled bells, auxiliary lighting post, regular hook couplers, thick rim wheels, two switches: one for direction, one for changing from AC to DC operation **1500 2400 1600**

NOTE: 42s have been brass-plated to appear as 54s. However, a magnet test will readily distinguish between the two since a 42 with a brass-plated steel cab will attract the magnet, while a true 54 will not. Reproduction 54s in brass have also been made. Extreme care is required in purchasing an original.

60 Electric, 0-4-0, NYC S-type, uncatalogued F.A.O. Schwarz Special, same as 33, but rubber-stamped "FAOS 60", black **NRS**

61 Electric, 0-4-4-0, NYC-type, uncatalogued F.A.O. Schwarz Special, same as 42, but rubber-stamped "FAOS 61", black **— 1800 —**

62 Electric, 0-4-0, NYC-type, uncatalogued F.A.O. Schwarz Special, same as 38, rubber-stamped "FAOS 62", black **— 1800 —**

318 Electric, 0-4-0, 1924-32, New York Central S-type prototype. (Low-to-medium priced loco.) Brass name and number plates and inserts for windows, ventilators. Early versions with strap headlights, combination latch couplers, large gear Super motor, later versions with cast headlights, latch couplers, small gear Super motor. One pantograph, one whistle. Catalogued with 332, 337, 338, 339, 341, 309, 310, 312 as well as 100 and 500 series freight cars

(A) Dark gray, black lettering, strap headlights, combination latch couplers, nickel pantograph and whistle **110 225 100**
(B) Gray, black lettering, red pilots, brass handrails and trim **100 225 100**
(C) Mojave, brass trim, red lettering, red pilots **100 225 100**
(D) Pea green, cast headlights, red lettering, brass trim including ventilators, red pilots **150 250 150**
(E) State brown with cream stripe, black lettering, cream ventilators, windows and door window frame, cast headlight, red or State brown pilot **200 375 175**
(F) State brown without cream stripe, otherwise same as (E) **200 375 175**

318E Electric, 0-4-0, 1926-35, similar to 318, but with either pendulum-type or drum-type reversing unit

(A) Gray, black lettering, red pilots, brass handrails and trim **110 225 100**
(B) Mojave, brass trim, red lettering, red pilots **110 225 100**
(C) Pea green, cast headlights, red lettering, brass trim including ventilators **110 225 100**
(D) State brown with cream stripe, black lettering, cream ventilators, windows, and door window frame, cast headlight, red or State brown pilots **175 375 150**
(E) State brown without cream stripe. Otherwise same as (E) **175 375 150**
(G) Black, red lettering, red pilots **250 500 225**

380 Electric, 0-4-0, 1923-27, Chicago, Milwaukee, St. Paul & Pacific, Olympian prototype. (Shares prototype with 10 and 381.) Introduced with 402 as first of new generation of electrics. Brass insert plates provide window, door and letter boards. Early models with hook couplers, later combination latch and finally latch couplers. Strap headlights first followed by large celluloid insert headlights, and cast headlights. Early ones with large gear Super motor, later small gear Super motor, with high coupler for 200 series cars, 13-1/2". Over the years, the 380 was catalogued with three different series of passenger cars: the 18, 19 and 190 set, the 319, 320 and 322 set, and the 428, 429 and 430 set. It also came with both the 10 series freights and later with 200 series freight cars. Bowes comment

(A) Maroon, black lettering, nickel pantograph, extra large nickel whistle, cast headlights, regular latch couplers, small-gear Super motor, red pilots, Sattler Collection **120 250 150**
(B) Maroon with black lettering, large nickeled bell, extra large nickeled whistle, large celluloid insert headlights, combination latch couplers, red pilots **120 250 150**

Classic Era Standard Electrics

408 E(B) — 381 E (Williams Reproduction) — 408 (A)

9 E — 10 E — 9 E

380 E — 380 — 380 E

318 E — 9 E — 8 — 318

402 E (C) — 9 — 402 (F)

(C) Mojave with black lettering, extra large nickeled bell and extra large whistle, large celluloid insert headlights, hook couplers or combination latch couplers, large gear Super motor, red pilots **175 375 175**

(D) Dark green with cast headlights, red lettering, large nickel whistle, brass pantograph, combination latch coupler, red pilots **150 325 175**

(E) Same as (A) but pedestal headlight, early production, Fincham Collection **NRS**

(F) Same as (C) but early version with brass ends painted mojave, Ely Collection **350 500 300**

380E 1926-29, similar to 380 but with pendulum-type reversing unit. Some with 2 weights added to frame for traction, "E" stamped on door, or "380E" on number plate. Note that version with weights brings $25.00 more in excellent condition

(A) Maroon, red lettering, cast headlights, latch couplers, red pilots **120 250 150**

(B) Maroon, black lettering, large celluloid insert headlights, combination latch couplers, red pilots **NRS**

(C) Mojave, black lettering, cast headlights, red pilots **175 350 175**

(D) Dark green, black lettering, cast headlights, latch couplers, red pilots **160 325 175**

381 Electric, 4-4-4, 1928-29, Olympian prototype, largest and most elaborate locomotive ever constructed by Lionel.* Bild-A-Loco motor, State green body, apple green sub-frame, and black frame, hand reversing with special brass plate numbered "381" **1250 2500 1500**

381E Electric,* 4-4-4, 1928-36. Same as 381 but with reversing unit. Plate numbered "381E"

(A) State green body, apple green sub-frame **1200 2250 900**

(B) State green body, red sub-frame **1500 2800 900**

381U Electric, 4-4-4, 1928-29. Kit version of hand reversing 381. Kit included parts for stationary motor and 8 sections of track. "Excellent" price requires assembly tools and original box.

(A) Plate numbered "381U" **1850 3750 1800**

(B) Plate numbered "381" **1600 3000 1600**

384 Steam, 2-4-0, 1930-32, with 8-wheel "384T" tender, Super motor, one-piece die-cast frame and pilot, black body with brass domes, handrails, bell and stack and copper piping. Brass plate on cab with black lettering: "No. 384 LIONEL LINES". Hand reversing, tender with copper or nickel journals

(A) Green stripe on frame edge, brass windows in cab **225 400 230**

(B) Green stripe on frame edge, green windows in cab **225 400 230**

(C) No stripe on frame edge, brass windows in cab **225 400 230**

384E Steam, 2-4-0, 1930-32, similar to 384 but with E-unit reversing, red lettered brass plate on cab reads "No. 384E LIONEL LINES"

(A) Green stripe on frame edge, brass windows **235 410 230**

(B) Green stripe on frame edge, green windows **235 410 230**

(C) No stripe on frame edge, brass windows in cab **235 410 230**

385E Steam, 2-4-2, 1933-39 with 384T, 385TW or 385W tenders, Bild-A-Loco motor, die-cast frame, separate steel boiler and pilot, hinged boiler front for lamp access, Pennsylvania style Keystone plate on cab reads "LL", E-unit, 23-1/2", number board on boiler front reads "385E". Came with and without chugger, with and without whistle. For use with 500 series freights and passenger cars with lower coupler heights, Leip comment

The following is a catalogue listing of locos and tenders:

1933 385E with 384T tender, chugger in loco
1934 385E with 384T tender, chugger in loco
1935 385E with 385TW tender, chugger in loco, whistle in tender
1936 385E with 385W tender, chugger in loco, whistle in tender
1937 385E with 385W tender, whistle in tender
1938 385E with 385W tender, whistle in tender
1939 385E with 385W tender, whistle in tender

(A) Dark gunmetal body with copper piping, domes, and brass whistle and bell, red painted drivers, pilot and trailing truck wheels, solid pilot truck wheels. Comes with 384T tender with rectangular brass plate "LIONEL LINES" **290 600 250**

(B) Gunmetal body with nickel piping domes, stack, whistle and bell, black painted drivers, pilot and trailing truck wheels, spoked pilot truck wheels, gunmetal boiler bands. Comes with 384T tender with rectangular brass plate and "LIONEL LINES" in block lettering **290 600 250**

(C) Gunmetal body with nickel piping, domes, whistle, bell,stack, black painted drivers, pilot wheels and trailing truck wheels, spoked pilot wheels, gunmetal boiler bands. Comes with 385T or 385W tender with die-cast body often deteriorated, and long oval nickel and black plate that reads "THE LIONEL RAILWAY LINES" **325 675 310**

390 Steam, 2-4-2, 1929 only; Lionel reentered with steam in 1929 after a hiatus of six years as a response to the popular Ives steam engine line. Steel boiler and die-cast frame, separate headlight casting, hand reversing with Bild-A-Loco motor, 14". Less common than 390E. Black body and frame, orange stripe on frame. Some without orange stripe on frame edge. With 390T tender, brass and copper trim only **350 750 300**

390E Steam, 2-4-2, steel boiler and die-cast frame, pendulum-type E-unit with Bild-A-Loco motor, separate headlight casting, 14". 1929-31, 1933, with passenger car sets 309, 310, 312 or 424, 425, 426. Also came with 500 series freights unless it had 390X tender with 200 series trucks. Then it pulled 200 series freights

(A) Black body and frame, orange stripe on frame, brass domes **300 650 300**

(B) Same as (A), but copper and brass trim **300 650 300**

(C) Same as (B), but no orange stripe **300 650 300**

(D) Two-tone blue, brass domes and smokestack, with copper trim, cream-orange stripe on loco frame and on tender. Came with three "Blue Comet" cars: 420, 421, 422, 1930 only, Leip comment **550 1000 500**

(E) Two-tone green, copper domes, orange or apple green stripe on loco frame and tender. Rare. Never illustrated in the catalogue, it is found with matching green frame or lighter green frame, date unknown **700 1200 675**

392E Steam, 4-4-2, 1932-39, stamped steel boiler, hinged boiler front gave lamp access, die-cast frame, Bild-A-Loco motor, 16-1/2". Next to the top of the line model. Keystone plate on cab with red background, lettered "LL".

(A) Black body, copper and brass trim, red wheels, nickel motor sides. With 384 tender with green stripe, "384T" on bottom, nickeled leading truck, 1932 **525 1000 400**

(B) Same as (A), but with chugger and cab switch, tender not striped, 1932 **550 1100 420**

(C) Black body, copper trim, some with blackened domes, blackened leading trucks, black wheels. With large 12-wheel tender, "LIONEL LINES", brass plate with black background **850 1500 800**

(D) Gunmetal body, nickel trim, black wheels, blackened leading truck, 12-wheel large tender, 1935-39. Tender plates read "LIONEL LINES" on red background **800 1200 775**

(E) Same as (C) but red wheels **850 1500 800**

400E Steam, 4-4-4, 1931-40 with 12-wheel "400T" oil tender, "Bild-A-Loco" motor, whistle in tender, 1935-40, steel boiler, die-cast frame, hinged boiler front, Leip comment

(A) Black with copper and brass trim handrails held by brass clips, red and white number boards, red wheels. Tender has brass and copper trim, brass plates with black lettering and brass journals. Narrow "Bild-A-Loco" motor, 1931, Leip comment **900 1800 1000**

(B) Same as (A), but handrails held by turned brass posts, 1931-32 **900 1800 1000**

(C) Same as (B), but black number boards with white lettering, 1932-33 **900 1800 1000**

(D) Same as (B), but black number boards with white lettering, chugger with switch on firewall, 1932 **900 1800 1000**

(E) Gray with nickel trim, gray painted number boards, handrails held by turned nickel posts, black number boards with white letters, black wheels, motor side plates and leading and trailing truck frames, no chugger, with matching gray whistle with nickel trim and plate with red paint, 1935-40 **1200 2500 1200**

(F) Medium blue boiler, dark blue frame, with/without cream stripe on frame. Copper trim, brass boiler bands, handrails held by brass clips, red

---

* Electric, 4-4-4, Chicago, Milwaukee, St. Paul Olympian prototype. Reproduction by Williams Reproductions. Comes with dummy motor, but many have been powered by their owners with original Lionel motors

(A) Same as Lionel's but without quick release strip from motor to lights, "WRL" stamped into frame, "LIONEL" plates **— 300 —**

(B) Same as above, but with "Chicago, Milwaukee, St. Paul and Pacific" plates rather than "LIONEL" **— 275 —**

Classic Era Standard Steam

384 E

390 E

385 E

1835 E

392 E

and white number boards, red wheels. Matching "400T" tender with brass trim and name plates with black lettering, brass journal boxes, 1931 **1200 2200 1200**

(G) Medium blue boiler, dark blue frame, with/without cream stripe on frame.Copper trim blue painted boiler bands, handrails held by turned brass posts, black and white number boards, black wheels, matching tender with brass journals and trim, red painted brass plates, 1935 **1200 2200 1200**

(H) Light blue with dark blue frame, with/without cream stripe on frame. Nickel trim, blue painted boiler bands, handrails held by turned nickel posts, black and white number boards, black wheels. "400T" matching tender with brass trim and aluminum plates with red paint, 1936-40 **1400 2800 1200**

(I) Medium blue boiler, dark blue frame, copper and brass trim, copper boiler bands, handrails held by turned brass posts, black number boards with white letters, "400T" tender with brass trim and name plates with black lettering, brass journal boxes, 1933-34 **1200 2200 1200**

(J) Gunmetal, copper trim and brass boiler bands, handrails held by turned brass posts, black and white number boards, red wheels with solid pony wheels, tender has brass trim and plates, chugger mechanism **900 1800 1000**

(K) Crackle black loco and tender, loco with copper trim and boiler bands, handrails held by turned brass posts, black number boards with white lettering, red wheels, solid leading truck wheels, nickeled motor side plates and leading and trailing truck frames with chugger. Many restorations and fakes. Few originals are known to exist. **2500 4000 1200**

(L) Black with nickel trim. Very rare **2500 4000 1200**

(M) Dark blue with purplish dark blue frame, copper trim and brass boiler bands, with/without red stripe on frame. Very rare **2500 4000 1200**

(N) Black with red stripe on frame and tender. Very rare **2500 3750 1100**

NOTE: Nickel-trimmed 400s are very rare and hard to find with a good original frame.

402 Electric, 1923-27, 0-4-4-0, NYC S-prototype, two Super motors, 17-1/2". Nearly always found in mojave, hole punched in frame near end for auxiliary lighting post, two different sized holes. Catalogued with 418, 419 and 490 passenger cars as well as with either 10 series freight (Early) or 200 series freight cars (Later). Numerous 402 variations exist. A listing of some follows:

(A) Strap headlights, hook couplers, two large gear Super motors, two nickel bells, two extra large nickel whistles **225 450 225**

(B) Celluloid insert headlights with on-off switch, combination latch couplers, two large gear Super motors, two nickel bells and two extra large nickel whistles, black lettering on plates, Leip comments **225 450 225**

(C) Cast headlights, latch coupler, small gear Super motors, two medium sized nickel pantographs, two large nickel whistles, red lettering on plates **225 450 225**

(D) Cast headlights, latch couplers, small gear Super motors, two brass pantographs, one nickel whistle, one brass bell, 3/16" hole for lighting post **225 450 225**

(E) Same as (B), but latch couplers, regular large sized whistles **225 450 225**

402E Electric, 1926-29, 0-4-4-0, same as 402 but with pendulum-type reversing unit and small gear Super motors, mojave. Some with plates lettered "402E", others with plates numbered "402" with "E" stamped on cab door. Some variations listed, more believed to exist:

(A) Cast headlights, latch couplers, red lettering, two pantographs, two whistles **225 450 250**

(B) Cast headlights, combination couplers, red lettering, one pantograph, two whistles, one bell **225 450 250**

(C) Celluloid insert headlights, combination couplers, two bells, two whistles, black lettering **240 475 260**

408E* Electric, 1927-36, 0-4-4-0, NYC S-prototype, two motors. More elaborate version of 402 with added roof, side and end trim as well as two additional lights on each end. Two large folding pantographs, two whistles, 17-1/2". Excellent reproductions have been made by Williams Electric Trains.*

(A) Apple green, most common color, red pilots **500 1000 500**

(B) Mojave, combination or latch couplers, red pilots **500 1000 500**

(C) Two-tone brown body (known as State brown paint scheme) and roof with two Bild-A-Loco motors, or two Super motors, brown pilots **1700 2300 700**

(D) State brown body, dark brown roof with two Bild-A-Loco motors, brown pilots **1400 3000 675**

(E) State car dark green, uncatalogued. Rare. Usually a factory repaint to match the State Cars, red pilots **1500 3000 600**

1835E Steam, 2-4-2, 1934-39 with 384T, 1835T, 1835TW or 1835W tenders, chassis and motor identical to 385E, but different paint and trim scheme. See 385E for details. The 1835E was less expensive than the 385E and did not have a chugger, although in later years it did come with a whistle. Black boiler, cab and frame, black domes, stack and boiler bands, one nickel pipe on each side, black spoked drivers, pilot and trailing wheels. Pennsylvania-style keystone plate on cab reads "LL". The following is a listing taken from the catalogues:

1934: 1835E with 1835T tender, (Illustration shows 384T tender however)
1935: 1835E with 1835TW tender. Tender with whistle
1936, 1937, 1938, 1939: 1835E with 1835W tender. Tender with whistle

(A) 1835E with 384T tender **280 590 250**

(B) 1835E with 1835T, 1835TW or 1835W tender (Die-cast tender with long oval plate that reads "THE LIONEL RAILWAY LINES") **300 635 265**

1910 Early, Electric, 1910-11, 0-6-0, NYC S-prototype, dark olive green body with square hood, "New York, New Haven, and Hartford" in fancy gold script, large nickel bell, pedestal headlight, red trim on 8 ventilator flaps, four ventilator grills and long pilots. Raised monitor roof, long straight hook couplers. One direction only, the two center wheels are cast-iron and are powered, while the other four wheels are stamped steel and not powered, 9-3/4". Came with two short (7-1/2") gondolas. Price for loco only **500 1200 600**

1910 Late, Electric, 1912 only, 0-6-0, NYC S-prototype, dark olive green body with round hood, same body as 33, "NEW YORK CENTRAL LINES" gold stamped in oval, large nickel bell, pedestal headlight, one direction only, gold painted ventilator grills, red pilots and window trim. Came with two short (7-1/2") gondolas. Price for loco only **450 1000 500**

1911 Early, Electric, 1910-12, 0-4-0, NYC S-prototype, square hoods, nickeled bell, pedestal headlight, auxiliary lighting post, 8 ventilator flaps, 4 ventilator grills, long red pilots, cast-iron wheels, long straight hook couplers.

(A) Dark olive green body with "New York, New Haven, and Hartford" in fancy gold script **425 800 450**

(B) Maroon body with "NEW YORK CENTRAL LINES" gold rubber-stamped inside oval **325 700 350**

(C) Dark olive green body with "NEW YORK CENTRAL LINES" in gold block lettering **325 700 350**

1911 Late, Electric, 1913, 0-4-0, NYC S-prototype, round hood, same body as 38, "NEW YORK CENTRAL LINES" in gold stamped block lettering, gold painted ventilators and handrails, nickeled bell and pedestal headlight, iron wheels, long crinkle hook couplers, short red pilots, red window trim and side rods **325 700 350**

1911 Special, Electric, 1911-12, 0-4-4-0, NYC S-prototype, maroon body with square hood, and eight ventilator flaps, larger body than regular 1911. Large nickel bell, pedestal headlight, auxiliary lighting post, gold painted handrails, long red painted pilots, side rods, long straight hook couplers, gold stamped "1911 SPECIAL"

(A) Gold rubber-stamped in fancy script "New York, New Haven and Hartford" **375 800 400**

(B) Gold rubber-stamped in block lettering "NEW YORK CENTRAL LINES" **375 800 400**

1912 Electric, 1910-12, 0-4-4-0, NYC S-prototype, dark olive green body with square hood, 8 red ventilator flaps, 4 red ventilator grills, gold painted handrails, red painted pilot, one motor, one dummy motor, side rods, two large bells, auxiliary lighting post, raised monitor section on roof, "1912" rubber-stamped in gold on side, reversing switch, sliding cab doors

---

*Williams Reproductions' 408E Electric, 0-4-4-0, NYC S-type prototype, dual dummy electric motors, most with "NYC" plates, some with "LIONEL" plates. "WRL" stamped on frame. Many have been powered by their owners with original Lionel motors.

(A) Apple green — 450 —
(B) Dark green — 450 —
(C) Two-tone brown — 500 —
(D) Mojave — 450 —

The Top of the Line 400 E

The Dual Motored Giant

408 E(E)

Classic Era Steam

400 E

392 E

392 E

(A) Thin rims, slide-on headlights, gold stamped "New York, New Haven and Hartford" in fancy script, short straight hook couplers, circa 1910-11 **1800 3200 1700**
(B) Thin rims, pedestal headlights, gold stamped "NEW YORK CENTRAL LINES" in block lettering, circa 1912 **1750 3000 1600**
(C) Thick rims, pedestal headlights, gold stamped "NEW YORK CENTRAL LINES" in block lettering, circa 1912 **1500 2700 1450**

1912 Special, Electric, 1911, 0-4-4-0, NYC S-prototype. Same as 1912, but polished brass body with red painted ventilator flaps and grills, pilots and drivers. Two large brass bells, auxiliary lighting post, long straight hook couplers, sliding cab doors, no lettering on sides, soldered on headlight, thin rims. This locomotive and the early Lionel 7 in brass are the most prized of the early Lionel series. As with the Lionel 7, great care must be exercised by buyers searching for originals since fine, unmarked reproductions have been made. **1500 2700 1700**

TROLLEYS, INTERURBANS AND TRAILERS

1 Trolleys 1-8
(A) Cream body, orange band and roof, with cream solid clerestory, rubber-stamped "No. 1 Electric-Rapid Transit No. 1", four wheels, five windows without embossed frames on each side, L-shaped solid steps, early New Departure Motor with friction drive, short frame, 5-1/8", open platform roof 8-1/2" long, circa 1906 **1000 2000 1000**
(B) White body, blue band and roof, with solid white clerestory, rubber-stamped "No. 1 Electric Rapid Transit No. 1", four wheels, five windows without embossed frames on each side, L-shaped solid steps, New Departure Motor with gear drive, short frame, 5-5/8", open platform, roof 8-1/2" long, circa 1907 **900 1900 1000**
(B-1) Matching non-powered trailer **700 1700 900**
(C) Cream body, blue band and roof with solid cream clerestory, rubber-stamped "No. 1 Electric Rapid Transit No. 1", four wheels, six windows with embossed frames, L-shaped solid steps, Standard motor, frame 5-7/8", roof 9-9/16" long, open platform, 1908 **800 1700 900**
(C-1) Matching non-powered trailer **700 1600 800**
(D) Same as (C), but lettered "No. 1 CURTIS BAY No. 1" **1100 2100 1100**
(E) Blue body, cream window band, blue roof with cream clerestory, rubber-stamped "No. 1 Electric Rapid Transit No. 1", four wheels, six windows with embossed frames, open rung steps, Standard motor, frame 5-7/8" long, roof 10-15/16" long, open platform with maroon posts, light, circa 1910 **1000 1800 950**

2 (A) Yellow body, red band, light blue squared roof with yellow open clerestory, rubber-stamped "No. 2 ELECTRIC RAPID TRANSIT No. 2", four wheels, six windows without embossed frames, open rung steps, Standard motor, 5-7/8" long, open platform with light blue posts, short straight hook couplers, 1906 **800 1700 900**
(A-1) Matching non-powered trailer **700 1600 800**
(B) Yellow body, red band, yellow rounded end roof with yellow clerestory with partial openings, rubber-stamped "No. 2 ELECTRIC RAPID TRANSIT No. 2", four wheels, six windows with embossed frames, wire suspended L-shaped steps, Standard motor, frame 5-7/8" long, closed platform, long straight hook couplers or long crinkle hook couplers, 1908-1909 **800 1700 900**
(B-1) Matching non-powered trailer **700 600 800**
(C) Red body, yellow window bands, doors, rounded end roof, and clerestory with partial openings, rubber-stamped "No. 2 ELECTRIC RAPID TRANSIT No. 2", four wheels, six windows, Standard motor, frame 5-7/8" long, closed platform with offset window, hook couplers, one light on platform end, hand reversing, 1910-12 **800 1700 900**
(C-1) Matching non-powered trailer **800 1700 900**
(D) Red body, yellow window bands and doors, rounded end yellow roof, and clerestory with partial openings, rubber-stamped "No. 2 ELECTRIC RAPID TRANSIT No. 2", four wheels, six windows with embossed frames, wire suspended L-shaped steps, Standard motor, frame 5-7/8" long, closed platform, long straight hook or crinkle hook coupler, one light, flush platform window and lower panel, 1913-16 **800 1700 900**
(D-1) Matching non-powered trailer **700 1600 1300**
(E) Same as (D), but platform window offset from lower platform panel, 1910-12 **700 1600 800**

3 (A) Cream body, orange band and roof with straight ends, open clerestory, rubber-stamped "No. 3 ELECTRIC RAPID TRANSIT No. 3", eight wheels, solid three-rivet trucks, nine windows without embossed frames, Standard motor, roof 13-7/8" long, open platform with posts, short straight hook couplers, 1906-07 **1400 3000 1500**
(B) Cream body, light orange band, orange roof with straight ends, open clerestory, rubber-stamped "No. 3 ELECTRIC RAPID TRANSIT No. 3", eight wheels, solid, three-rivet trucks, nine windows with embossed frames, Standard motor, roof 13-7/8", open platform with posts, short straight hook couplers, 1908-09 **1400 3000 1500**
(C) Same as (B) but cream body, dark olive green band and roof **1400 3000 1500**
(D) Same as (B) but cream sides,dark olive green band and roof, and open, three-rivet trucks **1400 3000 1500**
(D-1) Matching non-powered trailer **1300 2700 1400**
(E) Same as (A) but orange sides, dark olive green band and roof, and solid three-rivet trucks **1400 3000 1500**
(F) Dark green body, roof and lower platform ends, cream windows, doors and clerestory roof, maroon suspended L-shaped steps and coupler supports, rubber-stamped "No. 3 ELECTRIC RAPID TRANSIT No. 3", eight wheels, open three-rivet trucks, nine windows, embossed frames, Standard motor, roof 15-1/4" long, closed platform with offset windows **1400 3000 1500**
(G) Green body, roof, and lower platform end, cream windows, door and clerestory roof, maroon suspended L-shaped steps and coupler supports, rubber-stamped "No. 3 BAY SHORE No. 3", eight wheels, open single-rivet trucks, nine windows, embossed frame, Standard motor, roof 15-1/4" long, closed platforms with flush ends, one headlight, long straight hook couplers **1650 3500 1500**
(H) Same as (G) but lettered "No. 3 ELECTRIC RAPID TRANSIT No. 3" **1400 3000 1500**
(I) Same as (F) but green coupler supports and steps **1450 3200 1500**

4 (A) Cream body, windows, and clerestory roof, dark olive green band and roof, rubber-stamped "No. 4 ELECTRIC RAPID TRANSIT No. 4", eight wheels, closed three-rivet trucks, open steps, nine windows, embossed frames, two Standard motors, 13-7/8" long roof, open platform with posts, no headlights, short straight hook couplers **2000 4500 2000**
(B) Same as 4(A) but with interior light and headlight **2000 4500 2200**
(C) Dark olive green body, roof and platform ends, cream windows and clerestory roof, rubber-stamped "No.4 ELECTRIC RAPID TRANSIT No. 4", eight wheels, open three-rivet trucks, nine windows, embossed frames, open steps, two Standard motors, roof 13-7/8" long, open platform with posts, no headlights, short straight hook couplers **2000 4500 2200**
(D) Green body, roof, and platform ends, cream windows, doors and clerestory roof, maroon steps and coupler supports, rubber-stamped "No. 4 ELECTRIC RAPID TRANSIT No. 4", eight wheels, open three-rivet trucks, nine windows, embossed frames, suspended L-shaped steps, two Standard motors, 15-1/4" long roof, closed platform,flush ends, headlight, long straight couplers **2000 4500 2200**

8 (A) Cream body,doors, clerestory roof and platform ends, orange roof and band, rubber-stamped "No. 8 PAY AS YOU ENTER No. 8", eight wheels, open three-rivet trucks, nine windows, embossed frame, Standard motor, 17-3/4" long roof, large closed platform, offset windows on platforms. Based on No. 3 body with long vestibules adapted for No. 8 1908-09 **1400 3250 1500**
(B) Largest Lionel trolley: dark green sides, roof, platform and lower panels, cream windows, door, clerestory roof, red steps and coupler supports, rubber-stamped "No. 8 PAY AS YOU ENTER No. 8", eight wheels, open single-rivet trucks, eleven windows, embossed frames, large perforated steps, one Standard motor, 20-1/4" long roof, one headlight, no couplers, offset windows on platforms, large vestibule **1400 3250 1500**
(C) Same as (B) but rubber-stamped "8 PAY AS YOU ENTER 8"* **1400 3250 1500**
(D) Same as (B) but green steps and coupler supports **1400 3250 1500**

*Williams Reproduction No. 8 Trolley is the same as Lionel's 8(c), but has tab-and-slot construction, rather than soldered joints, and a can type motor with two diodes rather than the original type of motor; dark olive and cream; came with redwood box; stamped "Made by Williams Reproductions Limited, Laurel, Md." on trolley floor.

Trolleys, Trailers and Interurbans

8 Reproduction

1 (B)

2 (D)

2 (D-1)

1 (A)

3 (A)

1010 (B-1)

3300 (A)

9 Motor Car

(A) Matches 8 (A), cream body, doors, platform ends, and clerestory roof, orange roof and side band, rubber-stamped "No. 9 PAY AS YOU ENTER No. 9", eight wheels, open three-rivet trucks, nine windows, embossed frames, two Standard motors, 17-3/4" long roof, closed platform, offset windows on platforms. Based on No. 3 body with long vestibules adapted for Nos. 8 and 9, 1909 **3000 5000 3000**

(B) Matches 8 (B) except two motors **3000 5000 2750**

10 Interurban

(A) Maroon body and roof, high black knobs soldered to roof, solid clerestory and gold painted steps with many small holes, gold windows and coupler supports, gold rubber-stamped "INTERURBAN" and "NEW YORK CENTRAL LINES", gold painted wire handrails, open three-rivet trucks, ring and disc reverse, two large black wooden airtanks, short crinkle hook couplers, slide-on headlight with bracket, two doors, matching unpowered trailer, 1010(A) **600 1400 700**

(B) Dark olive green body and roof, high black knobs soldered to roof, solid clerestory, gold painted steps with many small holes, gold and maroon window trim and gold painted coupler supports, gold rubber-stamped "10 INTERURBAN 10" and "NEW YORK CENTRAL LINES" on sides, open three-rivet trucks, two large black wooden airtanks, removable floor, maroon doors, short crinkle hooks, slide-on headlight with bracket, matching trailer, see 1010(B) **600 1400 700**

(B-1) Same as (B) but low black knobs **600 1400 700**

(C) Maroon body and roof, seven windows, closed vestibules, high black knobs soldered to roof, solid clerestory, gold painted steps with many small holes, green and gold window trim, gold painted coupler supports, gold rubber-stamped "10 INTERURBAN 10" and "NEW YORK CENTRAL LINES" on sides, open three-rivet trucks, two large, black, wooden airtanks, removable floor, green doors, short crinkle hooks, slide-on headlight with bracket, matching trailer, see 1010(C) **600 1400 700**

(D) Dark olive green body and roof, seven windows, closed vestibules, no knobs, removable roof with one thumb screw and pierced clerestory with blue painted celluloid, gold painted steps punched with many small holes, maroon and gold trim, red painted celluloid window material for upper window section, gold painted coupler supports, gold rubber-stamped "10 INTERURBAN 10" and "NEW YORK CENTRAL LINES" on sides, open three-rivet trucks, two large, black, wooden airtanks, maroon doors, long straight hook couplers, slide-on headlight with bracket, single motor, ring and disc reverse, matching trailer, see 1010(D) **600 1400 700**

(E) Same as 10 (D) but open single-rivet truck **600 1400 700**

(F) Same as 10 (D) but open single-rivet truck and gold rubber-stamped "10 W.B.& A. 10" on lower side and "INTERURBAN" above window **1750 2750 1600**

(G) Same as 10 (D), but elaborately pierced clerestory with tabs, single-rivet open trucks, gold painted stamped steps with three holes, matching trailer, see 1010(G) **600 1400 700**

(H) Similar to 10 (D) but elaborately pierced clerestory with tabs, single-rivet open trucks, gold painted stamped steps with three holes, pedestal headlight, lighting post for trailer on vestibule, matching trailer, see 1010(H) **600 1400 700**

100 Trolley

(A) Blue body, roof and ends, white windows, doors, clerestory, five windows, offset windows on closed end platforms, maroon steps and coupler supports, one headlight, short crinkle hook couplers, turned door knobs, gold rubber-stamped "100 ELECTRIC RAPID TRANSIT 100" 5-7/8" long frame, 10-7/8" long roof, 1910 **900 1800 1300**

(A-1) Matching non-powered trailer, see 1000(A) **900 1800 1300**

(B) Blue body, roof and ends, cream windows, doors, clerestory, five windows, embossed window frame, flush windows on closed end platforms, maroon couplers, steps and coupler supports, one headlight, short straight hook couplers, stamped door knobs, gold rubber-stamped "100 ELECTRIC RAPID TRANSIT 100", 5-7/8" long frame, 10-7/16" long roof, 1912-14 **700 1500 1000**

(B-1) Matching unpowered trailer, see 1000(B) **700 1500 1000**

(C) Same as 100(B) but red sides, roof and ends, cream windows, doors and clerestory **700 1500 1000**

(D) Same as 100 (B) but rubber-stamped "100 LINDEN AVE. 100" **900 2000 1000**

(E) Red body, roof and ends, cream windows, doors, clerestory, six windows, embossed window frames, flush windows on end platforms, black couplers, coupler supports and steps, one headlight, long straight hook couplers, stamped door knobs, rubber-stamped "100 Electric Rapid Transit 100", 5-7/8" long frame, 11-1/2" long roof, 1914-15 **700 1500 1000**

(F) Blue body, roof and ends, cream windows, doors, clerestory, six windows, embossed frames, flush windows on end platforms, nickel plated couplers, maroon coupler supports and suspended L-shaped steps, two headlights, long crinkle hook couplers, rubber-stamped "100 Electric Rapid Transit 100", 5-7/8" long frame, 11-1/2" long roof, 1915 **700 1500 1000**

101 Summer Trolley

(A) Smallest Lionel summer car with five benches with blue ends, blue roof and ends, yellow clerestory, maroon posts and base side, gold rubber-stamped "101 ELECTRIC RAPID TRANSIT 101", maroon painted short crinkle hook couplers, maroon coupler supports, Standard motor, 5-7/8" long frame, 10-3/8" long roof, 1910. Matching non-powered trailer, see 1100(A) **800 1800 800**

(B) Same as (A) but blue base side, cream posts, 5-7/8" long frame **800 1800 800**

(C) Same as (A) but five benches, red roof and ends, yellow posts, black side, black painted short hook couplers, black coupler supports, 5-7/8" long frame **800 1800 800**

200 Trailer

(A) Matches 2(C) Trolley, but non-powered and rubber-stamped "No. 200 ELECTRIC RAPID TRANSIT No. 200" **NRS**

202 Summer Trolley: Medium sized, summer car with six benches with red ends, red roof and ends, yellow clerestory, and posts, black base, sides, gold rubber-stamped "202 ELECTRIC RAPID TRANSIT 202", black painted long straight hook coupler, Standard motor, manual reverse, matching non-powered trailer, see 2200. **800 2400 1000**

303 Summer Trolley: Largest Lionel summer car with eight cream benches,and dark olive ends, dark olive green roof and ends, yellow clerestory and posts, maroon base and side, gold rubber-stamped "303 ELECTRIC RAPID TRANSIT 303", one Standard motor, two four-wheel trucks, 15" long roof, one headlight, matching non-powered trailer, see 3300. **1300 2800 1400**

1000 Trailer

(A) Matches 100 (A) but not powered, gold rubber-stamped "1000 ELECTRIC RAPID TRANSIT 1000" **NRS**

(B) Matches 100 (B) but not powered, gold rubber-stamped "1000 ELECTRIC RAPID TRANSIT 1000" **NRS**

1010 Trailer

(A) Matches 10 (A) Interurban, but no motor **600 1400 800**

(B) Matches 10 (B) Interurban, but no motor **600 1400 800**

(B-1) Matches 10 (B-1) Interurban, but no motor **600 1400 800**

(C) Matches 10 (C) Interurban, but no motor **600 1400 800**

(D) Matches 10 (D) Interurban, but no motor **600 1400 800**

1100 Trailer

(A) Matches 101 (A) but not powered, gold rubber-stamped "1100 ELECTRIC RAPID TRANSIT 1100" **NRS**

2200 Trailer

(A) Matches 202 but not powered, gold rubber-stamped "2200 RAPID TRANSIT 2200" **1100 2500 1100**

3300 Trailer

(A) Matches 303 but not powered, gold rubber-stamped "3300 ELECTRIC RAPID TRANSIT 3300" **1400 3000 1400**

The No. 202 Summer Trolley

Chapter II

STANDARD GAUGE FREIGHT CARS

By Henry Edmunds and Roland E. LaVoie

During the years from 1906 to 1940, Lionel produced four basic series of Standard Gauge freight cars: the 10, 100, 200 and 500 series. Very early in its history, Lionel instituted the practice of a "deluxe" series and a "regular" series of freight cars. The 10 series, produced from 1906 to 1926, became the "deluxe" series when the 100 series was introduced in 1910. When a major production shift occurred in the mid-twenties, the 200 series replaced the 10 series and the 500 series replaced the 100 series. The 100 and 500 series freight cars are significantly smaller than their 10 and 200 counterparts. However, most of the construction techniques between a deluxe series and its regular counterpart are very similar and, in a great many cases, identical except for size.

Construction of the 200 and 500 freights was fairly uniform. Most of the differences found in the variations concern the use of nickel or brass trim or combinations of paint colors. For that reason, the variations of the later cars are easy for the collector to spot. However, such is not the case with the 10 and 100 freights.

To the beginning enthusiast the earlier freight cars present a bewildering variety of configurations.[1] With experience, however, these varieties became more familiar and patterns became visible. The usual question is why a particular change was made. Unfortunately, the 60 to 80 years separating us from the men and women who made the trains means that first-hand information is usually lost. However, a more general explanation is available. Lionel was a small scale manufacturing company with annual production in the high hundreds or low thousands. Management consequently made manufacturing and design changes readily to control or reduce costs. Sometimes this involved taking advantage of special material purchases and substituting the new for the old. Other times, a change was intended to solve the problem of worn or broken tooling. Finally, changes were sometimes made to make a better product.

Another reason for the variety of the 10 and 100 cars is simply their great age. Examples of old and flaking paint have been found where the car was repainted outside the factory very soon after it was made. Over the years, many cars have had trucks, couplers, brakewheels and other parts replaced outside the factory. Truly excellent examples of these cars have helped clarify the situation, but such cars are very hard to find. When an unusual variation turns up for sale which is presented as original, the purchaser is urged to exercise extreme caution.

Up to this time, manufacturing variations of 10 and 100 series cars have been given little attention. Consequently, the market does not usually differentiate value, cash wise, among varieties. With increased study and interest, we expect increased price differentiation between the harder and easier to find varieties.

We recognize that the astonishing number of varieties which have turned up, especially among the older cars, will lead to some confusion because most collectors will have no certain way to make judgements about scarcity. That is where you, the readers, come in. For the next edition of this book, we would like inventories of collections from as many collectors as possible. We would then be able to establish the relative scarcity or commonness of the varieties listed.

A great many people assisted the writers of this chapter in its preparation. Rev. Robert E. (Bob) Pauli and George Koff graciously allowed us to examine their extensive collections, and they shared with us their expertise developed over many years of collecting these cars. Numerous dealers allowed us to look over the pieces on their tables. Al Weaver sent in beautiful slides of his extensive collection. James Sattler shared photos with us and gave us a long list of variations in his collection. When editing time came, David Ely spent many hours giving us a chronology, new varieties and corrections for the 10 and 100 series cars. Philip Graves dramatically expanded our manuscript with new information on production variations in the 200 and 500 series cars. These two gentlemen caught a number of errors and made this a much more accurate chapter. Also making significant contributions were Roger Bartelt, Birk Leip and Woody Hoffman.

THE 10 SERIES FREIGHT CARS

These freight cars were introduced by Lionel in 1906 as the first Standard Gauge freight cars made by the company. Between their introduction and the cessation of their production in 1926, many changes in their construction occurred with frequent overlapping. These changes somewhat obscure the dating of the cars, but in general there are four readily identifiable phases of construction. Chronologically, they are:

PHASE I. EARLY "LIONEL MANUFACTURING CO."

The earliest cars of the 10 series show a lemon-yellow undercoat, and the bottom is neither stamped nor embossed. The color of the undercoating was changed to flat red a few years afterward, possibly when the early closed-side truck was replaced by the three-rivet open-side truck. In later production during this period, the underside was painted the same as the base color of the car.

PHASE II. LATER "LIONEL MANUFACTURING CO."

These cars, definitely manufactured prior to 1918, have their undersides painted the same color as the car. However, the bottom of the car is boldly embossed in large block letters, "LIONEL MFG. CO." In 1918, Lionel changed its corporate name to the "Lionel Corporation".

PHASE III. EARLY "LIONEL CORPORATION"

These cars are essentially the same as Phase II, but their undersides carry neither an embossing, nor rubber-stamped black lettering. Great care must be used in dating cars from this phase. They may indeed belong to a transitional period between the embossing the the rubber-stamping. On the other hand, the undersides may have once been rubber-stamped but repainted outside or even within the factory. They may also be cars which missed either the embossing or the rubber-stamping

[1] However, Marx and prewar American Flyer enthusiasts claim that their favorites produced even more varieties. Some American Flyer enthusiasts have been known to wonder aloud if their Chicago Flyer ever produced two or three pieces which are exactly the same.

10 Series Freights

12 (A) 11 (A) 12 (B)

13 (A) 14 (A) 15 (C)

16 (B)

13 (D) 14 (I) 15 (E)

16 (F) 17 (A) 17 (E)

process. Examples of these cars with original paint are readily observable. However, more research is needed to determine whether they represent a legitimate phase of construction. Other clues from couplers and trucks can help date these cars - assuming the couplers and trucks have never been replaced.

PHASE IV. LATER "LIONEL CORPORATION"

These cars, representing the last period of construction, are rubber-stamped with the car's number in black on the underside. Also rubber-stamped in black (sometimes gold) is the legend "MADE IN U.S.A. THE LIONEL CORPORATION NEW YORK" in three lines below the number.

Trucks and couplers are often helpful in assigning a 10 series car to a particular phase of construction. The earliest cars (1906-08) have closed-side three-rivet trucks. From 1908-10, another three-rivet truck was used which has open slots and embossed springs. In these cases - and no others - the wheels and axles turn as one unit. All later trucks feature wheels which turn individually. In 1911, a single-rivet open-sided truck was introduced. It has a large eyelet or rivet fastening the bolster to the side frame. There are at least three major varieties of the 10 series truck with one rivet on each side holding the side frame and bolster together. We believe the earliest version had two crimps on each side where the bolster was bent to form vertical sections. The bolster's vertical section was stamped out such that it matched the side frame, and was not visible through it. A later version eliminated the crimping at the bend over area. The third version did not have the crimping and the vertical section of the bolster and was rectangular and readily visible behind the side frame. We believe that several different kinds of rivets were used to join the side frames and bolster, but we do not know which type of rivet went with which truck version.

The 1911 version of the 10 series truck has two crimps where the bolster is bent and the bolster is stamped out to match the side frame. Bartelt photograph.

The couplers show similar variety. The early cars from 1906 to 1914 use a straight L-shaped hook which can be short (5/16") or long (1/2"). About 1910, Lionel began to install these hooks with a crinkle at the bent end, presumably to keep them from popping out of the coupler slots. As before, there were short and long versions of these couplers, which were used until 1918. In 1917, Lionel began to install by far the most common coupler

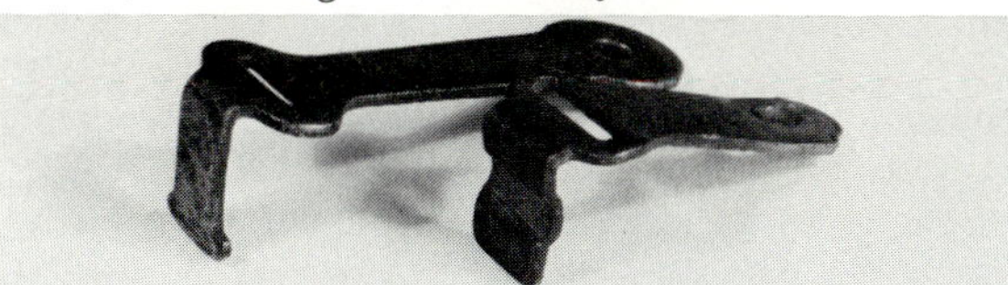

TOP: Hook coupler with ears. BOTTOM: Long crinkle hook coupler. Bartelt photograph.

used on the 10 series. It replaced the crinkle with two projecting nibs or ears on the bottom of the bent end. This coupler was used until production ended in 1926.

An unusual fate befell the 10 series in its last year of production. In 1926, Lionel began manufacturing its 500 series to replace the 10 series. American Flyer, then beginning its manufacture of Standard Gauge trains in Chicago, purchased an unknown quantity of Lionel 10 series bodies. They then stamped the cars with "American Flyer" underneath the body and mounted them on American Flyer trucks. These cars are now very rare and highly prized. For further information, refer to the short article on these cars by Bob Robinson and Ed Pinsky in the Autumn 1978 issue of the **Atlantic Division Express** and to Volume III, page 107 of the McComas-Tuohy series on Lionel Standard Gauge.

	Gd	Exc	Rst

11 Flat Car, 1906-1926. Some of the earliest production have handrails running the length of the car; most models were without handrails, end bolsters or stops were usually painted black.

I. EARLY "LIONEL MANUFACTURING CO." PRODUCTION Yellow or maroon underframe, no embossing, Type I or II trucks

	Gd	Exc	Rst
(A) Maroon body, two brakewheels, three-rivet Type II open-side trucks, no handrails, short hook couplers	50	100	50
(B) Same as A, but handrails and 3-rivet closed-side trucks, short straight coupler, Ely comment	32	50	25

II. LATER "LIONEL MANUFACTURING CO." PRODUCTION Embossed "LIONEL MFG. CO." on car underside

	Gd	Exc	Rst
(C) Brown body, two brakewheels, handrails, single-rivet flex trucks, long hook couplers, rubber-stamped "PENNSYLVANIA" in sans-serif lettering, Ely comment	32	50	25
(D) Maroon body, two brakewheels, handrails, single-rivet flex trucks, long hook couplers	32	50	25
(E) Orange body, two brakewheels, no handrails, single-rivet flex trucks, long hook couplers, black rubber-stamped "PENNSYLVANIA R.R." on side	75	125	50
(F) Red body, two brakewheels, no handrails, hook couplers with ears, single-rivet flex trucks	35	65	25

III. EARLY "LIONEL CORPORATION" PRODUCTION No embossing or stamping on car floor

	Gd	Exc	Rst
(G) Brown body, two large 1" brakewheels on same side of car, Type V trucks, "PENNSYLVANIA R.R." rubber-stamped in black sans-serif lettering, Ely Collection	32	50	25

IV. LATER "LIONEL CORPORATION" PRODUCTION Rubber-stamped "MADE IN U.S.A./THE LIONEL CORPORATION/NEW YORK" on underframe in black or gold in three lines, either with or without car number.

	Gd	Exc	Rst
(H) Brown body, two brakewheels, no handrails, hook couplers with ears, single-rivet flex trucks	35	65	25
(I) Same as (H), except rubber-stamped "PENNSYLVANIA R.R." in black on car side, Kotil comment	35	65	25
(J) Gray body, two brakewheels, no handrails, hook couplers with ears, single-rivet flex trucks	35	65	25
(K) Maroon body, two brass brakewheels, no handrails, hook couplers with ears, single-rivet flex trucks with embossed screw slot on bottom bolster. The brass brakewheels have the same construction and application techniques as their black counterparts. Koff Collection	32	50	25
(L) Same as (K), but has coupler brackets and two black brakewheels, Koff, Weaver, and Ely Collections	32	50	25
(M) Same as (K), but only one brakewheel, open-sided flex trucks and wheels keyed to axles, Edmunds observation	32	50	25
(N) Maroon body, black painted handrails (possibly not original), Type V trucks, coupler slots in frame lettered "PENNSYLVANIA R.R." in sans-serif black letters, Ely Collection	32	50	25

12 Gondola, 1906-1926, earliest construction has either yellow or flat red undercoating, but some with these colors are also embossed, many variations are found in trim colors. Most examples are lettered "LAKE SHORE". In Phase I and II cars, only the "L" and the "S" in "LAKE SHORE" are capitalized. All the letters are in capitals on the later cars.

I. EARLY "LIONEL MANUFACTURING CO." PRODUCTION Yellow or red undercoating, no embossing or rubber-stamping.

100 Series Freights

112 (A) — 112 (C) — 112 — 112

113 with 180 series trucks — 113 (B) — 114 (A) — 114 (B)

116 (D) — 116 (D) — 116 (E) — 116 (B)

117 with 180 series trucks — 117 (B) — 117 (C) — 117 (D)

(A) Red body, body edges not rolled, soldered corner braces, black rubber stamped "LAKE SHORE", early Type I three-rivet flex trucks with solid sides, short hook couplers, yellow undercoat, brakewheel soldered to outside of body, Ely comment **45 80 25**

(B) Same as (A), but no yellow undercoating **45 80 25**

(C) Red body, black rubber-stamped "LAKE SHORE" and "CAPACITY 80000 LBS. WEIGHT 35000 LBS.", three-rivet trucks with solid sides embossed "PAT. PENDING", black painted short hook couplers held on by escutcheon pins, yellow undercoat. The top of the body edge is rolled over to form a rim which is painted black. There are soldered corner braces on the rim. Two black painted brakewheels have shafts which go through the body rim, Sullens Collection **45 80 25**

(D) Same as (A), but Type II open-sided three-rivet flex trucks, one brakewheel mounted on top lip of body, Ely comment **45 80 25**

II. LATER "LIONEL MANUFACTURING CO." PRODUCTION Embossed "LIONEL MFG. CO." on underside. The earliest examples from this period retained yellow or flat red undercoating.

(E) Red body, dark olive green lower stripe, yellow undercoating, black rubber-stamped "LAKE SHORE", Type II three-rivet open-side flex trucks, short crinkle hook couplers, two green painted brakewheels, Ely comment **45 80 25**

(F) Red body, dark green lower body edge, flat red undercoat, black rubber-stamped "LAKE SHORE" 2-3/4" long, Type II three-rivet open-sided flex trucks, long crinkle-hook couplers, black brakewheels with red painted shaft, Ely comment **45 80 25**

III. EARLY "LIONEL CORPORATION" PRODUCTION No embossing or rubber-stamping

(G) Brown body, black painted body rim, single-rivet flex trucks, Type II data lines and "LAKE SHORE 65784" rubber-stamped in black, two gold painted brakewheels, hook couplers with ears, no coupler brackets, no underside stamping, Koff Collection **45 80 25**

(H) Gray body, gold rubber-stamped lettering "ROCK ISLAND LINES", two brakewheels, hook couplers with ears, single-rivet flex trucks **32 50 25**

(I) Brown body, black rubber-stamped "LAKE SHORE 65784", dark olive green painted body edge, four lines of data rubber-stamped in black, "CAPACITY 60000 LBS/WEIGHT 34500 LBS/LENGTH INSIDE 38 FT/M.C.B. COUPLERS AIR BRAKE", hook couplers with ears, brakewheels do not reach floor, Ely Collection **45 90 25**

(J) Light brown body, light brown lower body edge, rubber-stamped "LAKE SHORE 65784" in black, two lines of data on right: "Capacity 20,000 LBS, Weight 80,000 LBS", large brakewheels, Ely Collection **45 90 25**

IV. LATER "LIONEL CORPORATION" PRODUCTION data lines on sides vary as follows:

Type I: two lines, "CAPACITY 20000 LBS/WEIGHT 10000 LBS"

Type II: two lines, "CAPACITY 60000 LBS/WEIGHT 36500 LBS"

Type III: two lines, "CAPACITY 60000 LBS/WEIGHT 34500 LBS"

Type IV: four lines, "CAPACITY 60000 LBS/WEIGHT 34500 LBS/LENGTH INSIDE 38 FT/M.C.B. COUPLERS AIR BRAKE"

Rubber-stamped in black on bottom, "MADE IN U.S.A./THE LIONEL CORPORATION/NEW YORK" in three lines, most often with car number.

(K) Dark gray body, green painted upper rim and lower body edge, single-rivet flex trucks (blackened on sample observed), two brakewheels, Type IV data lines and "LAKE SHORE 65784" rubber-stamped in black, hook couplers with ears, coupler brackets, Koff, Weaver, and Ely Collections **32 50 25**

(L) Same as (K), but only one green painted brakewheel present, Koff Collection **35 65 25**

(M) Gray body and lower body edge, pea green painted body rim, Type I data lines and "LAKE SHORE" rubber-stamped in black, hook couplers with ears, coupler brackets, two brakewheels **32 50 25**

(N) Same as (M), except no data lines and dark green painted rim **35 55 25**

(O) Gray body, pea green painted body rim and lower body edge, gold lettered "ROCK ISLAND LINES", Type I data lines, hook couplers with ears, coupler brackets, two brakewheels, understamping in gold, Ely Collection **35 55 25**

(P) Same as (J), except black rubber-stamped "LAKE SHORE" only with no data lines **32 50 25**

(Q) Gray body, pea green painted body rim, Type II data lines and "LAKE SHORE" rubber-stamped in black, hook couplers with ears, no coupler brackets, two brakewheels, Kotil comment **32 50 25**

(R) Same as (Q), but dark green body rim and coupler brackets, Kotil comment **32 50 25**

(S) Gray body, green body rim, "LAKE SHORE 65784" rubber-stamped in gold, Type I data lines at upper left, single-rivet flex trucks, hook couplers with ears, two brakewheels, Ely Collection **32 50 25**

(T) Red-brown body, dark green body rim, Type III data lines and "LAKE SHORE 65784" rubber-stamped in black, blackened single-rivet non-flex trucks, hook couplers with ears, no coupler brackets, two brakewheels, Kotil comment **50 85 25**

13 Cattle Car, 1906-1926, usually made with either four or five slats on door and five open slots on side, usually found in either pea green or apple green. On some samples, one of the vertical dividing lines for the side slats of the body may be stamped out of line on the last two rows of slats.

I. EARLY "LIONEL MANUFACTURING CO." PRODUCTION Yellow underframe and usually two-piece roof construction

(A) Yellow underframe, flat sides, five slats on both doors and sides, two brakewheels, each on left, two-piece roof with second piece forming walkway, green body, Type I three-rivet solid-side trucks, short hook couplers, Ely comment **Unlettered 32 50 25**
Lettered 75 150 50

(B) Same as (A), except three-rivet open-sided trucks, brakewheels on right, Ely comment **Unlettered 32 50 25**
Lettered 75 150 50

II. LATER "LIONEL MANUFACTURING CO." PRODUCTION Embossed "LIONEL MFG. CO." on underside

(C) Green body, three-rivet solid side trucks, long crinkle hook couplers, five slats in doors and sides, two brakewheels, one-piece roof, embossed "LIONEL MFG. CO." on underside **Unlettered 32 50 25**
Lettered 60 120 40

III. EARLY "LIONEL CORPORATION" PRODUCTION No embossing or rubber-stamping

(D) Dark green body, embossed sides, hook couplers with cars, no brakewheels, Type V trucks, four door slots, Ely Collection
Unlettered 32 50 25
Lettered 60 120 40

IV. LATER "LIONEL CORPORATION" Rubber-stamped with car number and "MADE IN U.S.A./THE LIONEL CORPORATION/NEW YORK" in three lines on car bottom below number. Horizontally embossed stiffeners are present on the slats of these late production cars, Graves observation

(E) Pea green body, five slots in doors and sides, one horizontal dividing bar uneven on last two rows of slats near base of body, single-rivet flex trucks, hook couplers with ears, no coupler brackets, no brakewheels, one-piece roof, Koff Collection **32 50 25**

(F) Same as (E), except horizontal dividing bars evenly stamped, apple green body and coupler brackets, Weaver Collection **35 60 25**

14 Box Car, 1906-1926, most samples are lettered for "C. M. & ST. P." in rubber-stamped black lettering, usually painted red, yellow-orange or orange. Early production shows considerable variations.

I. EARLY "LIONEL MANUFACTURING CO." Yellow painted underframe and body interior, no embossing or stamping, usually two-piece roof

(A) Red body, thin black vertical stripes, no embossing on frame or body, yellow painted frame and body interior, two-piece red painted roof, black painted brakewheel at each end held by escutcheon pins, black lettered "C. M. & ST. P./19050" to both left and right of doors in two lines, door handles made from escutcheon pins, short hook couplers held in place by escutcheon pins, closed-side three-rivet trucks, Sullens Collection **32 50 25**

(B) Same as (A), but three-rivet open-sided trucks, red painted brakewheel on right, short crinkle hook couplers, Ely Collection **32 50 25**

(C) Same as (A), but body and door sides are embossed, short hook couplers, Type III trucks, unpainted brakewheel on left, Ely Collection **32 50 25**

(D) Same as (C), but numbered "54087", no black lines or embossing on sides, brakewheel on left, long crinkle hook couplers **35 60 30**

(E) Same as (D), but yellow-orange body **32 50 25**

(F) Red body with thin black striping, yellow underframe, embossed sides, two-piece roof, one brakewheel, closed-side three-rivet trucks, short hook couplers, lettered "NYC & H. R. R.R. 5906" on sides **40 65 30**

II. LATER "LIONEL MANUFACTURING CO." PRODUCTION Embossed "LIONEL MFG. CO." on underside

(G) Yellow-orange body, embossed sides, three-rivet closed-side trucks, long crinkle hook couplers, black rubber-stamped lettering "NYC & H. R. R.R. 4351", Sattler Collection **35 60 25**

(H) Yellow-orange body, embossed sides, single-rivet flex trucks, numbered "98237", hook couplers with ears **32 50 25**

(I) Orange body, embossed sides, no black stripes, rubber-stamped "C. M. & ST. P 98237" twice on both sides in black, single-rivet flex trucks, hook couplers with ears, no coupler brackets, no brakewheels, one-piece roof, no underside markings, Koff Collection **32 50 25**

IV. LATER "LIONEL CORPORATION" PRODUCTION Rubber-stamped on car frame with car number and "MADE IN U.S.A./THE LIONEL CORPORATION/NEW YORK" in three lines

(J) Same as (I), but rubber-stamped frame and coupler slots on frame, Ely Collection **32 50 25**

(K) Same as (J), but doors are a brown-orange color clearly different from car body color, door handles stamped from door itself rather than separately attached, Weaver Collection **32 50 25**

(L) Special "Harmony Creamery" issue, dark green embossed sides, gold rubber-stamped "BALTIMORE & OHIO" high on sides, railroad name separated by door, rubber-stamped gold "MILK INSULATED TANK SERVICE" in three lines at left of door and "HARMONY CREAMERY PITTSBURGH PA" in two lines at right of door, single-rivet flex trucks, hook couplers with ears, coupler brackets, number "8118" on lower left of car sides. Very rare, produced for promotional purposes only, Graves comment **NRS**

15 Oil Car, 1906-1926. All varieties of this car have a black girder supporting the tank and attaching the couplers; early versions had wooden painted domes and tank ends; all had gold painted handrails. Later production features metal domes and ends; steps are found on the sides of the tank near the ends and are of three types: simple, U-shaped steps on earliest production; four-piece gold painted soldered steps later on and one-piece gold painted steps with three holes on the last versions of the car. Early cars have long slots for couplers with stops soldered in. The listings below are grouped by body colors for the user's convenience.

I. RED TANK BODIES

—EARLY "MFG." PRODUCTION

(A) Rubber-stamped "PENNSYLVANIA RR 416" in black, three-rivet closed-side trucks, short hook couplers, red dome, U-shaped steps, wooden ends and dome **40 75 30**

—LATER "MFG." PRODUCTION

(B) Same as (A), except three-rivet open-sided trucks **40 75 30**

(C) Rubber-stamped "PENNSYLVANIA RR" in black without number, single-rivet flex trucks, hook couplers with ears, two gold handrails, black wood dome, three-hole steps, black metal ends **35 65 25**

II. MAROON TANK BODIES

—EARLY "MFG." PRODUCTION

(D) Rubber-stamped "PENNSYLVANIA RR 416" in black, three-rivet open-sided trucks, short hook couplers, maroon dome, U-shaped steps, wooden ends **32 50 25**

(E) Rubber-stamped "PENNSYLVANIA RR 416" in black, three-rivet closed side trucks, long crinkle hook couplers, maroon dome, four-piece steps, wooden ends **32 50 25**

—LATER "LIONEL MANUFACTURING CO." PRODUCTION

(F) Rubber-stamped "PENNSYLVANIA RR" in sans-serif gold letters without number, three-rivet open Type II trucks, long straight couplers, coupler stops near end of girder, black dome, four-piece steps, wooden ends, Ely comment **32 50 25**

(G) Rubber-stamped "PENNSYLVANIA" in gold sans-serif lettering, single-rivet flex trucks, hook couplers with ears, two gold painted handrails, on each side, black metal dome, four-piece soldered steps, black metal ends, Kotil comment **32 50 25**

(H) Same as (G), except wooden tank ends, long crinkle hook couplers and coupler slots on frame, three-rivet Type II trucks, Ely Collection **32 50 25**

—EARLY "LIONEL CORPORATION" PRODUCTION

(I) Same as (G), but long crinkle hook couplers and "PENNSYLVANIA RR" in gold serif rubber-stamped lettering, Sattler Collection **32 50 25**

(J) Rubber-stamped "PENNSYLVANIA RR" in black, single-rivet flex trucks, hook couplers with ears, two gold handrails, black wood dome, three-hole steps, black metal ends **32 50 25**

—LATER "LIONEL CORPORATION" PRODUCTION

(K) Same as (G), but three-hole steps and "PENNSYLVANIA" in gold serif lettering, Weaver Collection **32 50 25**

(L) Same as (G), but three-hole steps, Koff and Sullens Collections **32 50 25**

III. BROWN TANK BODIES

—LATER "MANUFACTURING CO." PRODUCTION

(M) Rubber-stamped "PENNSYLVANIA" in gold sans-serif lettering, single-rivet flex trucks, hook couplers with ears, wood dome, two gold handrails on each side and black metal ends, Ely Collection **35 55 25**

—EARLY "LIONEL CORPORATION" PRODUCTION

(N) Same as (M), but three-hole gold steps, short coupler slot **35 55 25**

(O) Same as (N), but brown wooden dome and sans-serif gold lettering, Lotstein Collection **35 55 25**

(P) Same as (O), but serif gold lettering, Ely and Sullens Collections **45 65 25**

16 Ballast (Dump), 1906-1926, a popular operating car with levers at the ends to dump the load by opening the car sides, measures 10-3/4", found in red, maroon, brown and dark green colors with a variety of trim and girder colors as well as variations in trucks and couplers. Listed by body colors for user's convenience. The prototype for this car can still be observed on the Strasburg Railroad near the TCA Museum in Strasburg, PA.

I. BROWN BODIES

—EARLY "LIONEL MANUFACTURING CO." PRODUCTION

(A) Black trim, three-rivet trucks, short hook couplers and yellow girder **65 150 40**

—LATER "LIONEL MANUFACTURING CO." PRODUCTION

(B) Black trim, black girder, rubber-stamped "PENNSYLVANIA 65784", "CAPACITY 20000 LBS, WEIGHT 10000 LBS" in sans-serif gold lettering **32 50 25**

(C) Black trim, black frame, rubber-stamped as in (B) except weight is "34500 LBS", Kotil Collection **35 55 25**

II. MAROON BODIES

—EARLY "LIONEL MANUFACTURING CO." PRODUCTION

(D) Dark green trim, yellow girder, three-rivet open-sided trucks, short straight hook couplers, lettered "PENNSYLVANIA 65784" in serif black letters, two lines of data **65 150 40**

—LATER "LIONEL MANUFACTURING CO." PRODUCTION

(E) Same as (D), but black girder and short crinkle hook couplers **32 50 25**

—EARLY "LIONEL CORPORATION" PRODUCTION

(F) Same as (E), but single-rivet flex trucks and hook couplers with ears **32 50 25**

III. RED BODIES

—EARLY "LIONEL CORPORATION" PRODUCTION

(G) Black trim, black girder, single-rivet flex trucks, hook couplers with ears, rubber-stamped "PENNSYLVANIA 76399" in sans-serif gold lettering **40 75 25**

IV. DARK GREEN BODIES

—LATER "LIONEL CORPORATION" PRODUCTION

(H) Maroon trim, green girder, single-rivet flex trucks, hook couplers with ears, "PENNSYLVANIA 65784" in black sans-serif lettering, "16" stamped on end, two lines of data on right, Weaver and Ely Collections **32 50 25**

(I) Same as (H), but serif lettering and "16" rubber-stamped on car ends, Ely comment **32 50 25**

17 Caboose, 1906-1926. This car occurs in early, middle and late construction styles and comes in red, maroon, and brown body colors. Cupola sides are found in both smooth and embossed sides, and the cupola roof can be found with rounded or squared ends. Nearly all examples are rubber-stamped "NYC & H. R. R.R." in black, and there are different numbers below that stamping, the most common being "4351". All listings are stamped "NYC & H. R. R.R. 4351" unless otherwise noted.

I. EARLY "LIONEL MANUFACTURING CO." PRODUCTION Yellow underframe, no embossing or rubber-stamping

(A) Red body, black-lettered "NYC & H. R R.R./51906." (Note that "H. R R.R." is correct. There is no period after the second "R".) Yellow undercoat on both sides of frame and inside car, black stripes on body side, sides not embossed. Yellow painted frame with black steps. Platform end plate is a separate piece of metal soldered to the frame. Car ends each have a large door flanked by large window cutouts. Black main window awnings, black painted main roof and cupola roof. Red painted smooth-sided cupola with two rectangular windows on each side. Inside the car, there is a bench along part of each side in front of the window. Each bench has a pin to hold a figure of a train crewman. (This is somewhat similar to the arrangement found on early Standard Gauge trolleys.) Three-rivet closed-sided trucks embossed "PAT. PENDING", short straight hook couplers held by escutcheon pins, Sullens and Ely Collections **75 150 45**

(B) Same as (A), but three-rivet open-side trucks, Ely comment **75 150 40**

(C) Red body, no undercoat or stamping on underside, single-rivet flex trucks, black main roof, integral black steps, embossed cupola sides, awnings on cupola windows but not on main windows (reverse of A), squared black cupola roof, number 342715 **75 150 40**

(D) Brown body, no undercoat or stamping on underside, hook couplers with ears, rubber-stamped "NYC & HRR 4351" (note one "R" not present), brown platform, black main roof, soldered black steps, black cupola roof, cupola windows smaller than usual, Kotil Collection **75 150 40**

II. LATER "LIONEL MANUFACTURING CO." PRODUCTION Embossed "LIONEL MFG. CO." on underside. All sides have smooth body sides without awnings unless otherwise stated.

(E) Brown body and underside, single-rivet flex trucks, hook couplers with ears, no coupler brackets, brown end platform with integral black painted steps, black main roof, smooth cupola sides, square brown cupola roof, Koff Collection **60 120 30**

(F) Brown body, hook couplers with ears, rubber-stamped "NYC & HRR 4351" (note absence of one "R"), brown platform, black main roof, soldered black steps with two risers, smaller windows, brown cupola roof, Kotil Collection **60 120 35**

(G) Maroon body, number 5906, single-rivet flex trucks, black main roof, integral black steps, embossed cupola sides, awnings on cupola but not on main windows, square black cupola roof, Ely comment **60 120 35**

(H) Red body, number 342715, single-rivet Type V flex trucks, long crinkle hook couplers, black main roof, integral red steps, embossed cupola sides, cupola has stamped awnings, square black cupola roof, Ely comment **60 120 35**

(I) Same as (H), but no awnings and maroon body, Ely comment **60 120 35**

III. EARLY "LIONEL CORPORATION" PRODUCTION No embossing or rubber-stamping

(J) Same as (D), but three "R's" in "NYC & H. R. R.R." lettering, three-hole steps and normal cupola window size, brown cupola and roof, Ely comment **75 150 40**

IV. LATER "LIONEL CORPORATION" PRODUCTION Rubber-stamped "17" and "MADE IN U.S.A./THE LIONEL CORPORATION/NEW YORK" in three lines on car bottom

(K) Maroon body, number 4351, single-rivet flex trucks, hook couplers with ears, no coupler brackets, black main roof, soldered black steps with three punched holes (similar to 15 oil car), smooth cupola sides, maroon cupola ends, no awnings, square black cupola roof, Koff and Weaver Collections **32 50 25**

(L) Same as (K), except cupola is embossed and has rounded roof **32 50 25**

(M) Red body, rubber-stamped lettering differs in height and thickness from earlier samples, number 4351, single-rivet flex trucks, hook couplers with ears, black main roof, soldered three-hole steps, embossed cupola sides, no awnings, rounded black cupola roof **35 60 25**

(N) Same as (M), except brown body and rounded maroon cupola roof **35 60 25**

(O) Brown body, embossed sides, square black cupola roof, black main roof, three-hole black steps, number 4351, hook couplers with ears, Ely Collection **35 60 25**

THE 100 SERIES FREIGHT CARS

The 100 Series of freight cars began in 1910, with the introduction of the 112 gondola and 116 ballast cars. Two years later, Lionel began sales of the 113 cattle car, 114 box car and 117 caboose. No other types of cars were introduced between these years and the cessation of production in 1927, when the 500 Series replaced these cars.

Although construction techniques did not vary much during the production run of the 100 Series, there are numerous variations in paint, lettering, couplers and trucks. Essentially, the details on couplers, undersides and general construction found in the 10 Series apply to the 100 Series as well. The main difference between the two series is that the 100 Series cars are much smaller than the 10 Series. The same underside treatments given to the 10 Series apply to this series, with one major exception: several of the 100 Series cars have the number rubber-stamped on the sides or ends instead of the underside. In those cases, the underside is stamped "MADE IN U.S.A./THE LIONEL CORPORATION/NEW YORK" in black without the number. The wheels of the 100 Series cars, it should be noted, are significantly smaller than their 10 Series counterparts. As a result, the 100 Series cars sit lower upon the track.

Three different types of trucks are found on the 100 Series cars. In general, they resemble those of the 10 Series, but they are smaller in proportion to the car sizes. The earliest of these cars possess flex trucks in two varieties. One type has the end of the bolster below the wheel axle holes pointed. On the other type, the end is rounded. Either type can have a large rivet at the center of its connecting bar or a small rivet hole. By far, the most common truck is a non-flex open truck with black painted sides. The earliest version of these trucks was nickel-plated and probably used only on passenger cars. As in the 10 Series trucks, three kinds of underside crossbars can be found - totally smooth, with two smooth bumps or with two slotted bumps. Coupler variations follow those of the 10 Series.

112 Gondola, 1910-1926. Over the 16 years of production of this car, a great number of variations were produced. Although the four main stages of production are well represented in the following listings, not all of these cars follow a definite pattern of development. Most of them are rubber-stamped "LAKE SHORE 65784" in black; exceptions are noted below. There are four main types of data lines rubber-stamped in black on the car sides.

Type I: two lines, "CAPACITY 80000 LBS/WEIGHT 30000 LBS"

Type II: two lines, "CAPACITY 80000 LBS/WEIGHT 35000 LBS"

Type III: two lines, "CAPACITY 20000 LBS/WEIGHT 10000 LBS"

Type IV: four lines, "CAPACITY 60000 WEIGHT 34500/LENGTH INSIDE 36 FT/M.C.B. COUPLERS/AIR BRAKE"

I. EARLY "LIONEL MANUFACTURING CO." PRODUCTION 7" cars, some versions embossed "LIONEL MFG. CO."

(A) Dark olive green body only 7" long, red body rim, rubber-stamped "LAKE SHORE" only in gold, Type II flex trucks, Type I data lines, short crinkle hook couplers, embossed "LIONEL MFG. CO." on car floor **45 75 30**

(B) Dark olive green body only 7" long, red body rim and bottom edge, rubber-stamped "N.Y.N.H. & H." in gold, Type I flex trucks, Type I data lines, long crinkle hook couplers, unmarked body floor, Weaver Collection **40 75 35**

(C) Same as (B), but embossed body floor and long straight hook couplers, Ely Collection **40 75 35**

(D) Same as (C), but short crinkle hook couplers attached outside body, Ely Collection **40 75 35**

(E) Same as (C), but olive interior, red lower body edge and long crinkle hook couplers, Type II trucks, Ely Collection **40 75 35**

II. LATER "LIONEL MANUFACTURING CO." PRODUCTION Embossed "LIONEL MFG. CO." on car floor, 9" bodies

200 Series Freights
212 (A)
219 (A)
211 (A)
214 (B)
213 (A)
214 (A)
215 (A)
216 (A)
217 (A)
212 (E)
218 (A)

(F) Red body, green body rim, black rubber-stamped lettering, Type III black non-flex trucks, Type II data lines, Bergstrom Collection **35 55 30**

(G) Cherry red body (markedly different from usual red), red body rim, black rubber-stamped "LAKE SHORE" only, Type III black non-flex trucks, Type II data lines, Bergstrom Collection. This is a highly unusual body color. However, a panel of experienced collectors has determined that it is probably genuine. This determination is based in part upon the reporting of a second example and the finding of a 117 caboose in the same color from the same collection. See entries for 112 (BB) and 117(L). Further reader comments invited. The presence of black non-flex trucks on this sample is troublesome. **40 60 30**

(H) Red body, black body rim, black rubber-stamped "LAKE SHORE" only, Type II data lines, long crinkle hook couplers, no coupler brackets, Weaver and Ely Collections. We have had a report that some of these cars came with nickel-plated couplers and that these were used as salesmen's samples. Reader comments invited. **35 55 30**

(I) Maroon body, green body rim, rubber-stamped "N.Y.C. & H.R.R.R. 65784" in black, Type III data lines, Type III black non-flex trucks, hook couplers with ears, no coupler brackets, Porcellini Collection **35 55 30**

(J) Same as (I), except medium brown body and darker brown body rim, Koff Collection **35 55 30**

(K) Chocolate brown body, Type IV data lines, rubber-stamped "LAKE SHORE 65784" in black, hook couplers with ears, Ely Collection **35 55 30**

(L) Same as (K), but dark brown body, "N.Y.C. & H.R.R.", Type II data lines and numbered "76399", Ely Collection **35 55 30**

III. EARLY "LIONEL CORPORATION" PRODUCTION No embossing or rubber-stamping on car undersides

(M) Maroon body, maroon body rim, black rubber-stamped lettering, Type III black non-flex trucks, Type III data lines, Bergstrom Collection **35 55 30**

(N) Same as (M), except Type IV data lines, Bergstrom Collection **40 60 25**

(O) Light gray body, black rubber-stamped lettering, no data lines, Type II flex trucks, lettered "LIONEL LINES" at car ends, Edmunds observation **32 50 25**

(P) Brown body, brown body rim, rubber-stamped black lettering, Type III black non-flex trucks, hook couplers with ears, no coupler brackets, Type IV data lines, Pauli Collection **40 60 25**

(Q) Same as (P), but Type III data lines **35 55 25**

(R) Same as (Q), but green body rim, Ely Collection **35 55 25**

(S) Same as (Q), but rubber-stamped "PENNSYLVANIA" **40 60 25**

(T) Same as (Q), but rubber-stamped "N.Y.C. & H.R.R." **35 55 25**

(U) Same as (S), but red body **40 60 30**

(V) Same as (T), but red body **40 60 30**

IV. LATER "LIONEL CORPORATION" PRODUCTION Rubber-stamped "MADE IN U.S.A./THE LIONEL CORPORATION/NEW YORK" in black in three lines with car number on bottom

(W) Gray body, green rim, black rubber-stamped "LAKE SHORE" lettering, Type III black non-flex trucks, hook couplers with ears, coupler slots in frame, Type III data lines, Koff, Porcellini, and Smith Collections **32 50 25**

(X) Same as (W), except darker gray body, Koff and Porcellini Collections **35 55 25**

(Y) Same as (W), except lettered "ROCK ISLAND LINES" in black **35 55 25**

(Z) Same as (Y), but light gray body, dark green rim, gold lettering on sides and base, Ely Collection **35 55 25**

(AA) Same as (X), except gray body rim and rubber-stamped without car number on bottom, Bergstrom Collection **32 50 25**

(BB) Same as (W), but cherry red body (see entry G), pea green rim and black "LAKE SHORE" lettering, Type III data lines, coupler brackets, Ely Collection **40 60 30**

113 Cattle Car, 1912-1926. One of the main variations found on this car is the presence of four or five horizontal embossed slats on the doors and body sides, usually made in pea green or apple green.

I. and II. "LIONEL MANUFACTURING CO." PRODUCTION Embossed "LIONEL MFG. CO." on car floor; no examples have been reported which can be assigned to the earliest production. Reader contributions are requested.

(A) Medium green body, five embossed slats, Type III black non-flex trucks, hook couplers with ears, no coupler brackets, two brakewheels, embossed "LIONEL MFG. CO." on car floor, Koff Collection **40 60 30**

(B) Same as (A), but four slats and long crinkle-hook couplers, Ely Collection **40 60 30**

(C) Same as (A), but pea green body **35 55 25**

(D) Same as (A), but Type II trucks set closer to car center by 1/2 inch, long crinkle hook couplers, four slats and embossed floor, Ely Collection **40 60 30**

III. EARLY "LIONEL CORPORATION" PRODUCTION No embossing or rubber stamping on car floor

(E) Apple green body, four embossed slats, Type III black non-flex trucks, hook couplers with ears, no coupler brackets, two brakewheels, Pauli Collection **45 75 30**

(F) Same as (E), except pea green body, Porcellini Collection **40 60 30**

IV. LATER "LIONEL CORPORATION" PRODUCTION Rubber-stamped on car floor in black with car number and "MADE IN U.S.A./THE LIONEL CORPORATION/NEW YORK" in three lines below number

(G) Pea green body, four embossed slats, Type III black non-flex trucks, hook couplers with ears, coupler brackets, two brakewheels, rubber-stamped "MADE IN U.S.A./THE LIONEL CORPORATION/NEW YORK" in three lines with car number on floor, Pauli and Bergstrom Collections **35 55 25**

(H) Same as (G), but rubber-stamped in gold on car bottom instead of black, Ely Collection **35 55 25**

(I) Apple green body, five embossed slats, Type III black non-flex trucks, hook couplers with ears, coupler brackets, two brakewheels, same rubber-stamping as (E), but number 113 stamped on one end of car instead of car bottom, Koff and Weaver Collections **40 60 30**

114 Box Car, 1912-1926. Early versions of this car came in red, but most were done in orange or yellow-orange. All known examples are rubber-stamped "CM & ST P" in black on both sides of the door, but the car numbers vary. All versions feature vertical embossed ribs on the sides.

I. and II. "LIONEL MANUFACTURING CO." PRODUCTION All reported versions from this period have embossed car floors. No examples have been reported which reflect the earliest period of production. Reader comments are requested.

(A) Red body, number "54087", Type II flex trucks, long crinkle hook couplers, embossed "LIONEL MFG. CO." on floor, small sans-serif black lettering, Ely comment **60 120 35**

(B) Yellow-orange body, number "54087", Type III black non-flex trucks, short hook couplers, no coupler brackets, two brakewheels, embossed as in (A), Weaver Collection **40 60 30**

(C) Same as (B), but orange body, small sans-serif lettering and long crinkle hook couplers, Ely Collection **40 60 30**

(D) Same as (B), but large serif letters and numbered "98237", Kotil and Ely Collections **35 55 25**

III. EARLY "LIONEL CORPORATION" PRODUCTION no embossing or rubber-stamping on car floor

(E) Same as (D), but no embossing, hook couplers with ears, Ely Collection **35 55 25**

(F) Same as (E), but small sans-serif lettering, 54087, "LIONEL LINES/N.Y./MADE IN/U.S.A." stamped on end and larger 1" brakewheels on right side of car ends, Ely Collection **35 55 25**

IV LATER "LIONEL CORPORATION" PRODUCTION Rubber-stamped black lettering on car floor; "MADE IN U.S.A./THE LIONEL CORPORATION/NEW YORK" in three lines below car number

(G) Orange body, number "98237", Type III black non-flex trucks, hook couplers with ears, coupler slots in base, two brakewheels, rubber-stamped "MADE IN U.S.A./THE LIONEL CORPORATION/NEW YORK" in three lines on bottom with car number, Pauli, Weaver, and Porcellini Collections **60 120 35**

(H) Same as (G), but numbered "62926" **40 60 30**

(I) Same as (G), but number of car stamped on one end rather than bottom, Koff Collection **40 60 30**

116 Ballast Car, 1910-1926. This smaller version of the 16 operating car works differently from its "big brother". Instead of a lever on the end, the operating lever is on the side of the 116 car. It releases two flaps so that the

200 Series Freights
212 (B)
219 (B)
211 (B)
THE LIONEL LINES
214 (A)
213 (B)
214 (A)
215 (C)
216 (B)
217 (B)
LIONEL
217
220 (A)
THE LIONEL LINES
218 (B)

load dumps out the car bottom, not its side. Both of these features are more prototypical than on the 16. It had been thought that all examples were stamped "N.Y.N.H. & H.R.R." in black or gold, but several exceptions have been found. When the car floor is marked at all, it is embossed "LIONEL MFG. CO." Early versions have Type I or II flex trucks; later ones have Type III black non-flex trucks. Most observed samples have hook couplers with ears. Where data lines are present, one end of the car side is marked "CAPACITY 50000 LBS" and the other end "WEIGHT 30000 LBS". The data numbers are found with or without commas.

I and II "LIONEL MANUFACTURING CO." PRODUCTION Embossed car floors and/or earlier trucks. No example has been reported which can be assigned reliably to the earliest period of production. Reader comments are requested.

(A) Maroon body, maroon body edge, rubber-stamped "N.Y.N.H. & H." only in gold, data lines, car number rubber-stamped on side at lower right in gold, Type I flex trucks, long straight hook couplers, no coupler brackets, embossed car bottom, Pauli Collection **40 60 30**

(B) "N.Y.N.H. & H.R.R." in 5/16" letters and black paint on floor ends, Type II trucks, long crinkle hook couplers, data lines, maroon ends, Ely Collection **40 60 30**

(C) Same as (A), but lighter maroon, black paint on floor ends and long crinkle hook couplers, Ely Collection **40 60 30**

(D) Same as (C), but lighter maroon color, 1/2" letters, "LIONEL LINES/N.Y./MADE IN U.S.A." stamped in gold on end, Ely Collection **40 60 30**

(E) Same as (D), but dark maroon with 1/2" gold lettering, Ely Collection **40 60 30**

(F) Same as (B), but data lines and 2-1/2" long lettering, Ely Collection **40 60 30**

(G) Chocolate brown body, black body edge and lettering, Type II trucks, hook couplers with ears, embossing, lettering size varies from 1/2" to 5/8", Koff and Ely Collections **40 60 30**

(H) Same as (G), but gold sans-serif lettering, Koff and Ely Collections **40 60 30**

III. EARLY "LIONEL CORPORATION" PRODUCTION No embossing on floor, later production characteristics

(I) Maroon body, maroon body edge, rubber-stamped black lettering, Type II flex trucks, coupler brackets, data lines, no embossing, Porcellini Collection **35 55 25**

(J) Same as (I), but green body edge and gold lettering, long crinkle hook couplers without brackets, Weaver Collection **35 55 25**

(K) Dark brown body, black lettering, Type II flex trucks, hook couplers with ears, Ely Collection **40 60 30**

(L) Same as (K), but red-brown body, Ely Collection **40 60 30**

(M) Same as (K), but chocolate brown body, Ely Collection **40 60 30**

(N) Dark green body, maroon body edge, rubber-stamped gold lettering, data lines, coupler brackets, Type II flex trucks, no embossing, Porcellini Collection **35 55 25**

(O) Gray body, green body edge, rubber-stamped black lettering, Type II flex trucks, coupler brackets, data lines, car number on end, no embossing, Porcellini and Ely Collections **35 55 25**

IV. LATER "LIONEL CORPORATION" PRODUCTION Type III black non-flex trucks, no embossing

(P) Dark green body, maroon body edge, rubber-stamped gold lettering, data lines, Type III black non-flex trucks, no coupler brackets, no embossing, Pauli and Weaver Collections **40 60 30**

(Q) Same as (P), but number stamped in black on car end and black lettering, Ely Collection **40 60 30**

(R) Same as (P), except has coupler brackets and car number rubber-stamped in gold on right lower side of car, Pauli Collection **50 75 35**

(S) Brown-red body, green body edge, Type III black non-flex trucks, coupler brackets, rubber-stamped black lettering, data lines, no embossing, Koff Collection **40 60 30**

(T) Same as (O), but Type III black trucks, Ely Collection **35 55 25**

117 Caboose, 1912-1926. All known examples of this car have embossed vertical ribs and are rubber-stamped "NYC & HRRR 4351" in black or gold. The lettering varies in size and thickness. Cupola roofs can be rounded or squared. Curiously, very few examples have turned up which lack the rubber-stamped lettering on the bottom used after 1918. More research is needed on the early production of this car.

I and II "LIONEL MANUFACTURING CO." PRODUCTION All cars listed here are embossed "LIONEL MFG. CO." on their floors. No examples have been reported which can be assigned reliably to the earliest phase of production. Reader comments are requested.

(A) Dark brown body, black main roof and brown cupola roof, Type III trucks, long crinkle hook couplers, Ely Collection **32 50 25**

(B) Medium brown body, small sans-serif lettering, black cupola roof, long crinkle hook couplers, Type V trucks, Ely Collection **32 50 25**

(C) Red body, black main roof, small sans-serif lettering in black, red cupola sides, squared black cupola roof, hook couplers with ears, no coupler brackets, black non-flex trucks, Weaver Collection **32 50 25**

III EARLY "LIONEL CORPORATION" PRODUCTION No embossing or rubber-stamping on car floor

(D) Red body, black main roof and rounded cupola roof, long crinkle hook couplers, small lettering, Ely Collection **35 50 30**

(E) Brown body, black main roof and cupola roof, small lettering and hook couplers with ears, Ely Collection **35 50 25**

(F) Same as (E), but large lettering and brown cupola roof, Ely Collection **35 50 25**

IV. LATER "LIONEL CORPORATION" PRODUCTION Rubber-stamped lettering in black "MADE IN U.S.A./THE LIONEL CORPORATION/NEW YORK" in three lines below rubber-stamped car number

(G) Brown body, black main roof, Type III black non-flex trucks, hook couplers with ears, no coupler brackets, rubber-stamped black lettering, black steps, brown cupola sides, squared brown cupola roof **32 50 25**

(H) Maroon body, black main roof, Type III black non-flex trucks, hook couplers with ears, no coupler brackets, rubber-stamped black lettering, black steps, red or maroon cupola sides, rounded black cupola roof, Pauli, Ely, Weaver, and Koff Collections **40 60 30**

(I) Same as (H), except maroon cupola sides, rubber-stamped gold lettering and coupler brackets, Porcellini Collection **32 50 25**

(J) Red body, black main roof, Type III black non-flex trucks, hook couplers with ears, rubber-stamped black serif lettering, red cupola sides, black rounded cupola roof, Weaver and Ely Collections **32 50 25**

(K) Same as (J), but red cupola roof, Ely Collection **32 50 25**

(L) Cherry-red body (strikingly different from usual red), black main roof, rubber-stamped black lettering, Type III black non-flex trucks, hookcouplers with ears, coupler brackets, black steps, normal red cupola sides, black cupola roof, rubber-stamped frame, but without car number, Bergstrom Collection. See note under 112 (G). **40 60 30**

OIL LABEL TYPES ON LIONEL STANDARD AND 0 GAUGE FREIGHT CARS

During the early to middle production run of the 200 and 500 series, Lionel pasted a label with oiling instructions on the car's underside. (The practice was apparently discontinued some time in 1933; we invite reader comments.) Reverend Robert Pauli has identified three different oil labels used on Lionel cars. They are as follows:

Type I: Picture of an 800 Series small 0 Gauge car frame viewed from its left side; label has no red border outline and red lettered instructions with block printing style. We do not know for sure if this 0 Gauge label has in fact been seen on very many 200 and 500 Series trucks. We invite reader comments.

Type II: Picture of a 10 Series four-wheel truck with electric roller pickup as viewed from its right side, no border on label, red lettered instructions in block printing style.

Type III: Picture of a 200 Series four-wheel truck with electric roller pickup as viewed from its left side, red border outline on label and red lettered instructions in serif printing style.

200 Series Freights

BRAKEWHEEL AND COUPLER DEVELOPMENT

by Philip Graves

PART I: BRAKEWHEELS

The nickel and brass brakewheels used on the 200 and 500 Series freight cars are very useful in assigning a particular car to its date of manufacture. In addition, the examination of these brakewheels, together with an analysis of other variables such as plates, trucks, and couplers, can help the collector determine whether or not the car was altered after it left the factory.

As with all the variables on these cars, Lionel's production changed according to a regular, predictable pattern. There are four types of brakewheels which can be found:

TYPE I: Brakewheel with wheel spokes flaring outward towards rim.

TYPE I: EARLY PRODUCTION

Three-piece construction consisting of a hub, a wheel and an L-shaped brake shaft. The brakewheel is inserted from the bottom of the shaft up to the point where the shaft bends. A hub with a slot to fit over the bent shaft is then crimped around the wheel hub. The assembly is mechanical. The soldered wheel is 5/8" in diameter, and all material used is brass. See Figure 1 below.

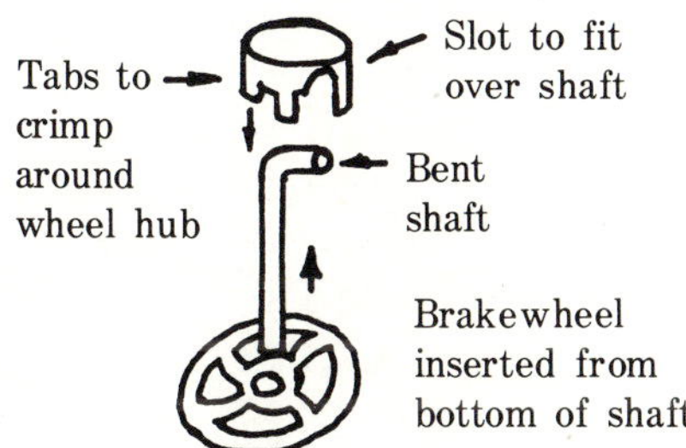

FIGURE 1: TYPE I and TYPE II

TYPE II: MIDDLE PRODUCTION

Same materials and assembly as Type I, but the brakewheel is larger, measuring 3/4" in diameter.

Note: The Type I and Type II brakewheels differ in other ways besides size. In the larger Type II brakewheel, the wheel spokes are of uniform diameter from hub to rim, and the hub is flush with the rim surface. In the smaller Type I brakewheel, the wheel spokes flare outward where they meet the rim, and the hub is recessed below the rim surface.

TYPE II: Brakewheel with uniform size wheel spokes.

TYPE III: LATER PRODUCTION

Two-piece construction consisting of a 3/4" brass brakewheel soldered directly to the brass brake shaft, which is straight instead of L-shaped. As the wheel is placed on the shaft, a detent in the wheel is filled with solder. See Figure 2 below.

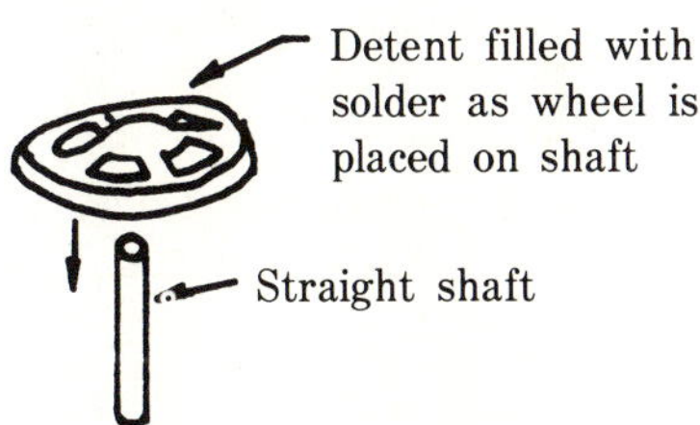

FIGURE 2: TYPE III and TYPE IV

TYPE IV: LATEST PRODUCTION

Same as Type III, but all material is nickel instead of brass.

PART II: COUPLERS

Another way of dating the production of the 200 and 500 Series freight cars is to examine the latch couplers on the cars. The latch coupler was introduced in 1923. Its first version included a horizontal tab with a slot so that the car could be coupled to the earlier hook couplers. This early latch coupler, known more commonly as the "combination" coupler, is not found on the 200 and 500 Series cars. There are two clearly different later types of latch couplers which are used:

Drawings by Ralph E. Graves

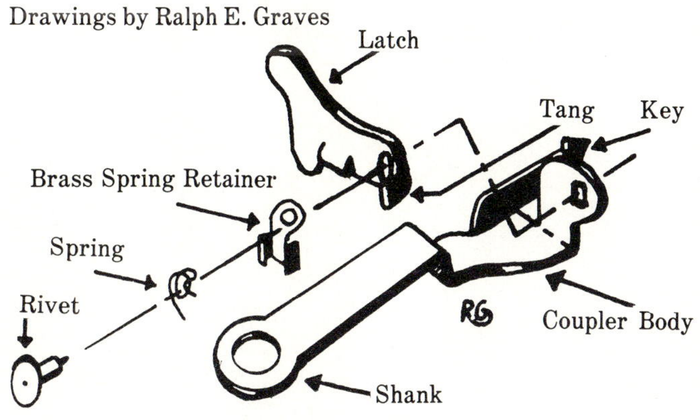

FIGURE 3: TYPE II

200 Series Freights
380
218
219
220
214 R
215
216
217
437
214
213
212
208 Tool Box
Contents of
LIONEL
217

TYPE I: EARLY TO MIDDLE PRODUCTION

This coupler was of five-piece construction. The shank, latch and rivet were nickeled, and there was a brass spring retainer and a wire spring. A tang on the latch was bent towards the shank end of the coupler. There was no flange on the lower surface of the latch. The wire spring was shaped to fit its retainer. The rivet was perfectly round. See Figure 3.

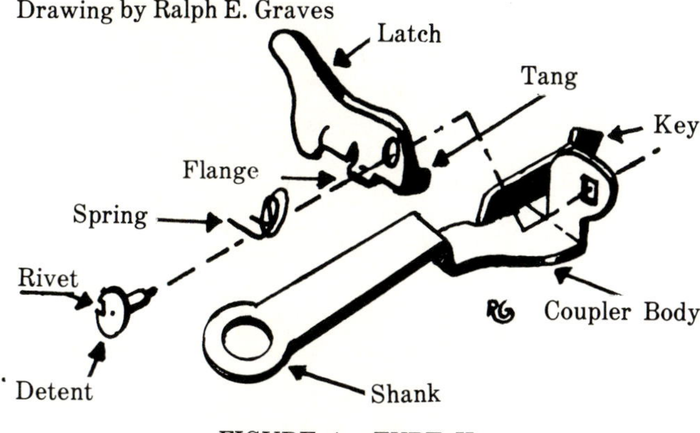

FIGURE 4: TYPE II

TYPE II: MIDDLE TO LATE PRODUCTION

This coupler was of four-piece construction because Lionel's engineers were able to modify it so that the brass spring retainer was omitted. As before, the three main parts were nickeled and the spring was made of wire. The tang on the latch was bent outward towards the key end of the coupler, rather than inward towards the shank. A flange was added to the lower surface of the latch to retain one end of the spring. The other end of the spring (shaped differently from its Type I predecessor) was held by a detent cut out of the rivet head. See Figure 4.

THE 200 SERIES FREIGHT CARS

These very large cars, introduced in 1926, represent a magnificent achievement in toy train construction. All of the varieties, regardless of scarcity, are highly prized by collectors today. The 200 Series, intended to replace the 10 Series, all had black frames. However, the colors on the cars showed far more variety and were much brighter (if less realistic). Lionel paid a great deal of attention to play value in these cars. The 218 dump cars operate manually, as do the magnificent 219 crane cars, which are among the most highly prized of this series. The 217 caboose was the first Lionel caboose to be lighted.

As far as is known, the 200 Series only had one type of truck. It has a small squared cutout at the center of the crossbar, embossed springs and black paint. The wheel journal boxes are mounted separately and are either copper or nickel.

Most of these cars possess nickel or brass trim in profusion. Plates on the sides of the cars have red or black lettering; sometimes they possess an oval border in red or black. Even small pieces of trim such as box car door handles are often brass. The 218 and 219 cars feature knurled operating knobs of solid brass, and on the dump car even the entire end bolsters are made of solid brass in a few versions.

All of the 200 Series freight cars are 12-1/2" long (although the huge boom on the crane car doubles its total length). They all possess latch couplers.

211 Flar Car, 1926-1940, originally sold with lumber loads, all have latch couplers, black bodies and "211 THE LIONEL LINES 211" rubber-stamped on the sides of the car in gold. These cars, as well as the floodlight and oil cars, may have the brake stands in reversed positions due to the car frame being placed in the punch press upside down. Bohn comment

(A) Nickel journals, brass Type I brakewheels, nickel stakes, Type I couplers and Type II oil label, Graves and Hoffman Collections **60 80 40**

(B) Copper journals, brass Type II brakewheels, nickel stakes, Type II oil label and Type II couplers, Koff and Weaver Collections **60 80 40**

(C) Nickel journals, nickel Type IV brakewheels, nickel stakes, Type II couplers, no oil label, trucks mounted with retaining washer instead of cotter pin, Graves Collection **60 80 40**

212 Gondola, 1926-1940, originally sold with barrell loads, all have latch couplers and two plates, one of which reads "LIONEL LINES" and the other "NO. 212 CAPACITY 80000 WEIGHT 30000"

(A) Gray body (earliest color), 1926 only, nickel journals, brass black-lettered plates, brass Type I brakewheels, Type I couplers and Type II oil label, Koff and Graves Collections **75 90 45**

(B) Maroon body, copper journals, black-lettered brass plates, brass Type II brakewheels, Type II oil label **60 80 40**

(C) Same as (B), but no oil label, Koff Collection **60 80 40**

(D) Same as (B), but nickel journals, Graves, Hoffman, and Weaver Collections **60 80 40**

(E) Medium green body, nickel journals, black-lettered nickel plates, nickel Type IV brakewheels, no oil label, trucks secured by horseshoe clip, Type II couplers, Graves Collection **75 100 50**

(F) Dark green body, nickel journals, brass plates, brass Type II brakewheels, Type II oil label, very rare, Graves and Weaver Collections **85 140 50**

213 Cattle Car, 1926-1940, all have latch couplers and black frames

(A) Mojave body, maroon roof and door guides, nickel journals, black-lettered brass plates, brass trim, brass Type I brakewheels, Type I couplers **145 195 80**

(B) Terra-cotta body, pea green roof and door guides, nickel journals, brass plates and trim, Type II oil label, brass Type I brakewheels, Type I couplers, Koff and Graves Collections **125 175 80**

(C) Same as (B), except Type III brakewheels, copper journals, Type II couplers **125 175 80**

(D) Same as (B), but maroon roof and door guides. Made as department store special, Graves observation **125 175 80**

(E) Cream body, maroon roof and door guides, nickel Type IV brakewheels, Type II couplers, nickel journals, no oil label, trucks secured with horseshoe clip **145 195 80**

Note: The 1979 edition listed two 213 varieties as having orange bodies. We have concluded that these are terra-cotta varieties. Reader comments are requested.

214 Box Car, 1926-40, all have latch couplers, black frames and large double doors. Left side plate reads "LIONEL LINES"; right side plate reads "NO. 214/AUTOMOBILE/FURNITURE", Hoffman observation

(A) Terra-cotta body, dark green roof and door guides, nickel journals, brass trim, brass Type I brakewheels, brass plates with borders, Type II oil label, Type I couplers **170 270 120**

(B) Cream body, orange roof and door guides, nickel journals, brass plates and trim, brass Type II brakewheels, Type III oil label, Type II couplers, Graves, Weaver and Hoffman Collections **150 250 100**

(C) Same as (B), but cream-yellow body clearly different from (B), Koff Collection **170 270 120**

(D) Yellow body, brown roof and door guides, nickel journals, nickel trim, nickel Type IV brakewheels, Type II couplers, no oil label, trucks secured with horseshoe clips **150 250 100**

(E) Same as (D), but brass trim and brakewheels **170 270 120**

214R Refrigerator Car, 1929-1940, two small doors, plate across top reads "LIONEL VENTILATED REFRIGERATOR", harder to find than most 200 series freights, did not come with sets, black frame and latch couplers

(A) Ivory body, peacock roof, nickel journals, brass plates, brass trim and brass Type II brakewheels, Type II couplers, Type II oil label, Koff Collection **375 550 200**

500 Series Freights

512 (A)

516 (C)

513 (A)

514 (E)

515 (A)

514 Refrigerator

517 (A)

511 (B)

(B) Same as (A), but white body, clearly a different color from (A), Weaver Collection **375 550 200**

(C) White body, light blue roof, nickel journals, nickel plates, nickel trim and nickel Type IV brakewheels, Type I couplers, no oil label, trucks secured by horseshoe clip **500 700 300**

(D) Same as (E), but brass plates, Sattler Collection **525 725 325**

215 Tank Car, 1926-1940, black frame and latch couplers. Reportedly, the small domes used on these and the 500 Series Cars are of two types. The first type was a smooth top; this variety had a very short production period compared to the second type, which had a fine mesh grid across the top of the dome, Sattler comments. Which cars are found with the smooth-top small domes? Are there similar differences in the large domes? Reader comments are requested.

(A) Pea green tank, brass trim and domes, red-lettered brass plates, nickel journals, brass Type II brakewheels, Type II couplers, Type II oil label **120 150 70**

(B) Same as (A), but smaller turned brass domes are screwed into tank, top of the largest dome flat or ridged, small domes or smooth-surfaced, Ely Collection **130 175 75**

(C) Ivory tank, brass trim and domes, brass plates, red-lettered "SUNOCO" decal, copper journals, brass Type III brakewheels, Type II couplers, Type III oil label **120 150 70**

(D) Same as (C), but no "SUNOCO" decal **120 150 70**

(E) Silver tank, black-lettered "SUNOCO" decal, nickel journals, nickel plates, nickel trim, nickel Type IV brakewheels, Type II couplers, no oil label **130 175 75**

(F) Same as (E), but brass trim **140 190 80**

(G) Light tan tank, black-lettered "SUNOCO" decal, copper journals, brass trim, brass plates with varied lettering (one has black "LIONEL LINES" lettering, the other red "NO. 215" lettering), no oil label. Probable factory error concerning color of tank and plates, Koff Collection **130 175 NRS**

(H) Same as (B), but numbered plate reads "No. 215/OIL CAR" in red letters, Ely Collection **130 175 75**

216 Hopper Car, 1926-1938, all known varieties are dark green, all have black frames and latch couplers

(A) Nickel journals, red-lettered brass oval plates, one plate has "LIONEL/LINES" in two lines separated by a double horizontal line (see illustration), the other plate reads "NO. 216/CAPACITY/20,000/CU. FT./110,000 LBS" in four lines, brass Type I brakewheel, no oil label, Type I couplers, Graves and Hoffman Collections **175 250 120**

"LIONEL LINES" BRASS PLATE

(B) Same as (A), but copper journals, Weaver Collection **175 250 120**

(C) Same as (A), but early 200 Series trucks with larger rectangular cutout in middle of truck frame between embossed springs, rather than small cutout in more common later 200 trucks, Koff Collection **180 275 130**

(D) Copper journals, black-lettered brass plates, brass Type III brakewheels, Type II couplers **175 250 120**

(E) Nickel journals, black-lettered nickel plates, nickel Type IV brakewheels, Type II couplers, trucks secured with horseshoe washer **275 400 150**

217 Caboose, 1926-1940, black frame, latch couplers, rear illumination

(A) Orange body, maroon main roof, maroon plates rubber-stamped in gold lettering, nickel journals, dark green platform railing, no window inserts, maroon doors, all-maroon cupola, Type I couplers **300 350 150**

(B) Same as (A), but black platform railing, Edmunds observation **250 325 125**

(C) Red body, peacock main roof, peacock doors, nickel journals, black-lettered brass plates, brass platform railings, brass window inserts, red cupola, with peacock front and rear, Type II oil label, Type II couplers, Graves Collection **120 150 70**

(D) Same as (C), but copper journals and no oil label, Weaver Collection **135 175 75**

(E) Same as (C), but all peacock cupola **135 175 75**

(F) Same as (C), but cream doors with peacock inserts, Koff Collection **150 190 80**

(G) Red body, white door, copper journals on oxide-treated truck frames, red main roof, black lettered aluminum plates, nickel platform railings, aluminum window inserts, all red cupola, Visnick observation **135 175 75**

(H) Light red body, light red main roof, nickel journals, black-lettered aluminum plates, aluminum platform railings and window inserts, light red cupola, Type II couplers, no oil label **120 150 70**

218 Dump Car, 1926-1938, operating bin controlled by one knob (sometimes two) on a geared rod. When bin tilts, the side of the car opens and the load empties. All samples have black-lettered brass plates, black frames, nickel journals and Type II latch couplers. Replacement gears are available for decayed gears.

(A) Mojave body, die-cast gears, two brass knobs, brass ends, Type II oil label, Koff Collection **175 225 100**

(B) Same as (A), except one brass knob, Weaver Collection **160 200 100**

(C) Mojave body, die-cast gears, one brass knob, mojave painted metal ends, Type III oil label, Koff Collection **175 225 100**

(D) Green body, maroon painted metal ends, early production circa 1926, probably a special promotion for a department store, Graves observation **NRS**

(E) Gray body, brass ends, probably a department store special, Graves observation **NRS**

219 Crane Car, 1926-1940, a very popular car then and now because of its immense play potential and sheer size. Lionel described it, quite rightly, as "an accessory that has won the admiration of every boy". One knob rotates the cab, another raises or lowers the boom and a third controls the hook. The car has a nickel clamping device to attach it to the rails to keep it from toppling when it lifts loads. All have black frames and latch couplers. One plate reads "LIFTING CAPACITY 20 TONS" on rear of cab.

(A) Peacock cab, dark red boom, dark green cab roof, nickel journals, steel-cut working gears (probably replacements), red windows, brass handrails, plates and knobs, dark green tool boxes, brass pulleys, Type I oil label, Koff and Hoffman Collections **120 175 75**

(B) Same as (A), except copper journals and black die-cast gears, Type II oil label, Type II couplers, Pauli, Weaver, and Graves Collections **140 190 80**

(C) Same as (A), except peacock windows and black die-cast gears, Type II oil label, Koff, Weaver, and Graves Collections **100 150 70**

(D) Same as (A), except green boom and red cab roof, Edmunds observation, reader comments requested. **NRS**

(E) Yellow cab, light green boom, red roof, nickel journals, nickel handrails and nickel knobs, red windows and tool boxes, Type II couplers, no oil label, trucks secured with horseshoe clips, Graves Collection **170 230 100**

(F) Same as (E), but copper journals, Weaver and Cirillo Collections **195 260 120**

(G) Ivory cab, red windows, roof and tool boxes, light green boom, black knobs, nickel handrails **250 325 150**

(H) Cream body, red boom, red roof, nickel journals, red windows, aluminum plates, black knobs, nickel pulleys, Kent Collection **120 230 100**

(I) White body, green boom, red roof, nickel journals, red windows, steel-cut gear wheels (probably replacements), brass knobs and plates, red tool boxes, brass pulleys, no oil label, LaVoie observation **275 350 150**

(J) Same as (I), but black die-cast gears and knobs, Weaver Collection **220 290 130**

(K) Dark blue cab body with doors at rear of cab sides rather than front, Young and Ely observations. Further details and confirmation are needed; this is a very unusual piece. **NRS**

220 Floodlight Car, 1931-1940, the last 200 series car introduced, it shares its base and lights with 820 0 Gauge cars. All have on-off switch, Type II latch couplers, and are rubber-stamped in sans-serif gold lettering "220 THE

500 Series Freights

512 (B) 516 (B) 511 (C)

514 (D) 514R (B) 513 (C)

520 (B) 515 (C) 515 (I)

517 (B) 515 (E) 515 (D)

LIONEL LINES 220" on frame sides, have black frames and no oil labels on any varieties

(A) Terra-cotta base, copper journals, brass light housings, brass handrails, Koff, Graves, and Weaver Collections **170 250 120**

(B) Same as (A), except nickel journals **170 250 120**

(C) Green base, nickel journals, nickel light housings and nickel Type IV handrails **190 275 120**

THE 500 SERIES FREIGHT CARS

In 1927, Lionel introduced a smaller version of the 200 Series to replace the equivalent 100 Series, which had a dated and drab look by this time. This group of freight cars, the 500 Series, complemented the larger, deluxe 200 Series and were painted in brighter and less realistic colors. Other features possessed by this and the 200 Series were brass or nickel plates and ornamentation, journal boxes on the trucks and latch couplers.

Initially, the 500 Series was composed of six cars: a gondola, a refrigerator car, an oil car, a lumber car, a cattle car and a caboose. Lionel's initial 500 series line differed in several interesting ways from its initial 200 series line. In the 200 series, the stock car and the box car were quite different in their side treatment (although the external dimensions are similar). The 213 stock car has stamped-out slats while the 214 box car has moderately embossed large rectangular patterns. In the 500 series, Lionel used modifications of the 513 die to produce the 514 refrigerator. The 514 refrigerator has the same slatted sides as the 513 but without the slats being punched out. Lionel did change the plate location for the 514 refrigerator and added a long plate along the roof line.

The original 200 series, while having both a box and a cattle car, did not have a refrigerator car. But the 500 series line started with a stock and a refrigerator car in the 500 series line.

Lionel's initial line - as we indicated - included a 514 refrigerator car. This car was offered for 2 years, 1927-1928, and then was replaced in 1929 by the 514R which is basically the same car but with an "R" added to the brass plate. Since the 514R refrigerator was made two years later than the 514 refrigerator, some design differences are evident. (We request our readers to compare the following details with their cars.) The 514 refrigerator has the Type I latch couplers with the spring retaining brass insert while the later 514R refrigerator has the Type II latch couplers without the spring retaining brass insert. The 514 refrigerators have truck king pins with holes for cotter pins while the 514R refrigerators have king pins with grooves for the offset washers.

The 514 refrigerator has large slots on its truck sides, while the 514R refrigerator has the small hole on its truck sides.

When Lionel changed the refrigerator car number to 514R in 1929, it created a new 514 box car. This car again used the 513 body without the slots punched out and retained the plate locations and door mechanisms of the original 513. With this change, the 500 series box car numbering exactly paralleled the 200 series numbering. In addition, the refrigerator cars of both series have had similiar numbering - 214R and 514R respectively.

In 1928 Lionel added the 516 hopper to the 500 series line. (The 200 series line had had a hopper since its 1926 inception.)

The last cars added to both the 200 and the 500s series line were the floodlight cars - the 220 and the 520. Both cars shared the same superstructure and light unit. This superstructure was also used on the 820 0 Gauge floodlight car. The 500 series cars also show other variations: oil labels, latch couplers, brakewheels and plate lettering. These variations are discussed in some detail with the introduction to the 200 Series cars.

There were only two varieties of trucks used on the 500 Series. One variety, the early and less common type, has black journals and a large rectangular slot cut out of the side panel. The second type has a much smaller hole in the side frame with the ends of the bolster bar swaged through the hole. In this truck, the journal boxes are copper or nickel instead of black. All of the 500 Series cars are built on a deeply embossed frame, 11-1/2 inches long.

Even though the 500 Series could be called "Son of the 200 Series", it became half of an extremely attractive line of freight cars manufactured during the Classic Period. As in the deluxe series, Lionel paid attention to play value, although not with operating cars. Lionel supplied lumber loads, barrels, and fake coal piles for the hopper, and the doors on these cars opened. It was with rolling stock like this that Lionel consolidated its position as the preeminent manufacturer of toy trains in the United States.

511 Flat Car, 1927-1940, all have latch couplers and are rubber-stamped "LIONEL LINES" in either silver or gold on frame sides. The car came with a long wooden block scribed on its sides and top to resemble a lumber load. The original wooden load brings a $3.00 premium in the car's price.

(A) Dark green body, nickel journals, rubber-stamped gold lettering, brass stakes and Type II brakewheels on left side of car ends, number rubber-stamped in gold on car bottom, Type II couplers, Type II oil label, Koff, Graves, Hoffman, and Pauli Collections **50 70 30**

(B) Same as (A), except brakewheels on right side of car ends, copper journals and nickel stakes, Koff and Hoffman Collections **35 50 20**

(C) Same as (B), but medium green body and nickel journals, Weaver Collection **35 50 20**

(D) Same as (B), but brakewheels and stakes both nickel, Lotstein Collection **35 50 20**

(E) Very dark green body (almost black), copper journals, rubber-stamped gold lettering, nickel stakes, brass Type II brakewheels on left of car sides, car number rubber-stamped in gold on car bottom, no oil label, Lotstein and Weaver Collections **35 50 20**

(F) Dark green body, copper journals, rubber-stamped silver lettering, nickel stakes, brass Type II brakewheels, Sattler Collection **35 50 20**

(G) Medium green body, nickel journals, rubber-stamped silver lettering, nickel stakes, Type IV brakewheels, Type II couplers, no oil label, trucks secured with horseshoe clip **35 50 20**

(H) Same as (G), but gold rubber-stamped lettering, Graves Collection **35 50 20**

512 Gondola, 1927-1939, all had black frames and latch couplers, 11-1/2 inches long, came with a set of barrels ($3-5 premium in price of cars listed below) and/or tool box with tools (see Accessory section for prices). Early and middle production cars had two supporting stanchions for each brakewheel. Later production cars eliminate the lower stanchion so that only one stanchion remains, Graves observation

(A) Peacock body, brass plates, nickel journals, Type II oil label, brass Type II brakewheels, Type II couplers, Graves Collection **40 55 25**

(B) Same as (A), except no oil label, Bergstrom Collection **40 55 25**

(C) Same as (B), but copper journals, Koff, Hoffman, and Weaver Collections **40 55 25**

(D) Same as (C), but lighter peacock body, Pauli Collection **60 80 35**

(E) Peacock body, brass plates, nickel journals, brass Type III brakewheels, no oil label, Type II couplers, trucks secured by horseshoe clip, Graves Collection **40 55 25**

(F) Green body, nickel journals, nickel plates, brass brakewheels, Weaver Collection **55 70 30**

(G) Same as (F), but nickel Type IV brakewheels, no oil label, Type II couplers and trucks secured by horseshoe clip **55 70 30**

(H) Same as (F), but darker green body, Edmunds observation **55 70 30**

500 Series Freights

513 Cattle Car, 1927-1938, all have black frames and latch couplers, data lines on one plate read "CAPACITY 60000 WEIGHT 20000"

The other plate is lettered "LIONEL LINES", but the plates differ. On the orange-bodied cars, the black lettering of this plate is much heavier and more bold than the thin-lettered plate found on the olive green-bodied cars. We need to know whether these differences are in fact associated with the body colors and whether these thick or thin-lettered plates also appear on other 500 series cars, Weaver photographs and observations

(A) Olive green body, orange roof and door guides, nickel journals, brass plates and trim, brass Type II brakewheels, Type II couplers, Type II oil label, Pauli, Graves, and Weaver Collections **50 80 35**

(B) Orange body, pea green roof and door guides, brass plates and trim, nickel journals, brass Type II brakewheels, Type II couplers, Type I oil label, Pauli and Hoffman Collections **50 80 35**

(C) Same as (B), but Type III oil label, Graves Collection **50 80 35**

(D) Same as (B), but plates have no borders, Edmunds observation. Further confirmation requested **50 80 35**

(E) Same as (B), but copper journals and Type II oil label, Koff and Weaver Collections **50 80 35**

(F) Cream body, maroon roof and door guides, nickel Type IV brakewheels, Type II couplers, nickel journals, nickel plates and nickel trim, no oil label, rare, reader verification requested **NRS**

514 Refrigerator, 1927-1928, black frame and latch couplers. Note: This car differs from the 514 box; it has a long, narrow plate along the top of the side which reads "LIONEL VENTILATED REFRIGERATOR". This car has "NO. 514" plates; it differs from the later 514R refrigerator car, whose plates read "NO. 514R". Since its double doors open outward, it does not possess door guides as does the 514 box car. All have Type II latch couplers and Type II brakewheels. Reader comments are requested concerning the relative scarcity of this car compared to the 514R version.

(A) White body, white doors, peacock roof, brass plates, nickel journals, brass Type II brakewheels and trim, Weaver Collection **250 475 150**

(B) Same as (A), but cream body with cream doors, Sattler Collection **225 300 125**

(C) Ivory (not white or cream) body, ivory doors, peacock roof, nickel journals, brass trim, brass plates, Type II brass brakewheels, Type II oil label, Type II couplers, Pauli, Koff, and Graves Collections **300 700 150**

(D) Cream body, cream doors, flat dark Stephen Girard green roof, nickel journals, brass trim, brass borderless plates, Type II oil label, Pauli Collection

This car, more than any other example found in all the research done on the 500 Series, illustrates the exasperating dilemmas faced in collecting these cars. It was examined by three experienced collectors by placing it alongside an example with a peacock roof and comparing it with color charts. There is no way this car should have anything but a peacock roof. And yet, there it sits, defying analysis.

The car is obviously a factory error, but how could such a thing come to pass? One easy answer is to assume that the car was on display in a shop window, where sunlight faded the roof. One would also expect fading of other paint in that case, and no other colors show signs of deterioration. In addition, the bluish tinge to Lionel's peacock color is absent on this roof.

Another hypothesis has to do with production. We are not certain of the exact method, but Lionel used a spray-painting technique whereby the paint (either pre-mixed or in pellet concentrates) was put in metal sprayers. If the level of paint had been allowed to run low in the spray canister, enough condensation could have formed to "wash out" the paint on a small number of cars. Another car we have found might bear out this hypothesis. See the entry for the 517(H) caboose, where the main roof was a flat light red - including the cupola front and rear - but the cupola roof, which is a separate piece, is the normal red. (To further complicate the caboose, one of the cupola windows was not punched out - a possible double factory error!)

A third hypothesis is that Lionel tried a pre-production sample of a different shade of color for this car's roof, and that it somehow slipped out of the factory. If this car is, in fact, a pre-production sample, it must be extremely rare. Unfortunately, there is no way to prove this hypothesis after all these years.

Since we have uncovered two examples in the 500 Series where the roofs are a flatter gloss and a lighter color than the normal production run, we may have a chance to see if other examples exist. If they do, we have perhaps uncovered a major factory variation due to a painting quality control lapse. We hope this discussion will send collectors rummaging through their 500 Series cabooses, box, cattle and reefer cars - and their 200 Series as well - to report any further variations to us. **275 600 —**

514 Box Car, 1929-1940, black frame and latch coupler, one plate reads "CAPACITY 60000 WEIGHT 20000"

(A) Cream yellow body, orange roof and door guides, copper journals, brass trim, brass Type II brakewheels, brass plates with borders, Type II couplers, no oil labels, Koff and Pauli Collections **75 100 40**

(B) Same as (A), but nickel journals and Type II oil label, Graves Collection **75 100 40**

(C) Yellow body, brown roof and door guides, nickel journals, nickel trim, nickel Type IV brakewheels, nickel plates, Type II couplers, no oil label, trucks mounted with horseshoe clip, Hoffman Collection **75 100 40**

(D) Same as (C), but brass Type III brakewheels, Weaver Collection **75 100 40**

(E) Same as (C), but "514" plate replaced by "LIONEL LINES" plate and "514" rubber-stamped on underside of frame **90 125 50**

(F) Cream body, green roof and door guides, copper journals, brass trim, brakewheels and plates. Although the authenticity of this car has been questioned, a photograph of it has been reported, and it is pictured in the 1932 Lionel catalogue as part of set 361E on page 22. We would like to hear from a collector who possesses this car, Graves observation **NRS**

514R Refrigerator Car, 1929-1940, black frame and latch couplers, long narrow plate on top of side reads "LIONEL VENTILATED REFRIGERATOR", double doors open outward

(A) Ivory body, peacock roof, nickel journals, brass trim, Type II brass brakewheels, brass borderless plates, Type II oil label, Type II couplers, Hoffman Collection **120 150 70**

(B) Ivory body, light blue roof, nickel journals, nickel Type IV brakewheels, no oil label, Type II couplers, trucks mounted with horse-shoe clip, nickel trim, nickel plates, Sattler Collection **375 700 200**

(C) Same as (A), but cream body, Koff Collection **135 175 70**

(D) Same as (A), but white body and copper journals, Weaver Collection **120 150 70**

515 Tank Car, 1927-1940, black frame and latch couplers. See 215 entries for discussion of dome types

(A) Burnt orange tank, nickel journals, brass trim, brass handrails, Type II couplers, Type III oil label, Pauli, Koff, Weaver, and Hoffman Collections **90 125 60**

(B) Same as (A), but Type II oil label, Graves Collection **90 125 60**

(C) Ivory tank, copper journals, brass trim, brass handrails, brass borderless plates, no oil label, Pauli and Hoffman Collections **90 125 60**

(D) Same as (C), but "SUNOCO" decal added, Weaver Collection **90 125 60**

(E) Light tan tank, copper journals, brass trim, brass handrails, Type III brakewheels, brass borderless plates, no oil label, Koff Collection **120 150 70**

(F) Same as (C), but nickel journals **120 150 70**

(G) Silver tank, "SUNOCO" decal, copper journals, brass trim, brass Type III handrails, brass plates, Type II couplers, no oil label **75 100 40**

(H) Same as (G), but handrails are nickel **75 100 40**

(I) Silver tank, "SUNOCO" decal, nickel journals, nickel trim, nickel Type IV handrails and nickel plates, Type II couplers, no oil label, Hoffman Collection **75 100 40**

(J) Same as (I), but plates are brass **75 100 40**

(K) Orange body, red "SHELL" decal, nickel journals, nickel trim, nickel handrails, Type IV brakewheels and nickel plates, trucks mounted with horseshoe clip (Very rare) **550 900 200**

516 Hopper, 1928-1940, black frame and Type II latch couplers, all with red body, the coal load brings a premium of $10.00.

(A) Copper journals, stamped steel coal load, brass ladders and trim, black-lettered brass bordered plates, brass Type II brakewheels, Pauli Collection **90 125 60**

(B) Same as (A), but nickel journals, Koff Collection **90 125 60**

(C) Same as (B), but no coal load, Weaver Collection **80 115 50**

(D) Same as (A), but nickel journals, plates and trim, Type IV nickel brakewheels **90 125 60**

Standard Freight Sets

(E) Nickel journals, brass ladders and trim, brass plates, coal load, brass Type III brakewheels, rubber-stamped gold lettering with capacity data. This car was only available as part of a special coal train led by the black No. 318 engine, Koff, Graves, and Weaver Collections **150 250 70**

(F) Same as (E), but no coal load **140 240 60**

(G) Same as (E), but plates entirely absent from car, as are their mounting slots. Probable factory error, very rare, Pauli Collection **500 750 NRS**

Note: We have had a report of a car in silver colors with nickel journals, either with or without capacity data stamping. Further sightings are requested to determine whether this color is original.

517 Caboose, 1927-1940, black frame and Type II latch couplers

(A) Pea green body, red main roof, nickel journals, brass railings, brass borderless plates, orange windows, green cupola roof, red cupola ends, Type I oil label, Pauli and Hoffman Collections **60 85 40**

(B) Same as (A), but Type II oil label, Graves Collection **60 85 40**

(C) Same as (A), but copper journals and brighter red roof and cupola ends, Koff Collection **60 85 40**

(D) Same as (A), but brass window inserts, Koff and Weaver Collections **75 100 50**

(E) Same as (A), but apple green body, Bergstrom Collection **75 100 50**

(F) Red body, red main roof, nickel journals, silver painted railings and window inserts, borderless aluminum plates, red cupola, trucks mounted with horseshoe clip, Weaver Collection **75 100 50**

(G) Same as (F), but brass plates **75 100 50**

(H) Same as (F), but lighter flat red main roof, normal red cupola roof, one cupola hole not punched on car observed; probable factory error. This is an intriguing car because of its flat light red roof. For a discussion of how this car could have been produced this way, see the extended discussion about a similar car at entry 514 (D), Lotstein Collection **90 125 60**

(I) Same as (E), but "NO. 517" plate replaced by "LIONEL LINES" plate and number rubber-stamped on underside of frame **90 125 60**

(J) Red body, black main roof, red cupola with black ends, orange windows, brass railings, brass plates, nickel journals. This was a special "coal train" caboose only available in a set with three special 516 hopper cars and a 318 locomotive **175 325 120**

520 Floodlight Car, 1931-1940, all have black frames and Type II latch couplers. Early versions had brakewheels on left side of car ends; later cars had them on right side. All have on-off light switch; same unit appeared on 820 0 Gauge cars. All samples rubber-stamped "LIONEL LINES" in gold on side of frame

(A) Terra-cotta base, brass Type III handrails, brass light casings, copper journals, rubber-stamped "520" on underside of frame, Weaver and Hoffman Collections **70 100 40**

(B) Same as (A), but nickel journals **70 100 40**

(C) Green base, nickel Type IV handrails, nickel light casings, nickel journals, rubber-stamped "520" on underside of frame, Graves, Hoffman, and Weaver Collections **95 140 50**

Large Early Passenger Car Sets

Chapter III

STANDARD GAUGE PASSENGER CARS

Gd Exc Rst

18 Pullman, 1906-27, part of largest early series passenger cars. Came with matching 19 Combine and 190 Observation.

(A) Dark olive green body and roof, solid clerestory, maroon doors and window sills, gold painted window dividers, clear celluloid windows, red speckled upper window celluloid, red speckled celluloid lavatory windows, roof not removable, doors do not open, three high wood knobs fastened to roof, open three-rivet trucks, short crinkle couplers, gold painted pinhole steps, gold rubber-stamped on sides "18 PULLMAN 18" and "NEW YORK CENTRAL LINES", gold painted door handle made from a nail end, not lighted, red primer on underside, 1906-10 **400 750 350**

(B) Similar to (A), but low knobs, optional lighting kit available, 1911-12, serif letters but no scroll design **400 750 350**

(C) Dark olive green body and roof, maroon doors and window sills, gold painted window dividers, clear celluloid windows, red speckled celluloid in upper window section, removable roof, doors open, single-rivet trucks, regular hook couplers, gold rubber-stamped "18 PULLMAN 18", black painted wood air tanks attached to floor underside, embossed "LIONEL MANUFACTURING CO." on floor, three-hole steps, pierced clerestory with tabs to hold celluloid, grooved diaphragms, matches 19 and 190, 1914-17 **70 150 70**

(D) Light orange body and roof, cream window sills and doors, gold painted window dividers, clear celluloid lower windows, red speckled upper windows, blue celluloid lavatory windows, stamped brass door handles, removable roof, doors open, single-rivet trucks, large crinkle hook couplers, gold rubber-stamped "18 PULLMAN 18" and "NEW YORK CENTRAL LINES" on side, smooth diaphragms. Matches 19 and 190, sold with brass 7 or 54 as top of the line set, 1916-17 **225 375 175**

(E) Dark olive green body and roof, maroon doors and window sills, gold painted window dividers, clear celluloid lower windows, blue speckled celluloid in upper window, removable roof, doors open, single-rivet trucks, regular hook couplers, gold rubber-stamped "PARLOR CAR" with scrollwork and "NEW YORK CENTRAL LINES" on sides, "18" on ends, floor not embossed, usually black rubber-stamped "LIONEL CORPORATION" on floor underside or end, three-hole steps, pierced clerestory with tabs to hold celluloid, plain diaphragms. Matches 19 and 190, 1918-23 **80 125 80**

(F) Dark olive green, similar to 18 (E), but combination latch couplers or latch couplers, interior light bracket, roller pickup on one truck, 1923-27 **80 125 80**

(G) Similar to 18 (E), but dark orange sides and roof, gold window sills. Came with brass 7 or 54 as top of line set with matching 19 and 190, 1920-23 **200 325 170**

(H) Similar to 18 (E), but mojave body and roof, combination latch couplers or latch couplers with interior light bracket and roller pickup on one truck. Matches 19 (G) and 190 (H), 1923-27 **175 300 150**

(I) Same as (E), but no rubber-stamping on bottom, "PARLOR CAR" lettering below windows in gold on sides within scrollwork, rubber-stamped "18" in gold on right side of car ends and "LIONEL/LINES/N.Y./Made in U.S.A." in four lines in gold on left side of car ends, Schuppner Collection **NRS**

(J) Same as (I), except gold rubber-stamped "Made in U.S.A./THE LIONEL CORPORATION/NEW YORK" on car bottom, Sattler Collection **NRS**

(K) Same as (J), but light olive green, Sattler Collection **NRS**

19 Combine

(A) Matches 18 (A) and 190 (A). Gold rubber-stamped, in sans-serif lettering, "PULLMAN" and "NEW YORK CENTRAL LINES". Extremely rare **600 800 225**

(B) Matches 18 (B) and 190 (B). Extremely rare **700 900 250**

Features of an 18-Series car from the mid 20's. Top: A 10-Series truck with electrical pickup and rectangular vertical bolster section that reaches the bottom edge of the side frame. Bottom: Wooden air tanks and a Type II oil label. Graves comments, Bartelt photographs.

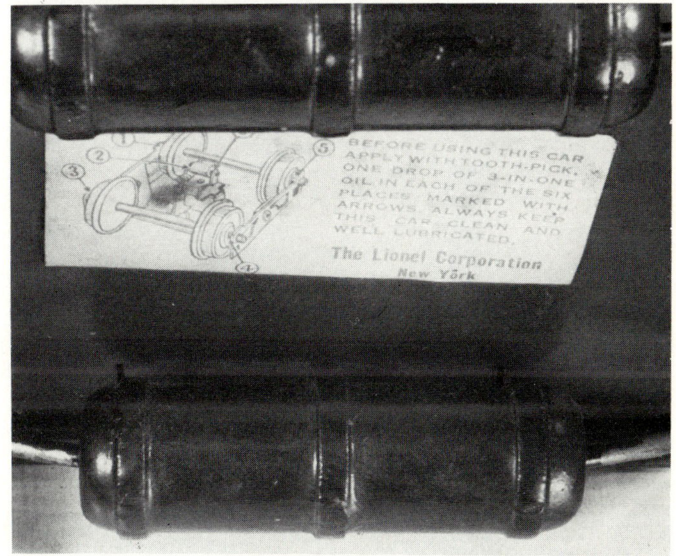

(C) Dark olive green, matches 18 (C) and 190 (C) or 190 (D) **80 150 70**

(D) Dark olive green, matches 18 (E) and 190 (F) **80 125 80**

(E) Dark olive green, matches 18 (F) and 190 (H) **80 125 80**

(F) Dark orange, matches 18 (G) and 190 (H) **200 325 170**

(G) Mojave, matches 18 (H) and 190 (I) **175 300 150**

(H) Matches 18 (J), Sattler Collection **NRS**

(I) Matches 18 (K), Sattler Collection **NRS**

18, 19, 190 Passenger Cars

19 (A)

18 (A)

18 (D)

18 (G)

190 (F)

No. 35 with three hole soldered steps. Note combination latch with triangular retaining plate. Also note barely visible slots punched in car floor for later steps but not used. (1923)

Later construction with solid two-riser step fastened to body by tabs (1924-25). Bartelt photographs.

29 Day Coach

(A) Dark olive green body and roof, gold rubber-stamped "No. 29 N.Y.C. & H.R.R.R. No. 29" on sides. Nine windows, body with large clerestory openings, body same as No. 3 trolley, solid platform on lower panel-ends, three-rivet open trucks, 1908 **475 700 400**

(B) Similar to 29 (A), but platform lower panel-ends open with twin railing, three-rivet open trucks, 1909 **475 700 400**

(C) Same as 29 (B), but rubber-stamped "PENNSYLVANIA R.R." **500 750 450**

(D) Maroon body and roof, gold rubber-stamped "No. 29 NYC & H.R.R.R. No. 29" on sides. Ten windows, platform ends open with twin railings, three-rivet open trucks, three high ventilators, nonremovable roof with no clerestory openings, short crinkle hook couplers, black painted wood airtank on each side, black steps pierced with many small holes, not illustrated, 1910 **800 1000 750**

(E) Same as 29 (D), but dark olive green body and roof **800 1000 750**

(F) Dark green body and roof, gold rubber-stamped "No. 29" twice on each side, "NEW YORK CENTRAL LINES" above windows, ten windows, platform ends open with twin railings, three-rivet open trucks, three low ventilators, nonremovable roof without clerestory openings, short crinkle hook couplers, black painted wood airtank on each side, black steps pierced with many small holes, 1911. Extremely rare **2000 3000 —**

(G) Dark olive green body and roof, maroon band through windows, gold rubber-stamped "29 NEW YORK CENTRAL LINES 29" on sides beneath windows, ten windows, platform ends open with twin gold painted railings, single chain on each platform, single-rivet open trucks, removable roof with pierced clerestory, large crinkle hook couplers, black painted wood airtanks on each side, airtanks smaller than those on earlier 29s, three-hole gold painted steps, 15-1/4", 1912-14 **450 675 350**

(H) Dark green body and roof, gold rubber-stamped "29 NEW YORK CENTRAL LINES 29" on sides beneath windows, ten windows, platform ends open with twin gold painted railings, single chain on each platform, single-rivet open trucks, removable roof with pierced clerestory and tabs for holding celluloid strip, large crinkle hook couplers, black painted wood airtanks on each side, airtanks smaller than those on earlier 29s, three-hole gold painted steps, 15-1/4", 1915-27 **375 600 275**

(I) Same as 29 (G), but gold rubber-stamped "29 PENNSYLVANIA R.R. 29" on sides beneath window, 15-1/4" **400 650 300**

(J) Same as (I), but rubber-stamping is "29 PENNSYLVANIA LINES 29", Sattler Collection **NRS**

31 Combine

(A) Maroon body and roof, wood grained baggage doors, gold rubber-stamped "PULLMAN" in elaborate scroll beneath windows, "NEW YORK CENTRAL LINES" above windows, black 100 series trucks, regular hook couplers, gold painted three-hole steps, clear celluloid lower windows, blue speckled celluloid upper window, only baggage door opens, passenger doors at both ends, combination latch couplers, metal airtanks, 1921-25, 10-3/4" **60 85 55**

(B) Same as 31 (A), but orange sides and roof, maroon baggage doors **70 95 60**

(C) Same as 31 (A), but dark olive green sides and roof, doors at one end only **55 80 50**

(D) Same as 31 (A), but brown sides and roof **60 85 55**

(E) Orange sides and roof, wood-grained baggage doors, white window curtains, rubber-stamped "NEW YORK CENTRAL LINES" and "PULLMAN" **70 95 60**

32 Mail

(A) Maroon sides and roof, matches 31 (A). Four wood-grained baggage doors, no passenger doors **60 85 55**

(B) Orange sides and roof, matches 31 (B), four baggage doors and four passenger doors **70 95 60**

(C) Dark olive green sides and roof, matches 31 (C) **55 80 50**

(D) Brown sides and roof, matches 31 (D) **60 85 55**

(E) Same as 31 (E) **60 85 55**

There are three distinct series of 35 and 36 passenger cars, early (A-B), middle (F-J) and late (N-R).

35 Pullman, first series. Two embossed ribs under windows, gold rubber-stamped on sides between ribs "35 PULLMAN 35" and above windows "NEW YORK CENTRAL LINES", single-rivet, closed side trucks, long crinkle hook couplers, gold painted steps with three holes, red speckled celluloid in upper windows, clear celluloid in lower windows, gold painted window dividers, removable roofs, oval lavatory windows, embossed handrails, 1912-13

(A) Dark olive green, maroon window sills **80 100 70**

(B) Dark blue made as special for Montgomery Ward. Extremely rare **250 450 200**

35 Pullman, second series 35 (F)-(I). Smooth sides, gold rubber-stamped "PULLMAN" with elaborate scroll beneath windows, "NEW YORK CENTRAL LINES" above windows, "35" on ends, embossed "LIONEL MANUFACTURING CO." on floor, large crinkle hook couplers, gold painted steps with three holes, blue speckled celluloid in upper windows, clear celluloid in lower windows, gold painted window dividers, removable roofs, square bottom lavatory windows with gold painted outline

(F) Dark olive green, maroon window sills **30 50 30**

Small and Medium Size Early Passenger Cars

(G) Same as (F), but gold rubber-stamped "CHESAPEAKE & OHIO" above windows **55 130 50**

(H) Maroon, green window sills **30 50 30**

(I) Orange, maroon window sills **40 90 40**

(J) Same as (H), but standard latch couplers and solid brass steps, Sattler Collection **NRS**

35 Pullman, third series 35 (N)-(R).* Smooth sides, gold rubber-stamped "PULLMAN" with elaborate scroll beneath windows, "NEW YORK CENTRAL LINES" above windows, "35" on one end, rubber-stamped "LIONEL CORPORATION" on ends or bottom, 100 series trucks, regular hook couplers, gold painted steps with three holes, blue speckled celluloid in lower windows, removable roofs, square bottom, lavatory windows with gold painted outlines. Gold rubber-stamped on bottom "Made in USA" and "The Lionel Corporation New York"

(N) Dark olive green, maroon window sills **30 40 30**

(O) Maroon, green window sills **25 35 20**

(P) Orange, maroon window sills **35 70 30**

(Q) Brown **30 40 30**

(R) Same as 31 (D), all orange **35 70 30**

36 Observation, first series. Matches 35 Pullman first series, but gold rubber-stamped "36 Observation 36" between ribs, long observation deck

(A) Matches 35 (A) **75 100 70**

(B) Matches 35 (B) **200 370 175**

36 Observation, second series. Matches 35 Pullman, second series. Gold rubber-stamped "OBSERVATION" with long deck

(F) Matches 35 (F) **35 50 30**

(G) Matches 35 (G) **65 135 60**

(H) Matches 35 (H) **35 50 30**

(I) Matches 35 (I) **50 90 40**

(J) Matches 35 (J), Sattler Collection **NRS**

36 Observation, third series. Matches 35 Pullman, third series. Gold rubber-stamped "OBSERVATION", short deck

(N) Matches 35 (N) **30 40 25**

(O) Matches 35 (O) **30 40 25**

(P) Matches 35 (P) **45 90 40**

(Q) Matches 35 (Q) **30 40 25**

(R) Matches 35 (R) **30 40 25**

180 Pullman

(A) Maroon body and roof, gold rubber-stamped "180 PULLMAN 180" on sides beneath windows, "NEW YORK CENTRAL LINES" above windows. Dark olive green doors, no openings in clerestory, black diaphragms, large crinkle hook couplers, black painted wood airtanks, gold painted steps pierced with many small holes, single-rivet 100 series truck, red undercoat on underside of floor, floor embossed "LIONEL MANUFACTURING CO.", 1911-13, 12-1/2" **100 150 90**

(B) Maroon body and roof, gold rubber-stamped "PULLMAN" in elaborate scroll beneath windows, "180" on ends. Dark olive green doors, pierced clerestory with tabs to hold celluloid, black diaphragms, regular hook couplers, black painted wood airtanks, three-hole, gold painted steps, single-rivet 180 series trucks, underside painted maroon to match sides, floor embossed "LIONEL MANUFACTURING CO.", 1914-17, 12-1/2" **80 100 70**

(C) Same as 180 (B), but brown body and roof **90 130 80**

(D) Maroon body and roof, similar to 180 (B), but floor not embossed. Rubber-stamped "THE LIONEL CORPORATION" on ends or bottom, 1918-21 **80 90 70**

(E) Brown body and roof, similar to 180(B), but floor not embossed. Rubber-stamped "LIONEL CORPORATION" on ends or bottom, 1918-21 **90 130 80**

181 Combine

(A) Maroon body and roof, matches 180 (A) **100 140 90**

(B) Maroon body and roof, matches 180 (B) **80 100 70**

(C) Brown body and roof, matches 180 (C) **90 125 80**

(D) Maroon body and roof, matches 180 (D) **80 100 70**

(E) Brown body and roof, matches 180 (E) **80 100 70**

(F) Yellow orange body and roof, orange doors, gold rubber-stamped "PULLMAN" in elaborate scroll beneath windows, "NEW YORK CENTRAL LINES" above windows, black diaphragms, removable roof, pierced clerestory **225 275 200**

182 Observation

(A) Maroon body and roof, matches 180 (A) and 181(A). Observation rail with scalloped top edge, long deck, 1911-13 **100 140 90**

(B) Maroon body roof, matches 180 (B) and 181 (B). Observation rail with fan-blade design and smooth top edge, long deck **80 100 70**

(C) Brown body and roof, matches 180 (C) and 181 (C). Observation rail with fan-blade design and smooth top edge, long deck, 1914-17 **80 100 70**

(D) Maroon body and roof, matches 180 (D) and 181 (D). Observation rail with fan-blade design and smooth top edge, short deck, 1918-21 **80 100 70**

(E) Brown body roof, matches 180 (E) and 181 (E). Observation rail with fan-blade design and smooth top edge, short deck, 1918-21 **90 125 80**

(F) Yellow orange body and roof, orange doors, matches 181 (F). Observation rail with fan-blade design and smooth top edge, long deck **225 275 200**

190 Observation

(A) Matches 18 (A) and 19 (A), vertical slat rail on long observation deck **300 600 250**

(B) Matches 18 (B) and 19 (B), vertical slat rail on long observation deck, also see (J) below **300 600 250**

(C) Matches 18 (C) and 19 (C) (also see 190 (D)). Interlocking spoke-wheel design rail with scalloped top edge on long observation deck **60 125 55**

(D) Matches 18 (C) and 19 (C). Fan-blade design rail with flat top railing on long observation deck, 1914-18 **90 135 80**

(E) Matches 18 (D) and 19 (D). Fan-blade rail with flat top railing, long observation **250 375 225**

(G) Matches 18 (F) and 19 (F). Fan-blade design with flat top rail on short observation deck, 1923-27 **90 125 80**

(H) Dark orange sides and roof, matches 18 (G) and 19 (G). Fan-blade design rail with flat top railing, short observation deck **225 350 200**

(I) Matches 18 (H) and 19 (H). Fan-blade design rail with flat railing top, short observation deck **180 250 175**

Top: An 18 (I) Parlor Car. Note closely-spaced "NEW YORK CENTRAL LINES" lettering and chairs inside windows. Bottom: A 190 Observation with widely spaced "NEW YORK CENTRAL LINES" lettering. Style of lettering differs at top, but not on bottom!

Classic Era Passenger Cars
380
320
319
319
322
1835 E
1835 W
310 (J)
309 (J)
312
318
310 (C)
309 (C)
312 (C)
318
310 (E)
309 (E)
312 (E)
384
384 T
309 (G)
312 (G)
LIONEL LINES

309 Pullman 1924-39, illuminated, latch couplers (except (A)), came with 310 Baggage and 312 Observation. Two different lettering styles can be found on these cars. One type features serif style lettering within scrollwork. The other type features plain block lettering without scrollwork, Sattler observation. See illustration below.

Top: "PULLMAN" lettering in larger serif letters within scrollwork. Bottom: Smaller serif letters, more widely spaced, without scrollwork.

(A) Maroon body and roof, mojave window inserts, wood-grained door, large door windows, stamped "NEW YORK CENTRAL LINES" above windows, 100, 200 or 500 series trucks, combination latch couplers, 1924 **70 150 70**

(B) Same as (A), but stamped "THE LIONEL LINES", 1927-29 **70 150 70**

(C) Mojave body and roof, maroon window inserts, wood-grained door, nickel journals, large door windows, stamped "NYC LINES", 1925-26 **70 150 70**

(D) Same as (C), but stamped " THE LIONEL LINES" **70 150 70**

(E) Pea green body and roof, orange window inserts and door, large or small door windows, nickel journals, stamped "THE LIONEL LINES", 1927-30 **70 150 70**

(F) Light brown body, dark brown roof, cream window inserts and doors, large or small door windows, stamped "THE LIONEL LINES", nickel or copper journals, 1930-33 **85 175 80**

(G) Maroon body, terra-cotta roof, cream window inserts and doors, large door window, stamped "NEW YORK CENTRAL LINES" above windows, nickel journals, 1931 **70 150 70**

(H) Apple green body, dark green roof, cream window inserts, apple green door with small window, rubber-stamped "THE LIONEL LINES", copper journals, 1934-35 (rare) **100 200 90**

(I) Light blue body and door with small window, dark blue roof, cream window inserts, rubber-stamped "THE LIONEL LINES", copper journals, 1934 **85 175 80**

(J) Pale blue body, silver roof, window insert and door, with small window, rubber-stamped "THE LIONEL LINES", nickel journals, 1935-39 **70 150 70**

(K) Light blue body and roof. Blue color identical to that found on 514 R and late 814 R freight car roofs. Gold rubber-stamped "THE LIONEL LINES" on insert below windows. Nickel journals, rubber-stamped Lionel identification on bottom. This car came as part of a set with an accompanying 390 E "Blue Comet" locomotive, a matching 310 baggage and a 312 observation. This collector had color samples from the cars examined by a chemist using x-ray spectroscopy. Levels of barium, lead and strontium in this car's paint were compared to paint samples from confirmed Lionel 514 R and 814 R refrigerator car roofs. The parallels in these levels of chemicals established beyond doubt that the paint on this car is genuine Lionel factory paint. This set is presently the only known example of this paint scheme, and it may in fact be one-of-a-kind. Editor's Note: The authentication process used is commendable. Adair Collection **NRS**

310 Baggage 1924-39, illuminated, latch couplers, 13-1/4". Came with 309 Pullman and 312 Observation.

(A) Matches 309 (A) with dark green baggage door **0 150 70**

(B) Matches 309 (B) with dark green baggage door **70 150 70**

(C) Matches 309 (C) with dark green baggage door **70 150 70**

(D) Matches 309 (D) with dark green baggage door **70 150 70**

(E) Matches 309 (E) with orange baggage door **70 150 70**

(F) Matches 309 (F) with cream baggage door **80 175 80**

(G) No baggage car made to match 309 (G) **— — —**

(H) Matches 309 (H) with apple green baggage door **100 200 90**

(I) Matches 309 (I) with light blue baggage door **80 175 80**

(J) Matches 309 (J) with silver baggage door **70 150 70**

(K) Matches 309 (K), Adair Collection **NRS**

312 Observation 1924-39, illuminated, latch couplers, 13-1/4". Came with 309 Pullman and 310 Baggage.

(A) Matches 309 (A) **70 150 70**

(B) Matches 309 (B) **70 150 70**

(C) Matches 309 (C) **70 150 70**

(D) Matches 309 (D) **70 150 70**

(E) Matches 309 (E) **70 150 70**

(F) Matches 309 (F) **80 175 80**

(G) Matches 309 (G) **70 150 70**

(H) Matches 309 (H) **100 200 90**

(I) Matches 309 (I) **70 150 70**

(J) Matches 309 (J) **70 150 70**

(K) Matches 309 (K), Adair Collection **NRS**

319 Pullman 1924-27, medium sized passenger car of Classic Era, came in a variety of colors with different trucks. Rubber-stamped with different road names, mostly "LIONEL LINES" or "NEW YORK CENTRAL LINES". Combination latch, later latch couplers, brass steps, 13-1/4"

(A) Maroon body and roof, wood-grained doors, mojave windows and number boards, 200 series trucks, rubber-stamped "LIONEL LINES" **70 100 70**

(B) Same as (A), but rubber-stamped "NEW YORK CENTRAL LINES". **100 145 90**

(C) Same as (A), but rubber-stamped "ILLINOIS CENTRAL" **100 145 90**

(D) Same as (A), but rubber-stamped "LIONEL ELECTRICAL RAILROAD" **100 145 90**

320 Baggage, 1925-27. (See 319 for background on series which includes 319 and 320.)

(A) Maroon sides and roof, wood-grained doors, mojave windows and number boards, 200 series trucks, rubber-stamped "LIONEL LINES" **70 100 70**

(B) Match for 319 (B) not known to exist. Comments requested.

(C) Same as (A), but rubber-stamped "ILLINOIS CENTRAL" **100 145 90**

(D) Same as (A), but rubber-stamped "LIONEL ELECTRICAL RAILROAD" **100 145 90**

322 Observation 1924-27.(See 319 for background on series which includes 319 and 320.)

(A) Maroon sides and roof, wood grained doors, mojave windows and number boards, 200 series trucks, rubber-stamped "LIONEL LINES" **70 100 70**

(B) Same as (A), but rubber-stamped "NEW YORK CENTRAL LINES" **70 100 70**

(C) Same as (A), but rubber-stamped "ILLINOIS CENTRAL" **100 145 90**

(D) Same as (A), but rubber-stamped "LIONEL ELECTRICAL RAILROAD" **100 145 90**

Late Small Standard Passenger Sets

332 Baggage. This car comes with two different small, late Standard Gauge passenger series. The first series consisted of the 332 Baggage plus 337 Pullman and 338 Observation. The 337 and 338 have single undivided windows. The second late, small series consisted of the 332 plus 339 Pullman and 341 Observation. The cars are 12 inches long and feature enameled inserts to create windows and number boards. All have 500 series trucks, latch couplers, nickel journals - without brass plates. They are rubber-stamped "RAILWAY MAIL" and "332" on each side and have black metal airtanks with nickel ends.

(A) Red body and roof, cream doors, windows and number boards, rubber-stamped "THE LIONEL LINES" **45 75 50**

(B) Peacock body and roof, orange doors, windows and number boards, rubber-stamped "THE LIONEL LINES" **45 75 50**

(C) Gray body and roof, maroon doors, windows and number boards **45 75 50**

(D) Olive green body and roof, red doors, windows and number boards **50 90 50**

(E) State brown body, dark brown roof, cream doors, windows and number boards, gold rubber-stamped "THE LIONEL LINES" and "RAILWAY MAIL" **60 100 60**

(F) Peacock body, dark green roof, orange doors, windows and number boards **60 100 60**

(G) Peacock body and roof, red doors, orange windows and number boards, catalogued 1929 only **75 125 75**

(H) Peacock body, dark green roof, orange windows, doors and number boards, with "IVES LINES" decals over "THE LIONEL LINES" rubber-stamping **90 140 90**

(I) Beige body, maroon roof, maroon windows, doors and number boards **120 175 100**

337 Pullman (See 332 for background) Ten single undivided windows, rubber-stamped "NEW YORK CENTRAL LINES" or "THE LIONEL LINES" above windows, four brass steps, illuminated, 1925-32, 12"

(A) Red body and roof, cream doors, windows, and number boards, matches 332 (A), rubber-stamped "THE LIONEL LINES" **45 75 45**

(B) Mojave body and roof, maroon windows, doors and number boards, rubber-stamped "NEW YORK CENTRAL LINES" **45 75 45**

(D) *Olive green body and roof, red doors, windows and number boards, matches 332 (D) **50 90 45**

(E) Olive green body and roof, maroon windows, doors and number boards **45 75 45**

(F) Pea green body and roof, cream windows, doors and number boards **65 120 60**

(J) Olive green body and roof, maroon windows, doors and number boards, rubber-stamped "ILLINOIS CENTRAL" **NRS**

338 Observation (See 332 for background, matches 337 Pullman.) Ten single, undivided windows, brass observation railing, 12"

(A) Red, matches 337 (A) **45 75 45**

(B) Mojave, matches 337 (B) **45 75 45**

(D) Olive green and red trim, matches 337 (D) **50 90 45**

(E) Olive green and maroon trim, matches 337 (E) **45 75 45**

(F) Pea green, matches 337 (F) **65 120 60**

(J) Olive green, matches 337 (J) **NRS**

339 Pullman 1925-33. (See 332 for background on series.) Six windows divided horizontally and vertically, rubber-stamped "NEW YORK CENTRAL LINES" or "LIONEL LINES" above windows, four brass steps, illuminated, 12"

(B) Peacock body and roof, orange doors, windows and number boards, matches 332 (B), rubber-stamped "THE LIONEL LINES" **45 75 45**

(C) Gray body and roof, maroon doors, windows and number boards, matches 332 (C) **45 75 45**

(E) State brown body, dark brown roof, cream doors, gold stamped windows and number boards, matches 332 (E), rubber-stamped " THE LIONEL LINES" **60 100 55**

(F) Peacock body, dark green roof, orange doors, windows and number boards **60 100 55**

(H) Peacock body, dark green roof, orange windows, doors, and number boards, with "IVES LINES" decals over "THE LIONEL LINES" rubber-stamping **90 140 90**

*Letters assigned to variations are not in strict alphabetical order since they refer to related car variations.

(I) Beige body, maroon roof, windows, doors, and number boards **120 175 100**

341 Observation 1925-33. (See 332 and 339 for background on series.)

(B)* Peacock body and roof, orange doors, windows and number boards, matches 332 (B), rubber-stamped "THE LIONEL LINES" **45 75 45**

(C) Gray body and roof, maroon doors, windows and number boards, matches 332 (C), rubber-stamped **45 75 45**

(E) State brown body, dark brown roof, cream doors, windows and number boards, matches 332 (E), rubber-stamped **60 100 55**

(F) Peacock body, dark green roof, orange doors, windows and number boards, rubber-stamped **60 100 55**

(H) Peacock body, dark green roof, orange windows, doors and number boards, with "IVES LINES" decals over "THE LIONEL LINES" rubber-stamping **90 140 90**

(I) Beige body, maroon roof, windows, doors and number boards **120 175 100**

412 Pullman 1929-35, brass plates with "CALIFORNIA" in black lettering with either serif or sans-serif letters, brass trim only on steps, handrails, name plates. Part of "State Car" series: 412, 413, 414, 416; the largest Lionel passenger cars ever made (21-5").* Interior trim included two washrooms with sinks and toilets, interior doors and individual passenger seats. Earlier cars have die-cast axle journals. They do decay and replacements are available. Later cars have stamped brass journals. Two body rivet designs are found. The later includes a new row of rivets outlining the car end section.

(A) Lighter green body, dark green roof, apple green window inserts, roof ventilators usually light green, a few are dark green **850 1200 800**

(B) Same as (A), but yellow window inserts, usually came with 400E **875 1250 825**

(C) Light brown body, dark brown roof, yellow window inserts, roof ventilators light or dark brown, some have yellow doors, came with 408E **900 1350 850**

413 Pullman "COLORADO", 1929-35, matches 412

(A) Matches 412 (A) **850 1200 800**

(B) Matches 412 (B) **875 1250 825**

(C) Matches 412 (C) **900 1350 850**

414 Pullman "ILLINOIS", 1929-35, matches 412

(A) Matches 412, 1929 only (A) **875 1400 900**

(B) Matches 412 (B), reader verification requested **NRS**

(C) Matches 412 (C) **925 1500 950**

416 Observation 1929-35, "NEW YORK", matches 412; celluloid insert on rear railing either "TRANSCONTINENTAL LIMITED" or "LIONEL LINES"

(A) Matches 412 (A) **850 1200 800**

(B) Matches 412 (B) **875 1250 825**

(C) Matches 412 (C) **900 1350 850**

418 Pullman 1923-32.* This car with the matching 419 and 490 formed the first large passenger car series of the Classic Era. Introduced with the 402 as the top of the line set in mojave, these cars later appeared in apple green. In 1927, a diner, 431, was added to the series. The cars have been expertly reproduced by Williams Electric Trains.**

(A) Mojave body and roof, maroon window trim, wood lithographed doors, 10 series trucks, combination latch couplers, gold rubber-stamped "PARLOR CAR" below windows on side and "NEW YORK CENTRAL LINES" above windows, four brass step units, pierced clerestory on roof, two

*Note that reproductions have also been made from a lighter weight steel with plates lettered "LION LINES".

**Williams Electric Trains has manufactured reproductions of the 418, 419, 490, 431 and 428, 429 and 430. WRL is embossed on major pieces of the body including the top ledge inside the car where the metal tabs hold the window material, inside of interior bulkheads and under vestibule ends. The cars are available in four colors, mojave, orange, dark green and apple green. Window inserts are available in red, maroon and orange. The cars are available with 200 series trucks or six-wheel, 418 style trucks. Decals with "NEW YORK CENTRAL LINES", and the numbers "418", "419", "490", "431", "428", and "429", and "430", are available. Hence it is expected that combinations of trucks, colors, window inserts and numbers not originally created by Lionel will occasionally be offered for sale. The value of the cars in excellent condition, properly assembled is about $150, except for the 431 diner which brings $200.

The State Sets

The Blue Comet And Stephen Girard Sets

408 E
419
431
408
419
431
9
429
9E
492
429

knurled screws hold roof to body, light inside car, one pickup roller, gold rubber-stamped "418" on one end only, four black airtanks with nickeled ends, usually with oiling instruction label on bottom, 1923-24 **175 250 175**

(B) Same as (A), but maroon doors, 1923-24 **175 250 175**

(C) Same as (A), but six-wheel trucks with nickel journals, latch couplers, 1925 **185 275 185**

(D) Same as (A), but six-wheel trucks, nickel journals, latch couplers, maroon doors **185 275 185**

(E) Same as(A), but six-wheel trucks, nickel journals, latch couplers and orange window trim with maroon doors, gold rubber-stamped "THE LIONEL LINES" or "NEW YORK CENTRAL LINES" above windows **185 300 185**

(F) Same as (A), but apple green body and roof, six-wheel trucks, nickel journals, latch couplers and red window trim with maroon doors **185 300 185**

419 Combination 1923-32, part of 418, 419, 490 series. (See 418 for background.) Combination cars or "combines" for short, carry a mixed consist of passengers, baggage and small freight items. It has three large passenger windows, a lavatory window and two windows in baggage compartment on each side, two regular doors and one large baggage door on each side, gold rubber-stamped on lower side "BAGGAGE" and "PARLOR CAR" and "419" on end

(A) Matches 418 (A) **175 250 175**
(B) Matches 418 (B) **175 250 175**
(C) Matches 418 (C) **185 275 185**
(D) Matches 418 (D) **185 275 185**
(E) Matches 418 (E) **190 300 185**
(F) Matches 418 (F) **215 325 200**

Blue Comet Cars: 420, 421 and 422, specially painted locos. Catalogued initially with the 390E and later with the 400E, their striking colors, deluxe interior fittings, and size have made them specially prized.

420 Pullman 1930-40, "FAYE", latch couplers, 18-3/4"

(A) Medium blue with dark blue roof sections and vestibules, cream windows with brass trim, plates and cast journals **525 750 550**

(B) Same as (A), but brass stamped journals **525 750 500**

(C) Lighter blue with dark blue roof sections and vestibules, cream windows, mostly nickel trim, brass plates, nickel journals, frosted window glazing **575 825 600**

(D) Same as (C), but diaphragms painted lighter blue, all nickel trim **650 900 675**

421 Pullman 1930-40, "WESTPHAL" matches 420

(A) Matches 420 (A) **525 750 550**
(B) Matches 420 (B) **525 750 550**
(C) Matches 420 (C) **575 825 600**
(D) Matches 420 (D) **650 900 675**

422 Observation 1930-40, "TEMPEL", matches 420 and 421

(A) Matches 420 (A) **525 750 550**
(B) Matches 420 (B) **525 750 550**
(C) Matches 420 (C) **575 825 600**
(D) Matches 420 (D) **650 900 675**

424 Pullman 1931-40, brass plates "LIBERTY BELL", part of the Stephen Girard Series: 424, 425 and 426. These are late, medium sized passenger cars, 18-1/2" long, found with Stephen Girard (light green) bodies and roofs, accented with dark green vestibules and roof areas. Six-wheel trucks, cream window inserts, operating doors, bench sides run longitudinally . All with brass plates and nickel or brass trim. Blue speckled celluloid upper windows, clear celluloid lower windows, roof opens on hinges and latches; latch couplers

(A) "LIBERTY BELL", brass trim **325 500 350**
(B) "LIBERTY BELL", nickel trim **350 600 375**

425 Pullman 1931-40, brass plates "STEPHEN GIRARD" (See 424 for background.)

(A) Brass trim **325 500 350**
(B) Nickel trim **350 600 375**

426 Observation 1931-40, "CORAL ISLE" (See 424 for background). Keystone on observation railing lettered "PENNSYLVANIA LIMITED"

(A) Brass trim **325 500 350**
(B) Nickel trim **350 600 375**

427 Diner, similar to 431 but was to have four-wheel, 200 series trucks while 431 was catalogued with six-wheel trucks. 427 was catalogued in 1930 and to the best of our knowledge was not made. 431 diners almost always have six-wheel trucks as catalogued. However, two examples of 431 diners with factory affixed 200 series trucks have been discovered. It is argued that these are really 427 diners misnumbered 431! We will leave this controversy to our readers... **Not Manufactured**

428 Pullman 1926-30. Part of 428, 429 and 430 series which featured 200 series trucks in contrast to the closely related 418, 419 and 490 series with six-wheel trucks. Other than the trucks, colors and lettering appear identical. The cars have been expertly reproduced by Williams Electric Trains. (See footnote 418 for more information.)

(A) Dark green body and roof, maroon window inserts, wood lithographed doors, latch couplers, gold rubber-stamped "PARLOR CAR" on lower sides, "428" on one end, and "THE LIONEL LINES" above windows **225 300 200**

(B) Same as (A), but maroon doors **225 300 200**

(C) Same as (A), but orange window inserts and maroon doors **225 300 200**

(D) Orange body and roof, apple green window inserts and doors, gold rubber-stamped "PARLOR CAR" on lower sides, "428" on one end, "THE LIONEL LINES" above windows. **250 400 225**

429 Combine 1926-30. (See 428 for background on series.) Combination is part passenger, part baggage. It has three large passenger windows, a lavatory window and two windows in the baggage compartment on each side as well as two regular doors and one large baggage door on each side. Gold rubber-stamped on lower side "BAGGAGE" and "PARLOR CAR". "429" stamped on end.

(A) Matches 428 (A) **225 300 200**
(B) Matches 428 (B) **225 300 200**
(C) Matches 428 (C) **225 300 200**
(D) Matches 428 (D) **250 400 225**

430 Observation 1926-30. (See 428 for background on series.) The Observation has an open rear deck with brass railings. It has been reproduced, see footnote to 418.

(A) Matches 428 (A) **225 300 200**
(B) Matches 428 (B) **225 300 200**
(C) Matches 428 (C) **225 300 200**
(D) Matches 428 (D) **250 400 225**

431 Diner 1927-32 Part of the 418, 419 and 490 series and/or the 428, 429 and 430 series. (See 418 and 428 for background on each series.) The Diner was generally not included in sets and is much scarcer than the other cars. It includes 8 tables and 32 chairs in the dining room and a small kitchen with stove and table. One light is provided for dining with one pickup roller attached to one truck providing the necessary current. The windows have blue speckled celluloid in upper window section. The car comes with four brass steps and usually a roof attached with 2 knurled screws, although a few cars are known to have hinged roofs, probably for dealer display. The car usually has six wheels, 418 style trucks, although it is reported with 200 series trucks. Four black metal airtanks, latch couplers, and nickel journals adorn the car.

(A) Mojave body, orange window inserts, maroon doors, six-wheel trucks, gold rubber-stamped "THE LIONEL LINES" above windows and "431" on one end only, knurled screws hold roof to body **300 450 350**

(B) Same as (A), but hinged roof with several small hinges **400 600 400**

(C) Same as (A), but maroon window inserts **300 450 350**

(D) Dark green body, orange window inserts, 200 series trucks, gold rubber-stamped "THE LIONEL LINES" above windows, "431" gold stamped on one end only **350 600 375**

(E) Orange body, apple green inserts, six-wheel trucks, gold rubber-stamped "THE LIONEL LINES" above windows, "431" on one end only **350 600 375**

(F) Apple green body, red window inserts, six-wheel trucks, gold rubber-stamped "THE LIONEL LINES" above windows, "431" on one end only **350 600 375**

490 Observation 1923-32. Part of 418, 419, 490 series. (See 418 for background.) The Observation has an open rear deck with brass railing. Reproductions available, see 418 for details.

(A) Matches 418 (A) **175 250 175**
(B) Matches 418 (B) **175 250 175**

(C) Matches 418 (C) **185 270 185**
(D) Matches 418 (D) **185 270 185**
(E) Matches 418 (E) **190 285 185**
(F) Matches 418 (F) **215 325 185**

1766 Pullman 1934-40. These cars are Ives designs produced by Lionel under the Ives name in 1932. In 1934 they appeared with Lionel plates. There are two matching cars: 1767 Baggage and 1768 Observation. They have six-wheel trucks, latch couplers, lights, roof latch mechanisms. Earlier cars have terra-cotta sides, maroon roofs and fishbelly, cream windows and doors and brass trim. Later cars have red sides, maroon roofs and fishbelly, aluminum windows and doors and nickel trim. However, all catalogue illustrations show the earlier cars.
(A) Terra-cotta with brass trim **300 450 325**
(B) Red with nickel trim **300 400 325**

1767 Baggage 1934-40. (See 1766 for background.)
(A) Terra-cotta with brass trim **300 450 325**
(B) Red with nickel trim **300 400 325**

1768 Observation 1934-40. (See 1766 for background.)
(A) Terra-cotta with brass trim **300 450 325**
(B) Red with nickel trim **300 400 325**

1910 Pullman 1909-10, dark olive green body and roof, maroon doors and window sills, gold painted window dividers, celluloid windows, roof not removable, doors do not open, three high wood knobs fastened to roof, open, three-rivet trucks mounted close to car ends, short straight hook couplers, gold rubber-stamped on sides "1910 PULLMAN 1910" in letters without serifs. First Lionel closed vestibule passenger car. **400 1100 350**

Chapter IV

0 AND 0-27 LOCOMOTIVES

by Robert Pauli

About 1913, The Lionel Manufacturing Company introduced a group of trains smaller than either Lionel's original 2-7/8" gauge line or the 2-1/8" "Standard Gauge", then in its seventh year of production. Lionel made a smaller line for two reasons. First, the smaller trains would sell for less, increasing the potential market and providing profits by increasing volume. Secondly, smaller trains would fit into smaller spaces, again increasing market size. This concept of making smaller and smaller trains to create and serve new markets has continued to this day.

In those early years, though, Lionel was a small firm with stiff competition at home and abroad. Imported trains (and other toys), especially those from Germany, were readily available at attractive prices. People believed they were better than American toys. But World War I, beginning in 1914, brought a halt to those imports. Amid patriotic fervor, "Made in the U.S.A." gained new importance, and production rapidly climbed. Among the many toy train manufacturers was a firm with energetic sales pitches and quality products proudly identified as LIONEL ELECTRIC TRAINS.

If seven is a lucky number, then seven hundred, the number of Lionel's first little electric type 0 Gauge locomotive, certainly benefited from it. The 700 headed a series of electric type engines on Lionel's new 0 Gauge rails, comprising several four-drive-wheel companions: 701, 706, 728, and 732. The larger 703 had a pair of four-wheel pilot trucks flanking its drivers, plus a sturdy little Lionel electric motor. Many of those motors still run well! Two proposed locomotives (702 and 704) were not produced; nor was the steam type 710, with a four-wheel tender, even though it was catalogued. It's likely that a pilot model - a handmade prototype - was constructed, and the catalogue illustration was based upon it. Intensive study of both Lionel trains and catalogues has disclosed some of these prototypes. In 1976, an entire train was discovered, the factory prototype of Lionel's Standard Gauge **BLUE COMET**! Its blue 390E and three coaches (made with parts from at least 3 State cars and 9 309-310-313 series cars) did not match production sets, but they matched Lionel's 1930 catalogue illustrations perfectly. For detailed descriptions, see two articles: John Daniel, "The **BLUE COMET** Mystery", **TOY TRAIN OPERATING SOCIETY BULLETIN**, March 1977, Vol. 12, No. 3, pp. 4-5; and Dr. Gerald Wagner, "Lionel Factory Prototype **BLUE COMET** Set", **THE TRAIN COLLECTORS' QUARTERLY**, Spring 1977, Vol. 23, No. 2, pp. 16-17, 28.

After 1916, Lionel altered the 700 series locomotives and renumbered them as the 150, 152, 154, and 156. The 156 was substantially larger and came with a pair of four-wheel pilot trucks. Lionel also responded to patriotic fervor at the outbreak of World War I (The Great War was its working title until it was assigned a number) by manufacturing a menacing gray twin-barreled four-driver dreadnought (203) in 0 Gauge. But a steam locomotive, 151, catalogued at the same time, followed 710 to oblivion. In 1918, the little 158 marked the end of an era. Its two pedestal-type headlights gave way to cheaper strap headlights. In 1923, Lionel introduced the 153. Like the 154, it reversed by hand lever; otherwise, it was identical to the 152.

In 1921, Lionel brought out a new version of the 156: the 156X. To eliminate continued derailments, Lionel removed both the 156's four-wheel pilot and trailing trucks and their mounting holes as well, and added an "X" on the box but not on the locomotive. The 156 was still the largest locomotive in Lionel's 0 Gauge fleet, but now it looked somewhat bare whizzing around curves. Unfortunately, youthful operators had less to do - no need to rerail pilot trucks for Dad, no need to remove them from the engine, either. Lionel had already done that!

Making the most of the "Roaring '20s", Lionel designed a new group of four-driver electric type locomotives and numbered them for the decade - the 200 series. It comprised the 253 (New Haven style box cab), 254 (Milwaukee Road **OLYMPIAN** electric or "bi-polar"), and the big, boxy, burly, twin-motor 256 with eight-drive-wheels. None had any derailment-prone pilot wheels. The following year (1925), a new single-motor box cab (251) graced Lionel's catalogue, with a smaller four-drive-wheel revision of the 700-150 N.Y.C. "S" class electrics arriving in 1926. In 1927, Lionel installed its new Super-Motor in box cab electric 248 - a pretty and inexpensive little item.

In the late 1930's, Lionel's middle-of-the-line die-cast steamers were also numbered in the 200 series with 224, 225, 226, 227, and 229 among them. The lucky number 700 was used again, gracing the boxes of Lionel's renowned 700E, the 0 scale New York Central Hudson, exactly 1/48th actual size. Yet that number was printed only on the box. No. 5344, the number of the real locomotive Lionel modeled, adorned the cab and headlight.

To the confusion of many Lionel railroaders, Lionel made two types of 0 Gauge track. The gauge, the distance between the outside rails (1-1/4"), was identical; the difference was the radii of the curves. 0 Gauge track, with big, heavy-duty rails and ties, had a 15" radius for Lionel's top-of-the-line locomotives and cars. In 1934, a 36" radius ("Special Model Maker's track") was offered for Lionel's scale model of the Union Pacific's sleek yellow and brown streamliner, the **M-10000**. Many modelers with spacious layouts liked these wider curves, providing continuous sales, so these special 0 Gauge curved sections stayed in the catalogue for the next 20 years. In 1938, this track was christened 072 (0 Gauge, 72" diameter curves), and trains that used it were called the 072 series. By 1942, they comprised the **M-10000**, the **HIAWATHA**, the scale Hudson, the Pennsylvania Railroad B-6 0-6-0 switcher, and scale freight cars. In 1936, for even more realism, Lionel introduced straight and curved sections (and switches) in this series with solid steel "T" rails. This track remained in the catalogue through 1942, but the market for it was too limited to justify continued production after World War II. That was also true of the entire 072 series. Those trains looked beautiful and ran well, but they required a lot of space and money. A few dedicated modelers were willing to sacrifice whole rooms and make the considerable investment required, but most of Lionel's customers were not. Proof of that is evident in Lionel catalogues. The entire 072 series comprised only a few items - the Hudson, the B-6 switcher, a handful of freight cars with scale trucks and couplers, and a single basic set of passenger cars (the **M-10000** cars were repainted and the ends were modified for the **HIAWATHA** and the scale Hudson's **RAIL CHIEF**). These few items cannot begin to compare with

Armored Locomotive No. 203

the vast variety of lower-priced, more compact, more popular 0 Gauge locomotives and cars.

Lionel took those features a step further with 027 trains, though with far less fanfare. That track (0 Gauge, 27" diameter curves) first appeared during the bleak days of the Great Depression with Lionel's clockwork trains. Its rails and ties were smaller and lighter to keep the price down. Its tight curves required less space, and they often provided a thrill as speeding little locomotives flipped off the curves. Lionel did not deign to run anything but its lowest-priced trains on that track. As time passed and the grip of the Great Depression eased somewhat, Lionel began to see other possibilities. People were moving (many were forced) into smaller homes, and that inexpensive track was a space-saver. In fact, it had appeal. Suppose there would be a few more trains to choose from in that price range? People could buy them and, later on, they could move up to 0 Gauge. In 1937, Lionel announced a new line of remote control trains - the 027 series, with Lionel features at a low price. They weren't called starter sets, but that was their purpose. They sold well, and 027 sets have been featured in Lionel catalogues to this day.

The differences between 0 and 027 tracks are obvious when sections of each are placed side by side. 0 Gauge has big, heavy-duty rails. Ties are curved upward at the bottom to keep from digging into the carpet or scratching the floor. 027 has smaller, lighter rails. The trains they support aren't as heavy, so the ties come straight down. Most 027 trains were made in great quantities, and they were purchased for children who weren't gentle with them. Higher-priced 0 Gauge trains commanded more respect; generally they have survived in better condition. Although collectors usually prefer 0 Gauge trains, some 027 items are now hard to find, and what once sold for a dollar or two now brings substantial sums, for example, the various Lionel windup handcars. These little items came to Lionel's aid during the Depression years, for they sold for one or two dollars and generated substantial revenue, not only through sales, but also through publicity for the rest of the line by the Lionel brochure packed with each one.

It is misleading to think that the Mickey Mouse, Donald Duck and Peter Rabbit handcars were the only source of financial salvation for Lionel in those troubled Depression years . A contemporary feature news article called "The Mouse That Saved A Train Company", or some such title, certainly gave that impression. However, the inventive and creative streamliner sets were the real shot in Lionel's financial arm.

Like other Lionel trains, the earliest 0 Gauge cars and locomotives were available in two series, one larger, the other smaller. In early Standard Gauge, Lionel had offered the larger 10 series and the smaller 100 series. Later in Standard Gauge, Lionel offered the larger 200 and the smaller 500 series. As shall be seen in the 0-027 freight car section, a similar progression occurred, but with infinitely more complications, especially in the later years.

It is fascinating to conjecture what Joshua Lionel Cowen would have said if, in 1915, he had known that his 0 Gauge line, originally presented as a less expensive alternative to his real pride and joy, the Standard line, would overtake and eventually eliminate the bigger trains by 1940. Whatever the case, these smaller trains showed the same logical, orderly progression of change found in the Standard trains, even if the changes were more complex. In retrospect, it is fortunate that the smaller gauge prevailed. The thought of die-cast, realistic locomotives in Standard Gauge is awesome; what train table would have held them? If one looks very closely, one can trace the development of these trains and their operating principles right through today. Today's 0 and 027 switches, for example, have not changed much operationally since their introduction nearly a half century ago. The continuity between all of Lionel's 0 and 027 trains shows just how skillfully Joshua Lionel Cowen designed and marketed his product from the beginning.

4 Electric, 0-4-0, 1928-32, CM St P & P Olympian; similar to 254 but with Bild-A-Loco motor and curved hand reversing slot in hood side. Brass trim, nickel journals (1928-30) or copper (1931-32), die-cast headlight; embossed lettering; black frame, latch couplers, 9-1/4".

(A) Orange body, black frame, brass trim **450 700 400**

(B) Gray body with apple green stripe, black frame, brass trim, pea green hatches, Sherer Collection **475 800 400**

(C) Orange body, weights on each end of one-piece frame. Part of department store set made for Macy's, Sherer Collection **NRS**

4U "You build it", 4 set in kit form, 1928—29. Kit includes the 4 loco, 8 sections of curved track and parts for winch; orange body, black frame, brass trim. Must be unbuilt and in original box with instruction sheet to command full price. **900 1000 600**

150 Early, electric, 0-4-0, 1917, New York Central (NYC) S-type cab, 700 body type. Dark green body, red window trim, black frame, nickel pedestal headlight and bell, hook couplers mounted with rivet to frame, rubber-stamped "NEW YORK CENTRAL LINES" in oval and "150", no reversing, 7". **65 90 60**

150 Late, electric, 0-4-0, 1918-25, NYC S-type cab, nickel strap headlight and bell, hook couplers mounted in slots in frame, black frame, rubber-stamped "NEW YORK CENTRAL LINES" in oval and "150", no reversing, 6".

(A) Maroon **35 50 35**

(B) Dark green **40 60 40**

(C) Brown **40 60 40**

(D) Dark olive green **70 90 40**

(E) Mojave **100 180 40**

(F) Peacock **135 230 40**

(G) Maroon, shorter 5 inch cab, embossed gold painted railings, embossed brown painted window frames, ventilator grills not painted darker color, strap headlight with 249-style wiring connection, Edmunds Collection **NRS**

151 Steam, 0-4-0, catalogued in 1921 but never made **Not Manufactured**

152 Electric, 0-4-0, 1917-27, NYC S-type, nickel strap headlight and bell, rubber-stamped "NEW YORK CENTRAL LINES" in oval on cab and "152", early models non-reversing, later ones hand-reversing with reverse rod at end. Hook couplers mounted in slots in frame as of 1918, black frame, 7". Early models have early wire trim, later models have brass tab-fastened handrails and latest production has nickel tab handrails. Handrails on this and the 153 loco can also be stamped instead of wire. Sometimes the late nickel handrails flank the side doors as well as the ends, Kotil and Ely comments

(A) Dark green, coupler mounted with rivet, pedestal headlight, 1917 **40 60 40**

(B) Dark olive green, 1918 **50 70 40**

(C) Dark gray **50 70 40**

(D) Light gray **80 100 40**

(E) Mojave **100 120 40**

(F) Peacock **100 120 40**

(G) Dark green, no letters or numbers, strap headlight, large nickeled bell, brass rails on ends and sides, hook couplers with ears, Type II motor, 5-3/4" body, pickup plate reads "FOR 0 GAUGE TRACK/MANUFACTURED BY/THE LIONEL MANUFACTURING CO./NEW YORK", 1917, Merrill Collection **NRS**

153 Steam, 0-4-0, catalogued in 1921 but never made **Not Manufactured**

153 Electric, 0-4-0, 1924-25, NYC S-type, same as later 152s with hand-reversing rod at end. Nickel strap headlight and bell, rubber-stamped "NEW

*Includes 0, 0-27, Winner, Lionel Ives and Lionel Jr. in strictly numerical order.

O Gauge Early Electrics

Late Die-Cast Steamers

226 E black — 2226 W

225 E black — 2235 W

224 E black — 2224W

229 black — 2689W

238 E — 265 W

Scale And Semi-Scale Switchers

227 Prototype in brass

227 2227B

701 701T

203 2203T

1662 2203T

YORK CENTRAL LINES" and "153" on cab, hook couplers mounted in slots in frame, 7". Handrails can be brass (earlier) or nickel (later). Two types of handrails can be found. One type is wire with soldered stanchions. The other is a shorter one-piece type. Koff and Ely comments

(A) Dark green	**60**	**90**	**50**
(B) Dark olive green	**70**	**110**	**50**
(C) Gray	**75**	**110**	**50**
(D) Mojave	**90**	**125**	**50**

154 Electric, 0-4-0, 1917-23, NYC S-type, nickel strap headlight and bell, hook couplers mounted in slots in frame, with straight or curved roof ends, "NEW YORK CENTRAL LINES" and "154" rubber-stamped on cab, hand-reversing. Wire handrails are fastened by Y-shaped metal holders flanking the door and on the lower area. Ely comment

(A) Dark green body, narrow frame, shell has metal base for vertical screw mount to frame, early coupler mount, MFG motor, Ely Collection **NRS**

(B) Same as (A), but red window trim, Ely Collection **NRS**

(C) Same as (B), but wide base, Ely Collection **NRS**

(D) Same as (C), but top of roof is rounded instead of square at ends, Ely Collection **NRS**

156 Electric, 4-4-4, 1917-23, NYC S-type, front and rear pilot trucks with solid die-cast wheels with red discs inside rims, nickel headlight and nickel bell, hook couplers mounted in slots in frame as on 1918, "NEW YORK CENTRAL LINES" in oval and "156" on cab, hand-reverse, 10".

(A) Dark Green	**375**	**500**	**275**
(B) Maroon	**425**	**550**	**300**
(C) Olive green	**475**	**650**	**325**
(D) Gray	**525**	**750**	**350**

156 Electric, 0-4-0, same as 156 above, but no front and rear pilot trucks, 1922.

(A) Dark green	**350**	**500**	**275**

156X Catalogue number for 156 without pilot trucks, 1923-24.

(A) Maroon	**325**	**450**	**225**
(B) Olive green	**375**	**500**	**225**
(C) Gray	**450**	**650**	**225**
(D) Brown	**400**	**550**	**225**

158 Electric, 0-4-0, 1919-23, NYC S-type, same as later 150 but with two stamped imitation headlights, same as on Winner loco, no bell, hook couplers mounted in slots in frame, black frame, rubber-stamped "NEW YORK CENTRAL LINES" and "158", no reversing, 6". Buyer beware! This engine is easily faked by changing the headlights on a 150 and relettering the engine, Bohn comment

(A) Gray	**50**	**75**	**25**
(B) Black	**60**	**80**	**30**

(C) Dark green body, red window trim, strap operating headlight, nickeled bell, hook couplers mounted within slots in black frame, rubber-stamped "NEW YORK CENTRAL LINES" within oval and "158", no reverse, 5", brass plate on bottom of motor reads "THE LIONEL CORPORATION", possible factory repaint, Sattler Collection **NRS**

201 Steam switcher, 0-6-0, 1940-42, flat black, nickel bell, rubber stamped "201" under cab window, with Magic Electrol (DC-coil-reversing mechanism), zinc alloy die-cast superstructure, boiler is same casting as 1662 which is smaller than the scale or semi-scale switcher, operating front box couplers, middle wheels flangeless; headlight is centered on smokebox door, 8-1/2". 2201 Tender, slope-back, back-up lights, "LIONEL LINES" rubber-stamped on side

(A) 201 and 2201 B (bell)	**325**	**500**	**240**
(B) 201 and 2201 T (without bell)	**300**	**350**	**225**

203 Steam switcher, 0-6-0, 1940-42, same as 201 but without Magic Electrol

(A) 203 and 2203B (bell)	**300**	**450**	**250**
(B) 203 and 2203T (without bell)	**275**	**450**	**225**

203 Armored locomotive, 0-4-0, 1917-21, electric, two guns within a turret face forward

(A) Olive green, plate on bottom of motor reads "LIONEL MANUFACTURING CO.", 1917, Sattler Collection **NRS**

(B) Same as (A), but gray body, Ely Collection **NRS**

(C) Same as (B), but plate on bottom reads "THE LIONEL CORPORATION", 1918-21, Sattler Collection **NRS**

204 Steam 2-4-2, 1940-41, uncatalogued. Sold in sets only. Used same casting as 1684. "204" rubber-stamped in white under cab window, nickel-finished drive and connecting rods with crosshead, 229M-25 motor with roller pickups and Baldwin disc drivers, bakelite bottom motor plate with embossed lettering: "MADE IN/THE/U.S. OF/AMERICA/THE/LIONEL/CORP./NEW YORK". End gear on armature shaft turns an intermediate gear which meshes with gears cast as part of wheels. Motor held in boiler by screw which goes across boiler just behind steam chest, and second screw running across boiler behind and above rear drivers. Shiny metal handrails, 1684-7 bell and 1684-6 whistle which is simply a metal shaft with a collar. This locomotive uses an unusual method of tender linkage; a round stud is pressed in place under cab floor. Detailed cab interior, including firebox doors and gauges. This engine has been reported with other motors whose originality has not been confirmed. We would also like to learn the set number and contents which come with this loco, Peca Collection

(A) 1689 tender with black 204	**20**	**40**	**20**
(B) 1689 tender with gunmetal 204	**30**	**60**	**25**
(C) 2689 tender with gunmetal 204	**30**	**60**	**25**
(D) 2689 in black with black 204	**20**	**50**	**20**

INTRODUCTION TO THE 224, 229, 1664 and 1666 LOCOMOTIVES

Three of these four locomotives were introduced in 1938. The fourth, the 229, joined the line in 1939. The 1666 and 1664 were catalogued as 0-27, while the 224 and 229 were offered as 0 Gauge. To the best of our knowledge, all four share the same boiler, but come with four different motors. The 0 Gauge motors have heavy duty roller pickups, while the 0-27 motors have sliders. The second difference is the drivers. The 0-27 motors have plain spoked drivers, while the 0 Gauge motors feature the more detailed Baldwin disc drivers. The 0 Gauge motor is heavier and larger than the 0-27 and is shared with both the 225 and 226 locomotives. The heavier motor probably could pull at least two or three more cars.

After World War II, the basic casting used for all four of these engines reappeared with the 224 and 1666.The prewar cab was squared off and it came with either a post or a locomotive hook that mated with the tender coupler bar slot. The postwar cab is rounded and the locomotive no longer had a post. It only has a shorter shank hook which mated closely with the tender bar slot.

224/224E Steam, 2-6-2, 1938-42, zinc alloy die-cast superstructure, stamped "224E" on metal plate under cab window, E-unit reversing, 10-1/8"

(A) Black with 2224 plastic tender	**45**	**75**	**40**
(B) Gunmetal with 2224 die-cast tender	**80**	**140**	**65**
(C) Gunmetal with 2689 sheet metal tender	**45**	**75**	**40**
(D) Black with 2224 die-cast tender	**80**	**140**	**65**

225/225E Steam, 2-6-2, 1938-42, die-cast superstructure, stamped "225 LIONEL LINES" (or 225E) on metal plate under cab window, E-unit reversing, 10-1/2". Tender has four-wheel trucks with/without whistle, Kotil comment.

(A) Black with 2235 die-cast tender	**160**	**225**	**90**
(B) Black with 2245 die-cast high truck tender	**160**	**225**	**90**
(C) Black with 2235 plastic tender	**150**	**200**	**80**
(D) Gunmetal with 2225 sheet metal waffle top tender	**150**	**200**	**80**
(E) Gunmetal with 2235 die-cast tender	**160**	**225**	**90**
(F) Gunmetal with 2265 sheet metal waffle top high truck tender	**150**	**200**	**80**

226 Steam, 2-6-4, 1938-41, die-cast superstructure, stamped "226" or "226E LIONEL LINES" on metal plate below cab window, E-unit reversing, 11-3/4". 2226 tender has 12 wheels, whistle, reads "LIONEL LINES" **250 375 140**

227 Steam, 0-6-0, 1939-42, die-cast superstructure, Pennsylvania Railroad (PRR) B6 0-6-0 switcher. Tubular track version of full scale 701 switcher (701 switcher and tender 708 set). Flat black, "8976" rubber-stamped under cab window and "PENNSYLVANIA" on tender; "227" cast in boiler front plate. Teledyne DC couplers both on front of engine and rear of tender; E-unit reversing, 9-5/;8". Black slope-back tender, tinplate trucks, has low couplers made for use with 2600 series cars

(A) 227 with 2227 T (without bell)	**450**	**700**	**350**

Later 0 Gauge Electrics
LIONEL
LIONEL
LIONEL LINES No256
251 (A)
251 (C)
256 (D)
254 (C)
254E (C)
254E (A)
253 (I)
4
253 (D)
253 (A)
253 (H)
253 (G)
249 (J)
252 (E)
252 (A)
252 (B)
250 (A)

(B) 227 with 2227 B (bell) **475 750 375**

228 Steam, 0-6-0, 1939-42, same as 227 but with "228" cast in boiler front, high couplers for use with 2800 series cars

(A) 228 with 2228T (without bell) **450 700 350**

(B) 228 with 2228B (bell) **475 750 375**

229 Steam, 2-4-2, 1939-42; die-cast superstructure, uses same boiler casting as 224, gunmetal or black; "229" rubber-stamped or in nickel under cab window, E-unit reversing, 10-1/8". This locomotive shows an interesting progression of variations. The earliest versions have a number plate mounted through slots on the cab. Later, the plate is dropped and the number rubber-stamped on the cab, but the slots for the plate are still present (Lionel most likely wanted to use up its supply of cabs with slots). Then the slots disappear when the locomotive is made with its high-coupler 2666 tenders, which were meant for 2800 freight cars. In the latest production, the location of the E-unit is changed to the rear of the cab just in front of the sand dome. This change is accompanied by a motor with a different number plate from earlier production (specifics needed - reader comments invited). Ely observations

(A) Black with 2689T sheet metal tender **35 50 20**

(B) Black with 2666T plastic tender **35 50 20**

(C) Black with 2666W plastic tender **35 50 20**

(D) Gunmetal with 2689W sheet metal tender **45 70 20**

(E) Black with 2689W sheet metal tender, Kotil Collection **35 50 20**

230 Steam, 0-6-0, 1939, same as 227 but coupler operated by remote uncoupling track (RCS), described as 900 in catalogue, 9-5/8" **700 1100 450**

231 Steam, 0-6-0, 1940; PRR B6 0-6-0 switcher,catalogued as 901 in 1939. Same as 228 but coupler operated by RCS, 9-5/8" **700 1100 450**

232 Steam, 0-6-0, 1940-42, PRR switcher, same as 230 but with Magic Electrol (DC operating coil controls reversing unit), 9-5/8". With ringing bell only **700 1100 475**

233 Steam, 0-6-0, 1940-42, same as 231 but with ringing bell only and Magic Electrol reversing. "8976" rubber-stamped under cab window, "233" cast in boiler plate, 9-5/8". **700 1100 475**

238/238E Streamlined steam, 4-4-2, 1936-38, 1939-40 uncatalogued, PRR torpedo type; die-cast superstructure; nickel plates, trim and journals; "PENNSYLVANIA" on side, "238" or "238E" under cab window, gunmetal 1936-38, black 1939-40, 10-3/8". Sheet metal, waffle top tender with "LIONEL LINES" on nickel plates

(A) With 2225T tender **150 200 135**

(B) With 2225W tender **150 200 135**

(C) With 265 tender **150 200 135**

(D) With 265W tender **150 200 135**

(E) With 2265 with high trucks **150 200 135**

248 Electric, 0-4-0, 1926-32, NYC, no reversing, early engines (1926-27) have strap headlight, combination couplers, spoked wheels and single reduction motor. Engines from 1928 on, have cast headlight, latch couplers, disc wheels and double reduction motor. Some models after 1930 have no handrails or holes for same; most of these are bodies returned to Lionel after Ives stopped production. (Ives had used Lionel bodies on an Ives frame for 3260).

(A) 1926-27, dark green body, black frame and brass ventilators and number boards, number board rubber-stamped "LIONEL" and "248" **65 110 30**

(B) 1926-27, same as (A), but maroon ventilators and number boards **65 110 30**

(C) Same as (A), but with "LIONEL" and "248" etched in brass, and later style motor **60 100 30**

(D) Same as (B), but with later style motor, wheels and couplers **60 100 30**

(E) Orange body, brass ventilators and number boards, "LIONEL" and "248" etched on number boards, and strap headlight **60 100 30**

(F) Same as (E), but peacock inserts **60 100 30**

(G) 1929-30, red body, black frame and brass ventilators and number boards **60 100 30**

(H) 1929-30, olive green body, black frame and orange ventilators and number boards **70 120 30**

(I) 1931-32, terra-cotta body and cream ventilators and number boards **75 125 30**

(J) Orange body, strap headlight, brass doors, brass ventilators and name/number boards painted black with letters etched through in brass, brass pantograph and whistle, combination latch couplers **60 100 30**

(K) Same as (G), but cream ventilators and number boards, Kotil Collection **NRS**

(L) Same as (F), but single cast headlight, Sattler Collection **NRS**

(M) Same as (I), but cast headlight and no handrails, Ely Collection **NRS**

249/249E Steam, 2-4-2, 1936-37, 1938-39 uncatalogued; die-cast zinc frame, sheet metal superstructure, same boiler and frame as 261, 261E, 262, 262E, but with new valve gear, marker lights and piping; nickel trim; E-unit reversing, "249", or "249E" under cab window, black wheels with thick or thin rims, 9-3/4". Tenders have two four-wheel trucks, "LIONEL LINES" stamped on nickel plates

(A) Gunmetal **100 150 65**

(B) Satin black **115 170 65**

250E "Hiawatha" streamlined Atlantic type steamer, 4-4-2, 1935-42, Milwaukee Road; requires 0-72 track with 12-wheel tender; die-cast superstructure, nickel plates, trim and journals. Gray and orange tender with black frame. Later 250Es have a thicker boiler casting to add weight for traction, 13-1/4". Tender coupler differs for passenger or freight sets.

(A) With 250W tender (has manual coupler for freight cars) **600 1000 450**

(B) With 250WX tender (has rear drawbar for passenger cars) **600 1000 450**

(C) With 2250W tender (has electric coupler for freight cars) **600 1000 450**

250 Early, Electric, 0-4-0, 1926, New York Central (NYC) S-type. No reversing slot in hood top. Sold with 93 set (629 and 630 passenger cars); same body as 252; brass trim; 0 Gauge sized stamped headlights; combination latch couplers, non-reversing, 8"

(A) Dark green body **150 200 100**

(B) Peacock body **175 250 100**

(C) Yellow-orange body **175 250 100**

250 Late, Electric, 0-4-0, 1934, uncatalogued; same body as 252, but with 250 number plate; has reversing slot in hood, some have "E" stamped on doors, latch couplers, copper journals, 8". These locomotives have reversing units, Sattler observation

(A) Yellow-orange body; terra cotta frame **100 150 60**

(B) Terra-cotta body, maroon frame **115 170 70**

251 Electric, 0-4-0, 1925-32, NYC box cab, second largest 0 Gauge electric, brass trim, nickel (or copper in 1931-32) journals, embossed "LIONEL" and "251", latch couplers, two pantographs and whistles, hand-reversing, black frame 10"

(A) Gray body, brass trim, strap headlights **175 250 140**

(B) Gray body, black frame, red trim, strap headlights **175 250 140**

(C) Red body, ivory trim, with ivory stripes, cast headlights **200 300 140**

(D) Same as (C), without ivory stripe **185 275 140**

251E Electric, 0-4-0, 1927-32, NYC box cab; same as 251 but with E-unit reversing, 10"

(A) Red body, black frame, ivory trim, with ivory stripe, cast headlight **200 300 140**

(B) Gray body, black frame, red trim, strap headlight **175 250 140**

(C) Same as (A), without ivory stripe **185 275 140**

(D) Same as (B), but cast headlight, Kotil Collection **NRS**

252 Electric, 0-4-0, 1926-32, NYC S-type; same as early 250, but with hand-reversing, brass trim; nickel (and copper from 1931-32) journals; one die-cast headlight, latch couplers, 8"

(A) Green peacock body with brass railings on either side of door and two brass railings on hood top surface. Nickel headlight, brass pantograph at one end, brass reverse unit lever and brass whistle at other end. Embossed brass door with black line in lower door panel and black door handle. Fillister head screw at each end holds body to frame, two brass flag stanchions at each end, Type I latch coupler at each end, large single gear motor, armature shaft carries large gear with nut which meshes with wheel gears (early Super motor). The nickel finished brush plate has bent extensions forming legs which attach directly to the motor side frame. Copper finished pick-up springs; brass plate fastened on copper spring reads: "FOR 0 GAUGE TRACK/MANUFACTURED BY/THE LIONEL CORP./NEW YORK". Frame has square corners, but at reverse lever end an inserted black painted sheet metal piece goes across the two sides and supports the hand-reverse unit. Integral frame arms hold motor in place. Sample examined has replacement red disc wheels; originals currently not known **90 125 50**

The Top Of The Line 256

256 (A)

256 (C)

256 (D)

(B) Olive green body 90 125 50
(C) Dark green body 100 150 50
(D) Terra-cotta body, maroon frame, with/without cream stripe 110 165 50
(E) Yellow-orange body, terra-cotta frame 110 160 50
(F) Yellow-orange body, black frame 110 155 50
(G) Maroon body, MACY Department Store Special 150 300 60
(H) Same as (D), but black frame and cream stripe, Hundertmark Collection NRS
(I) Same as (B), but spoked wheels and combination latch couplers, Schuppner Collection NRS

252E Electric, 0-4-0, 1933-35, same as 252, but with E-unit reversing, with/without rubber-stamped "E" on door, 8"
(A) Terra-cotta body, maroon frame 110 165 50
(B) Yellow-orange body, terra-cotta frame 90 125 50
(C) Terra-cotta body and frame 110 180 50
(D) Same as (A), but black frame, cream stripe and "E" on door, Kotil Collection NRS

253 Electric, 0-4-0, 1924-32, New Haven-type, brass trim; nickel (and copper after 1930) journals and headlights, latch couplers; hand-reversing, 9"
(A) Peacock body, black frame, orange trim 80 125 50
(B) Dark green body, black frame, brass trim 90 140 50
(C) Dark green body, black frame, orange trim 90 140 50
(D) Mojave body, black frame, brass trim 95 150 50
(E) Pea green body, black frame, brass trim 150 275 50
(F) Gray body, black frame, brass trim, uncatalogued 175 310 60
(G) Stephen Girard green body, dark green frame, cream trim (with 603, 603, 604 cars or large 800 freight cars) 110 310 60
(H) Red body, black frame, brass trim 175 310 60
(I) Red body, black frame, orange trim, uncatalogued 175 310 60
(J) Terra-cotta body, maroon frame, cream trim 150 275 60
(K) Maroon body, black frame, brass trim 250 475 60

253E Electric, 0-4-0, 1931-36, New Haven-type, same as 253 but with E-unit reversing, "E" rubber-stamped on cab 1931-32, then embossed, 9"
(A) Stephen Girard green body, black frame, cream trim 75 125 60
(B) Terra-cotta body, maroon frame, cream trim 125 225 60
(C) Stephen Girard green body, dark green frame, cream trim with "E" rubber-stamped on number plates 85 190 60

254 Electric, 0-4-0, 1924-32, Milwaukee Road-type, hand-reversing, brass trim, black frame, nickel (or copper in 1931-32) journals, 9-1/2", latch couplers

For a comprehensive analysis of the 254 see our article at the end of this chapter.
(A) Type I in dark green or mojave, 1924-25 70 150 70
(B) Type II in mohave, 1926-27 70 150 70
(C) Type III in olive green 1926-27 70 150 70
(D) Type IV in olive green, 1928-29 70 150 70
(E) Type IV in olive green and orange, 1928-29 80 170 70
(F) Type V in olive green and red, 1920-32 80 170 70
(G) Type V in olive green, 1920-32 80 170 70

254E Electric, 0-4-0, 1927-34, same as 254, but with E-unit "Distant Control" reversing. "E" embossed on number plate (or rubber-stamped in 1927-28) on side door, 9-1/2". Slot for reverse lever is on both sides of loco at the same end. There is no reverse lever; an E-unit is present instead, and there is no bracket for the reverse lever, Edmunds comment
(A) Olive green body, red striped cab and red hatches, Sherer Collection NRS
(B) Same as (A), but no cab stripes, Sherer Collection NRS
(C) Apple green body, orange-striped cab and hatches NRS
(D) Same as (C), but no cab stripes NRS
(E) Orange body, Sherer Collection NRS
(F) Pea green body, no external "E" identification, side-saddle mounted reversing unit, late 1934 production, Sherer Collection NRS
(G) Same as 254, version (E), but labeled "254E" instead of "254", Sattler Collection NRS

255E Steam, 2-4-2, 1935-36, only with sets. Die-cast zinc frame, sheet metal superstructure, nickel trim, black wheels, gunmetal finish. Same boiler and frame as 260E but less valve gear and no chugger, 11-5/8". With 12-wheel, 263W gunmetal tender, nickel trim 400 600 250

256* Electric, 0-4-4-0, 1924-30, B.&M. Hoosac Tunnel-type; first 0 Gauge double motor engine. Orange only with black frame, hand-reversing, 11-1/2"
(A) "LIONEL" with frame outline and "256" rubber-stamped, nickel trim, brass windows, spoked wheels, stamped Standard Gauge headlights with celluloid inserts, one pantograph 500 900 300
(B) Same as (A), but without frame outline around "LIONEL" 375 600 250
(C) Same as (B), but with brass trim, disc wheels, cast headlights 350 500 250
(D) "LIONEL LINES" and "256" on brass plate with small letters and frame outline, brass trim, green windows, disc wheels, cast headlights, two pantographs, two whistles 475 800 300
(E) Same as (D), but with larger letters and without frame outline on plate 475 750 300

257 Steam, 0-4-0, 1930; 1931-32, uncatalogued. Same boiler and frame as Early 258, some with Ives plates; Ives loco had a tender base with a different number; die-cast zinc frame, sheet metal superstructure, black gloss finish, brass and copper trim, red-spoked wheels, non-reversing, 8-1/4"
(A) With/without orange stripe and four-wheel 257 tender with/without orange stripe 65 120 65
(B) With uncatalogued crackle black tender 85 175 65
(C) Without stripe with four-wheel 259 tender, uncatalogued 60 100 60

258 Early, Steam, 2-4-0, 1930, same as 257, but with hand-reversing; 8-1/4"
(A) With four-wheel 257 tender 65 100 65
(B) With eight-wheel 258 tender (black with orange stripe) 75 115 75

258 Late, Steam, 2-4-2, 1941, uncatalogued; same boiler and frame as 259 and 259E, but with 0-27 E-unit reversing motor, "258" rubber-stamped under cab window, 9-7/8". With 1689 sheet metal eight-wheel tender rubber-stamped "LIONEL LINES"*
(A) As described above 35 50 25
(B) Same, but gunmetal, slightly harder to find than black version NRS

259 Steam, 2-4-2, 1932. Same boiler, cab and sheet metal frame as Late 258, red-spoked drivers and red solid pilot and trailing wheels, circular "L" enameled plate under cab window, hand reverse, 9-7/8". With four-wheel 259 tender with brass ladder and copper journals 35 50 25

259E Steam, 2-4-2, 1933-34, 1936-38 and 1939-40 uncatalogued. Same as 259 but with E-unit reversing. Nickel trim, black wheels, round "L" enameled plate under cab window, 9-7/8"
(A) Black with 1689 or 2689 tender, 1936-40 uncatalogued 45 60 30
(B) Black with four-wheel 259 tender 45 65 30
(C) Black with eight-wheel die-cast 262 tender, 1934 50 70 35
(D) Gunmetal with 1689 or 2689 tender 50 70 35
(E) Same as (B), but nameplate on bottom has word "gauge" misspelled as "guage", Claxton Collection NRS

260E Steam, 2-4-2, 1930-35, die-cast frame, sheet metal superstructure, gloss finish to 1934, then semi-gloss, brass or copper trim 1930-34, then nickel, E-unit reversing, light in firebox, chugger 1933-35, 11-5/8"
(A) Black body, green frame, with eight-wheel 260 tender, 1931-33 300 400 225
(B) Black body and frame, cream stripe, with eight-wheel tender, 1930 350 425 250
(C) Black body, green frame, with 12-wheel 260 tender, 1934-35 350 425 250
(D) Dark gunmetal body and frame, nickel trim, 12-wheel 263 tender, 1934-35 (check frame for warping and cracks) 400 550 250
(E) Dark gunmetal body and frame and 12-wheel 263 tender with whistle, 1935 (check frame for warping and cracks) 400 575 250

261 Steam, 2-4-2, 1931, similar to 262 except non-reversing. Die-cast zinc frame and sheet metal boiler and cab, black gloss finish; brass/copper trim, red-spoked wheels, 9-3/4". With four wheel black 257 brass trimmed tender 120 175 60

261E Steam, 2-4-2, 1935; same as 261 but with E-unit reversing, nickel trim, black wheels, 9-3/4". With eight-wheel black "261T" sheet metal tender in nickel trim 120 175 70

262 Steam, 2-4-2, 1931-32, similar to 261 but with hand-reversing (lever in cab) copper and/or brass trim, 9-3/4"
(A) With eight-wheel die-cast "262T" tender with orange striping 90 135 60

*Two different reproductions have been made

260 and 263

260E B) 260T

260E (A) 260T

260E (D) 263T

255E 263W

263E (A) 263W

263E (B) 263W

Small Steamers

258 (B) 258T

261 257T

262 (B) 262T

249E (B) 265W

249 (A) 265W

259E (D) 1689T

Small O Streamliner Sets

(B) All copper trim and tender, does not have orange striping **90 135 60**

262E Steam, 2-4-2, catalogued 1933-34, available through 1936, same as 262 but with E-unit reversing

(A) Gloss black finish, copper and brass trim, red wheels, drum-type E-unit, die-cast 262T tender **120 190 70**

(B) Satin black finish, nickel trim, black wheels with pressed steel gears and open spokes, drum-type E-unit, sheet metal "262T" tender **135 220 75**

(C) Same as (B), but drivers have cast-in gears **135 220 75**

(D) Satin black finish, nickel trim, black drivers without rims, drum-type reversing unit, 249E boiler front, sand piping forms triangle with frame on left side, as with 249, 265T streamlined tender with nickel journals, tender rubber-stamped on underside, Type II latch coupler, Young Collection **NRS**

(E) Gloss black finish, all copper trim, red wheels, drum-type E-unit, sheet-metal 262T tender **110 175 70**

263E Steam, 2-4-2, 1936-39, similar to 255E/260E. Die-cast zinc frame, which is often warped or cracked, sheet metal superstructure, no chugger, whistle; nickel trim. Round "L" enameled plate on tender side, E-unit reversing, 11-5/8". Gunmetal versions can have one boiler pipe coming from each dome or two pipes from the front dome only. Early 255-260 type tenders have a center section inset across the front casting; later tenders lack this insert. The 263W and 2263W tenders come in gunmetal or blue. The "L" logo plate is brass on early versions and chrome on later versions, Kotil comment.

(A) Gunmetal body and frame and matching 12-wheel 263 tender **300 450 250**

(B) Blue Comet Engine used in Blue Comet set, blue body, dark blue frame and matching tender **350 550 250**

264E Streamlined Steam, 2-4-2, 1935-36 catalogued; 1937-38 and 1940 uncatalogued, NYC Commodore Vanderbilt-type, die-cast steam chest and cab, sheet metal boiler, die-cast cab without fire box doors inside, without eccentric rods, with "L" circular plate on locomotive front, nickel plates, trim and journal boxes, nickel plate "COMMODORE VANDERBILT" on engine side. 1935 models have wide nickel rim drivers, after 1936 rims are narrow, 9-3/4". Tenders have four-wheel trucks, nickel trim, and nickel plate "LIONEL LINES". The die-cast engine cab is often cracked or deteriorated; check for damage or replacement. Engines with reproduction cabs or damaged cabs will have lower values than those shown here. There are two cab castings on both this and the 265E. The earlier casting has a plain cab interior. The later version has a firebox cast inside the cab, Kotil comment

(A) With 261T sheet metal tender, 1935 only, red, "Red Comet" engine **165 325 80**

(B) With 261T sheet metal tender, 1935 only, black, uncatalogued **110 200 80**

(C) With 261TX drawbar sheet metal tender, 1935 only, black uncatalogued, reader verification requested **NRS**

(D) With 265 sheet metal waffle top streamlined tender, 1936, red **165 300 80**

(E) With 265W sheet metal waffle top streamlined tender, 1936 and 1940 (1940 uncatalogued), black **165 300 80**

(F) With 265W sheet metal waffle top streamlined tender, 1936, red, "Red Comet" engine **165 300 80**

(G) With 265W sheet metal waffle top streamlined tender, 1936, black **110 200 80**

(H) "The Red Comet" set, with either 264(A) or 264(F) and two matching red 603 Pullmans and one matching 604 Observation (the set) **225 500 120**

265E Streamlined Steam, 2-4-2, 1935-39, NYC Commodore Vanderbilt. Same as 264E, but with eccentric rods. 1935 models have wide nickel rim drivers, after 1936 rims are narrower. 1935 models have plain cab, after 1936 cab's wall has firebox doors, improved motor installed in 1937. 265E has the same cab problems as the 264E, check this out carefully; 9-3/4". Tenders have four-wheel trucks, nickel trim, nickel side plates reading "LIONEL LINES"

(A) With 261TX drawbar, sheet metal tender, 1935, black **125 190 80**

(B) With 265T/265W sheet metal, waffle top, streamlined tender, 1936, gunmetal **120 180 75**

(C) With 265TX/265WX drawbar, sheet metal, waffle top, streamlined tender, 1936-38, light blue, "Blue Streak" engine **350 475 80**

(D) With 2225T/2225W sheet metal, waffle top, streamlined tender, 1938-39, black **120 180 75**

(E) With 265T sheet metal, waffle top, streamlined tender, 1936. Some were chrome plated (only 10 chrome plated locomotives were made for display purposes) **120 180 75**

(F) "Blue Streak Set", Set No. 295E. Consisted of 265E(C) engine and matching 617 coach, 619 baggage and 619 observation. Lead passenger car has special coupler to mate with 265 tender. Cars are light blue with white window stripe. Price for set: **500 950 250**

(G) Same set as (F), but loco and tender are black instead of blue, and cars are medium blue without window stripe **NRS**

289E Streamlined Steam, 2-4-2, uncatalogued, c. 1937, NYC Commodore Vanderbilt; die-cast superstructure (same as 1689 with 0 Gauge motor) nickel plates, trim and journals. Sold in sets only, 9-1/8", 1689 tender with/without whistle, four-wheel trucks

(A) Black **125 175 70**

(B) Gunmetal **140 200 70**

450 Electric, 0-4-0, 1930, uncatalogued, New Haven-type, similar to 253, but with brass plates on side and with "MACY SPECIAL" and "450" in script lettering, solid disc wheels, two cast headlights, brass whistle and pantograph, 9"

(A) Red with black frame **NRS**

(B) Apple green with dark green frame **NRS**

616E/616W Streamlined Diesel, 1935-41, Boston and Maine's "Flying Yankee", articulated train, sheet metal construction except for die-cast top of power car and die-cast end of observation car, frosted celluloid windows, double reduction gear motor, nickel trim

(A) Set: 616E/616W Power car with black die-cast top and chrome body, two 617 chrome Coaches with two doors on each side, 618 Observation all chrome, all vestibules have chrome skirts, all cars have fluted sides, 1935 **125 225 100**

(B) Set: 616E/616W Power car with dark gunmetal nose and chrome rear half, two 617 chrome Coaches with one door on each side, 618 Observation with chrome front and dark gunmetal tail section, all vestibules have chrome skirts, all cars have fluted sides, 1936-41 **100 150 100**

(C) Uncatalogued set: 616 Power car with silver painted body with red die-cast top, only one 617 Coach painted silver, two doors on each side, 618 Observation painted silver, vestibules are painted silver, cars have smooth sides **150 275 100**

(D) Uncatalogued set: Same as (C) but 617 has only one door on each side and all cars have fluted sides **150 275 100**

(E) 616E/616W Power car as described in set (A) **25 45 25**

(F) 616E/616W Power car as described in set (B) **35 60 30**

(G) Same as (B), but die-cast top of power car and end of observation car are painted dark olive green instead of dark gray, possible Baltimore-area department store special, Hundertmark Collection **NRS**

636W Streamlined Diesel, 1936-39, Union Pacific's City of Denver with articulated cars. Sheet metal construction except for die-cast diesel power car, frosted celluloid windows, nickel trim, some with rubber-stamped "LIONEL LINES", double reduction motor, trailer cars have fluted sides

(A) Yellow and brown set, 636W, 637 Coach, 637 Coach and 638 Observation **200 300 200**

(B) Two-tone green set, uncatalogued, 636W, 637 Coach, 638 Observation **275 600 200**

(C) 636W loco only in yellow and brown **60 100 60**

(D) 636W loco only in two-tone green **NRS**

(E) Same as (A), but all yellow vestibules between cars instead of brown vestibule tops, Sattler comment **NRS**

(F) Same as (A), but dark reddish brown and yellow with reddish-brown vestibule tops, "LIONEL LINES" rubber-stamped on 636 unit, Sattler and Ely comments **NRS**

(G) Same as (F), but all yellow vestibules, Sattler comment **NRS**

700 and 150
Series Electric Locomotives

by Lou Redman

0 Gauge electric-type locomotives, which established Lionel's reputation for quality motors, formed the 700 series and were first catalogued in 1915. Starting in 1916, they became the 150 series. The series, based on the New York Central's S-1 type locomotive, was manufactured until 1927, when the 250 series was introduced. According to Irving Schull, curator of Lionel's train collection before it was sold in 1960, 0 Gauge locomotives were first made for Christmas sales in 1913. *

Lionel, in 1915, assigned the following numbers to its 0 Gauge locos: 700 (5-3/4" long), 706 (reversible 701), and 703 (7", reversible, 4-4-4). These lengths describe the body, not the frame, and are provided to clarify the relationship between the locos and between the series. No locos numbered 702 or 704 have ever been observed, and we assume that, although catalogued, they were not manufactured. The 702 and 704 would have had a 2-4-2 wheel arrangement.

As production and time progressed, the 700 became the 150. Handrails changed from raised wire, to embossings, or to stampings clipped on the bodies. However, the first 150 mentioned above is not the common 1917 brown 150 with a "Manufacturing" motor, or the more typical 1918 maroon with a "Corporation" motor. The first 1916 150 was a much larger loco: it had wire handrails, as did the others in the series.

The words MANUFACTURING and CORPORATION date production to either before or after 1918. In August, 1918 Lionel incorporated, and thereafter the name plate on the third-rail pickup assembly reads "LIONEL CORPORATION". A common misconception about the 700/150 series electrics is that the 700 series with the Manufacturing motor was made until 1917 and that the 150 series with the Corporation motor appeared in 1918. This misconception was laid to rest in my 1966 TCA Quarterly article (see Table 1).

Other than different motors, how can 700 and 150 bodies and frames be identified? On a 700, three holes were punched in the top of the body, near each end, for mounting a pedestal headlight and a bell. On the frame, the hook couplers were rivet-mounted and the earliest 700s had Type 1 motors with iron wheels and no axle bearings. Cab windows were trimmed in red, as were all locos in the 700/150 series, except maroon or brown locos, which had dark olive green trim. Only the earliest 700, 701, 703 and 706 have gilt-painted ventilators. (See photograph.) Handrails were wire, mounted on stanchions and soldered to the body.

There were two differences between the first 700s and the 1916 700s with Type 2 motors. Wheels were die-cast on Type 2 motors instead of cast-iron, and the ventilators were not gilded. However, as with the Type 1 motors, there were no axle bearings.

Conversation with Lou Redman, 1957.

A 1915 700

The Type 2 motor illustrated is from a 703, has die-cast, spoked wheels and no axle bearings. Although the catalogue shows die-cast pony wheels, the loco has, in fact, stamped, tin wheels, held onto the threaded axle-ends with nuts. The 1916 703 as depicted in the catalogue shows a variation in pony trucks (compared with the passenger car trucks pictured on the 703). This variation has never been found, nor has a passenger car with that truck. As mentioned earlier, the loco does not have gilt ventilators.

Type 1 Motor

Type 1 Motor - 1913-15: Triangular brush plates, brush and spring in tube with threaded cap. Field and armature wound with green, cotton-covered wire. Note differences in side plates between this and Type 2.

Type 2 Motor

Type 2 Motor - 1916-17: Same brush plate as Type 1, but in a different position. Note difference in side plate. This side plate continues until end of production in 1927. Otherwise same as Type 1.

The next entry — appearing the same year (1916) as the 700 with a Type 2 motor — was the dark green 150, 5-3/4 inches long, with two slots at one end in addition to the three holes for mounting a STRAP rather than a PEDESTAL headlight. This loco could be called a transition model between the 700 and 150 series. By 1917 the changeover to the new numbers was complete with the introduction of the smaller 150 (5 inches), the 152 (former 700), the 154 (former 701) and the 156 (former 703). The catalogue cuts remained virtually unchanged until 1923. One exception was the new 158, appearing in 1919, with a new cut.

A 1916 "transition" 150

The "new" 158 was really the smaller 150 with two dummy headlights, instead of a working headlight and bell. One wonders why the new loco was made at all, since the price difference between it and the 150 was between 75¢ and $1.50. Given the cost of making and stocking the dummy headlights, different rubber-stamps and the consequent production problems, the 158 hardly seems worth the trouble. Interestingly, the dummy headlights reappear nine years after 158 production ceased on the Winner locos of 1932.

Now we come to an oddity in the numbering system — the 203 armored loco (see catalogue). From 1917 through 1919 Lionel catalogued and sold the 203 armored loco, a tank-like body surmounted by a two-gun turret. In 1917 a Type 2 motor was used, in 1918-1919, a Type 4. (Note that the Type 3 motor appears on only the brown 150 with MANUFACTURING plates.)

A typical "little boy" of the line: the 1918 150

Type 3 Motor

Type 3 Motor - 1917: Armature and field wound with varnish-covered wire. Dog-leg brush holder, brushes mounted in cap retained in hole in spring bronze strip.

We have now arrived at 1918, and the production of CORPORATION motors. By Christmas the Type 4 motor was in all locos with axle bearings. The addition of axle bearings is one item that CAN be dated to the change from MANUFACTURING to CORPORATION production. Of course, it was probably coincidental. In 1918 all headlights became the strap type with only one hole and one pair of slots punched in each end of the top of the body. Coupler mountings were simplified with just a rectangular slot in the end sill to mount the hook couplers. Handrails continued to be wire as late as 1924 when the 153 (a reversible 152) was introduced. 1924 is probably the last year of Type 4 motor production, and Type 5 appeared in 1925 on the 150 and 152, until the last 152 in 1927.

Type 4 Motor

Type 4 Motor - 1918-25: Same as Type 3, except brushes are crimped into fingers punched into the spring bronze strip. Most common motor found on 150 series.

The bigger 154 includes some special variations. The 154 derived from the 701. The 701 had a narrow frame, 2-1/8 inches wide. The first 154 with MANUFACTURING plates also has a narrow frame. Later 154s were 2½ inches wide, the same width as the 703, 156 and 156X. The 701 cab was secured to the frame by a vertical screw, through an L-shaped metal stamping soldered into the cab end. The later 154s were secured to the frame with a horizontal screw, an ear with threaded hole being formed upward out of the frame (without the L-shaped stamping). The vertical screw mounting also appeared on the 706 (the reversible 701). The reverse switch is of special interest. At first it was mounted on a bracket *inside* the *motor* side plates. This made it necessary to extend the switch lever, which was done by riveting a metal arm to the fiber switch lever (see picture of Type 2 motor). This construction also appears on the MANUFACTURING and the CORPORATION Type 4 motor of 1918. When the frame was made 2½ inches wide, the reversing

A "Little Boy" 150 in front of a "Big Boy" 156

assembly was mounted on the frame, and the fiber reverse lever protruded through a slot in the frame. Other peculiarities of wide frame 154s are their square-cab or round-cab roof-ends and their half-moon punch in the body ends to clear the mounting screw for the reversing switch. This punch-out occurs only on the 154 cabs. The earlier, square-cab roof-end is punched only on one end. Later, production became more sophisticated: the half-moon was punched out on both ends, allowing the body to be installed on the frame without reference to direction.

Now let's move along to the "Big Boys" of the line: the 703, 156 and 156X. These bodies are 7 inches long, their frames are made from the truss-like portion of the 701 and 154 frames, with an extra long cow-catcher platform to create the longer frame. Only the 150 and 158 have one-piece frames. All others have 4 pieces — two truss sides and two cow-catcher platforms. The very scarce 156X was made in 1922-24 with and without sets, and as a separate loco only in 1924, when the 156 was no longer made. The 156X usually comes in maroon and is catalogued in that color, but the catalogue also says that "the 156X is the same as the 156 except for pilot trucks". This description has caused considerable argument among collectors, however, we should remember two relevant facts: a true 156X of whatever color should show no wear on the pilot truck retaining slot in the end platform and the motor truck frame should not have a pilot truck retainer. (That's the purpose of the two horizontal slots in each end of the motor frames — to hold the retainer.)

Round and square cab roofs of two 154s

Type 5 Motor

Type 5 Motor - 1926-27: Brush plate only changed to square type. Fiber plate holds brush tubes; brush springs made from formed wire.

Again, the collector can only wonder why the 156 and 156X were made, because the price difference was small. The 156X sold for $12.75 while the 156 sold for $14.25. In sets the 156X and two maroon passenger cars (it was sold only with passenger cars which should be maroon) sold for $16.25. The 156 with *three* cars sold for $20.00. Why not, just market a 156 with 2 cars!

The following table has been prepared to summarize the information just provided.

Brush Holders from Type 3 and Type 4 Motors.

Type 3 Motor: On the left, has dog-leg brush holder with brushes mounted in grommet retained in hole in phos-bronze strip.

Type 4 Motor: On the right, has brushes mounted in fingers punched from phos-bronze strip.

700/150 SERIES ELECTRIC LOCOMOTIVES

YEARS MFD	LOCO NUMBERS + CAB LENGTH 5"	5¾"	6"	7"	Special	MOTOR TYPE	AXLE BEARINGS	WHEELS	COUPLER MOUNTING	HEAD-LIGHT	NAME-PLATE roller	HOOD PUNCHING Holes-Slots FRONT	REAR	HAND-RAILS
1913-1915		700	701	703		1	No	Iron	Rivet	Pedestal	None	3-h	3-h	Wire
1916		700	(706) 701	703		2	No	Die-cast	Rivet	Pedestal	Mfg**	3-h	3-h	Wire
		150	(706)			2	No	Die-cast	Rivet	Strap	Mfg	3-h, slots	3-h	Wire
1917		152	154	156*		2	No	Die-cast	Rivet	Pedestal or Strap	Mfg	3-h, slots.	3-h, slots.	Wire
					203	2	No	Die-cast	Slot	None	Mfg			None
	150					3	No	Die-cast	Slot	Strap	Mfg	1-h, slots,	1-h, slots.	Embossed
1918	150					4	Yes	Die-cast	Slot	Strap	Corp	1-h, slots.	1-h, slots.	Embossed
					203	4	Yes	Die-cast	Slot	None	Corp			None
1925	158					4	Yes	Die-cast	Slot	Dummy	Corp	1-h, slots.	1-h, slots.	Embossed
		152				4	Yes	Die-cast	Slot	Strap	Corp	1-h, slots.	1-h, slots.	Wire or Stamped
		153	154			4	Yes	Die-cast	Slot	Strap	Corp	1-h, slots.	1-h, slots.	Wire
				156		4	Yes	Die-cast	Slot	Strap	Corp	1-h, slots.	1-h, slots.	Wire
				156X		4	Yes	Die-cast	Slot	Strap	Corp	1-h, slots.	1-h, slots.	Wire or Stamped
1926-1927		152				5	Yes	Die-cast	Slot	Strap	Corp	1-h, slots.	1-h, slots.	Stamped

*With solid die-cast wheels; all others are spoked.
*Mfg = MANUFACTURING; CORP = CORPORATION

Half-moon punch in 154

If you have a 150 in a different color(s), let us know about it.

In closing, let us review colors. The most common color is dark green, as on the Lionel 216 hopper. The following is a complete list of known colors:

All 700 series are dark green
150 (5-3/4" cab) is dark green
150 (5" cab) comes in brown, maroon, dark green, olive green, mojave and peacock
152 comes in dark green, light gray, dark gray, dark olive green and peacock
153 comes in dark green and dark olive green
154 comes in dark green and olive green
156 comes in dark green
156X comes in maroon and olive green
158 comes in gray, black and dark green

If your 150 comes in a different color, it just proves that ALL the information will probably never be known about Lionel's paint pot. Also, misnumbered locomotives have been found, which can only be classified as production line mistakes, or as "individually" painted engines. For example, we have seen 5" long bodies numbered 150 and 158 in dark green with headlights and bells! While watching for a variation to come along, keep in mind the "Quaker connection". Apparently, in 1916 Lionel lettered and numbered some 700s for Quaker Oats. "Quaker" appears in the oval where "NEW YORK CENTRAL LINES" is usually rubber-stamped. Two Quaker Oats numbers have turned up: 728, which is really a 700, and 732, which is really a 701. Both have Type 2 motors, hence fixing their manufacture to 1916.

5344
NEW YORK CENTRAL
700EW
700W
5344
NEW YORK CENTRAL
700K
700K5
The Scale
Hudson
No763-E
LIONEL LINES
763E (A)
2263W
No763-E
LIONEL LINES
LIONEL LINES
763E (B)
2226WX
No763-E
LIONEL LINES
LIONEL LINES
763E (C)
2226WX

700 Electric, 0-4-0, 1913-16, NYC S-prototype, same body as Early 150. Dark green body with red window trim, hook couplers mounted to frame by rivet, non-reversing, rubber-stamped "NEW YORK CENTRAL LINES" in oval and "700", 7"

(A) Body is 5-3/4" long, Type 1 motor, iron wheels, rivet coupler mounting, pedestal headlight, no name plate on pickup roller assembly, three holes on hood on front and rear, wire handrails, gilt ventilators **250 300 110**

(B) Same as (A), but Type 2 motor, die-cast wheels, "LIONEL MFG CO." on plate on pickup roller assembly **225 250 100**

LIONEL TRAINS AND THE NEW YORK CENTRAL'S 5344

by Roger Arcara

Mention the New York Central Railroad's "Hudson" locomotive 5344, and most collectors of model trains will think of the Lionel 700EW, with the prototype road number stamped on its cab. Why did Lionel choose that particular number for the true-scale Hudson? And was the 700EW the only Lionel model of the 5344? The answers are not so simple as some may believe.

Hudson 5344, built by the American Locomotive Co. in 1931, was the last of its class, J1e, and official company photographs of it were taken to be the latest New York Central passenger locomotive until the J3 class was de-veloped in the later 1930's. Lionel worked from Alco and New York Central plans and pictures in preparing production implements for their true-scale Hudson, so it is likely that the 700EW was stamped with the New York Central's roster number 5344 because the photographs were of that particular Hudson — at least as it originally appeared.

Here the story becomes complicated, because when the Lionel model was put on the market in 1937, with appropriate publicity, the prototype 5344 had not appeared the way Lionel modeled it for about three years. It seems that 1934 was the Year of the Streamliners in the U.S.A., with the widely publicized Union Pacific and Chicago, Burlington & Quincy motor trains capturing headlines and newsreel footage. The New York Central, for their own good reasons, elected to remain with steam power, but chose No. 5344, already several years old, to be the first steam locomotive in America to be streamlined. A sheet-metal jacket, designed in the Case School of Science in Cleveland, and resembling a black, upside-down bathtub, was fitted to this Hudson in December, 1934, and the 5344 then went forth into the world of publicity with the name "Commodore Vanderbilt" on its side. In August, 1935, roller bearings and Scullin disc driving-wheels replaced the original equipment.

Within a year of its first appearance, toy models of the "Commodore Vanderbilt" showed up in the Lionel catalogue. The 0-Gauge 264E and its slightly more detailed companion, the 265E, came on the market in 1935. Crude 2-4-2 types, they nevertheless had to be models of the New York Central's No. 5344, the only steam locomotive then streamlined in this fashion. (It is true that the Rexall Drug Company later paid to have a New York Central 4-8-2 streamlined in this form and painted blue and white to match its exhibition train, which toured the country in 1936, but the toy train makers intended their toy models, with but one possible exception, to be "Commodore Vanderbilt" locos, of which there was only one prototype, the 5344. The blue 265E with the train of blue articulated passenger cars having a white window-band did resemble the Rexall train, and may have been inspired by the latter, but was never promoted as a model of it.)

By the time the 700EW appeared late in 1937, appearing as its prototype had last appeared in 1934, Lionel had the "Commodore Vanderbilt" situation well in hand. In addition to the 264E and the 265E, there was the 027 1689E, which appeared in 1935 and was made for several years. Its die-cast body was later slightly modified to accommodate an 0 Gauge motor, and it thus became the uncatalogued 289E. In those Depression years, Lionel was also making low-priced wind-up trains, and from 1935 to 1937 they offered the red 0-4-0 wind-up "Commodore Vanderbilt" types, 1508 (ringing bell and battery-powered headlight, 1935) and 1511 (working whistle, 1936-37).

To recapitulate: Lionel manufactured the 264E in black and in red; the 265E in black, in blue, and in gunmetal gray; the 1689E and the 289E, each in black and in gunmetal gray; and the 1508 and 1511, each in red (although black versions were illustrated in the catalogues, they seem not to have been made) — a total of eleven toy versions of the No. 5344 in its "Commodore Vanderbilt" guise before the true-scale 700EW was put on the market as a model of the same locomotive as it originally appeared. Thus, Lionel produced a total of twelve versions of the one New York Central locomotive 5344.

What about the Lionel 763EW and 773 models? They do not qualify for this enumeration, since these simplified Hudsons did not bear the road number 5344, and could have represented the whole New York Central J1 class. The same is true of the Lionel 4-6-4 types 646 and 2046. The Lionel 00-gauge Hudsons also do not qualify, since they bore the prototype number 5342.

In 1938, the New York Central applied new, gray, bulbous streamlined jackets designed by Henry Dreyfuss to ten of its new class J3 Hudsons, which were slightly larger and more powerful than those of class J1. These streamliners, 5445 to 5454, thus became class J3a. Since the J1e 5344 streamliner did not match the new style, and was thought to be rather ugly in comparison, its "Commodore Vanderbilt" jacket was removed in July, 1939, and it was then fitted with a Dreyfuss-style jacket to match the J3a class. The no. 5344 was one of the very few locomotives to be streamlined in two different styles — and all the while, Lionel was producing their scale model of it in its original, unstreamlined form!

After World War II, Lionel made the 027 221, a small 2-6-4 version of the Dreyfuss streamlined Hudsons, but this could have represented any one of eleven actual New York Central locomotives, of which 5344 was just one. Due to maintenance problems caused by the jackets, and to the fact that Diesel locomotives were taking over the prestige passenger trains in the late 1940's, the New York Central removed the streamlining from its steam locomotives around 1948. The era of streamlined steam locomotives was just about over in the U.S.A.; the publicity emphasis was more and more on Diesels. The change did not go unnoticed at Lionel; the 221 was discontinued at just about the same time as the 2333 Diesel models were introduced. Not long afterwards, the New York Central, with a surprising disregard for history, scrapped all of its J-class Hudsons — including the 5344.

700E Steam, 4-6-4, 1937-42 NYC Hudson, scale per NMRA Standards for 0-72 T-rail; black zinc alloy die-cast superstructure, nickel plates, rubber-stamped "5344" below cab window and on headlight, 14-1/8"; "NEW YORK CENTRAL" on tender's side. [1]

(A) 700E with 700/700W 12-wheel black die-cast tender, weighing 3 lbs. 1 oz. Must be all original and have the wooden display board to bring the full price. [2] **1700 2600 1200**

700EWX Steam, 4-6-4, 1937, same as 700E but with modified drivers for tubular rails. Needs original box to bring the full price **1900 2800 1200**

700K Steam, 4-6-4, 1938-42, same as 700E but in six kits, sold as unbuilt gray

Large 0 Gauge Sets

752 W (A)
753
753
754
752 W (F)
753
754
250 E
250 WX
782
783
784
700 E (A)
700 W
792
793
703 E
2263 W
2615
2613
2613
763 E (C)
2226 WX
2623
UNION PACIFIC
LIONEL LINES
752W
THE MILWAUKEE ROAD
NEW YORK CENTRAL
5344
LIONEL LINES

primer engine in original boxes **2000 3100 1200**

701 Electric, 0-4-0, 1913-16, NYC S-prototype, dark green body with red window trim, hook couplers mounted to frame by rivet, 8" long, non-reversing. Rubber- stamped "NEW YORK CENTRAL LINES" in oval and "701"

(A) Body is 6" long, Type 1 motor, iron wheels, rivet coupler mounting, pedestal headlight, no name plate on pickup roller assembly, three holes on hood on front and rear, wire handrails, gilt ventilators **240 380 180**

(B) Same as (A), but Type 2 motor, die-cast wheels, "LIONEL MFG. CO." on plate on pickup roller **200 350 160**

(D) Same as (B), but unpainted ventilators, Sattler Collection

701 Steam, 0-6-0, catalogued 1940. See 708 for description of loco and tender

702 Electric, 0-4-0, catalogued 1915 but not manufactured **Not Manufactured**

703 Electric, 4-4-4, 1913-16, NYC S-prototype, dark green body with red window trim, hook couplers mounted to frame by rivet, non-reversing, rubber-stamped "NEW YORK CENTRAL LINES" in oval and "703", 10"

(A) Body is 7" long, has Type 1 motor, iron wheels, rivet coupler mounting pedestal headlight, no name plate on pickup roller assembly, three holes on hood on front and rear, wire handrails, gilt ventilators. Stamped pony and trailing wheels secured by nuts **1000 1300 700**

(B) Same as (A), but Type 2 motors, die-cast wheels, "LIONEL MFG. CO." name plate on pickup roller assembly, stamped pony and trailing wheels secured by peening axles **950 1200 700**

704 Electric, 2-4-2, catalogued 1915 but not manufactured **Not Manufactured**

706 Electric, 0-4-0, 1913-16, NYC S-prototype, dark green body with red window trim, same as 701, but with reversing

(A) Same as 701(A), but reversing **275 375 250**

(B) Same as 701(B), but reversing **250 300 250**

708 Electric, see entry for 701

708 Steam, 0-6-0, 1939-42, scale PRR B6 switcher, built to NMRA standards for 0-72 T-rail track. Zinc alloy die-cast superstructure, flat black, "8976" rubber-stamped under cab window, "PENNSYLVANIA" on tender's side; "8976" cast in smokebox door, E-unit reversing, 9-5/8". 708 with 7091 scale slope-back tender with back-up light **950 1500 700**

710 Steam, 0-4-0, catalogued in 1915 but never made **Not Manufactured**

728 Electric, similar to 700 electric, special promotion, rubber-stamped "Quaker" instead of "NEW YORK CENTRAL LINES" within oval, dark green body with gold painted ventilators, cast iron wheels, Ely Collection **NRS**

DIE CASTING AND THE M-10000

by Rev. Philip Smith

Lionel's crowning achievements in die-casting — the 0 scale Hudson and Pennsy B6 switcher — have won regard as bench marks in American model railroading. As we look through catalogues from preceding years, it's tempting to consider the products listed there as crude and toylike. However, Lionel's scale trains were not poised in the sky waiting to drop out of heaven. Their history lies within those early trains. It lay there latent until a desperate drive for survival turned Lionel's management and employees in a new direction. Our brief account begins in 1934, which began as the bleakest year in Lionel's history.

By 1934, Lionel was nearly bankrupt. It hadn't shown a profit since 1930, when the Great Depression made toy trains a distant luxury instead of a Christmas tradition. Pinning its hopes on something new and different, Lionel cooperated with the Union Pacific to introduce a 1/45th scale model of the UP's new streamliner, the M-10000. In February 1934, the M-10000 began a triumphal publicity tour, capturing headlines and the public's imagination. Competing railroads touted the Zephyr, the Flying Yankee, and the Hiawatha. The New York Central hopped on the bandwagon by streamlining one of its famous Hudsons — No. 5344, the prototype of Lionel's 0-scale masterpiece (700EW) that would be introduced in 1937.

Buoyed by all that publicity, Lionel trains sold well enough to rescue the company. Furthermore, the M-10000 rolled in a new direction. Its success plainly showed that a competitive edge existed for realistic trains. Lionel took advantage of that by introducing models of all the aforementioned streamliners, built as closely as possible to railroads' original blueprints. Gradually, other trains in the line were affected, thanks to advancing technology.

Until the 1930's, Lionel had manufactured its trains and accessories by bending, cutting, and punching holes in sheets of steel. It was hard enough to model the flat or gently curved contours of contemporary electric locomotives and trolleys. Manufacturing a scale model steam locomotive, with its round boiler and complex details, would have involved so many extra steps in production that the finished model would have cost a fortune. A few dedicated scale modelers were willing to pay that price. The vast majority of Lionel's customers were not. To solve that problem, Lionel turned to a new technique — die-casting.

In that process, a mold (called a "die") was fashioned by hand with all the details of the finished model. After that, molten metal was injected into the die under tremendous pressure, forcing metal into every nook and cranny. As the metal hardened, it took on all the details of the die. When it cooled, it could be painted and lettered. Although each die was expensive, it greatly reduced manufacturing costs, since it produced a detailed item in one operation. Lionel experimented with this technique by making simple items like wheels and frames. As employees became more experienced, they began to make whole locomotives. Lionel's sheet steel construction could still be used for smooth, sleek streamliners. Die-casting opened the doors to a line of detailed, affordable, rugged trains like the ones people saw every day, the trains that shipped their goods, the trains on which they traveled.

Lionel's triumph in die-casting was its 0-scale New York Central Hudson, introduced in 1937. In a way, it combined both worlds. A few intricate details that might have broken when removed from the die, such as long pipes and handrails, were mounted by hand. But that was affordable only because most details were formed by the die. Die-cast cars shared Lionel catalogues through 1942, when World War II halted toy train production. Afterwards, higher postwar labor costs and a new technology - injection molded plastics - combined to make sheet metal construction a practice of the past.

---

1 A reproduction of the 700E has been made by Hudson Products using a centrifugal casting method rather than a high pressure die-casting method. The major castings are usually made from soft metals and subsequently hardened and sometimes plated. Most Hudson Products locos are marked Hudson Products on the plate on the pickup assembly. These locos came with All Nation motors which are quite different from the Lionel motors.

2 Reproduction tenders: (1) Madison Hardware tenders originally used original Lionel tender bodies with reproduction coal piles, frames, and trucks. Some of the reproduction parts were very heavy and crude, weighing 3 lbs. 5 oz. (2) Hudson Products tender, weighing 2 lbs. 8 oz., used a soft cast metal, some read "Hudson Products" on base; (3) E. C. Kraemer's one piece plastic version weighing 1 lb. 10 oz. The weight for the original 700T tender was with whistle whereas reproduction tenders are without whistle, except for Madison Hardware's copy, which featured a whistle as an option in 1964-65.

The Mickey Mouse Circus Set, No. 1536
(See 1508 for description)

752E/752W Diesel, 1934-41, Union Pacific's City of Salina (M 10000); 0-72, sheet metal construction except for die-cast cab front and top over motor, die-cast underbody which often warps or cracks, reproduction underbodies available. Frosted celluloid windows, rubber-stamped "UNION PACIFIC" (over window), "LIONEL LINES" and unit number below on sides. (1934 catalogue shows "LIONEL LINES" rubber-stamped above window, car type below, but to date none has been found.) Some with motor name plate misspelled "GUAGE", the misspelling does not affect its value.

The U.P. came in both three and four car sets, in both aluminum and yellow and brown. Although aluminum is harder to find, yellow/brown brings the premium price as it is in greater demand, probably because of its very attractive appearance.

(A) Four car set in yellow and brown: 752W or 752E Power Unit, 753 Coach, 753 Coach and 754 Observation with yellow sides, brown roof, ends and underbody **450 650 350**

(B) Same as (A), but in aluminum finish **400 590 300**

(C) Three car set in yellow and brown; otherwise same as (A) **325 500 250**

(D) Three car set in aluminum; otherwise same as (B) **300 450 225**

(E) 752E in yellow and brown **150 225 90**

(F) 752E in aluminum **130 200 75**

(G) 752W in yellow and brown **150 225 90**

(H) 752W in aluminum **130 200 75**

763E Steam, 4-6-4, 1937-42, NYC Hudson, modified scale, similar to 700E but with less detail, runs on 0-72 tubular track, zinc alloy die-cast superstructure, E-unit reversing, "No. 763-E" underneath "LIONEL LINES" under cab window, nickel trim, 14-1/8"

(A) Gunmetal with 12-wheel 263 or 2263W oil tender **800 1200 650**

(B) Gunmetal with 12-wheel 2226X/2226WX tender **1500 2200 950**

(C) Black with 12-wheel 2226WX tender **900 1400 750**

1000 Electric, 0-4-0, 1930, Winner, catalogued but not made **Not Manufactured**

1010 Electric, 0-4-0, 1931-32, Winner, New Haven-type, lithographed "WINNER LINES". dummy headlight, no reverse, hook couplers, disc wheels, offered originally only in sets, 5". Either light orange or tan with green roof **35 50 25**

1015 Steam, 0-4-0, 1931-32, Winner, black, copper trim, hook couplers, nonreversing, offered originally only in sets, 7", with 1016 black and orange four-wheel tender lithographed "WINNER LINES" **35 50 30**

1030 Electric, 0-4-0, 1932, Winner, New Haven-type, lithographed "WINNER LINES", non-reversing, dark orange body and green roof, dummy headlight on top, operating headlight in cab front, hook couplers, offered originally only in sets, 5" **30 50 30**

1035 Steam, 0-4-0, 1932, Winner, operating headlight, hook couplers, nonreversing, originally offered only in sets, 7", with 1016 tender lithographed "WINNER LINES" **30 50 30**

1100 Handcar, "Mickey Mouse", catalogued 1935-37 with circle of two-rail track, uncatalogued 1934; clockwork, 10". With original boxes add $50-$75 to excellent

(A) Red base **400 500 275**

(B) Apple green base **500 700 275**

(C) Orange base **600 950 275**

(D) Maroon base, very rare, Sattler Collection **NRS**

1103 Handcar, c. 1935-37 (uncatalogued) "Peter Rabbit" Chick Mobile, with flanges for track or without flanges for floor operation, 8-7/8", yellow base, clockwork

(A) Track version: flanged wheels, yellow body, rabbit head measures 1-5/8" between ears, Sattler Collection **400 850 400**

(B) Same as (A), but floor version with non-flanged wheels, Ely Collection **400 850 400**

(C) Same as (B), floor version, but smaller rabbit which measures only 1-7/16" between ears, Sattler Collection **400 850 400**

1105 Handcar, "Santa Claus", 1935-36, clockwork, 10-1/2"

(A) Red base **575 900 400**

(B) Green base **625 1000 400**

1107 Handcar, "Donald Duck" rail car, 1936-37, clockwork with quacking mechanism, 9-3/8"

(A) White dog house, red base and red roof **450 800 300**

(B) White dog house, red base and green roof **425 700 300**

(C) Orange dog house, red base and green roof, Sattler Collection **NRS**

1506L Steam-clockwork, 0-4-0, 1933-34; with battery-powered headlight, ringing bell and brake, with a four-wheel 1502 black tender with red trim, lithographed "LIONEL-IVES LINES"

(A) 1506L and 1502 **70 100 40**

The 1506L "Lionel-Ives" clockwork loco and tender. Compare this with the illustration of the 1681 made a year later. Loco does not have a Lionel motor. Bartelt photograph.

1506M Steam-clockwork, 0-4-0, 1935, same as 1506L but with a 1509 "Mickey Mouse" light red stoker tender, 7-1/4". Sold only as set 1532 with 1515 Tank and 1517 Caboose **225 400 170**

1508 Steam, red sheet metal body, battery-powered headlight, clockwork-powered, main rod each side, nickel plate with black "LIONEL LINES" lettering, one nickel sand dome, stack, brake mechanism, ringing bell. "MICKEY MOUSE STOKER/®WALT DISNEY/MADE IN U.S. OF AMERICA/PAT. APPLIED FOR". This loco was part of set 1533, which contained a 1514 Erie box car, a 1515 tank car, and a 1517 NYC caboose. The set also included 8 curved and 2 straight pieces of special two-rail track and a windup key. A No. 1572 semaphore was present which had a black base, gray painted U-channel shafts, two semaphore flags riveted individually in place, a yellow flag with red trim and simulated printed green and red lenses. A windup key came with the set. The box was labeled "No. 1533 MECHANICAL FREIGHT SET", 1935

(A) 1508 and 1509 stoker tender **275 400 160**

(B) Set 1536 — the Mickey Mouse Circus Train Outfit. An assortment of cardboard figures and objects: 1508, 1509, 1536 diner, 1536 band car, 1536 animal car and tent, Mickey Mouse barker, circus tickets, auto, gas station and sign. Excellent condition requires a complete set of materials with original box **800 1200 —**

(C) Set 1536 without cardboard accessories **425 750 275**

1511 Steam-clockwork, 0-4-0, 1936-37, Commodore Vanderbilt-type, with whistle, no light, 7-1/2", with 1516 tender. Originally offered only in sets

(A) Black, 1936, 1511 and 1516 **25 40 25**

(B) Light red, 1937, 1511 and 1516 **40 65 25**

1588 Steam-clockwork, 0-4-0, 1936-37, torpedo-type, same casting as 1688, 9-1/2". Whistle, light, in black, with 1588 or 1516 tender, originally offered only in sets **90 125 50**

1651E Electric, 0-4-0, 1933, Lionel-Ives, New Haven-type, lithographed cab on 253 frame, lettered "LIONEL-IVES LINES", red cab with brown roof, black frame, brass trim, die-cast headlight, hand reversing, 9" **100 150 65**

1661E Steam, 2-4-0, 1933, Lionel-Ives, sheet metal frame and superstructure, hand-reversing, gloss black finish, brass and copper trim, red-spoked wheels, 8". With 1661 lithographed tender lettered "LIONEL LINES", originally offered only in sets **65 100 40**

1662 Steam, 0-4-0 switcher, 0-72, 1940-42, zinc alloy die-cast superstructure, flat black, white numbered "1662" under cab window, 8-1/2". With 2203 die-cast slope-back tender with back-up light. Sold only as set **130 200 75**

1663 Steam, 0-4-0 switcher, 1940-42, 0-27, same as 1662 but with Magic Electrol DC reversing (so that 1663 could run on same track with a 1666). With 2201 die-cast slope-back tender **160 250 100**

1664/1664E Steam, 2-4-2, 1938-42, 0-27, zinc alloy die-cast superstructure, nickel plate or rubber-stamped under cab window, nickel trim, E-unit reversing, 10-1/8". Came with "1689T", "1689W" in black or gunmetal and "2666T" or "2666W"

(A) 1664, black, 1940-42 **45 65 30**
(B) 1664E, black, 1939 **45 65 30**
(C) 1664E, gunmetal, 1938 **45 70 35**

1666/1666E Steam, 2-6-2, 1938-42, 0-27, same boiler as 1664/1664E but six drive wheels; came with "2666T", "2666W", "2698T", "2689W" and "1689W"

(A) 1666, black, 1940-42 **45 65 30**
(B) 1666E, black, 1939 **45 65 30**
(C) 1666E, gunmetal, 1938 **55 70 35**

A closer look at the 1666. Note the "universal" drawbar on the tender, which can be hooked to this type of loco or the type with a metal pin on the cab floor. It's a long reach to shovel scale coal from this tender! Bartelt photograph.

1668/1668E Steam, 2-6-2, 1937-41, Pennsylvania "Torpedo" streamlined locomotive, headlight and red classification lamps, drive and connecting rods, nickeled wire handrails, nickeled plate reading "1668-E LIONEL LINES 1668-E" (later version omits the "E") in black lettering, 1689 tender with or without whistle (1689T or 1689W), came with sets 1073 and 1074 in 1937-40 and sets 1073 and 1174 in 1941. Latch couplers, Griesbeck, Kotil, Claxton and LaVoie comments

(A) Gunmetal loco and tender **30 55 30**
(B) Black loco and tender **30 55 30**

1681 Steam, 2-4-0, 1934-35, Lionel Jr., sheet metal frame and superstructure, nickel trim, hand reversing, originally only in sets with four-wheel 1661 lithographed tender, 8"

(A) Black and red frame, 1934 **20 30 20**
(B) Red frame, 1935 **30 40 20**

Lionel's whimsical 1681 "Lionel Jr." 2-4-0 loco. Note the resemblance to the 1509L Lionel-Ives clockwork loco illustrated previously. Bartelt photograph.

1681E Steam, 2-4-0, 1934-35, Lionel Jr., same as 1681, but with E-unit reversing

(A) Black with red frame, 1934 **20 30 20**
(B) Red with red frame, 1935 **30 40 20**

1684 Steam, 2-4-2, 1942 (possibly in black in 1940-41 and gunmetal, 1940), 0-27 die-cast superstructure, E-unit reversing, rubber-stamped "1684" under cab window, 9-1/4". With/without whistle in "1689T", "1688T", "2689T" or "2689W". Cast motor frame or stamped motor frame, Kotil comment

(A) Black 1684 **30 50 20**
(B) Gunmetal 1684 **45 65 30**
(C) Same as (A), but with 1664-type motor, screw on rear motor mount, motor mounting rods across boiler interior have spacers on each end to center the motor inside the casting, Claxton Collection **30 50 20**

1688E/1688 Steam, 2-4-2, 1936, Lionel Jr., PRR torpedo, same casting as 1668, E-unit reversing, nickel plate and trim, 9-1/2". Originally sold in sets

(A) Gunmetal 1688E with "1689T" or "1689W", 1936-38 **30 50 20**
(B) Gunmetal 1688 with "1689T", 1939-40 **30 50 20**
(C) Black 1688 with "1689T", 1939 **30 50 20**
(D) Gunmetal 1688E with open forward facing cab windows and winged keystone as shown in 1936 catalogue, Ely Collection **NRS**

1689E Steam, 2-4-2, 1936-37, Lionel Jr. & 0-27, NYC Commodore Vanderbilt, same casting as 289E, only in sets, 9-1/4"

(A) Black **15 20 15**
(B) Gunmetal with "1689T" or "1689W", 1936 **20 25 15**
(C) Black, uncatalogued, without markers and with 1689T, 1689W or 1588 four-wheel tender, Blackman Collection **25 30 20**

Lionel's sleek 1689E. The streamlined skirts over the steam cylinders differ from the catalogue illustration of this engine. Bartelt photograph.

1700E Diesel, 1935-37, Lionel Jr. & 0-27, sheet metal, nickel plate reading "LIONEL LINES", 9-5/8"

(A) Set 1065: 1700E Power car, 1701 Coach and 1702 Observation, aluminum and light red, 1935 **50 65 50**
(B) Same as (A), but in chrome with light red. 1935 **55 65 55**
(C) Set 1071E: 1700E, 2 1701s, 1702, 1936-37, in chrome and light red **60 80 60**
(D) 1700E Power car, 1701 Coach and 1702 Observation, Hiawatha orange and Hiawatha gray (1936), smooth sides, Sattler Collection **NRS**
(E) 1700E Power car, 1701 Coach and 1702 Observation, Union Pacific brown and Union Pacific yellow (1936), smooth sides, Sattler comment **NRS**
(F) Hiawatha orange with Hiawatha gray stripe in skirt area rather than chrome lower panel sides. This particular set has four units (1700ED Power car, two 1701 Coaches and a 1702 Observation). It was acquired with its original boxes from its first owner. This example is the only known surviving set of what probably was a department store special, Degano Collection **NRS**

1816/1816W Diesel-clockwork, "Silver Streak", 1935-37, sheet metal, nickel plate reading "LIONEL LINES", 9-5/8"

(A) Set 1535: 1816, 1817 Coach and 1818 Observation in chrome and orange, 1935 **65 100 50**
(B) Same as (A), but with whistle **70 120 50**

5344 See 700 E
8976 See 227, 228, 229, 230, 706 and 708

"PAPER TRAIN"

50 1943, actually a cardboard train whose black engine is number "224". The 2224 Tender reads "LIONEL LINES". It comes with a 2812 red gondola with a red, white and blue Lionel "L", and black frame; a 61100 yellow Box with a brown roof and a red, white and blue Lionel "L", and a red 47618 Caboose. Accessories include a crossing signal, gate, three figures, assorted baggage, heavy paper track, wooden axles. Reportedly, very difficult to assemble, let alone actually run on its track. (For complete set) **200 300 —**

THE LIONEL 254

by Bruce C. Greenberg

The basic assumptions of this article are based that (1) Lionel was a well-organized company that made year-by-year production improvements and (2) that by careful data collection and analysis annual production changes can be identified and documented. It must be recognized, however, that since these trains were made between 50 and 60 years ago, there are problems of "post" factory changes. Nevertheless, with systematic data gathering and the compiling of identical cases, it is to identify many versions as true factory production. This method, however, leaves some cases indeterminate.

The key to this analysis is systematic data gathering. Each reporter who volunteered (or in some cases I volunteered) described on each of his pieces using the same reporting supplied by the author. Reporters were urged to report anything that didn't fit - and some findings didn't. Some of these reports of items that didn't fit led me to revise my data collection form and my ideas.

This study of the 254 was spurred by a letter from Henry Edmunds, a long-time correspondent, about a new 254 variety. Henry was working on the Prewar Lionel Guide. He reported that he had seen a 254 with horizontal reverse slots on both rear sides of the pantograph end of the locomotive. He had puzzled over these reverse slots and wondered how the stamping could have gotten into the press the "wrong" way. He asked, "Is this piece one of a kind, or was it produced in some quantity?" Fortunately, at the next local trail meet, I had the opportunity to take a census of 254s.

I already knew from studying 240 - 250 series Prewar 0 electrics that features varied: motor, plate lettering color, content and probably style, wheels, couplers, trim finish and color. I hoped to sort these out along with slots and whatever else I found.

I made up a simple chart of characteristics and with a portable tape recorder walked through the hall looking for 254s. I explained to each person who had a 254 what I was doing and asked permission to pick up his piece. I asked each owner what information he had about the piece's origins, as this would provide some indication of originality (or change). In several cases, the seller had just acquired the piece from the original owner and the piece was complete, and showed its years of dust, decayed wheels and broken couplers. The motors appeared to be original or at least unchanged. One piece I observed was restored and the seller explained the changes he made. I saw several dubious pieces that had passed through several hands.

In the course of my walk, I discovered several new variables - three types of frames and thick and thin plate lettering. Consequently, I made two more trips around the hall to check on the new variables.

Later, after considering expected and unexpected findings, I developed a more complete reporting form which I sent out to eight friends. Of the eight, several reported additional variables and asked me to clarify and correct my variables. After incorporating their data, I sent copies of the reorganized data to them for further corrections and recommendations. Then, I prepared the final copy.

This report is only possible because of the interest of a number of people - such as Henry Edmunds - and the contributions of Roger Bartelt, who provided the exceptionally clear and sharp pictures of the electric motors, Joseph and Trip Riley, who graciously permitted us to photograph their engines, Joe Kotil and Leon Eggers, who provided extensive, detailed reports and made a number of helpful suggestions for improving the data collection. Warren Blackmar, Henry Edmunds, Bill Edson, Dave Ely, Phillip Graves, Woody Hoffman, Roland LaVoie and George Koff also assisted. I would like to thank Ken Sherer and Lou Redman whose prior work on motor typologies provided the basic perspective for this research.

Study conclusions:

There are three major types of 254 frames: rectangular (1924-25), two piece with corner gussets (reinforcing wedges) (1926-27) and one piece with corner gussets (1928) to the end of production.*

There are five major versions of the 254.

Type I (1924-25)

The earliest 254s have Type IV (detailed below) motors, red spoked wheels, rectangular frames, all nickel-finished trim and a strap headlight. They came with one reverse lever slot on the left rear and are finished in dark green or mojave. The lower door panel has a thick black outline. All lettering is black. Most came with combination latch couplers with slots, although some with only a latch appeared.

Type II (1926-27)

The second type came with Type V motors and two-piece frames with corner gussets, but retained the nickel trim of the earlier locomotives. An unusual feature is the horizontal reverse lever slots on both the left and right sides toward the rear.

Type III (1926-27)

The third 254 series also had Type V motors and two piece frames with corner gussets, but it featured new brass trim and cast headlights. These locomotives each had only one reverse lever slot on the left side toward the rear.

Type IV (1928-29)

This series includes locomotives with both manual and automatic reverse mechanisms. They commonly came in olive green and pea green. They had the new one piece frame with corner gussets, and new Type VI motors with solid center red wheels, was all brass and the couplers were latch only.

Type V (1930-34)

This type had a new Type VII motor, and an olive green body with red hatches and red painted body bottom edge, pea green body with orange hatches and with or without edge stripes. But of more interest are the locomotive's two hand-reverse slots - one on the left rear and one on the right rear. It was this characteristic, observed by Henry Edmunds, which spurred the entire analysis!

0 GAUGE MOTOR TYPES

This typology, originally developed by Lou Redman and Ken Sherer, was subsequently elaborated by the author.

MOTOR TYPES

1. 1913-15 Triangular brush plates, brush and spring in tube with threaded cap, field and armature wound with green cotton-covered wire. A photograph of this motor occurs earlier in this chapter.

2. 1916-17 Same triangular brush plate as Type 1 but rotated from 11 o'clock to 9:30. The side plate has a more gently rounded front end. The brushes and springs are mounted in tubes with threaded caps. A photograph of this motor occurs earlier in this chapter.

3. 1917 Irregular shaped (dog leg) brush holder, brushes are each mounted

* These dates are estimates. Reader comments would be appreciated.

in a cap and retained in the hole by a spring bronze strap. Armature and field are now wound with varnish covered wire. A photograph of this motor occurs earlier in this chapter.

3. 1917 Irregular shaped (dog leg) brush holder, brushes are each mounted in a cap and retained in the hole by a spring bronze strap. Armature and field are now wound with varnish-covered wire. A photograph of this motor occurs earlier in this chapter.

4. 1918-25 Same irregularly shaped dog-leg brush holder as Type 3 but brushes mounted in fingers punched into a phosphor-bronze strip. The gear side has a small pinion gear which meshes with a large intermediate gear held on by a nut. The intermediate gear meshes with gears mounted on the rear of the drivers. A photograph of this motor occurs earlier in this chapter.

5. 1926-27 The brush plate is changed to a square type held on by screws through two extension feet. The brush plate holder is constructed from a piece of fiber inserted into the metal cover. The brush tubes are mounted into the fiber plate and the brush springs are made from formed wire. The gear side has a small pinion gear which meshes with a large intermediate gear fastened by a nut. The intermediate gear meshes with gears mounted on the rear of the drivers. All Type 5 motors (except 156) have spoked wheels. Samples observed have red painted spokes. Fillister head screws hold the motor to the frames, Riley Collection, Bartelt photographs.

The brush side of a Type V motor.

The brush plate side of a Type VI motor.

6. 1928-29 Rectangular nickeled brush plate is held away from the rectangular motor side frame by spacers. The 1928 brush plate is a piece of red fiber laminated to the nickeled cover, in 1929 the fiber piece is black. The motor has solid disc wheels with two sets of double reduction gears. Each gear consists of a large fiber gear in front of which is mounted a small metal gear. Both gears are mounted on the same shaft. There is no gear cover. The commutator end of the armature shaft runs in a hole drilled in the brush plate.

7. 1930 The redesigned five-sided brush plate is now constructed of fiber which is held from the side frame by brass bushings to provide clearance for the brushes riding on the commutator. The commutator end of the armature shaft is supported by a hole drilled through the fiber. There is no bushing, the motor frame is rectangular and the motor has red painted solid disc wheels and double reduction gears. The pinion gear meshes with the two large fiber gears. Each fiber gear rides on the same shaft with a smaller metal gear. The small metal gears mesh with the gears mounted on the rear of the drivers. The motor side plate opening on the gear side is enlarged to allow easier armature removal. The outboard pinion end bearing (gear side) is supported by a fiber plate which covers the gears.

The brush plate side of a Type VII motor.

8. 1931-32 The five-sided brush plate is the same as on Type VII, but two pairs of intermediate gears are now a single steel intermediate gear. The fiber plate covering the gears resembles a triangle pointing down. It is reported that the fiber plate holds a bronze bearing for the armature shaft end while another hole in the fiber provides the bearing for the intermediate gearshaft. However, in our observed sample there was no bronze bearing for the armature shaft. Brass bushings provide clearance for the fiber plate. Our sample has side frames with a large extension at one end and short tabs at the other. It also has spoked wheels with steam bosses, Riley Collection, Bartelt photographs.

The brush plate side of a Type VII motor.

The following chart summarizes the five major types of 254s and the 4 which is a special version of the 254. Not all characteristics apply to each type: NR (not relevant) is used when appropriate. Some units were omitted either because of insufficient cases or very peculiar characterisics.

	TYPE I	TYPE II	TYPE III	TYPE IV - MANUAL	TYPE IV - AUTOMATIC	TYPE V
Locomotive Number	254	254	254	254	254E	254 E
1. Estimated production years	1924-25	1926-27	1926-27	1928-29	1928-29	1930
2. Body color	dark green or mojave	mojave	olive green	olive green/pea green	olive green/pea green	olive green
3. Hatch color	dark green or mojave	mojave	olive green	olive green/orange	olive green/orange	red
4. Body edge color (beading)	dark green or mojave	mojave	olive green	olive green/pea green	olive green/pea green	red or olive green *15
5. Headlight type and size *1	nickel-finished	nickel-finished	large cast *13	small cast	small cast	small cast
6. Pantograph finish	nickel	nickel	brass	brass	brass	brass
7. Whistle finish	nickel	nickel	brass	brass	brass	brass
8. Number of reverse slots	one	two	one	one	one	two
9. Slot location *2	left rear	left rear and right front	left rear	left rear	left rear	left and right rear *2
10. Hand reverse lever	yes	yes	yes	yes	yes	yes
11. Lever finish	nickel *3	nickel	brass	brass	brass	brass
12. Pendulum reverse unit	no	no	no	no	yes	no
13. Modern E unit *4	no	no	no	no	no	yes *16
14. Coupler type	latch with slot	latch with slot	latch with slot	latch	latch	latch
15. Fillister screw at ends	yes *5	yes	yes	yes	yes	yes
16.A. Plate lettering color and style *6		black	black	black	red	black
16.B. Plate lettering content		Lionel/254	Lionel/254	Lionel/254	Lionel/254	Lionel/254
17. Lower door panel line width *7	thick	thick	thin (1/64)	thin (1/64)	thin (1/64)	thin (1/64)
18. Door knob present	no	no	no	no	no	no
19.A. Door lettering present	no	no	no	no	no	yes
19.B. Door letter content	N.R.	N.R.	N.R.	N.R.	N.R.	"E" *17
20. Frame type *8	rectangular	two-piece gusset corners	two-piece frame, gusset corners	one-piece frame, gusset corners	one-piece frame, gusset corners	one-piece frame, gusset corners
21. Wheel type *9	spoked	spoked	spoked	solid	solid	solid
22. Wheel color	red	red	red	red	red	red
23. Frame trim:	A *10	B	B	B	B	B
A. Brass tank nickel spring, nickel ladder						
B. Brass tank nickel spring, brass ladder			A	A	A or B	A
24. Pickup: A-with ridge B-without ridge	B *11	B				
25. Motor type	4	5	5	6	6	7
26. Number of cases	5 *12	2	2	6	2	2

*1 Both large and small cast headlights have been reported. All reported original cast headlights have the green side on the left.
*2 The pantograph is located on the rear hood, the whistle on the front hood.
*3 One locomotive was reported with a brass lever.
*4 The modern E unit was introduced in 1933.
*5 Our research shows that all original 254s came with fillister head screws. This is a useful authenticity indicator.
*6 In our data collection we did not ask about style. Likely styles are: block without serifs, block with serifs or rounded with serifs, rounded without serifs.
*7 There are two line widths - thin which has been reported as 1/32 or 1/64 of an inch and as thick as 1/16 or 1/32. We need further clarification.
*8 There are three basic frames: the early frame with rectangular corners, the later frame with triangular (gusset) corners made from two pieces and the late one-piece frame with gusset corners.
*9 All wheels are two-piece construction with a die-cast center and nickel finished rim. Many locos now have replacement wheels. These are often marked "MEW".
*10 Dark green locos have "A" type frame trim while 2 out of 3 of the mojave locos have "B" type frame trim.
*11 Both dark green locos have "B" no ridge pickups while the mojave locos are evenly split between "A" and "B".
*12 All Type IV motors come with frames having rectangular corners
*13 Both samples had provision for cast headlights. However the original headlight was present on only one.
*14 Of the two cases, there is one A and one B.
*15 Two of the three cases had red beading, one had olive green.
*16 The lever serves as a cutout for either the pendulum reverse unit or the modern E unit. In the pendulum reverse case, the switch has only two contacts and it opens and closes the coil. In the case of the E-unit, there are four contacts. Their function is not entirely clear although it is likely that they control current to the coil.
*17 This is rubber-stamped. Cleaning the brass door readily removes rubber-stampings. However, traces can often be seen with magnification and strong lighting.

Chapter V

0 AND 0-27 FREIGHT CARS

by Robert Pauli

INTRODUCTION

From the beginning, Lionel created two series of 0 cars. One was the four-wheel diminutive 800 series consisting of the 800 Box Car, 801 Caboose, 802 Cattle Car, and the out of sequence 900 Ammunition Car (a gray 800 type Box Car) and the 901 Gondola Car. The other was the larger series of double truck cars, which were numbered in the 820's: 820 Box Car, 821 Stock Car, and 822 Caboose. In 1927 Lionel began a second generation of small four-wheel 0 Gauge with the 902 Gondola Car. This was a substantial improvement over the smaller 901. The second entry among these newcomers, the 831 Flat Car, also made its debut in 1927. These were preceded in 1924 by the 803 Hopper Car and the 804 Tank Car, which at first were only additions to the small, early 800 series. Four years later, when the 803 Hopper and 804 Tank were upgraded and united with the new 902 Gondola and 831 Flat Car, the Second Generation of 0 Gauge Lionel 800 Series freight cars was born, finally resulting in the following numbers: 803, 807, 809, 831, and 902. Later, these same car bodies, sporting new frames and new four-wheeled trucks, became the 650 series of freight cars: 651-657, 659, and 620. In 1938, when automatic box couplers were installed, these same cars became the 2650 series: 2651-2657, 2659, and 2620, with 2660, 3651, 3652, and 3659 as later operating versions.

A year before, in 1926, Lionel had introduced yet another eight-hundred series: the 810-817, 820 series of big classical tinplate freight cars. This series blossomed into the 2800 series.

The manual box coupler with two ribs on top was first offered in 1936. However, the older latch coupler was continued for less expensive sets until 1942, and possibly even into 1943, as Lionel made use of leftover parts during cleanup and changeover to World War II production. This resembled American Flyer's creative use of parts. The late set of 831, 809, 804, and 807, headed by a 259 loco with a four-wheeled tender, came from this concluding wartime year, 1942.

Some of Lionel's 0 Gauge production bore more than a passing resemblance to European production, as this comparison of a Lionel 805 with a French Hornby car shows. That is because Lionel's Standard and 0 cars were designed by La Precisa in Italy - and naturally the designers imitated the trains they saw around them. Bartelt photograph

Changes within each series will be discussed in the introductions to each car, preceding the first numbered car in that series. Wherever possible, color names follow the T.C.A. Color Chart. At times, a second word description will be given, and if a color is not a match, it will be further discussed. We will create additional standard descriptions for colors not on the T.C.A. Color Chart.

Bibliography:

Fraley, Donald S., M.D., ed. **Lionel Trains: Standard of the World, 1900-1943**. Train Collectors' Association, 1976. (T.C.A. Color Chart included in this book).

Penney, Madeline. "War and Peace with Meccano." **Toy Train Operating Society Bulletin**, Volume 16, Issue 6 (June 1982).

Editor's Note: The introductions to the various 0 Gauge sections were written by Robert Pauli and edited by Rev. Philip Smith and Bruce Greenberg. Other major contributors to this section were Roger Bartelt (photos), Philip Graves (variations and couplers), Ralph Graves (line drawings), Louis Bohn (couplers and variations), and David Ely (variations). Many others made contributions as well.

0 GAUGE COUPLERS

Before 1915 to about 1927, Lionel used a simple hook coupler with a slot on top and a vertical hook that resembled an inverted "L". Another type of hook coupler was used on some of the small four-wheel lithographed cars from 1933 to 1937. It was a simple long hook of medium width with a slot on top. The following is a list of these couplers:

TYPES OF HOOK COUPLERS USED ON LIONEL 0 AND 027 CARS

by Louis Bohn

TYPE I: LONG HOOK COUPLER WITH EARS: Long straight shank, widened area for slot, narrow tang slot, coupler tang has projecting ears. Typical uses: 820 Series, 800 Series and 901.

TYPE II: SHORT STRAIGHT HOOK COUPLER: Short straight shank, widened area for slot, wide tang slot, coupler tang is rounded at its end.

TYPE III: SKELETON-KEYHOLE COUPLER WITH EARS: Coupler shank is circular at its end and broadens as it goes outwards toward its widened area for coupler slot. Viewed from above, it resembles an old-fashioned skeleton keyhole to some extent. It is about the same length as Type II. Its coupler tang has projecting ears. Typical uses: mechanical series cars.

TYPE IV: STRAIGHT-HOOK SKELETON KEYHOLE COUPLER: Same construction and typical uses as Type III, but longer coupler tang without ears.

TYPE V: SHORT STUBBY COUPLER WITH EARS: Very short, narrow shank and very wide area for slot. Wide coupler slot. Coupler tang has projecting ears. Typical uses: "Winner" passenger cars.

TYPE VI: LONG STRAIGHT NARROW TANG COUPLER: Long straight shank, widened area for slot, wide slot, coupler tang, small, narrow and rounded at end. Typical uses: "Winner" tenders and mechanical freight cars.

TYPE VII: LONG PUNCHED HOLE COUPLER: Essentially similar to Type VI, but shank end is rounded, shank has punched hole at attachment and coupler tang is squared off.

TYPES OF LATCH COUPLERS

by Philip Graves

From about 1924-1928, a combination latch coupler was made with a slot to accommodate the earlier hook couplers, and from 1924 to World War II, the latch coupler held trains together. Some of the inexpensive lithographed cars had a less expensive latch coupler, but the 650 series cars retained their early high-quality latch coupler throughout production, except for those that were fitted with manual box couplers after 1936.

The manufacturing process used to attached these latch couplers to their cars was simple, direct and reliable. At one end, the coupler shank had a pendulum-shaped projection:

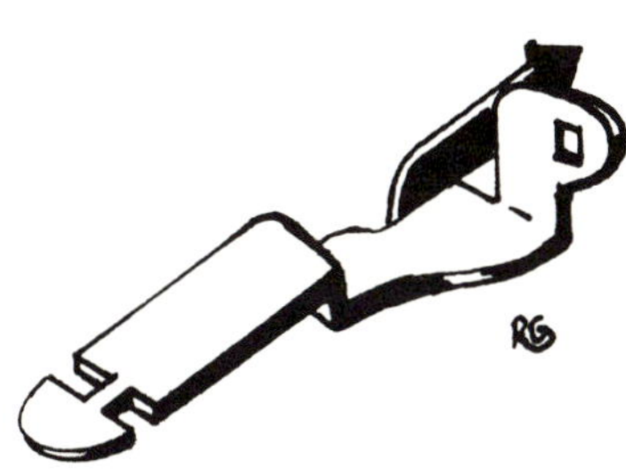

Before insertion into a slot in the car frame, the projection was bent upwards:

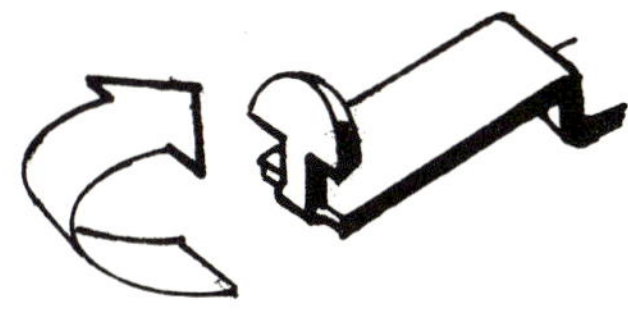

After the coupler shank's projection was inserted into the car frame, the projection was simply twisted one-half of a turn:

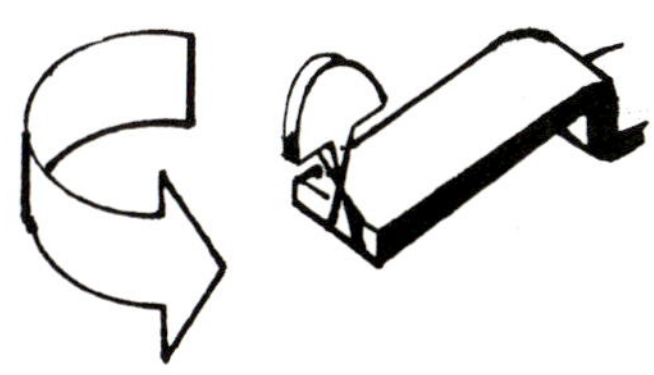

As with the Standard Gauge couplers of this kind, there were two basic types of these couplers. The earliest type had a separate brass spring retainer, and the tang of the latch was bent towards the shank end:

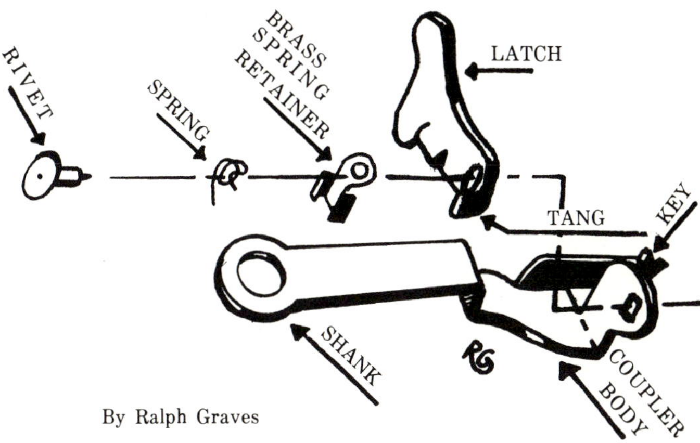

The Type II latch coupler, which was later, eliminated the separate brass spring retainer by using a flange on the bottom of the latch to secure one end of the spring and a cut-out in the rivet to serve as a detent for the other end. In addition, the tang of the latch now projected outward towards the key end of the coupler:

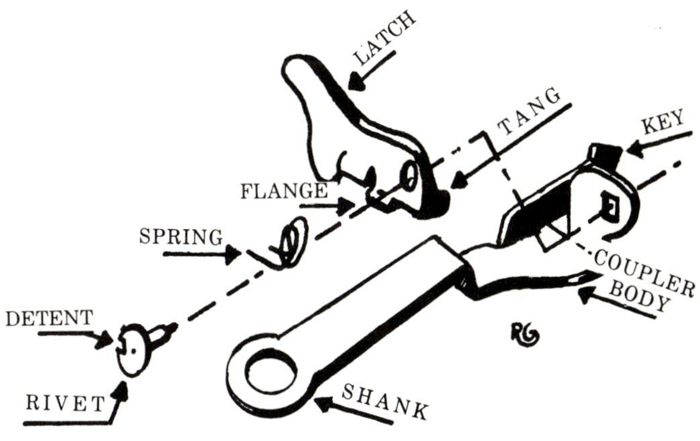

TYPES OF BOX COUPLERS

By Robert Pauli

From 1936-1942, three types of box couplers were used, each with manual and automatic versions. The 1936 box coupler was a box with two ribs on top. In 1938, that box was used on the automatic magnetic coupler mechanisms of the 2600 series cars which had a pointed end, and the different magnetic mechanism of the 2800 series cars, which had a blunt end. Passenger cars of higher quality also used the latter coupler and its larger, higher trucks.

The same double-ribbed 1936 box coupler was used on both the 1939 solenoid trucks of the 2600 series and the continuing magnetic trucks of the 2800 series. But in 1940, major changes took place. The box coupler was redesigned with a simulated knuckle and lift pin on top; a long vertical metal bar in back extended almost 1/2" below the box. That bar was necessary when smaller Type III trucks were installed on 2600 and 2800 series cars. To mate with older, higher couplers, this new coupler shank rose a full 1/4". The long metal bar was needed to reach the solenoid from that higher position. Some bars had spot-welded springs to keep them from sticking open. Furthermore, the solenoid was no longer riveted to the truck frame. Instead, the truck base was clipped to the axles, making the solenoid removable. The interchangeable truck shank was raised 1/8". The 2800 series continued with this coupler, and the 800 series came with a similar manual version, but the 2600 series changed again before or during 1941.

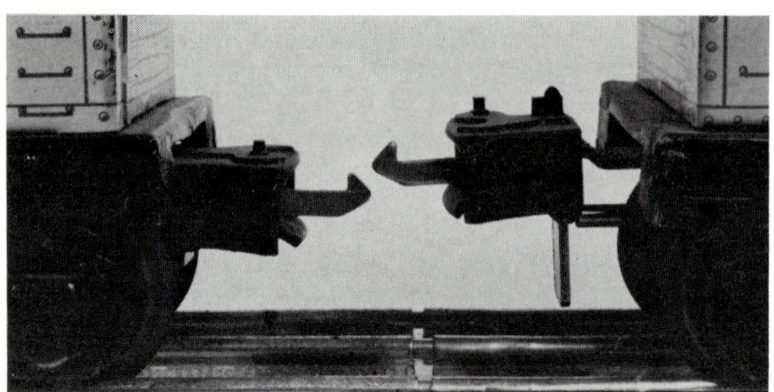

Oh, the problems caused by those high-rise and low-rise couplers. . . .

Two factors brought about this change. First, Lionel wanted its locomotives and cars to couple more closely, more realistically. Secondly, with World War II grimly looming, Lionel wanted to conserve vital material - metal - for military equipment the company was producing. To these ends, the coupler shank was lowered and shortened, saving about an ounce of metal on each car. With Lionel's vast production, that amounted to no small total. That brought the back of the box coupler underneath the frame, permitting the cars to couple more closely. Because of tight clearances, the simulated lift pin on the top of the box was omitted, and car frame openings on both ends were widened between 1/8" and 1/4".
widened between 1/8" and 1/4".

Manual box coupler production followed the automatic coupler production on the 650 series at least, and probably on all cars, beginning in 1936 with the double-ribbed box. In 1940, a simulated knuckle and lift pin were added for realism, but in 1941, the lift pin was removed, except on the 2800 and the 800 large series cars. Components from previous years were used up before new production began, but in 1942 all leftover parts were pressed into service in a scramble to offer at least a limited line of trains amid military production during the first full year of World War II. This raid on the Lionel parts bin accounts for many odd and interesting variations among these cars.

0 GAUGE TRUCK TYPES

By Robert Pauli

Since the publication of the last edition of this guide, major research has been conducted on these trucks. In general, the truck classifications have remained the same. However, myriad subdivisions within these nine types have been described. It appears that Lionel's experimentation with these trucks has been far more complex than initially realized, especially towards the 1936-42 box coupler era.

Why would Lionel spend such staggering tooling and manufacturing costs to change its truck-coupler assemblies? The answers to this question are deeply rooted in Lionel's history and are full of irony. The first reason is that right from the start, Lionel produced two different series of freight cars with different wheel, truck and coupler sizes. As long as simple hook couplers were used, there was enough vertical "play" so that the two different series would be capable of coupling. That changed when the latch coupler was introduced because the coupler's action was now horizontal instead of vertical. The large and small 0 Gauge freights now became mutually exclusive.

The second reason was market pressures of two types. Since Lionel had to offer a low-priced as well as a high-priced line, the frames could not be standardized without destroying Lionel's price structure. In addition, Lionel felt pressure to be first on the market with its coupler advances such as the manual box couplers of 1936 and especially the automatic box couplers of 1938-42. Many mistakes were made with this latter coupler, forcing Lionel to change trucks and couplers again and again. Features were combined into all sorts of strange conglomerations. The resulting complexity, especially with the Type III truck, is enough to make the most dedicated train scholar want to hide under a layout and babble incoherently!

Nevertheless, classifications of these trucks follow. Minor truck variations seldom have impact upon the value of a car, but major ones certainly do.

TYPE I: Semicircular hole in the side frame and three embossed rivets at each end. No journals. Used only on early passenger cars.

TYPE II A: Side frame has two rivets at each end, two more below axle hole and three rivets on bar between axle holes. Two squared cutouts with upper center corners rounded off. Used on early 603, 604, 610, and 612 cars. Several variations:

TYPE II A-1-A: Painted black, plain top

TYPE II A-1-B: Unpainted, plain top

TYPE II A-2: Unpainted, two small depressions on top surface

TYPE II A-3: Unpainted, two small depressions on top surface with two slots in depressions

TYPE II A-4: Unpainted, two small depressions with slots, nickel holder for fiber insulation in a third-rail roller which is mounted within the slots

TYPE II A-5: Same as II A-4, but chemically blackened

TYPE II B: A rare truck made only in 1926-27 with a dumbbell-shaped hole to accommodate axle and journal tabs. Note absence of all rivets but one.

TYPE III: All of the Type III trucks featured a narrow slot between the journals, two rivets between the journals and two rivets on either side of each of the journal boxes. Beyond that, the variations are extraordinarily complicated!

TYPE III-A: Narrow bolster bar with a single rib, two rivets above oblong slot on side. Couplers were mounted on the frame with this style truck. The truck was fastened to the frame by eyelet rivets.

TYPE III-B: Double ribbing on wide bolsters, two 1/8" diameter holes flank center hole. We have dated this from 1936.

TYPE III-Br: Same as III-B, but with pickup roller.

TYPE III-C: Same as III-A, but has a zig-zag shank extension to carry the searchlight car's center rail pickup.

TYPE III-D: Same as III-B, except for a straight shank extension to hold the first box coupler with two top ribs (1936).

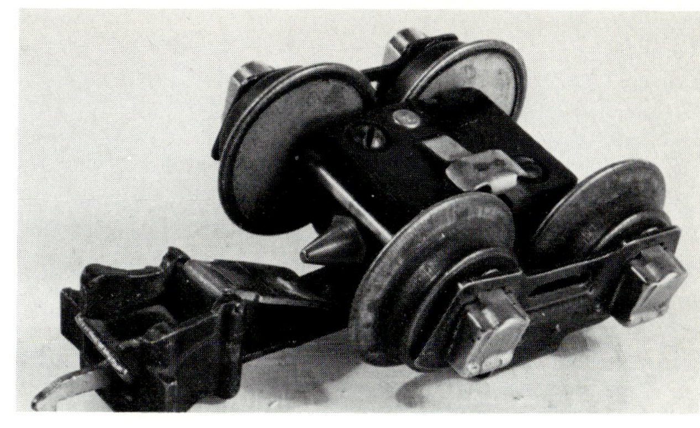

TYPE III-E: The 1938 revision of III-D to carry automatic magnetic couplers. Differences are small but obvious. A bakelite bottom plate is secured by long screws. The electromagnet is riveted in place. The coupler has a nickeled shoe and an L-shaped shank which is pulled down by the electromagnet. Type III-E also comes with brass or nickel pickup shoes designated III-Eb (brass) and III-Ec (copper).

We also have identified Type III-Es. The "s" stands for the solenoid mechanism. Some Type III-Es trucks are found with small fiber insulators to prevent the uncoupler or car mechanisms from operating when crossing switches. These are designated III-Esf. Some Type III-Es trucks are also found with a bakelite extension attached to part of the bottom plate. These are designated III-Esb.

TYPE III-F: The 1939 truck revision. In this year, Lionel replaced the electromagnet coupler with the solenoid coupler. Consequently, truck design changed for both the manual and the versions. The truck has a straight shank carrying the coupler and the ribbed box used since 1936. It usually has black journals. However, the extended L-shape stamped piece that fitted into the rear of the 1938 box was replaced by a small squared stamped steel piece. This square piece is pushed forward by the solenoid to raise the front of the coupler and cause uncoupling. The pickup shoe of the remote version was made from bakelite with only a small rivet making electrical contact with the special RCS track.

We call the 1939 manual coupler III-Fm and the 1939 solenoid version III-Fs (s for solenoid). There is a special version of this coupler with a center rail pickup roller mounted on a bakelite extension. We shall call this III-Fsb.

TYPE III-G: The 1940 truck revision. The box coupler was redesigned with simulated knuckles and lift pins. The coupler square stamping has grown larger and forms a rectangle. The solenoid (when present) attaches to the truck axles rather than being riveted to the frame. The contact shoes, if present, are bakelite with contact through a small rivet embedded in the shoe. There are two manual versions, III-Gm low and III-Gm high, and two solenoid versions, III-Gs low and III-Gs high.

The low versions, both manual and solenoid, have a 1/8" drop in the shank. The high versions, both manual and solenoid, have a 1/4" rise in the shank. The high versions were used for the last 2800 series cars with deep-dish frames and cut-out ends. Some III-G trucks are fitted with center rail pickup rollers. These roller assemblies are readily installed or removed. Solenoids are also readily added or removed from this truck. Some couplers' rear rectangles have springs spot-welded to their tails. The ease of installation (and removal) of parts created production economies. Some III-Gs and III-Gm trucks come with coupler boxes without simulated lift pins.

TYPE III-H: The 1941 truck revision. The truck was revised so that the back of the coupler nestled beneath the car frame, permitting very close car couplings. To achieve this effect, the shank was dropped downward, the simulated lift pin was removed to reduce clearance requirements, and the car frame openings at each edge were widened by 1/8", making the opening 1/4" wider. III-Hm is the manual version, III-Hs the solenoid version.

TYPE IV: This is a passenger truck used on 605, 606 cars and early 260 tenders. Three rivets are above each journal box and three more rivets are found on the bar between the journals. The outer edge of the bolster bars projects sharply inward towards the journal boxes. There is a large rectangular cutout in the bolster bar.

The left truck, Type III-E, is the 1938 electromagnet truck with the cone-shaped magnet core. This truck has a nickel finished shoe which shorts while crossing switches. The right truck has the later solenoid truck with the small diameter solenoid rod. This truck has a bakelite pickup shoe with fourth-rail electrical contact made only through the small metal rivet. This truck also has an electrical pickup roller for the center rail. This 1941 III-H coupler has a very short shank and small rear squares.

The left truck is the 1941 III-H shown in the photo preceding. The truck is the 1940 III-G solenoid mechanism truck. However, because of the 1/8" rise in the coupler shank, the solenoid rod would miss the coupler tail plate. To compensate, Lionel lengthened the coupler tail plate!

TYPE V-A: Used on 607 and 608 cars and 258T and 262T tenders. The ends of the bolster bars project sharply inward, as in Type IV, but the bolsters are flat. There are large rectangular side frame openings. A stud is riveted to the truck and fastened to the frame by a cotter pin and a brass washer. Nickel wheels with nickel backing, thick nickel axles and nickel (possibly copper) journals.

TYPE V-AR: Same as V-A, but with a center rail roller added.

TYPE V-B: Same as above, but slot is cut out of top bolster bar above cut-out rectangle for a reinforcing bar.

TYPE V-BR: Same as V-B, but with a center rail roller added.

TYPE VI-A: Flat bolsters, triangular side frame openings, a row of nine simulated rivets over journals. These trucks usually have a mounting stud riveted to the truck. The stud is fastened to the car by a brass washer secured by a C clip. Nickel or copper journals, nickel wheels with nickel backs, thick nickel axles. Rectangular slot above rivets.

TYPE VI-Ar: Same as VI-A, but with center rail pick-up roller.

TYPE VI-As: Same as VI-A, but with long shank extension for 1936 style manual box couplers with a 1/4" hole for a floating stud; stud is fastened to frame by a nickel washer and C clip, nickel axles.

TYPE VI-Ars: Same as VI-As, but with added center rail pick-up roller.

TYPE VI-B: U-shaped bolster, two triangular holes in truck side frame, long row of nine simulated rivets above journals.

TYPE VI-Bs: Same as VI-B, but long shank extensions with 1/4" hole, truck connected to frame by floating stud, C-clip and nickel washer hold stud to frame, nickel wheels with nickel backs, thick nickel axles, nickel journals only.

TYPE VI-Brs: Same as VI-Bs, but with added center rail pick-up roller.

TYPE VI-C: Similar to Type VI-B and Bs, but row of nine rivets does not go all the way across the truck. The crossbrace ends are swaged through a slot in the upper bolster bar similarly to the postwar staple-end metal trucks.

TYPE VII: U-shaped bolster, two triangular holes in truck side frame, two bars over each journal with three simulated rivets, a blank space above the spring simulation to make it easier to spread the tabs of the bolsters and a long shank extension about an inch wide.

TYPE VIII-A: Six-wheel truck with nickel wheels, large rectangular cut-outs in bolster bar, nickel wheels and nickel journals.

TYPE VIII-B: Same as III-A, but blackened wheels and journals. Used on late Madison-type passenger cars.

TYPE IX: Scale six-wheel truck, used only on 700E Hudson tender.

TYPE I: Red block lettering, no border, depicts four-wheel car frame.

TYPE II: Red block lettering, no border, right side view of four-wheel truck drawing with third-rail roller.

TYPE III: Small red serif lettering, red border, four-wheel truck drawing with a center rail roller viewed from the left side.

We believe that some cars, without oil labels, originally had labels, but had fallen off. Very careful study will often indicate the traces of remaining glue. It is important to note that replacement oil labels have been made. They are considerably cruder than the originals.

THE 650 SERIES

Because our listing is numerical for easy use, the 650 series is our starting point. The first 650 series of Lionel 0 Gauge freight cars was the smaller of two series to be offered to the public, and the bodies for these 650 cars can be traced to the second generation of smaller, four-wheeled cars, known as the 800 series: 803-807, 809, 831, and 902. A production system, begun in 1923 with this second generation of 800 series cars, continued through the 650 series and the 2650 series up through 1942.

The basic changes from the second generation of 800 series cars to the first 650 series cars occurred in the frame and trucks. (See the listings of Frame Types and Truck Types, especially Type III subclassifications.) Brass trim (1933-35) continued for a short while; then nickel trim (1935-42) replaced it. Black journals (1939-42) and finally totally black trim (late 1942) concluded the changes. The four-wheel frame of the 800 series was changed so that two four-wheel trucks could be added to the new Type 650-A frame. (See list of frames which follows.) That frame, together with the car bodies, became the basis for the 2650 series of automatic uncoupling freight cars in 1938.

Freight car bodies for both the 650 series and the 2650 series were taken directly from the second generation of small, four-wheel 800 series cars. In fact, the change was more of an upgrading than the beginning of a new series. These cars used latch couplers attached to a type 650-A frame with dime-sized truck depressions. Only the earliest four cars have completely brass trim, except for the nickel latch couplers, copper journals, and possibly some other copper trim, such as the small domes near the ends of the tank car body.

The second series of 650 cars have Type III-D trucks with two bolster ribs and manual 1936-39 box couplers with two top ribs. But more commonly, they have the final box coupler, the 1941 truck Type III-H without the simulated lift pin, partly recessed beneath the frame. To permit this coupler placement, Lionel created the Type 650-D frame.

The third series of 650 cars are those with decals and rubber-stamped lettering, Type 650-B frames and Type III-B trucks; these probably come from the 1940-42 era.

Other cars with other types of box couplers have been discovered, and it may be that more than just the gondola cars were manufactured, meaning that a fourth and fifth series of 650 cars may have been produced. Certainly their counterparts in the 1650 series do exist - one series for 1938, a second for 1939, a third dated 1940, and still another dated about 1941-42. We suggest this in light of Lionel's annual box coupler changes.

650 TYPE FRAMES

All 650-2650 Series frames are embossed with two lines of block lettering: "MADE IN/U.S.A.":

TYPE 650-B Two quarter-sized depressions containing two semicircular slots, two 7/8" and two elliptical holes for latch coupler retaining keys.

A full listing of all 650 type frames follows:

TYPE 650-A: Two dime-sized depressions for trucks, two semicircular slots for truck tabs, two 7/8" end slots for latch couplers, and two elliptical holes for the latch coupler retaining keys.

TYPE 650-B: Two quarter-sized depressions containing two semicircular slots, two 7/8" and two elliptical holes for latch coupler retaining keys.

TYPE 650-C: Two quarter-sized depressions and two 7/8" semicircular or elliptical holes.

TYPE 650-D: Two quarter-sized depressions, two 1-1/8" end openings, for 1941 box coupler without simulated lift pin.

TYPE 650-E: Two quarter-sized and deepened by 1/8" (dished down) depressions, two 1-1/8" end openings, for 1941 box coupler without simulated lift pin.

The 650 freight car series production began about mid-1933, with hoppers, tank cars, box cars, and cabooses with brass trim and copper journals. In mid-1935, flat cars, gondolas, stock cars, and manual dump cars were added, but with nickel trim. The Floodlight Car, 620, arrived late in 1937; it had nickel trim and came with the earliest type of frame, Type 650-A, and early type trucks, Type III-A and Type III-C, the latter being changed to accommodate a center rail roller. After remaining unchanged from 1935-38, the series went through many changes from 1939-42, when World War II brought toy train production to a halt. Spare parts were used to make the final sets, creating some of the more unusual cars; production may also have paralleled that of the 2600 series with the annual changing of coupler and truck types, including the changing of paint colors and the adding of decals. Probably both changes occurred.

The 650 freight cars have two Type III four-wheel trucks with four thin axles carrying eight wheels. There are "early" and "late" colors, four different kinds of couplers, and three different manually operated box couplers. All type 650 varieties of 6-1/2" frames have lettering stamped: MADE IN U.S.A. Any exceptions will be noted in the text.

The car frames are usually painted semi-gloss black, but there are exceptions. The 620 Floodlight car is painted "light red", the same color found on late 657 and 2657s. Also, the 650 flat car frame is painted "light green", which is a shade darker than "Stephen Girard Green", though lighter than "green". This color is also used on the base of a very common item, the 45N Watchman. We will call it "Light Green". In true train collector tradition, the first car in the 650 series is numbered outside of the series! It is the 620 Floodlight Car.

620 Floodlight Car with two four-wheel trucks

(A) 1937-38, aluminum painted die-cast light, large screw-base bulb, black rubber wire runs to electrical contact button, round glass reflector inside, round glass lens, round spring lens retainer, black yoke holds light with two small nickel hex-head bolts, four large wire handrails, two nickel brakewheels and stands, light red painted Type 650-A frame, latch couplers with shank keys, round black washer on bottom riveted to yoke with spring underneath, "No. 620/MADE BY/THE LIONEL CORP/NEW YORK", black rubber-stamping on frame bottom, one Type III-A truck, and one Type III-C truck with shank extension bent zig-zag downwards and bolted to a piece of black pressed fiberboard insulation which holds the third rail roller, small black bolt, black wheels with nickel backs, thin nickel axles, nickel journals, trucks fastened with eyelet rivets, Koff and Pauli Collections **15 25 12**

(B) 1939-41, same as (A), except for black journals, one Type III-B truck and one III-B truck with third rail roller, Type 650-B frame, Phillips screws hold light. Confirmation requested. **15 25 12**

(C) 1941-42, same as (B) with black journals, but with 92 gray painted floodlight **20 30 15**

651 Flat Car, painted light green (the same color as the 45N Gateman base); four-wheel trucks. These cars also have four curved nickel stakes and two nickeled brakewheels and stands.

(A) 1935-38, Type 650-A frame, latch couplers, "No. 651/MADE BY/THE LIONEL CORPORATION/NEW YORK" rubber-stamped in black lettering frame bottom, Type III-A trucks fastened with eyelet rivets, black wheels with nickel backs, thin nickel axles, nickel journals, Pauli and Koff Collections **10 20 8**

(B) 1939-41, same as (A) except for black journals, Type III-B trucks, Type 650-B frame. Confirmation requested. **NRS**

(C) 1942, four curved nickel stakes, two nickel brakewheels and stands, light green Type 650-D frame 1-1/8" end openings to accommodate Type III Hm trucks, rubber-stamping same as (A), black wheels with nickel backs, thin black axles, black journals, Pauli Collection **15 30 12**

652 Gondola Car, all have two four-wheel trucks and semi-gloss black painted frames.

(A) 1935-38, yellow painted sides and ends with two nickel brakewheels and stanchions, four small nickel plates, two in small serif lettering "LIONEL", two "No. 652", 650-A frame, Type III-A trucks, trucks secured by eyelet rivets, black wheels with nickel backs, thin nickel axles, Koff and Pauli Collections **12 25 11**

(B) 1939-41, same as (A), except Type 650-B frame, Type III-B trucks, black journals. Confirmation requested. **14 30 12**

(C) 1939, same as (A), except Type 650-C frame, Type III-D trucks, with black journals, each truck is secured by a nickel horseshoe clip which fastens to a stud riveted to the trucks, two nickel washers used as spacers between car frame and horseshoe clips, Pauli Collection **14 30 12**

(D) 1940-41, burnt orange sides and ends with two nickel brakewheels and stanchions, no plates, white rubber-stamped lettering "LIONEL" across car sides in panels 2 through 7, with "LL/652/218000" in first panel, overscored and underscored, "G-3/I.L. 40 6/I.W. 10 2" in last panel, Type 650-B frame, Type III-B trucks, black wheels with nickel backs, thin nickel axles, black journals, nickel Type II latch couplers, Pauli and Koff Collections **14 30 11**

652, TYPE (D)

(E) 1940, same as (D), except Type 650-C frame, Type III-G-M-low trucks, black horseshoe clips fastened to stud mounted on each truck, black wheels with nickel backs, thin nickel axles, black journals, Pauli Collection **15 35 12**

(F) 1940, same as (D), but box coupler has two ridges. Truck type and years not known. We want to know if this was factory production; this would be evidenced by other examples **NRS**

653 Hopper (Coal) Car, two four-wheel trucks.

(A) 1933-34, body painted Stephen Girard green (matches late 253 locomotive), two brass brakewheels and stanchions, a brass ladder at each end, brass wheel for manually unloading car, two brass plates on each side with small serif lettering, left plate reads "LIONEL/LINES", right reads "No. 653", Type 650-A frame, big rectangle punched out of the frame center to accommodate black manually operating hopper bin, Type III-A trucks secured by eyelet rivets, black wheels with nickel backs, thin nickel axles, copper journals, Koff Collection **13 25 15**

(B) Late 1934, same as (A), except nickel journals, Koff Collection **13 25 15**

(C) Late 1934, same as (A), except nickel journals and position of brass ladders. Both ladders are mounted at one end because the four ladder tab slots are stamped at wrong end of that one side. Probably that side was placed in hole stamping jig upside down and/or backwards. A most unusual car, Koff Collection **15 30 12**

(D) 1935-39, same as (A), except all nickel trim, plates, and journals, Koff and Pauli Collections **13 25 10**

(E) 1939-40, nickel trim and plates, black journals, box couplers. More information requested. **NRS**

654 Tank Car, two four-wheel trucks

(A) 1933, aluminum painted tank body, yellow SUNOCO decal with a red horizontal arrow pointing right, GAS above "SUNOCO" and "OILS" underneath, brass center dome above decal, two brass handrails with eight nickel stanchions, two brass ladders, two brass plates on each side with small serif lettering, "LIONEL/LINES" on left and "No. 654" on right, two copper end domes, Type 650-A frame, Type III-A trucks secured by eyelet rivets, black wheels with nickel backs, thin nickel axles, copper journals, Koff and Kotil Collections **12 25 10**

(B) 1934, same as (A), except brass end domes and copper journals. Confirmation requested. **12 25 10**

(C) 1935-38, same as (A), except all nickel trim domes, handrails, stanchions, ladders, plates, and journals, Pauli Collection **12 25 10**

(D) Early 1939, orange tank body with a red "SHELL" decal on each side centered above handrail, three nickel domes, two nickel handrails with eight nickel stanchions, two nickel ladders, four nickel plates, same lettering as (A), latch couplers, Type III-B trucks, black wheels with nickel backs, thin nickel axles, nickel journals, Pauli and Kotil Collections **14 30 12**

(E) Late 1939, same as (D) except black journals, Koff Collection **14 30 12**

(F) 1940, same as (D), but without plates and plate depressions, instead six close-cropped decals, two red "SHELL" decals, two decals with black lettering "LIONEL LINES T.L.C. 654" (overscored and underscored) "CAPY. 140000 LT. WT. 65000", and two other decals with black lettering, "UNITED STATES SAFETY APPLIANCES STANDARD A.R.A. SPEC. III T.L.C. 4-24-40", Type 650-B frame and Type III-B trucks, black wheels with nickel backs, thin nickel axles, black journals, nickel latch couplers, Pauli and Koff Collections **12 25 10**

(G) 1941, tank body painted 92 gray, nickel trim but no plates, four close-cropped decals, two with "S.U.N.X." "654 CAPY 100,000 LBS. LT.WT." "42,000 LIONEL LINES", two other decals have "SUNOCO" emblem as (A) above but with ten new lines of small lettering underneath, Type 650-E deep dish frame, Type III-Hm trucks, black wheels with nickel backs, thin nickel axles, black journals, Koff and Ely Collections **18 40 15**

(H) 1942, same as (G), except two black journals, copper handrails, and black axles, Pauli and Kotil Collections **18 40 15**

(I) Later 1942, same as (G), except all-black trim, including journals and thin axles, handrails fastened with cotter pins instead of stanchions, round-hole fastening points, Koff and Kotil Collections **18 40 15**

(J) Same as (C), but black journals, Sattler Collection **12 25 10**

655 Box Car with two four-wheel trucks

The Scale Series

97

714

716

716

716

717

715

T Rail Track
and Switch

(A) 1933-34, cream painted body and doors, maroon roof and door guides, brass door handles crimped on inside, brass ladders, brass brakewheels and stanchions, two brass plates on each side with small serif lettering, left plate reads "LIONEL/LINES" and right plate reads "No. 655", semi-gloss black painted Type 650-A frame, Type III-A trucks, copper journals, Koff Collection **15 30 15**

(B) 1934, same as (A), except nickel journals, Koff Collection **15 30 15**

(C) 1935-38, same as (A), except all nickel trim, door handles, brakewheels and stanchions, ladders, plates, and journals **15 30 15**

(D) 1939-40, cream body and doors, tuscan roof and door guides, nickel door handles tabbed on inside, nickel brakewheels and stanchions, nickel ladders, no plates, instead black rubber-stamped lettering, on left side, overscored and underscored, "LIONEL/LINES/655", to right of that data, "CAPY. 100,000/LD.LMT. 123100/LT.WT. 44200", on right side of the car, the L symbol inside a double circle on a black background with six lines of lettering underneath, Type 650-A frame, latch couplers, Type III-B trucks secured by eyelet rivets, black wheels with nickel backs, thin nickel axles, black journals, Pauli Collection **17 35 15**

(E) Late 1942, same as (D), except Type 650-D frame and all-black trim, door handles, brakewheels, stanchions, and ladders, box coupler without simulated lift pin, Type III Hm trucks with black wheels with nickel backs, thin black axles, and black journals, Pauli Collection **20 45 20**

656 Stock Car with two four-wheel trucks.

(A) 1935-39, light gray painted body and doors, vermilion roof and door guides, nickel trim, nickel door handles crimped up to 1938, tabbed thereafter, two nickel brakewheels and stanchions, two nickel ladders, and two nickel plates on each side, left plate reads "LIONEL/LINES", right plate reads "No. 656", Type 650-A frame, latch couplers, Type III-A trucks, black wheels with nickel backs, thin nickel axles, nickel journals, Pauli and Koff Collections **18 40 10**

(B) Same as (A), but with vermilion painted doors (confirmation of details requested) **18 40 16**

(C) Same as (A), but gray door guides (confirmation requested) **18 40 16**

(D) 1939-40, burnt orange painted body, doors and door guides, tuscan roof, nickel trim, nickel door handles tabbed inside, nickel brakewheels and stanchions, and nickel ladders, no plates, instead white rubber-stamped serif lettering, "LIONEL/LINES" on left and "LL/656" overscored and underscored on right, semi-gloss black painted Type 650-B frame, latch couplers, Type III-B trucks secured by eyelet rivets, black wheels with nickel backs, thin nickel axles, black journals, McErlean and Koff Collections **30 60 20**

(E) 1940, same as (D), but black rubber-stamped lettering and Type II latch couplers, Young Collection **30 60 20**

657 Caboose with two four-wheel trucks

(A) 1933-34, red painted body, roof, and cupola, two cream painted window inserts, brass end railings, two brass plates with small serif lettering on each side, "LIONEL/LINES" on left, "657" on smaller plate on right, Type 650-A frame, latch couplers, Type III-A trucks, black wheels with nickel backs, thin nickel axles, copper journals, Koff Collection **10 20 10**

(B) Late 1934, same as (A), except nickel journals, Pauli Collection **10 20 10**

(C) 1935-38, same as (A), but light red painted body, roof, and cupola, window inserts, aluminum end railings, two nickel plates with small serif lettering on each side, "LIONEL/LINES" on left, "657" on right on smaller plate, nickel journals, Pauli, Kotil, and Koff Collections **13 25 10**

(D) 1939, light red painted body, roof and cupola, cream painted window inserts, aluminum painted end railings, no plate slots, instead white rubber-stamped serif lettering, "LIONEL LINES" in center and number 657 underneath, Type 650-B frame, latch couplers, Type III-B trucks, black wheels with nickel backs, thin nickel axles, black journals, from uncatalogued set, Koff, Blackmar, and Kotil Collections **10 20 10**

(E) 1940, same as (D), but very light red painted body, roof, cupola, and both end railings, off-white window inserts, Pauli Collection **10 20 10**

(F) Late 1941, very light red painted body and end railings, tuscan roof and cupola, two off-white window inserts, white rubber-stamped lettering same as (D), Type 650-D frame, one Type III-B truck and one Type III-H-M truck, black wheels with nickel backs, thin nickel axles and thin black axles, black journals, Pauli Collection **12 25 10**

659 Dump Car with two four-wheel trucks

(A) 1935-38, manually operated, medium green painted tilting dump bin held in place by two nickel stands with locking mechanism, two nickel brakewheels and stands, Type 650-A frame latch couplers, black wheels with nickel backs, thin nickel axles, nickel journals, Pauli Collection **15 30 15**

(B) Same as (A), but black journals, Sattler Collection **15 30 15**

SCALE MODEL SERIES: 714-717 and 714K-717K

A glance through toy train catalogues printed before World War II will reveal that most locomotives, cars, and accessories were formed from sheet metal. They roughly resembled real ones, though many fine details (such as the complex piping on steam locomotives) were omitted. Those intricate details were too expensive to make and too time-consuming to apply on toy train mass-production lines. Furthermore, in the hands of youthful, enthusiastic operators, they would have broken easily.

Gradually, though, new technology brought a more realistic look to the Lionel Lines. In 1934, with its back to the wall, Lionel pinned its hopes for surviving the Great Depression on its M-10000, a 1/45 scale model of the Union Pacific's new yellow and brown streamliner. Unlike other Lionel trains up to this time, the M-10000 was formed in part from die-castings and in part from sheet steel. Unlike them, it looked exactly like the real thing. The sleek streamliner's success brought Lionel out of receivership and plainly showed the competitive edge gained by realistic trains. The following year (1935), Lionel introduced a second die-cast locomotive, the steam-powered streamliner: the HIAWATHA. Lionel saved the cost of new passenger car tooling by simply repainting the M-10000 cars. On the new steam locomotive, complex piping was conveniently covered by a smooth metal shroud. On real railroads, though, sleek streamliners were far outnumbered by ordinary, pipe-laden steam locomotives. Lionel brought that look to its trains by improving the same production technique that had been used to manufacture the M-10000 and HIAWATHA locomotives - die-casting.

In die-casting, a mold (die) was made incorporating details such as rivets and piping. Then molten metal was injected under pressure to force it into every nook and cranny. When the metal cooled, it had taken all the details of the die. Best of all, since those details were part of the whole casting, they weren't fragile. Lionel did not invent die-casting; Dorfan and Ives used it to provide very realistic locomotives while Lionel relied on its highly-touted sheet steel construction. Finally, Lionel began to employ it to make more realistic locomotives. Initially, only wheel frames were die-cast. As employees became more experienced, they die-cast locomotive bodies as well. Their efforts culminated in Lionel's renowned 0 scale series, built to National Model Railroad Association (N.M.R.A.) standards, including scale flanges and coupler height: the New York Central Hudson (1937), the Pennsylvania B-6 0-6-0 Switcher (1939), and the four-car series that is the subject of this section (1940, two years after Lionel had introduced similar cars in 00 scale). Like the Hudson (but not the switcher), they were available either ready-to-run (RTR) or in kits, signified by a "K" following the car number (714K, for example). Kits appealed not only to less prosperous customers, but also to a growing number of scale modelers who preferred to paint and number their own equipment.

This series ran from 1940 until 1942, when World War II halted toy train production. Since these cars had scale trucks and couplers, they were not compatible with Lionel's other locomotives and cars. Lionel remedied that by offering another series, the 2900 series whose cars were just as highly detailed as their scale counterparts, but had tinplate trucks and couplers to

Scale and Semi Scale Freights

2954

714 K

2955

715

2955

715

2956

716

2957

make them operable with other Lionel equipment.

The 714 Box Car, the 715 Tank Car, and the 716 Hopper Car had sprung Bettendorf trucks. The 717 Caboose had trucks with simulated leaf springs, the same ones used on the 701T Pennsy scale switcher tender. Slow speeds and comparatively light weight of the prototype Pennsylvania B-6 tender required nothing more substantial than those four-wheel trucks. Larger capacity and ballast-scorching passenger speeds of the New York Central Hudson's tender demanded heavy-duty Commonwealth six-wheel trucks. Counting those tender trucks, Lionel offered three different 0 scale trucks in all.

Two types of bodies were used. The Box Car was molded of "phenolic plastic", though many collectors refer to it as bakelite. The other three cars were cast with magnesium alloy. To the dismay of collectors and operators alike, pre-World War II die-cast items can (and do) deteriorate, expanding, warping, cracking, eventually crumbling. Before buying or trading, check for minute cracks. Look carefully along the edge of a locomotive or car. If the metal seems to bend instead of being straight, deterioration has begun.

714 Box Car, 1940-42, tuscan painted black "phenolic plastic" (bakelite) 10-3/4" body, tuscan painted roof walk, two tuscan painted sliding doors with two black door latches, four metal door guides, plastic air brake unit underneath, white rubber-stamped serif lettering with "PENNSYLVANIA 100800" on left overscored and underscored with three lines of information lettered beneath on the right side, the PRR tuscan keystone surrounded by a white circle, with six lines of information underneath followed, on another line below, by the prototype car number, and that followed by still another longer line of lettering extending still further to the right; four strap steps on bottom corners of sides at the ends, one black brakewheel on end, two scale sprung Bettendorf trucks with two NMRA scale couplers **150 250 150**

714 Box Car Kit, 1940-42, same as 714 when painted and assembled, except for 714K on decals. Kit brings "excellent" value only when complete and in gray primer, assembled or unassembled. **— 500 —**

715 Tank Car

(A) 1940, black painted die-cast metal tank body and 9" frame, two black handrails with four stanchions on each side, one stanchion of a different type on each end, one black brakewheel on stand, plastic air brake unit on bottom, "SHELL" decals in block lettering on left with "S.E.P.S. 8124" beneath and underscored, followed by two lines of information, decals on right have twelve lines of lettering, followed by the actual car number beneath, strap steps on corners under sides, scale Bettendorf sprung trucks with NMRA scale couplers, Sattler Collection **150 225 125**

(B) 1941-42 same as (A), except for decals, on left, "S.U.N.X. 715" with one line of lettering beneath, on right with ten lines of lettering beneath, "SUNOCO" symbol on yellow diamond with red arrow, Sattler Collection **200 375 125**

715K Tank Car Kit, 1940-42, same as the 715 cars above when painted and assembled, except for 715K on decals. Kit brings "excellent" price only when complete and in gray primer, assembled or unassembled **— 375 —**

716K Hopper Car, 1940-42, same as 716, but in unassembled kit with gray primer **— 700 —**

stamped serif lettering, "B & O 532000" overstamped and understamped on left, three lines of lettering underneath, prototype car number on right, below "new" date, "BALTIMORE & OHIO" across right side with one line of lettering beneath two lines of miniscule die-cast lettering **150 225 125**

717 Caboose, 1940-42, tuscan painted magnesium alloy casting, white rubber-stamped serif lettering, "717 Caboose N.Y.C. 19400" centered on both sides, with car number in smaller numbers at bottom center of sides, also "UNITED STATES SAFETY APPLIANCES STAND" in block lettering beneath cupola on both sides, and in three lines, two yellow plastic marker lamp simulations with a red painted surface simulating the rear lens, plastic air brake unit on bottom, a painfully obvious third-rail contact shoe on the center bottom of the car, (same arrangement as scale Hudson tender), two scale leaf-spring trucks with NMRA scale couplers. Although the 1941 catalogue (p.45) refers to this caboose as having a light, there is some question as to whether it was actually produced with a light. Reader comments are invited. **150 250 125**

to whether it was actually produced with a light. Reader comments are invited. **150 250 125**

717 Caboose Kit, 1940-42, same as 717 when painted and assembled, except for 717K on decals. Kit brings "excellent" price only when complete and in gray primer, assembled or unassembled. **— 350 —**

INTRODUCTION TO EARLY FOUR-WHEEL 800 SERIES 0 FREIGHT CARS

By Robert Pauli

FIRST GENERATION 800 SERIES

This first diminutive series of four-wheel freight cars went into production before 1915, probably about 1913. It continued, with only minor rubber-stamping variations, until about 1926. The 800 Box Car, 801 Caboose, and 802 Stock Car, came first. Later the 900 Ammunition Car (a gray 800 type Box Car) appeared with the 203 Tank Locomotive before 1917, at the outbreak of World War I. The final car in the series, the 901 Gondola Car, arrived about 1919. Cars made after that constitute the "second generation" of 800 series cars.

All these cars have 5-3/4" round-end frames painted semigloss black, with one large simulated step at each corner. There are two 7/8" slots on the rounded frame ends for the hook couplers, and two key-shaped holes in the frame top to fasten the couplers. Measurements of these frames, which we call Type 800-1, are approximate and are taken at the car frame center. Never made with trim, brakewheels, or journals boxes, these little cars all have two thick nickel axles and four nickel wheels with nickel backs. The open ends of the two nickel hook couplers look like the top half of a plus sign. This first small four wheel set should not be confused with the early larger 820 series, described later.

SECOND GENERATION #800 SERIES

About 1923, Lionel introduced two new cars in the 800 series that were more realistic than their predecessors: #803 Hopper and #804 Tank Car. Both cars had a new frame (Type 800-2) measuring 6-3/4" at center, one inch longer than the 5-3/4" Type 800-1 frame, probably to carry longer car bodies. This new frame had rounded ends, no holes for journals, and medium-sized spring simulations. It differed from the earlier frame by sporting a simulated air brake tank on the edge of the frame in the center of the car. Furthermore, the four single strap step simulations at the bottom corners had been replaced by simpler (and cheaper) double strap step simulations. An embossing surrounding each axle hole and simulated spring represented a single-axle truck like those mounted on contemporary 4-wheel cabooses (called "bobber" cabooses because of their unsteady ride) and diminutive steam switcher tenders. Each embossing looked like an inverted triangle, wide on top and squared off beneath the axle hole. Those embossings were joined in a single line at center that dropped down to outline the steps on the ends. The 7/8" end slots, formerly rounded, were squared off. The two slotted holes that accommodated two hook couplers remained. In addition to the slots for individual car body tabs and the large punched opening for the 803 hopper bin, there were two unused slots near the rounded ends. In three out of four frames in front of this author at the moment, there are two such slots at one end. In the fourth car there is but one. Paint fills these holes of the Type 800-2 frames. They are a remnant of original stamping for the #530 and #630 observation cars where they were used to fasten the observation deck railings in place. These frames, with these holes already in place, were then used in a second stamping process for whatever type of car body they were to receive.

The earliest of these cars have little trim, and no holes for additional trim. The first #803 (1923) hopper car has but one trim wheel, which is the large, early center brass (two-piece) wheel used to manually dump the car; Lionel used a handy part. The first #804 tank car (1923) came with one red center dome, and while a dome is necessary to most prototype tank cars, this is clearly an item that can be called trim on a toy train. The second #804 tank car (1924) has a brass center dome.

The Type 800-2 frames were 1/8" wider than the earlier Type 800-1 frame; hence, when Lionel attempted to put wheels and axles on these cars, they would not stay on due to that extra width. The problem was solved not by changing the die, but by adding four 1/8" spacers to the axles, outside the four wheels.

But the die was changed for the next group of car frames (Type 800-3). The hole for the axles was inset 1/8" on all four wheels. This changes the simulated trucks considerably; though all previous holes remain, including the two small slots for the observation deck railings, four holes have been added to the ends near each corner. These are most likely added for the 902 gondola, introduced in 1927 with two brakewheel stands that utilized two of these holes. This car and the 831 flat car, 807 caboose, 806 cattle, and 805 box were also introduced in 1927. In fact, the later round end of cars in this series (except for the 807 caboose, 831 flat car, and 804 tank car) all have these four round holes in the ends. But the telltale sign of this third round-end frame is the two small spring simulations above the axle holes. In brief, Type 800-3 frames have rounded ends, two small spring simulations, and no journals.

With more trim added to the gondola, box car, cattle car, caboose and (in 1927) flat car, it was not long before Lionel again changed the round-ended frame. This time, about 1929 (1928's production), nickel journals were added, with a slot placed above the axle hole for the top journal tab and the axle hole squared off for the bottom journal tab. All holes remained the same, including the slotted hole for the coupler, the four round holes in the ends, and the two unused observation deck slots, with the same exceptions. The caboose, flat car, and tank car do not have those four round ends, two small simulated springs, and nickel journals. Oddly enough, it seems that the first two cars of the 800 series, the 803 hopper and 804 tank car, were the last to receive trim, for all the other cars of the series now had brass brakewheel ladders except the caboose which had brass ends and no room for brakewheels. In 1930, once again the frames were changed. This time the round ends were removed and the new frame measured 6-1/2". Type 800-5 had square ends, two small unusual end slots, and lasted until 1938. In 1931 the final car was added to the series, the 809 manual dump car. Now that the cars had trim, the trim had to be changed: early large-center (two-piece) brakewheels gave way to later and simpler small-center (one-piece) brakewheels. The block lettered brass plates became serif lettered and, toward the mid-thirties, became nickel serif lettered plates. About 1930-31, nickel journals gave way to more colorful copper, and in 1933, the 650 series began to overshadow these second generation 800 series cars, but they persisted to the extent that some were built during the late 1930's and 1940's, with Type 800-6 frames that have smaller axle holes for smaller axles and two tab slots for each journal box.

FOUR-WHEEL FREIGHT CARS, 1915-1941

by David Ely and David Christianson

Lionel made four-wheel freight cars over many years and consequently the cars exhibit many changes in frame, coupler, lettering, journal, brakewheel and wheel design. The changes follow a relatively orderly progression which can be charted and analyzed.

Frame Types

There are five distinct frame types:

Type I: 5-1/2 inches long, rounded ends, no journals, single spring over axle

Type II: 6-1/2 inches long, rounded ends, no journals, single spring over axle

Type III: 6-1/2 inches long, rounded ends, no journals, double spring over axle

Type IV: 6-1/2 inches long, rounded ends, journals, double spring over axle

Type V: 6-1/2 inches long, square ends, journals, double spring over axle

Type I: 5-1/2 inches long, rounded ends, no journals, single spring over axle

Type III: 6-1/2 inches long, rounded ends, no journals, double spring over axle

Type V: 6-1/2 inches long, square ends, journals, double spring over axle

Comparison of rounded and square ends

Coupler Types

Type I: Hook couplers found with frames Types 1 and 2 and sometimes with Type 3

Type II: Latch couplers found with frames Types 3, 4 and 5

Lettering

Lettering also showed a chronological development:

Type I: Rubber-stamp

Type II: Brass plates with block letters

Type III: Brass plates with serif letters

Type IV: Aluminum plates with serif letters

Type V: Rubber-stamp (or decal)

Journals

Journals showed a progression similar to that of other Lionel equipment:

Type I: No journals

Type II: Nickel journals

Type III: Copper journals

Type IV: Nickel journals

Type V: Black journals

Brakewheels

Brakewheels show a chronological development:

Type I: No brakewheels

Type II: Larger brass, two-piece brakewheels of about 5/8 inch diameter

Type III: Two-piece brass brakewheels of about 1/2 inch diameter

Type IV: One-piece brass brakewheel of about 1/2 inch diameter

Type V: One-piece nickel brakewheel

Wheels

Wheels show a systematic development through time:

Type I: Early cars came with nickel wheels on thick axles and spacers between the wheels and frames

Type II: Nickel wheels and axles

Type III: Black wheels and thinner axles

FIRST SERIES 800 FOUR-WHEEL CARS

800 Box Car, 1915-26, four wheels, Type 800-1 frame, no trim, brakewheels, or journals, two nickel hook couplers (see above introduction for further details)

(A) Orange body, roof, and two unlettered metal sliding doors with simulated handles punched out of the doors, four black rubber-stampings, two on either side of the doors, in block lettering, "PENN.R.R.4862", "800" stamped beneath each door, Type 800-1 frame painted semi-gloss black (described in introduction) with gold serif lettering, "MADE IN U.S.A. THE LIONEL CORPORATION NEW YORK", nickel wheels and two thick axles, Pauli Collection **15 40 15**

(B) Same as (A), except "800" stamped on one end, not both sides **10 35 15**

(C) Yellow-orange body and roof, otherwise same as (B) **10 35 15**

(D) Same as (C), except maroon roof **25 45 15**

(E) Same as (B), except green body and roof **20 60 20**

(F) Same as (B), except different lettering on sides, WABASH 399 **15 50 20**

(G) Same as (B), except no lettering on frame and new stamping on one end, "LIONEL LINES/N.Y./Made in U.S.A." **15 40 20**

(H) Orange body, maroon roof, rubber-stamped black lettering, "PENN RR/6399" on each side of door (four places), vertical punched door handles, no embossed ribs on door, hook couplers with ears, rubber-stamped lettering on both ends, "LIONEL LINES/N.Y./MADE IN U.S.A.", Merrill Collection **15 50 20**

801 Caboose, 1915-26, four wheels, Type 800-1 frame, no trim, brakewheels, or journals, two nickel hook couplers (see introduction for further details)

(A) Maroon body and cupola, black roof, two rubber-stampings, one on each side between two window openings, in black sans-serif lettering, "WABASH/R.R./4890", "801" on one end, Type 800-1 frame with two end railings on each end, "MADE IN U.S.A./THE LIONEL CORPORATION/NEW YORK" stamped on bottom in gold, lines in serif lettering, nickel wheels and thick nickel axles, Pauli Collection **15 35 20**

(B) Same as (A) except body and cupola painted brown, no lettering on frame bottom, lettered "WABASH/R.R./4390", "801" in black serif lettering to left of door on one end, "LIONEL/LINES/N.Y. MADE IN U.S.A." to right of door on same end, black sans-serif lettering, four nickel wheels, two thick axles, Pauli Collection **25 45 20**

(C) Same as (B), except stamped "N.Y.N.H.&H." on sides **25 45 20**

(D) Red body, all red cupola, black main roof and frame, lettered in black "WABASH/R.R./4890", "801" on lower right corner of car side, Carlin Collection **15 35 20**

(E) Maroon body, all maroon cupola, black main roof and frame, hook couplers with ears, black rubber-stamped "WABASH/R.R./4390" on sides and "LIONEL/LINES/N.Y./MADE IN U.S.A." on one end only, Merrill Collection **15 35 20**

802 Stock Car, 1915-26, four wheels, Type 800-1 frame, no trim, brakewheels, or journals, two nickel hook couplers (see introduction for further details)

(A) Pea green body, roof, and two sliding doors lettered "UNION/STOCK/LINES" in black block lettering, 802 in black serif lettering on one end, no lettering on frame, four nickel wheels, two thick axles, Pauli Collection **20 40 20**

(B) Same as (A), but with "MADE IN U.S.A./THE LIONEL CORPORATION/NEW YORK" in gold serif lettering **10 40 20**

(C) Same as (B) except a lighter green paint, possible "light green" (light green is the color of the base of the 45N Watchman, a fairly common item) **20 50 20**

(D) Medium green body (possibly same as A), black frame with two springs over wheels, hook couplers with ears, rubber-stamped black sans-serif lettering on doors, "UNION/STOCK/LINES", punched door handle, black rubber stamped "LIONEL/LINES/N.Y./MADE IN U.S.A." on one end only, Merrill Collection **20 40 20**

The following cars (900 and 901) are part of the early four-wheel 800 series.

900 Ammunition Car (derived from 800 Box car)

(A) 1917-21, khaki painted body, roof and doors, four nickel wheels on two thick nickel axles, Type 800-1 frame, no trim, brakewheels, journals, or lettering, two nickel hook couplers (see introduction to 800 series for further details). This car came with an armored train pulled by Armored Motor Car 203, which looked like a World War I tank! Made by Lionel Manufacturing Company, Koff Collection. Note: This car can be faked easily by repainting on 800 box car, Bohn comment **60 125 30**

(B) Same as (A), but painted gray **60 125 30**

901 Gondola Car, 1919-25, four wheels, Type 800-1 frame, no trim, brakewheels, or journals, two nickel hook couplers, nickel wheels, thick nickel axles (see introduction to 800 series for further details)

(A) Lake Shore, circa 1919-21, khaki painted body, gold stamped "LAKE SHORE" in serif lettering centered on sides, "901" gold rubber-stamped on one end only, gold rubber-stamped on bottom, "MADE IN U.S.A./LIONEL CORPORATION/NEW YORK", Sullens Collection **40 75 30**

(B) Same as (A), but maroon painted body, black rubber-stamped "LAKE SHORE" in serif lettering centered on side, "901" black rubber-stamped on one end only, Sullens Collection **20 35 15**

Small 0 Freight Cars

809 804 805 807

653 654 656 657

2653 2654 2656 2657

2659 2652 655 2651

3659 2652 2655 3651

3652 2620 2657

(C) Maroon painted body, black rubber-stamped, "LAKE SHORE" in serif lettering centered on sides, one end stamped "LIONEL/LINES/ N.Y./MADE IN U.S.A." in small block lettering, underframe stamped in gold serif lettering "MADE IN U.S.A./THE LIONEL CORPORATION/NEW YORK", Pauli and Kotil Collections **20 35 15**

(D) Same as (C), but no underframe lettering, Bohn and Carlin Collections **20 35 15**

(E) Same as (A), but gray body, Bohn Collection **20 35 15**

(F) Same as (C), but white underframe lettering, Koff Collection **20 35 15**

(G) Same as (A), but gray body with black lettering, Koff and Kotil Collections **25 35 15**

(H) Pennsylvania, gray sides and ends, large gold rubber-stamped serif lettering "PENNSYLVANIA" on both ends, small black lettering on end, "LIONEL/LINES/N.Y./MADE IN U.S.A.", Type 800-1 frame painted semi-gloss black, frame stamped with gold serif lettering, "MADE IN U.S.A./THE LIONEL CORPORATION/NEW YORK", thick axles, nickel finished wheels, Pauli Collection **25 35 15**

(I) Pennsylvania, gray painted body, gold stamped sans-serif lettering "PENNSYLVANIA" centered on side, "901" gold rubber-stamped at each end, gold rubber-stamped on bottom "MADE IN U.S.A./THE LIONEL CORPORATION/NEW YORK", Sullens Collection **25 35 15**

SECOND GENERATION, 800 SERIES FOUR-WHEEL CARS

803 Hopper Car

(A) 1923 Early Car, dark green body, brass two-piece large center brakewheel mounted below center of side for manually unloading bin, no slots or holes for other brakewheels, large gold rubber-stamped serif lettering, "LIONEL" across both sides and "MADE IN U.S.A./THE LIONEL CORPORATION/NEW YORK" stamped diagonally on end opposite the one with two small slots for observation deck railings (for 530 and 630 observation cars), reporting marks and number in block lettering, "WEIGHT/60000 Lbs." beneath "LIONEL" to left of center, "CAPACITY/80000 Lbs." beneath "LIONEL" to right of center, number (803) on frame in medium-sized gold lettering on end with observation deck slots, black base for unloading bin, semi-gloss black painted Type 800-2 frame (earliest frame on this type of car) with medium spring simulations over axle holes, four spacers on axles, two nickel hook couplers, four nickel wheels with two thick nickel axles, Pauli Collection **20 25 15**

(B) 1924, same as (A), except for semi-gloss black painted Type 800-3 frame with two small simulated springs over axle holes, axle holes indented 1/8", eliminating need for spacers on axles, frame has two round holes for brakewheels near each end, number (803) in large gold rubber-stamped lettering on end opposite two observation deck slots, above diagonal serif lettering, two nickel latch couplers, Pauli Collection **20 25 15**

(C) 1925, same as (A), except with unused slots for brakewheel stanchions on body ends, semi-gloss black painted Type 800-4 frame with unused observation deck slots, frame lettered like (B), but toward opposite side, four nickel journals, four nickel wheels, two thick nickel axles without spacers, since frame is indented, two nickel latch couplers, Pauli, Kotil, and Koff Collections **20 25 15**

(D) 1925, same as (C), except gold stamping on opposite end, Koff Collection **20 25 15**

(E) 1926, same as (C), except two early two-piece brass brakewheels with two brass stanchions and slots for them at body ends, two of four holes in semi-gloss black painted Type 800-4 frame accommodate two long brass brakewheel rods, two nickel latch couplers, four nickel journals **20 25 15**

(F) 1927, same as (E) with brass brakewheels, rods, and stanchions, plus slots for them at body ends, two brass ladders as well, on sides near opposite ends, four nickel journals, two nickel latch couplers **20 25 15**

(G) 1928, same as (F), but with later one-piece, small center brass brakewheels, Koff Collection **20 25 15**

(H) 1929, Late Car, peacock body with early two-piece, large center brakewheel mounted below center of side for manually unloading bin, two brass one-piece small center brakewheels with rods and stanchions on ends, two brass ladders on sides near opposite ends, two brass plates on each side, one with "LIONEL/LINES" in block lettering, the other with "No. 803", Type 800-5 semi-gloss black painted frame with square ends, four nickel journals, two nickel latch couplers, four nickel wheels, two thick nickel axles, no rubber-stamped lettering **20 25 15**

(I) Same as (H), except early two-piece, small center brakewheels, probably to use up the inventory **20 25 15**

(J) 1930, same as (H), except serif lettering on brass plates **20 25 15**

(K) 1931, same as (H), except serif lettering on brass plates and four copper journals, Pauli, Sattler, and Kotil Collections **20 25 15**

(L) 1934, same as (H), except nickel plates with serif lettering, nickel small center brakewheels, and nickel journals **20 25 15**

804 Tank Car

(A) Mid-1923, Early Car, dark gray tank body, red painted center dome, gold rubber-stamped serif lettering "LIONEL TANK LINES" across both sides of tank, semi-gloss black painted Type 800-2 frame with round ends and single medium-sized spring simulations over axle holes, "MADE IN U.S.A./THE LIONEL CORPORATION/NEW YORK" in small gold serif lettering on frame bottom, two nickel hook couplers, four nickel wheels, two thick nickel axles with four nickel spacers **20 25 15**

(B) Late 1923, same as (A), except brass center dome (The Type 800-2 frame of the sample observed has only one of the usual two unused observation deck slots), Pauli, Koff, and Ely Collections **20 25 15**

(C) 1924, same as (A), except lighter gray tank body, brass center dome, number (804) rubber-stamped in gold block lettering above 3 lines of small gold serif lettering on bottom of frame, Pauli, Ely, Kotil, and Koff Collections **20 25 15**

(D) 1925, same as (C), except terra-cotta tank body with no lettering, brass center dome, Koff Collection **20 25 15**

(E) Early 1925, terra-cotta (close to burnt orange) tank body, brass center dome, black rubber-stamped serif lettering "LIONEL TANK LINES" across both sides, semi-gloss black painted Type 800-3 frame with two simulated springs, rounded ends, and an indentation over each axle hole that eliminates need for spacers on axles, Type 800-1 Oil Sticker on bottom of frame, perhaps for first time (instructions for oiling car printed in red block lettering without red border), four nickel wheels, two thick nickel axles, two nickel latch couplers, Pauli Collection **20 25 15**

(F) Late 1925, same as (C), except four nickel journals, semi-gloss black painted Type 800-4 frame with two slots for each journal, two small simulated springs above each journal, and rounded ends, number (804) printed on Type 800-1 Oil Sticker on bottom of frame, Pauli and Koff Collections **20 25 15**

(G) 1929, Late Car, aluminum tank body, three brass domes, two brass handrails on eight nickel stanchions, two brass ladders, semi-gloss black painted 6-1/2" Type 800-5 frame with square ends, no lettering or oil sticker on bottom of frame, two brass plates with block lettering on each side of tank, one with "LIONEL/LINES", the other with "No. 804", no Sunoco decals, four nickel wheels, two thick nickel axles, four nickel journals, two nickel latch couplers, Pauli and Koff Collections **20 25 15**

(H) 1931, same as (G), except four copper journals and serif lettering on all four brass plates, Pauli Collection **20 25 15**

(I) Same as (H), except copper end domes and Type 800-5 frame with two 3/16" holes, Koff Collection **20 25 15**

(J) 1935, aluminum tank body, two Sunoco decals lettered "GAS/SUNOCO/OILS", three nickel domes, two nickel handrails, eight nickel stanchions, two nickel ladders, four nickel plates with serif lettering, as (J), semi-gloss black painted Type 800-5 6-1/2" frame with square ends, no rubber-stamping or oil sticker, four nickel wheels, two thick nickel axles, four nickel journals, two nickel latch couplers, two 3/16" holes behind coupler fastening holes, Pauli Collection **25 30 15**

(K) 1939, yellow-orange tank body, two red "SHELL" decals, all nickel trim and plates, except four black journals, semi-gloss painted Type 800-6 frame, with smaller holes for two thin nickel axles and two slots for each journal, four black wheels with nickel backs, two nickel latch couplers **25 30 15**

(L) 1939, orange (yellow-orange) tank body, two red "SHELL" decals, all nickel trim and plates, except four black journals, semi-gloss painted Type 800-6 frame, with smaller holes for two thin axles and two separate slots for each journal box, two nickel latch couplers, four black wheels with nickel backs on two thin nickel axles **25 30 15**

(M) Similar to (L), but two additional close-cropped decals, two on left, in four lines of information, first two lines serif lettering, "LIONEL LINES", "T.L.D. 804" overscored and underscored, next two lines in block lettering, "CAPY 140000", "LT. WT. 65000"; other two decals have five lines of block lettering, "UNITED STATES", "SAFETY APPLIANCES", "STAN-

DARD", "A.R.A. SPEC. III", "T.L.C. 4-24-40", semi-gloss black painted, Type 800-6 frames with two 3/16" holes (1/2" behind holes for fastening latch couplers), four black journals, four black wheels with nickel backs on two thin nickel axles, Pauli Collection **35 45 20**

(N) Identical to (M), except three black domes, all other trim nickel (except four black wheels and four black journals) **25 30 15**

(O) Same as (A), but lettering on underframe is black instead of gold, Sattler Collection **20 25 15**

(P) Same as (J), but copper handrails, Kotil Collection **20 25 15**

805 Box Car

(A) Mid 1924-27, pea green body and doors, terra-cotta roof and door guides, two early round brass door handles, two early two-piece large center brass brakewheels with two brass stanchions on two long brass rods and two brass ladders all on ends, two brass plates on each side with block lettering, one on left "LIONEL/LINES", the other on right No. 805, semi-gloss black painted, Type 800-3 frame with two small simulated springs over each axle hole, no journals, Type 800-1 Oil Sticker with red lettering but no border, two nickel latch couplers, four nickel wheels on two thick nickel axles, no axle spacers, no rubber-stamped lettering **20 25 15**

(B) Mid 1926-Early 1927, terra-cotta body and doors, orange roof **20 25 15**

(C) Mid 1926-Early 1927, cream body and doors, orange roof and door guides **20 25 15**

(D) Mid 1926-Early 1927, pea green body and doors, maroon roof and door guides **20 25 15**

(E) Mid 1926-Early 1927, orange body and doors, maroon roof and door guides, two early round brass door handles, four brass spacers, Koff Collection **20 25 15**

(F) 1927, dark pea green body and doors, orange roof and door guides, Pauli Collection **20 25 15**

(G) Same as (F), but no oil sticker, Koff Collection **20 25 15**

(H) 1927, orange body and doors, pea green roof and door guides **20 25 15**

(I) Same as (F), except two small brass strap door handles and four nickel journals, Pauli Collection **20 25 15**

(J) 1929, same as (F), except two small brass strap door handles, and Type 800-5 squared off frame, four nickel journals, Type I oil sticker, Koff and Pauli Collections **20 25 15**

(K) 1931, same as (F), except two small brass strap door handles, two one-piece small center brass brakewheels with two brass stanchions and two brass connecting rods, two brass ladders on ends, two brass plates on each side, one with block lettering "LIONEL/LINES", the other with small serif lettering "No. 805", semi-gloss black painted Type 800-5 frame with square ends, four copper journals, two nickel latch couplers, four nickel wheels, two thick nickel axles, no rubber-stamped lettering, no oil sticker, Pauli Collection **20 25 15**

806 Cattle Car (Stock Car)

(A) Mid-1926 (when production began for 1926 selling season, among first cars) pea green body and doors, terra-cotta roof and door guides, small round brass door handle, two 803 Hopper-style large center brass two-piece brakewheels (originally manufactured for manual dump mechanism on 803 Hopper) with two long brass connecting rods and two brass stanchions, two brass ladders on ends, two brass plates on each side with block lettering, one with "LIONEL/LINES", the other with "No. 806", semi-gloss black painted Type 800-3 frame with two small simulated springs and indentations over axle holes, no journals, two nickel latch couplers, four nickel wheels, two thick nickel axles, no rubber-stamped lettering or oil sticker, Pauli, Sattler, and Koff Collections **25 35 18**

(B) 1927, orange body and doors, maroon roof and door guides, two small round door handles, two early large center (two-piece) brass ladders on ends, two brass plates on each side with block lettering as in (A), semi-gloss black painted Type 800-3 frame as in (A), two nickel latch couplers, four nickel wheels, two thick nickel axles, Type 800-1 oil sticker, Pauli Collection **20 30 15**

(C) Same as (B), except no oil sticker, Koff Collection **20 30 15**

(D) 1929, same as (B), except two late door handles, Type 800-4 frame, four nickel journals, Koff and Kotil Collections **20 30 15**

(E) 1929, orange body and doors, pea green roof and door guides, two brass strap door handles, early large center (two piece) brass brakewheels with two long connection rods and two brass stanchions, two brass ladders on ends, four brass plates, as (A), semi-gloss black painted 6-1/2" Type 800-5 frame, two nickel latch couplers, four nickel journals, four nickel wheels, two thick nickel axles, Type 800-1 oil sticker printed in red with no border, Pauli and Koff Collections **20 30 15**

(F) 1930, orange body and doors, maroon roof and door guides, two brass strap door handles, two early large center two-piece brass brakewheels with two long brass rods and two brass stanchions, two brass ladders, two brass plates on each side with small serif lettering, one with "LIONEL/LINES", the other with "No. 806", semi-gloss black painted 6-1/2" Type 800-5 frame with square ends and two unused 3/16" holes (perhaps used to hold frame during punching, painting, or drying), two nickel latch couplers, four copper journals, four nickel wheels, two thick nickel axles, no rubber-stamping or oil sticker, Pauli Collection **20 30 15**

(G) 1931, same as (F), except two small center one-piece brass brakewheels, semi-gloss painted black Type 800-5 frame without the two 3/16" holes, Pauli Collection **20 30 15**

(H) 1932, same as (G), except two 3/16" holes in frame again, Koff Collection **20 30 15**

Note: We have had a report of an orange 806 with a brown roof instead of maroon, but further details are lacking. Reader comments are requested.

807 Caboose

(A) 1927, peacock body, dark green cupola and roof, maroon window inserts, two brass end railings, two brass plates on each side with block lettering, one with "LIONEL/LINES", the other with number (807), semi-gloss black painted Type 800-3 frame with two small simulated springs over each axle hole, two unused slots for observation deck railings, two nickel latch couplers, four nickel wheels, two thick nickel axles, no rubber-stamped lettering, no oil sticker, Pauli and Koff Collections **20 25 15**

(B) Early 1928, vermilion body, peacock roof, cupola, and window inserts, otherwise as (A), Koff Collection **20 25 15**

(C) 1928, same as (B), but with Type I oil sticker on bottom of frame, Pauli Collection **20 25 15**

(D) 1929, same as (C), except semi-gloss black painted Type 800-4 frame with two slots for nickel journals flanking each axle hole, Type I oil sticker, no rubber-stamped lettering, Pauli Collection **20 25 15**

(E) 1930, same as (C), except semi-gloss black painted Type 800-5 frame, two unused observation deck slots still there, four nickel journals with appropriate slots, two nickel latch couplers, four nickel wheels, two thick nickel axles, no rubber-stamping lettering, no oil sticker, Pauli and Kotil Collections **20 25 15**

(F) Same as (E), except unused observation deck slots finally omitted, Type I oil sticker, Koff Collection **20 25 15**

(G) 1931, vermilion body, peacock roof, cupola, and window inserts, semi-gloss black painted Type 800-5 frame with two unused observation deck slots, two nickel latch couplers, four copper journals, no rubber-stamped lettering, no oil sticker, Koff Collection **20 25 15**

(H) 1931, same as (G), except two 3/16" holes have been punched 1/2" behind the holes for fastening the two nickel latch couplers, Pauli Collection **20 25 15**

(I) 1934, light red body, roof, and cupola, cream window inserts, two painted silver end railings, two different plates on each side, both with serif lettering, "LIONEL/LINES" on nickel plate, number (807) on brass plate, semi-gloss black painted Type 800-5 frame with two unused observation deck slots, plus two 3/16" holes, as (H), two thick nickel axles, no rubber-stamped lettering, no oil sticker, Pauli Collection **25 30 15**

(J) 1935, same as (H), except all nickel trim, nickel plates, nickel journals, no rubber-stamped lettering, no oil sticker, Pauli Collection **23 28 15**

(K) After 1936 but before 1939, same as (I), but with all nickel trim, Type 800-6 semi-gloss black painted frame with two unused observation deck slots altered to accommodate four black wheels with nickel backs on two thin axles, previously, one slot for each journal was part of axle hole; now, with smaller holes for thin axles, both slots are separate from axle hole, Pauli and Koff Collections **25 30 15**

(L) 1939, light red body, roof, and cupola, cream window inserts, two silver painted end railings, no plates, instead, white rubber-stamped serif lettering, "LIONEL LINES" across both sides with number (807) underneath, semi-gloss black painted Type 800-6 frame with small axle holes for thin nickel axles, two separate slots for journals, no lettering or oil sticker on frame, four black wheels with nickel backs, only one nickel latch coupler, Pauli Collection **25 30 15**

(M) 1942, same as (L), except black end railings and black journals, Kotil Collection **20 25 15**

809 Manual Dump Car

(A) 1930, orange tilting dump bin, rubber-stamped lettering on only one side in four lines, first line "No. 809" in block lettering, other three lines "MADE BY/THE LIONEL CORPORATION/NEW YORK" in serif lettering, two nickel stands, each with a locking handle, keep bin from doing its thing unexpectedly, two nickel stands at ends hold two brass one-piece small center brakewheels with brass rods, semi-gloss black painted Type 800-5 frame with square ends, two nickel latch couplers, four nickel wheels on two thick nickel axles, four nickel journals, frame has no lettering or oil sticker, Pauli and Kotil Collections **20 25 15**

(B) 1930, same as (A), except four copper journals, Koff Collection **20 25 15**

(C) 1930, same as (A), except four copper journals and medium green dump bin, Koff Collection **20 25 15**

(D) 1931, same as (A), except four copper journals and two unused 3/16" holes punched in frame toward center about 1/2" behind coupler fastening holes, Pauli Collection **20 25 15**

(E) 1932, medium green dump bin, locking levers, brakewheels, and lettering as (A), semi-gloss black painted Type 800-5 frame has unused 3/16" holes noted in (D), four nickel journals, four nickel wheels, two thick nickel axles, two nickel latch couplers, frame has no lettering or oil sticker, Pauli Collection **20 25 15**

(F) Same as (E), except no lettering, Pauli Collection **20 25 15**

(G) 1939, medium green dump bin, locking levers, brakewheels, and lettering as (A), semi-gloss black painted Type 800-6 frame with four black wheels on two thin nickel axles, four nickel journals, Kotil Collection **20 25 15**

(H) Same as (A), but with four black journals, probably four black wheels on two thin nickel axles and semi-gloss black painted Type 800-6 frame to accommodate thin axles **20 25 15**

(I) Same as (B), with four copper journals, but with medium green dump bin, semi-gloss black painted Type 800-5 frame with unused 1/16" holes, four nickel journals, four nickel wheels, two thick nickel axles, two nickel latch couplers, frame has no lettering or oil sticker **20 25 15**

(J) Same as (A), but serif style lettering, Kotil Collection **20 25 15**

831 Flat, 1927-34, this car is part of the second generation four-wheel cars - 803-807, 809 series including 902. The car shows the progression of frame types, brakewheel types, underside frame lettering, journal type and load development

(A) Circa 1926, black semi-gloss painted Type III frame, eight nickel stakes, Type II brakewheels, nickel hook couplers, nickel wheels on thick nickel axles, no journals, Koff Collection **15 20 15**

(B) Circa 1927, same as (A), but frame painted dark green, frame underside stamped "MADE IN U.S.A./THE LIONEL CORPORATION/NEW YORK" in small serif lettering and "831" in block lettering, nickel latch couplers, Koff Collection **15 25 15**

(C) Circa 1929, dark green painted Type IV frame, four nickel stakes, nickel journals, nickel latch couplers, Type II brakewheels, Type I oil sticker with "831" rubber-stamped in black block lettering on the sticker. The car had a load consisting of a single piece of wood scribed to simulate eight boards. The load underside had grooves running across between the stakes and a 1" diameter hole in the center, nickel wheels on thick nickel axles, Pauli and Kotil Collections **15 25 15**

(D) Same as (C), but Type V frame, Koff and Sullens Collections **15 25 15**

(E) Circa 1931, dark green painted Type VI frame, square ends, two springs, journals, unused slots 5/32" long at one end, 5/32" holes approximately an inch from each end, four nickel stakes, nickel journals, nickel latch couplers, nickel brakewheel stand, brass brakewheel post, small center one piece brass brakewheel. The car is gold rubber-stamped on the underside, "No. 831/MADE BY/THE LIONEL CORPORATION/NEW YORK" in block lettering, copper journals, nickel wheels and thick nickel axles. A one piece load consisting of a single block of wood is present. It is scribed to simulate eight boards, and its underside is grooved across the block between the stakes and the centered one-inch diameter hole. Pauli, Bohn, I. D. Smith, Sattler, and Koff Collections **15 25 15**

(F) Circa 1931, same as (E), but "No." omitted from underside frame stamping, Koff and Sullens Collections **15 25 15**

(G) Same as (E), but brakewheels on opposite sides of car ends, probably due to metal blank for frame being inverted when placed in punch press during manufacturing, Bohn Collection **15 25 15**

(H) Same as (C), but Type III brakewheel, Kotil Collection **15 25 15**

(I) Same as (E), but "831" stamping on bottom is below rest of lettering, not above it and no 1" diameter hole, Kotil Collection **15 25 15**

(J) Same as (E), but copper journals, Kotil Collection **15 25 15**

(K) Same as (E), but car is rubber-stamped "MADE BY/THE LIONEL CORPORATION/NEW YORK" "No. 831" in black block lettering, latch couplers, Pauli Collection **15 25 15**

(L) Circa 1939, bright green painted Type VI frame. The paint matches the base of the 45N Automatic Watchman. Four nickel stakes, nickel brakewheel stand, nickel brakewheel rod, one piece nickel 15/32" diameter, Type V brakewheel, 8 pieces of wood for load, nickel journals, black wheels with nickel backs, thin nickel axles, nickel latch couplers, black rubber-stamped on underside "No. 831/MADE BY/THE LIONEL CORPORATION/NEW YORK/IN U.S. OF AMERICA", Pauli, Sullens, Kotil, and Koff Collections **15 25 15**

(M) Circa 1940-42, same as (H), but black journals, Pauli Collection **15 25 15**

(N) Dark green painted Type IV frame, no journals or journal slots, 6-1/2" rounded ends, four nickel stakes, two springs and two slots on truck sides, two Type III brass brakewheels, latch couplers, gold stamped "831/MADE IN U.S.A./THE LIONEL CORPORATION/NEW YORK" on underside, Hoffman Collection **15 25 15**

(O) Same as (E), but Type III brass brakewheels and black rubber-stamped "831" on oil label on underframe. This is a highly unusual practice for Lionel. On this example, the number is just below the oil label text as if it were stamped there by design instead of accident. Reader comments are requested. Hoffman Collection **10 17 27**

(P) Same as (L), but copper journals, Sattler Collection **15 25 15**

(Q) Same as (D), but brass journals, Kotil Collection **15 25 15**

902 Gondola Car, this car is part of the second generation of 800 series cars; see introduction to 803 Hopper Car for further details.

(A) 1927, dark green sides and ends, Type II brakewheels, brass stanchions and brass posts for brakewheels, four small brass plates with block lettering, two on left "LIONEL", two on right "No. 902", Type III frame with two small holes on each end for brakewheel posts, couplers not present, most likely hook couplers, Type II nickel wheels on thick nickel axles, no journals **15 25 15**

(B) 1927, peacock sides and ends, two Type II two-piece large center brakewheel, brass posts and stanchions, four small brass plates with block lettering, two on left "LIONEL", two on right "No. 902", 6-1/2" long rounded ends, Type III frame with two small simulated springs above each axle hole, no journals, two small holes at each end for brakewheel posts, nickel latch couplers, nickel wheels on thick nickel axles, no rubber-stamped lettering on underframe, Type I oil label glued to bottom of frame, Koff and I. D. Smith Collections **15 25 15**

(C) 1927, same as (B), but plates reversed on one side, Pauli Collection **20 25 15**

(D) 1929, same as (B), but Type V frame, 6-1/2" long, square ends, journals, two springs, nickel journals, Pauli and Koff Collections **20 25 15**

(E) 1931, same as (B), but Stephen Girard green sides and ends, two Type IV brakewheels of one piece with small brass center, four brass plates now have small serif lettering, Type V frame, 6-1/2" long, square ends, journals, two springs, copper journals, no oil sticker, Pauli and Bohn Collections **25 30 20**

(F) Same as (D), but Type VI frame, punchings at one end but no round holes, Kotil Collection **20 25 15**

(G) Same as (E), but Type VI frame, Kotil Collection **25 30 20**

(H) Same as (E), but Type III frame, two Type IV brass brakewheels, four brass block lettered plates, copper journals and no oil label, Hoffman Collection **25 30 20**

LIONEL'S LARGER 0 GAUGE FREIGHTS: THE 800 and 2800 SERIES

We have already shown how the small counterpart to these cars, the 650 Series, had a complex history of development. This complexity even extends to speculation about different types of 650 cars produced from 1937-1942.

There is no such speculation about the larger series of 0 Gauge freight cars. The 800 series had some early color changes, but production remained fairly constant until the in-

Early 800 Series Freight

troduction of the manual box coupler in 1936, when the second series of these tinplate beauties appeared. In 1938, the 2800 series, with automatic magnetic couplers, made its debut and stayed pretty much the same until 1940. Then the 800 series with manual box couplers and the 2800 automatic coupler series received new paint, "deep dish" frames, and new trucks, Type III G-m-low for the manual 800, and the solenoid-equipped Type III G-s-low for the 2800. Both trucks have a long shank with a full 1/4" rise to allow the box coupler with the simulated lift pins to couple with earlier, higher couplers. Later 1941 Type III-G-s box couplers without the simulated lift pin appear on some late production sets. This same box coupler may have been used on some late production cars of the 800 series, and we number the manual coupler variety Type III-G-m, but we cannot at the moment give an example.

INTRODUCTION TO LIONEL'S 810 SERIES LARGE CLASSIC 0 GAUGE FREIGHT CARS

Lionel's first three large series 0 Gauge freight cars (820 Box Car, 820 Cattle Car, 822 Caboose) were never revised as were their smaller cousins in the 800 series. Instead, in 1926, Lionel introduced six new cars, displaying "this marvelous new series" on page 33 of the catalogue. "Our aim," Lionel modestly announced, "has been to express the individuality of every type of commercial freight car used on all railroads." All six cars sported heavy sheet steel frames with simulated truss rods. On real cars, those rods could be adjusted to keep wooden underframes from sagging. They also distributed the shock of hard couplings and the strains encountered in freight trains between the heavy wooden buffer at each end, sparing the underframe. Lionel's new trucks featured realistic journals and two simulated springs on each side. Few of these six cars (811 Flat Car, 812 Gondola, 813 Cattle Car, 814 Box Car, 815 Oil Car, 817 Caboose) were actually made in their catalogued colors. In addition to their display page, they were catalogued in one set (Outfit 299): 254 Milwaukee Road Olympian (or "bi-polar") electric locomotive, 814 Box Car, 813 Cattle Car, and 817 Caboose. Paging through Lionel's 1926 catalogue, one notices that these new cars seem to be replicas of Lionel's big 200 series Standard Gauge cars. Eventually, the 810 Crane, the 814R Refrigerator Car ("Reefer" for short), 816 Coal Car, and 820 Floodlight Car would round out this series.

Lionel lost no time. The 816 Coal Car arrived in 1927, catalogued in dark gray but made in olive green. In 1929, the 816 came in red, and the 814R Reefer arrived. The big, burly 810 Derrick rolled ponderously into view in 1930, operated manually via three knurled nickel handles and machine-cut gears. Taking its cue from the Standard Gauge 219 Derrick, 810 was illustrated with a brass handle, but it did not come that way. Finally, in 1931, the 820 Floodlight Car brought this early series to a bright conclusion with its twin brass searchlights. Strong evidence for the Standard Gauge roots of this series is the fact that Lionel used the same base for 820 and 220/520 Standard Gauge Floodlight Cars. The catalogue reported different lamps, though. The 820 uses 27 lamps; the 220/520, 28 lamps. Colors changed in 1935.

More extensive changes came in 1936 with Lionel's new manual box coupler. Throughout the series, frames were modified to accommodate the box coupler's long swivel shank. In view of these pronounced alterations, many collectors consider these "middle frame" cars a separate collectible series. In 1938, these manual box couplers were changed to automatic box couplers and the 2800 series was launched. Keeping an eye on sales appeal, Lionel designed its box couplers to mate with latch couplers on older cars. That meant that customers didn't have to buy whole new outfits. They could add these new cars to their rosters right away.

In 1939-40, the colors of both the 810 and 2810 series changed, adding totally new paint schemes. In 1940, new couplers were designed along with more frame changes. And in 1941, the coupler simulated lift pins were removed. There are three major collectible series and, in the view of many collectors, eight different series, as follows:

(1) 1926, short wheel base, early colors, nickel journals, latch couplers

(2) Later 1926, same as (1), except longer wheelbase

(3) 1928, same frame as later 1926, except new colors, nickel journals, latch couplers

(4) 1931, same frame as later 1926, same colors as 1928, except copper journals

(5) 1935, same frame as later 1926, same colors as 1928, except latch couplers

(6) 1936, new frame, new colors, nickel journals, box couplers

(7) 1940, late frame, late colors, nickel plates, nickel trim, box couplers

(8) 1941, late frame, late colors, decals, black trim including journals, box couplers

810 SERIES FREIGHT CAR FRAMES

TYPE I: Early 1926 only, painted semi-gloss black with two 7/32" diameter truck mounting holes, which are 1-5/8" from the ends and only 5-1/2" from each other, the frame is 8-13/16" long and has no depressions, two semi-circular slots for truck tabs, two 3/4" end slots, two slotted holes for fastening latch couplers.

TYPE II: Late 1926-35, usually painted semi-gloss black with two 7/32" diameter truck mounting holes which are 5-1/2" from each other, the frame is 8-13/16" long and has no depressions, two semi-circular slots for truck tabs, two 1-1/4" end slots, two slotted holes for fastening latch couplers.

TYPE III: 1936-39, painted semi-gloss black, two quarter-sized truck depressions each having two 7/32" truck mounting holes which are 1-5/8" from the ends and 5-1/2" from each other, the frame is 8-13/16" long. Two 3/16" diameter holes near center, two small elliptical holes near ends for mounting 1936 box couplers, slotted holes for fastening latch couplers are gone, two 1-1/4" end slots.

TYPE IV: 1940-42, painted various colors, two deep dish depressions containing two 7/32" diameter truck mounting holes, which are 1-1/8" from the ends and 6-1/2" from each other. These are considerably closer to the end than are previous styles. The frame is 8-13/16" long, 1-1/4" end openings (not slots), two 3/16" holes near center.

810 SERIES BOX COUPLERS

1936 style with two top ridges:

1940 style with simulated knuckle and lift pin:

1941 style with simulated knuckle, but no lift pin:

810 Crane

(A) 1930, terra-cotta cab, maroon roof, peacock boom, two nickel side frames on control mechanisms, brass hooks, black lead weight ball, brass pulley (same as Standard Gauge 219 Derrick hook), stem of hook passes through lead weight and is riveted to nickel pulley bracket, bracket riveted through center of pulley, two cream painted windows, two brass doors, four brass handrails, two brass plates on back of cab with black block lettering, upper plate, "LIFTING CAPACITY/10 TONS" with a line of space between data, on right, three times larger "No. 810", lower plate "MADE BY/THE LIONEL CORPORATION/NEW YORK" (Lionel Corporation in much lar-

Later 800/2800 Series Freights

ger lettering than other two lines), two nickel handles protrude from back of cab, third handle beneath cab, handles fastened by small nickel bolts (following the Standard Gauge 219 Derrick, the catalogue shows a brass handle, but 810 was not made that way), each handle fastened to large nickel shaft, bottom shaft extends through nickel stanchion and through "tunnel" in frame near center, shaft turns brass worm gear and rotates cab, maroon housing hides gear and secures cab to frame, two nickel plates hold boom and hook mechanism, one brass worm gear there, other gears black, Type II frame (frame, truck, and label definitions page 5), latch couplers, track clamp swings on large nickel rod riveted to frame (large nickel bolt tightens to track to support derrick as it lifts heavy objects), small spring-loaded clip keeps track clamp tucked underneath frame when not in use, clip secured to frame by small eyelet rivet, cab secured through hole in center of frame by nickel nut, brass washer(s), and large bolt inside cab, black Type V-B trucks, and nickel wheels on thick nickel axles, each truck is secured by a brass cotter pin and a brass washer mounted through a small hole in the brass truck stud, nickel journals, Pauli and Koff Collections **50 80 30**

(B) 1931, same as (A), except two brass windows and copper journals **50 80 30**

(C) 1934, same as (B), except (possibly) three brass handles (confirmation requested) **NRS**

(D) Early 1935, cream cab, vermilion roof, light green boom (matches base of 45N Automatic Watchman), nickel windows and doors, four nickel handrails on cab sides, two nickel plates on back of cab, lettering same as (A), except "N" in "No. 810" changed to serif "N", housing that secured cab to frame painted cream to match cab, middle period colors. (We need additional sightings to confirm the originality of this combination.) **50 80 30**

(E) Late 1935, same as (D), but with three black cast knobs fastened with three small black bolts **50 80 30**

(F) 1936, same as (D), but with three black finished die-cast knobs each fastened by a small nickel bolt, Type III frame with larger round hole on one end for dummy coupler shank (on 810 and 2810 Derricks only), black Type VI-A truck and Type VI-As truck's (see frame truck and label definitions), nickel journals, nickel wheels, thick nickel axles, 1936 box couplers, Type VI-As truck has long shank that connects with coupler shank via a stud and circular clip, Type VI-A truck has no shank, since a shank would foul the lowest knob on certain curves and derail the derrick, coupler shank fastened to frame by stud and circular clip. Later derricks have a cut in the side of the shank near the coupler to clear the knob on curves, Koff Collection **50 80 45**

(G) 1937, same as (F), except one Type VI-Bd truck and another Type VI-B truck with U-shaped bolster, Pauli Collection **50 80 30**

Note: A slight possibility exists that there may be an 810 Derrick similar to (D), or in late colors, with or without plates, and with late or 1936-type trucks and box couplers. Reader comments invited.

Note: Die-cast gears, like die-cast frames and bodies, tend to expand, warp, and crack. Replacement gears are available. When purchasing an 810 Derrick, or any item with die-cast components, check carefully for minute cracks and improper gear mesh. Deteriorated die-cast parts cannot be repaired, since the warped, brittle metal will crack and crumble whenever any attempt is made to work on it.

811 Flat Car

(A) Late 1926, maroon painted Type II frame, latch couplers, eight brass stakes, single large wooden block scribed to simulate ten beams, two brass early two-piece large center brakewheels with two short brass rods on two nickel brakewheel stands mounted on left side at each end, black Type V-B trucks, gold rubber-stamped serif lettering "THE LIONEL LINES" across frame sides, gold rubber-stamped number "811" in block numerals on frame bottom near center, above number is Type III oil label, nickel wheels, thick nickel axles, nickel journals, Sattler, Edmunds, Kotil, and Pauli Collections **30 40 20**

(B) 1927, same as (A), except for Type II oil label, Koff Collection **30 40 20**

(C) 1925, same as (A), but brakewheel stands mounted on right sides, Type II oil labels, Koff Collection **20 40 20**

(D) 1931, same as (A), but late one-piece small center brass brakewheels, Type VI-A trucks (see frame truck and label types definitions) with flat bolsters, small underline added to number (811), no oil label, copper journals, Koff Collection **20 40 20**

(E) 1935, aluminum painted Type II frame, eight separate beams, eight nickel stakes, nickel one-piece small center brakewheels with short nickel rods on nickel brakewheel stands, Type V-B trucks each fastened by a cotter pin and a nickel washer, black rubber-stamped serif lettering "THE LIONEL LINES" across frame sides, "811" on frame bottom, no oil label, nickel latch couplers, nickel wheels, thick nickel axles, nickel journals **20 40 20**

(F) 1937, same as (C), except with Type III frame, Type VI-A trucks with flat bolsters and long shank extensions riveted with truck mounting studs, trucks mounted on frame with two nickel washers beneath two circular clips, truck shank extensions to long coupler shanks via two small studs and two circular clips, nickel wheels, thick nickel axles, nickel journals **15 35 15**

(G) 1938, same as (D), except the two nickel brakewheels are reversed (mounted on right side) on both ends because their holes and slots are punched in the wrong positions, Pauli and Koff Collections **20 45 20**

(H) Same as (A), but brass journals and nickel stakes, Kotil Collection **15 35 15**

812 Gondola

(A) 1926, mojave sides and ends, early two-piece large center brass brakewheels, two short brass rods, two brass stanchions, two brass plates on each side with block lettering, "LIONEL/LINES" on left (large "L" covers both lines and begins both words), "No. 812" on right, semi-gloss black painted Type II frame, latch couplers, four small holes near ends for brakewheel rods, though only two are used, black finished Type V-B trucks, each truck is secured by a cotter pin with a brass washer, Type II oil label. The car originally came with a set of six barrels (0209), but these usually are long gone, nickel wheels, thick nickel axles, nickel journals, Pauli Collection **35 55 20**

(B) 1926, same as (A), except Type I oil label for four-wheeled cars, Koff Collection **35 55 20**

(C) 1927, dark green sides and ends, block lettering on all four brass plates, Type II oil label, otherwise as (A), Koff Collection **35 55 20**

(D) 1927, same as (C), except Type III oil label, Koff Collection **35 55 20**

(E) 1928-29, same as (C), except small serif lettering on all four brass plates, later one-piece small center brass brakewheels, no oil label, Koff Collection **35 55 20**

(F) 1931-32, mojave sides and ends, as (A), except with copper journals, late one-piece small center brass brakewheels, no oil label **35 55 20**

(G) 1931-32, pea green sides and ends (matches 815 Tank Car), otherwise as (A) **35 45 20**

(H) 1931-33, same as (C), with dark green sides and ends, but with small serif lettering on all four brass plates, two late one-piece small center brass brakewheels, no oil label, black Type VI-A trucks, nickel wheels, thick nickel axles, copper journals; the observed car has four brass washers to tighten up loose trucks, Pauli and Koff Collections **35 55 20**

(I) 1931-33, Stephen Girard green sides and ends, otherwise as (H), except for washers; the observed car has tight trucks with no washers; washers may have been installed only as needed, depending on tight or loose trucks, Pauli Collection **20 45 20**

(J) 1931-33, apple green sides and ends, two one-piece small center brass brakewheels, serif lettering on all four brass plates, otherwise as (H), including black Type VI-A trucks, Type II frame, no oil label, copper journals, additional information requested **20 45 20**

(K) 1936, green sides and ends, a shade darker than 45N Automatic Watchman base (note: this is an unusual color which we have been unable to match), two nickel one-piece small center brakewheels with two short nickel rods on two nickel stanchions, two nickel plates on each side, as (A), but with small serif lettering instead of block lettering, semi-gloss black painted Type III frame, black Type VI-As trucks, 1936-style box couplers, nickel wheels, thick nickel axles, nickel journals; each truck is fastened by a floating stud connected with a circular clip with a small tab that extends through an elliptical frame hole, Pauli Collection **25 75 15**

(L) 1937, 45N light green sides and ends, each truck stud is secured by a circular clip and a nickel washer, otherwise as (K), Pauli and Koff Collections **20 45 20**

813 Cattle (Stock) Car

(A) 1926, orange body and doors, pea green roof and door guides, early large horizontal thin brass door handles, early two-piece large center brass

Last 800/2800 Series Freights

813 | 2817 | 814R | 2820 | 2814 | 2816 | 3814 | 2812

brakewheels with two long brass rods on four brass stanchions, brass ladder on each end, two brass plates on each side with small serif lettering, "LIONEL/LINES" on left (large "L" covers both lines and begins both words), "No. 813" on right, overscored, underscored, and encircled, Type II frame painted semi-gloss black, latch couplers, black Type V-B trucks, Type II oil label, nickel wheels, thick nickel axles, nickel journals, Pauli and Claxton Collections **30 75 20**

(B) 1927, same as (A), except late small vertical brass door handles and Type III oil label, Koff Collection **30 75 20**

(C) 1931, same as (A), except late small vertical brass door handles, late one-piece small center brass brakewheels, Type VI-A trucks, Type II oil label, copper journals, Koff and Sattler Collections **30 75 20**

(D) 1932, same as (A), except late small vertical brass door handles, late one-piece small center brass brakewheels, no oil label, copper journals, Pauli Collection **30 75 20**

(E) 1934, orange body and doors, maroon roof and door guides, late nickel door handles, two late one-piece small center nickel brakewheels with two long nickel rods on two nickel stanchions, and nickel ladder at each end, nickel plates on each side as (A), with black serif lettering, "No. 813" on oval plate on right, overscored and underscored "LIONEL/LINES" on left plate as (A), Type II frame, latch couplers, faked simply from A/B by changing roof from C and door guides and journals, of less value, BUYER BEWARE! **30 40 20**

(F) 1937, cream body and doors, maroon roof and door guides, two late nickel door handles, two late one-piece small center nickel brakewheels with two long nickel connecting rods on two nickel stanchions, nickel ladder at each end, two nickel plates on each side with black serif lettering as (E), number on right oval plate overscored, underscored and encircled as (A), Type III frame painted semi-gloss black, 1936 style box couplers, long shank extensions pass through end slots, small tabs through elliptical frame holes, two black Type VI-B trucks with bolsters, connection made by two floating studs and two circular retaining clips, nickel wheels, thick nickel axles, nickel journals, no oil sticker, Koff Collection **50 90 45**

(G) 1940, tuscan painted body, doors, roof, and door guides, late nickel door handles, one (or two) late one-piece small center nickel brakewheels, with one long nickel connecting rod, one nickel stanchion, nickel ladder at each end, white rubber-stamped serif lettering instead of plates, "LIONEL/LINES" on left, on right, overscored and underscored, "LL/813", Type III-M trucks, 1940 style box coupler, a long vertical uncoupling bar below back of the box, black wheels with nickel backs, thin nickel axles, black journals, very rare **NRS**

(H) 1941, same as (G), except for one (or two) black one-piece late small center brakewheels, with long black rods on one (or two) black stanchion(s) and probably a black ladder, very rare **NRS**

Note: We also have a report of a version with trucks mounted closer to the center of the car frame than usual. Further information is needed; reader comments requested.

814 Box Car

(A) 1926, cream body and doors, orange roof and door guides, two early large horizontal thin brass door handles, two early two-piece large center brass brakewheels with two long brass rods on four brass stanchions, brass ladder at each end, three plates on each side, one on left, two on right, "LIONEL/LINES" on left plate in black small serif lettering (large "L" covers both lines and begins both words), upper right plate "No. 814" on brass oval plate in black serif lettering, overscored, underscored, and encircled, lower right brass plate "AUTOMOBILE/FURNITURE" in black sans-serif lettering, Type II frame painted semi-gloss black, latch couplers, black Type V-B trucks, Type II oil label, nickel wheels, thick nickel axles and nickel journals **20 70 35**

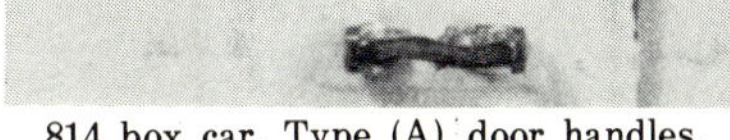

814 box car, Type (A) door handles.

(B) 1927, same as (A), except two late small vertical brass door handles, Pauli Collection **46 75 30**

(C) 1928, same as (A), except late small vertical brass door handles and Type III oil label, Koff Collection **35 75 30**

(D) 1929, same as (A), except late small vertical brass door handles, Type III oil label and copper journals, Pauli Collection **35 75 30**

(E) 1932, same as (A), except late small vertical brass door handles, late one-piece small center brass brakewheels each with long brass rod held on by two brass stanchions, brass ladder at each end, serif lettering on all plates (three on each side), Type VI-A trucks and copper journals, no rubber-stamped lettering, no oil label and nickel wheels on thick nickel axles, Pauli and Koff Collections **25 75 25**

814 Box Car Type (E) detail of door handle. Compare with (A)

(F) 1933, same as (E), but with pea green door guides **20 40 20**

(G) 1936, cream body and doors, maroon roof and door guides, colors of 813/2813 Cattle Car, nickel plates, large 1936-style box couplers, Sattler Collection **20 40 20**

(H) 1937, yellow body and doors, brown roof and door guides, nickel door handles, nickel plates with black serif lettering (three on each side) lettered as (A), late nickel brakewheels each with a nickel rod mounted with only one nickel stanchion, nickel ladder at each end, Type III frame painted semi-gloss black, 1936-style box couplers, Type VI-Bs trucks, eight nickel wheels with thick nickel axles (cf. 814R and 817). Note: Odd parts on this car suggest that it was part of a production run designed to use up excess inventory. At first, that would seem to be 1942, when Lionel was using any parts available to manufacture trains in the grip of wartime restrictions. We cite an earlier date (1937) because of this car's colors and nickel journals, Koff Collection **35 80 25**

(I) 1939, same as (H), but with standard parts, late one-piece small center nickel brakewheels each with a long nickel rod mounted by two nickel stanchions, semi-gloss black Type III frame as (H), black Type VI-As trucks, long coupler shanks have small tabs that fit elliptical frame holes, nickel wheels with nickel backs, thick nickel axles, nickel journals, no rubber-stamped lettering or oil label; one box coupler on this car has a shank for magnetic box couplers used on 2800-series cars! **30 75 25**

(J) 1940, orange body and doors, brown roof and door guides, late small black door handles, black one-piece small center brakewheels each with a long black rod fastened with a black stanchion, black ladder at each end, black rubber-stamped lettering instead of plates, "LIONEL/LINES/814" on left in large serif lettering, overscored and underscored, with three lines of reporting marks in small sans-serif lettering underneath, large double-circle Lionel "L" emblem on right with six lines of reporting marks underneath, Type IV frame, Type III-M trucks with 1940 manual box couplers, coupler boxes have simulated knuckles and lift pins plus long metal bar in back, 1/4" "high rise" shanks connect couples to trucks, black wheels, thin black axles and black journals **25 100 40**

(K) 1941, same to (J), but with nickel plates (three on each side) instead of rubber-stamped lettering, plates lettered as (A) **55 125 35**

(L) Same as (A), but blue door guides, Edmunds Collection **20 70 35**

(M) Same as (A), but larger early door handles mounted horizontally and Type I oil label, Claxton Collection **20 70 35**

814R Refrigerator Car ("Reefer")

Note: This is a scarce car, since it was not included in catalogued sets.

(A) 1929, ivory body, peacock roof, four doors on brass hinges, held closed by brass bar riveted to right door, early two-piece large center brass brakewheels each with a long brass rod mounted on two brass stanchions, brass ladder on each end, three brass plates on each side, as on 814 (A) box car, "LIONEL/LINES" on left plate in black small-serif lettering (large "L" covers both lines and begins both words), upper right plate "No. 814R" on oval plate in black serif lettering, overscored, underscored, and encircled, lower right plate, "VENTILATED/REFRIGERATOR" in black sans-serif lettering, Type II frame painted semi-gloss black, latch couplers, black Type V-B trucks, Type III oil label, nickel wheels, thick nickel axles and nickel journals, Pauli and Koff Collections **40 95 40**

(B) 1934 or 1935, white body and doors, light blue roof, either Type V-B trucks or Type VI-A trucks, nickel plates instead of brass plates, otherwise as (A) **55 120 50**

(C) 1936, same as (B), but with late one-piece small center nickel brakewheels each with a long nickel rod mounted by one nickel stanchion, nickel ladder on each end, six nickel plates (three on each side) lettered as (A) "VENTILATED/REFRIGERATOR" in serif instead of block lettering, nickel door hinges and nickel bar have replaced brass ones, Type III frame painted semi-gloss black, 1936-style box couplers with long shanks and small tabs that fit elliptical frame holes, nickel wheels with nickel backs, thick nickel axles and nickel journals, Pauli Collection **60 120 50**

(D) 1938, white body and doors, light blue roof, late one-piece small center nickel brakewheels each with a long nickel rod mounted by one nickel stanchion, nickel ladder at each end, black Type VI-Bs trucks with a long shank extension with a 1/4" hole, that hole fastened to 1936 box coupler's shank extension with a free-floating stud and a circular retaining clip, otherwise as (C), including six nickel plates (three on each side) with serif lettering, nickel door hinges and nickel bar, Type III frame painted aluminum, nickel journals, Koff Collection **60 130 35**

Note: Buyer Beware! If this price is rated too much above others, parts from those cars will be used to make this one. All it takes is a person who can paint and a "middle frame" car, about $25!

(E) 1940, flat white body and doors, brown roof, late black one-piece small center brakewheels each with a long black rod fastened by a black stanchion, black ladder at each end, eight small black door hinges and black bar have replaced nickel ones. No plates, instead, black rubber-stamped lettering in two pressed-in panels on each side, "LIONEL/LINES/814R" in serif lettering on left, overscored and underscored, with three lines of reporting marks in block lettering underneath, large double-circle Lionel "L" emblem on right, "VENTILATED/REFRIGERATOR" in serif lettering below "L", underneath that are three more lines of reporting marks in small black lettering, Type IV, black Type IIIH-m truck with 1940-style manual box couplers, black wheels, thin black axles and black journals; scarce, like other rubber-stamped cars in this series **200 500 60**

815 Tank Car

(A) 1926, pea green tank body and supports, large brass center dome, two smaller brass end domes, on each side there is a centered brass ladder connecting brass U-shaped handrails mounted by two brass stanchions, early two-piece large center brass brakewheels each with a short brass rod mounted by one nickel stand, two brass plates with black block lettering on each side of the tank body, "LIONEL/LINES" on left, "No. 815" on right, maroon painted Type II frame, black Type V-B trucks, nickel wheels, thick nickel axles and nickel journals, Type II oil label, Sattler Collection **35 75 25**

(B) 1927, same as (A), except Type II frame painted semi-gloss black, Koff Collection **35 75 25**

(C) 1927, same as (A), except brakewheels moved from left side of frame ends to right sides (for usual position, see photograph), black rubber-stamped data on oil label, "Nov 13 1927", Pauli Collection **35 75 25**

(D) 1931, same as (A), except copper journals **30 65 30**

(E) 1931, aluminum tank body and supports, large brass center dome, two smaller brass end domes, on each side there is a centered brass ladder connecting brass U-shaped handrails on four nickel stanchions, late one-piece small center brass brakewheels each with a short brass rod mounted on a nickel stand (on left side of frame ends, as usual), black serif lettering on all four brass plates (two on each side), semi-gloss black painted Type II frame with details as (A), black Type VI-A trucks, nickel wheels with nickel backs, thick nickel axles, copper journals, no oil label, Pauli, Sattler, and Koff Collections **25 55 25**

(F) 1932, same as (E), but with yellow "Sunoco" decal on both upper left sides, decal has horizontal red arrow pointing right, "GAS/SUNOCO/OILS" inside yellow diamond in black sans-serif lettering, "SUNOCO" larger than other two lines, Pauli Collection **35 75 25**

(G) 1936, aluminum tank body and supports, all nickel trim, domes, ladders, handrails, stanchions, plates with black serif lettering, as (E), late one-piece small center nickel brakewheels each with a short nickel rod on a nickel stand (on left side of frame ends, as usual), "Sunoco" decal, as (F), Type IIIK frame, nickel wheels with nickel backs, thick nickel axles and nickel journals. Pauli and Koff Collections **30 75 30**

(H) 1939, orange-yellow tank body and supports, "Sunoco" decal replaced with red "SHELL" decal in same position, all nickel trim and "middle frame", as (G), 1936-style manual box couplers, two Type VII trucks, nickel wheels with nickel backs, thick nickel axles and journals **35 75 35**

816 Coal Car

(A) 1927, olive green body, 1/2" wide bar across car top at center to brace sides, centered on one side is an early two-piece large center brass brakewheel connected to a long brass rod which opens and closes hopper chutes. The other end of the rod is held in place by a small brass retaining washer. Same style brakewheel and long rod, brass plates (two on each side) with block lettering "LIONEL/LINES" on upper left plate (large "L" covers both lines and begins both words), "No. 816" on upper right oval plate, "N" in small serif, numerals in block lettering, number overscored, underscored and encircled. Type II frame in two parts to accommodate hopper bins, Type V-B trucks and nickel wheels with nickel backs, thick nickel axles and thick nickel journals, Pauli and Koff Collections; Note: both truck tab slots are reversed from other Type II frame; they are punched toward the ends instead of the center. **40 90 35**

(B) 1931-34, red body, black serif lettering on upper right oval brass plate, otherwise as (A), Koff Collection **35 80 30**

(C) 1931-34, red body, black small serif lettering on upper left brass plate, otherwise as (A) **35 80 30**

(D) 1931-34, same as (C), except late one-piece small center brass brakewheels and hopper wheel, black Type VI-A trucks, nickel wheels with nickel backs, thick nickel axles and copper journals, Koff Collection **35 80 30**

(F) 1940, black body, black 1/2" wide bar across top of car at center to brace both long sides, late one-piece small center black brakewheels and hopper wheel, brakewheel rods, stanchions, ladders, no plates, instead white rubber-stamped lettering "LIONEL/LINES/816" on left in serif lettering, overscored and underscored, three lines of reporting marks underneath in block lettering, "NEW 9-40" in block lettering above left chute, black double-circle Lionel "L" with white background on upper right side, four lines of reporting marks in block lettering below "L", car classification (K4) below reporting marks in larger black lettering, two-piece Type IV frame, no room as (E), for unused 3/16" holes, Type III-G trucks, black wheels, thin black axles and black journals, rare **NRS**

(G) 1941, black body, brace, trim and Type IV frame, as (F), four nickel plates (two on each side of car) "LIONEL/LINES" on left plate, as (A), but in black small serif lettering, "No. 816" on right oval plate, as (A), one black Type III-G truck, as (F) and one Type III-H truck with 1941 box coupler, simulated lift pin omitted; probably made from parts inventory as World War II demands upon metal and other vital materials began to hinder toy train production **60 120 35**

817 Caboose. This car and its counterpart, the 2817, were never produced with lights, although its Ives and American Flyer equivalents were both lighted. The Lionel miniature train crew "sat in the dark", as it were.

(A) 1926, peacock body and cupola, dark green roof, two orange windows on each side, brass railing at each end with two translucent red simulated rear marker lights, "LIONEL LINES" on long brass center plate on both sides in black block lettering, overscored and underscored, "No. 817" on brass plate near bottom left corner in black block numerals, overscored and underscored, semi-gloss black painted Type II frame, latch couplers, black Type V-B trucks, Type III-1 oil label, no rubber-stamped lettering, nickel wheels with nickel backs, thick nickel axles and nickel journals, Pauli and Koff Collections **25 60 20**

(B) 1931, same as (A), but with copper journals, Koff Collection **25 60 20**

(C) 1932, same as (A), except two brass window inserts on each side, black serif lettering and numerals on brass plates (two on each side), black Type VI-A trucks, copper journals, no oil label or rubber-stamped lettering, Pauli Collection **25 60 25**

(D) 1933-34, red body and cupola, peacock roof, two brass window inserts (on each side), black serif lettering and numerals on brass plates (two on each side) lettered as (A), black Type VI-A trucks with copper journals, as (C), semi-gloss black painted Type II frame, as (A), no oil label or rubber-stamped lettering, Pauli and Koff Collections **40 85 30**

(E) 1935, light red body, roof and cupola, two nickel window inserts on each side, aluminum painted end railings with two translucent red simulated rear marker lights, black serif lettering on brass plates lettered as (A), semi-gloss black painted Type II as (A), black Type VI-A trucks, as (C), or two black Type VI-B trucks. Both types have triangular side frame openings and a long row of nine simulated rivets above their journals, nickel wheels with nickel backs, thick nickel axles and nickel journals **25 60 25**

(F) 1936, light red body, roof and cupola, two nickel window inserts on each side, aluminum painted end railings with two translucent red simulated rear marker lights, nickel plates (two on each side) with black serif lettering and numerals, lettered as (A), Type III frame painted semi-gloss black, black Type VI-B trucks, 1936-style manual box couplers, Pauli and Koff Collections **30 75 30**

(G) 1940-42, flat red body with matching end railings with two translucent red simulated rear marker lights at each end, brown roof and cupola, two white window inserts on each side, no plates, instead white rubber-stamped serif lettering "LIONEL LINES" in lower center panel of both long sides, "817" centered underneath, "UNITED STATES/SAFETY APPLIANCES/STANDARD" in lower left corner in white block lettering, Type N frame, 1940-style manual box couplers; we need to confirm this car's details **45 100 40**

(H) Same as (D), but inside of main roof is peacock, indicating a possible factory repaint, Edmunds Collection **40 85 30**

820 Floodlight Car

(A) 1931, terra-cotta painted base mounted on black painted Type II frame, floodlights, brakewheel and railings fastened to base instead of frame, two brass floodlights with nickel yokes on black stands, each floodlight held in place by two nickel hex-head bolts at ends of yoke, each round glass lens held in place by brass retaining ring, each floodlight has rear handles, a raised top, a nickel reflector behind a large bulb (27) in a screw-base socket, bulb contact button soldered to single coated wire covered with black woven cloth, four long thin brass railings, two late one-piece small center brass brakewheels each with a short brass rod on a nickel stand on left side of end of base, base contains two quarter-sized depressions for aforementioned black floodlight stands, big semicircular slot in base for wafer switch handle, small center depression with raised plus sign, small hole for nickel bolt and washer that secures wafer switch, latch couplers, "THE LIONEL LINES" stamped on both sides of frame in gold serif lettering, "820" stamped in gold block lettering on bottom of frame near wafer switch, frame has handrail holes, large center opening for wafer switch, two holes for contact roller wires to floodlights, slots for base tabs, Type V-Br trucks, nickel wheels with nickel backs, thick nickel axles and copper journals, Koff and Edmunds Collections **40 85 35**

(B) 1931, same as (A), except brakewheels on right side of end of base, Koff Collection **40 85 35**

(C) 1932, same as (A), except black Type VI-A trucks, Pauli Collection **40 85 35**

(D) 1933, same as (A), except brass journals **40 85 35**

(E) 1935, 45N light green base, two nickel floodlights, lenses held in place by nickel retaining ring, four long thin nickel railings, two late one-piece small center nickel brakewheels, each with a short nickel rod on a nickel stand on left side of base end, semi-gloss black painted Type II frame as (A), but "820" stamped in gold serif lettering, black Type VI-Ar trucks, nickel wheels with nickel backs, thick nickel axles and nickel journals **35 75 30**

(F) Early 1936, light green base and nickel components as (E), but with Type III frame, 1936 style box couplers, black Type VI-Ars trucks, Koff Collection **32 90 45**

(G) 1936-39, same as (F), but with black Type VI-Br trucks, Pauli Collection **45 100 40**

(H) 1941-42, 45N, light green base without depressions for floodlight stands, stands now part of one-piece die-cast yokes with Phillips-head bolt at each end to hold two 92 gray die-cast floodlights from smaller 2620 Floodlight Car, each with two rear handles, an open raised area on top to allow heat to escape and a nickel reflector behind a large bulb (27) in a screw-base socket, each glass lens secured by round retaining spring, four long thin nickel railings, two late one-piece small center nickel brakewheels each with a short nickel rod on a nickel stand on right side of base end, Type IV frame, large center opening to provide clearance for wafer switch, Type III-H trucks with black wheels with nickel backs, four thin nickel axles, black journals, 1941-style box couplers, distinctive 1/4" "high rise" of coupler shank makes couplers compatible with box couplers and latch couplers on 810 Series cars **45 100 40**

THE 820 SERIES

Even before Lionel's 0 Gauge line made its formal debut in the 1915 consumer catalogue, the company introduced its first large series 0 Gauge freight cars, the 820 series, comprising three body types, a box car (820), a stock (or cattle) car (821), and a caboose (822). Over the years, Lionel catalogued several different box car paint schemes. The caboose was shown in brown and maroon. The stock car, catalogued in 1915 and 1916, was probably made with a black roof during its first year of production. Some collectors believe that the same is true of the box car. Those two cars shared the same frame, which had square ends and measured 7-1/4" long over its center line. The caboose had a frame of its own, measuring 7" over its center line. The four steps and the two railings at each end were formed from the frame. This frame also had an integral coupler pocket, since there was no place for an end slot. Unlike the other two cars, the caboose came with a black roof throughout its production. All three cars are gems of tinplate construction with inwardly embossed board ribs on box cars, inwardly embossed (early) and outwardly embossed (late) ribs on cabooses, and inwardly embossed ribs between the cut-out slats of the stock car. They are hard to find in good or better condition. (The stock car is especially scarce.)

The stock car has a most unusual history. First catalogued in 1915-16, it disappeared from the line for nine years, reappeared in 1925-26 and then disappeared again, never to return. Some people believe that although catalogued in 1915-16, it was not made.

820 Box Cars

We have detailed observations of one early and three late 820 box cars, and sketchy information about a very rare 820 box car. We need more detailed information about early pre-1918 production and hope that our readers with such pieces will assist us by describing their pieces in detail, or better yet, send photos along with their descriptions.

Pre-1918 cars may be identified by the embossing "LIONEL MFG. CO." on the floor underside. However, it is possible that early cars are not embossed. We do not know. The following design elements also likely differ from those reported in the cars that follow:

1. Body color
2. Roof color
3. Door color
4. Actual lettering (show capitalization and lower case letters)
5. Style of lettering - block, script, heavy or light, with serifs or without serifs
6. Location of lettering - left of door, right of door, end, underframe, height
7. Coupler type - hook with nibs, straight long hook with no nibs, straight short hook
8. Coupler mounting procedure - slot through car floor with twist on coupler shank end, hole through coupler end and rivet or cotter pin
9. Presence (absence) of coupler support bar - how the coupler support bar was made - soldered in position
10. Door runner type - made from pressing in part of side and part of frame, separate piece soldered in position, location inside or outside
11. Frame type - length, end slots for couplers, distance of truck holes from frame end, separate truss rods soldered to frame, embossing on bottom, presence or absence of truck guide holes
12. Truck type
13. Presence of trim - brakewheels, ladders, door handles

820 Box Car

(A-E) Reserved for future listings

(F) ILLINOIS CENTRAL, probably pre-1918, orange-yellow painted body, roof and door, small maroon painted door handles formed from the doors, orange painted center spreader bar about 3/8" wide under roof, the eleventh rib on each side frames the door, black rubber-stamped "ILLINOIS CENTRAL RAILROAD" to the left of the door. The lettering is part of a complex herald consisting of a large diamond in front of a double circle. The large diamond is divided into four smaller diamonds and each diamond contains one word, "CENTRAL/MISSISSIPPI/VALLEY/ROUTE", on the right side of the door in black Railroad Roman type is "65784" centered on the side. Beneath the number and shifted to the right in black sans-serif lettering is "CAPACITY 20000 LBS./WEIGHT 30000 LBS." The car is lettered "LIONEL/LINES/N.Y./MADE IN USA" and "No. 820" on one end only. There is no lettering or embossing on the underframe. The car has complicated one piece frame 7-3/16" long, and the center 5" of the frame has been cut and formed, so that the center section is pressed up to provide the bottom door runner. The frame ends have 1" long slots to retain the nickel finished hook couplers. There is a 5/8" long semi-circular slot for the truck retaining tab. There are also coupler retaining slots that hold the T end of the coupler. These are 9/16" from the car end. The center spreader bar is soldered on each side to 2-3/4" long runners which are actually extensions of the side top and hold the door in place. The trucks are as illustrated and have 11 rivets.

These trucks are the same general style as the trucks observed on the later 820s but differ in their consistent rivet placement and three rivets at "A". We believe this is the earliest 820 model yet seen by the panel. Sullens Collection **50 75 35**

(G) Same as (F), but lettering is "CAPACITY 50,000 LBS/WEIGHT 30,000 LBS.", "65784" lettering is 1/4" high, "No. 820" in serif numerals at one end of car on left, "LIONEL/LINES/N.Y./MADE IN U.S.A." on same end of car on right, 7-3/16" long frame, no stamping on bottom, Type IIA-I-A trucks, tabs holding body to frame are parallel to frame ends, Kotil Collection **50 75 35**

(H-L) Reserved for future listings

(M) ILLINOIS CENTRAL, 1924-25, dark orange body, doors, and roof, small maroon painted door handles formed from the doors, orange painted center spreader bar about 3/8" wide under roof, simulated ribs created by inward embossing, door guides formed from top of body side and from frame on the inside of the car, black rubber-stamped "ILLINOIS CENTRAL" herald. The herald consists of a large diamond in front of a double circle lettered "ILLINOIS CENTRAL RAILROAD". The large diamond is divided by an X into four smaller diamonds and each diamond contains one word, "CENTRAL/MISSISSIPPI/VALLEY/ROUTE". The car has black painted Type II-A-1 trucks with plain tops. On the right side of the door the car has block lettering "65784" "CAPACITY 20000 LBS./WEIGHT 10000 LBS." The car is numbered "820" at one end below the center and is gold rubber-stamped with serif lettering "MADE IN U.S.A./THE LIONEL CORPORATION/NEW YORK" on the frame underside. Black semi-gloss painted Type 820-1 frame with side embossings that simulate truss rods, the frame is deepest in the center and tapers upward towards the trucks, then toward each end it deepens to meet the folded-down ends. The ends each have 1" wide slots for nickel hook couplers which fasten to the frame through this slot. The center of the slot is approximately 5/8" from the end, Bohn Collection **35 50 25**

(N) Same as (M), but frame not slit, Type IIA-I-A trucks, hook couplers with ears, "65784" numbers in slanted serif numerals 3/16" high, tabs holding body to frame are parallel to frame sides, Kotil Collection **35 50 25**

(O-R) Reserved for future listings

(S) UNION PACIFIC, orange painted body, doors and roof, inwardly embossed ribs, ten on each side of door, original doors missing, interior door guides formed from extension of the body side tops to form a top runner 2-3/4" long and on the bottom by a ridge 5" long pressed up from the base. The car has 3/8" wide orange painted center spreader bar supporting the roof. Viewed from the side, the frame is deepest in the center and tapers upward towards the truck. Then towards each end it deepens to meet the folded down ends. The ends each have 1" wide slots for nickel hook couplers. The hook couplers fasten to the frame through a slot about 9/16" from the frame end. We have studied the car lettering on both sides and believe that all the lettering on each side was produced by one rubber-stamp because the spacing of the letters is constant. The car is lettered "UNION/PACIFIC" in black serif type on the left side of the door with "820" shifted towards the left. To the right of the door is "65784" in italicized black serif numerals. Beneath the number and shifted slightly to the right is "CAPACITY 20000 LBS./WEIGHT 10000 LBS." The car has no end lettering or numbering. It is, however, gold rubber-stamped "MADE IN U.S.A./THE LIONEL CORPORATION/NEW YORK". The trucks are mounted in 1/8" diameter holes approximately 1-5/8" from the ends. The car has semi-circular slots towards each end to guide the truck tabs, Bohn Collection **35 50 25**

(T) Reserved for future listing

(U) UNION PACIFIC, circa 1925-26, orange painted body, doors and roof (orange roof resembles 250 Hiawatha orange), body orange is darker than roof orange. The car has inwardly embossed ribs, maroon painted small door handles formed from the doors, interior door guides formed from body and frame. The car has an 3/5" wide orange painted center spreader bar supporting the roof. The Type 820-1 frame is painted semi-gloss black with side embossings that simulate truss rods. The frame is deepest in the center and tapers upward towards the trucks. Then towards each end it deepens to meet the folded down ends. The ends each have 1" wide slots for nickel hook couplers. The hook coupler fastens to the frame through a slot about 5/8" from the frame end. The car is lettered "UNION PACIFIC" in black serif type on the left side of the door. Also on the left one line below "PACIFIC" is the number "820" shifted towards the left. The car is numbered "65784" in black serif type on the right side of the door centered on the side. Beneath the number and towards the right is "CAPACITY 20000 LBS./WEIGHT 10000 LBS" in black sans-serif lettering. There is no end lettering. The frame underside has gold rubber-stamped serif lettering, "MADE IN U.S.A./THE LIONEL CORPORATION/NEW YORK". The frame has a 1/8" diameter hole toward each end for the truck mounting screw; it also has semi-circular slots towards each end to guide the truck tabs. The observed sample had two Type II truck varieties, one Type II-A-3 unpainted truck with two small slotted unused depressions on bolster, and one Type II-A-4 truck with a nickel insulator bracket fastened in the two slotted depressions. This bracket accommodated black fiber insulation, which in turn held the third rail roller. The truck runs on nickel wheels on thick nickel axles. At first glance this car appeared to have maroon lettering. A better look revealed that it is actually faded black lettering, Pauli Collection **35 50 25**

(V) Same as (U), but load data lettering centered on right side, "LIONEL CORPORATION" not rubber-stamped on frame underside, two Type II-A-3 trucks, Koff Collection **35 50 25**

(W) Same as (S), but on left side of door "UNION/PACIFIC" only, on the right side of the door is 65784 and below and slightly to the right starting between the 6 and the 5 is "CAPACITY 20000 LBS./WEIGHT 10000 LBS", black rubber stamped on one end only "820" and gold rubber-stamped on underside "MADE IN U.S.A./THE LIONEL CORPORATION/NEW YORK"; these cars are numbered either on their sides or their ends, but not both, as far as is known, Sullens Collection **35 50 25**

In **LIONEL: STANDARD OF THE WORLD**, p. 37 a dark olive green 820 box is shown. The text indicates ATSF and 48522 lettering. We would like to provide a more complete description of this car. The following elements should be considered:

1. Actual lettering
2. Lettering style
3. Lettering location
4. Coupler type
5. Coupler mounting procedure
6. Coupler support bar - presence or absence, construction technique
7. Door runner type - how made, and location, inside or outside
8. Frame length, location of truck holes, presence or absence of truck guide holes
9. Truck type

821 Stock Car, so far reported only as late period (1925-26) production. We do not have any detailed reports on the early 1915-16 cars. The explanation may be simple; although catalogued, these cars were not produced. However, it is possible that these cars were made, but in very small numbers. If early period (1915-16) 821 cars exist, they may have floor embossing that reads "LIONEL MFG CO." Embossing, if present, would provide unambiguous identification. If early 821 cars exist, they may have distinctive lettering style, content and location, coupler type and mountings, truck types and even slot punchings. The earliest 820 box that we have seen, 820(F), has a distinctive frame and lettering. For a check list of characteristics, please see the immediately preceding section on 820 box cars. We look forward to reader reports.

(A-F) Reserved for future listings

(G) 1925-26, olive green sides, doors and roof, nine punched out vertical slots on each side of the door. Each slot is interrupted by a small center piece that is not punched out. The car has sans-serif black rubber-stamped lettering "UNION/STOCK/LINES" on the door with raised handle on each door, rubber-stamped "MADE IN U.S.A./THE LIONEL COR-

PORATION/NEW YORK" on bottom, no embossing, "821" on center of each end, hook couplers with ears are fastened by inside twist around 1" frame slot, no trim or brakewheels, Kotil Collection **16 35 15**

(H) Same as (G), but pea green sides, doors and roof, Bohn Collection **16 25 15**

(I) Same as (G), but medium green body and ends, orange roof, probable factory repaint or swap, "UNION/STOCK/LINES" in sans-serif lettering, no slits in frame for couplers, four end tabs parallel to frame ends and two center tabs parallel to frame sides, Type II-A-3 trucks, Kotil Collection **16 25 15**

(J) Maroon painted sides, doors and roof, black block style rubber-stamped door lettering "UNION/STOCK/LINES", black block numerals centered on one end "821". We need more information on this car. Please consult our checklist in the 820 section.

Note: Lionel had a design or manufacturing problem involving the axle nibs. The nibs were formed too far inward, allowing the wheels to fall down inside the rail. Lionel solved the problem by installing a small nickel washer behind each wheel to take up the extra space. Very difficult to find, Bohn comment **NRS**

822 Caboose. We have only observed one example of early production for this car. Reader comments on other examples are needed.

(A) 1913-15, brown painted body, cupola, and small cupola roof, semi-gloss black painted main roof, body sides with inward ribbing, two arched window cut-outs with embossed frames, centered between windows is black rubber stamped fancy serif lettering within a black stamped double oval lettered in three lines, "NEW YORK/CENTRAL LINES", with a very fancy "C", on one end in small black serif lettering to the left of door is "822" and to right of same door in four lines of very small black block lettering is "LIONEL/LINES/N.Y./MADE IN U.S.A." The last line is in extremely small lettering; ends have stamped door frames with cut-outs for windows, special stamped caboose frame, Type 822-2 (as opposed to Type 820-1 on other cars) painted semi-gloss black, with four step simulations on corners, two upraised end railing simulations, two coupler pockets pressed downward from frame to hold two early type hook couplers from falling onto third rail, two slotted holes to fasten coupler ends, and embossed rod simulations on sides, no lettering on bottom of frame, two Type II-A-1A trucks painted flat black with plain tops at bolster bars and without slots and depressions, each truck is fastened by a nickel bolt through a hole in frame, each truck has four nickel wheels with nickel backs on two thick nickel axles, Pauli Collection **40 55 25**

(B-F) Reserved for future listings

(G) Maroon painted body, cupola, and cupola roof, black painted roof, black double oval New York Central herald with black serif lettering "NEW YORK/CENTRAL/LINES" inside of the herald. The car is numbered "822" on the lower right corner of each side. Each end has a raised light area. The caboose frame is different from that used for the box and stock cars and has simulated steps at the corners, solid end railings and end coupler retainers. The retainers keep the nickel finished hook couplers from touching the center rail. The body has 27 embossed outward ribs, arched windows with embossed window frames and embossed end doors with small window in door. The side cupola windows are punched out. The cupola roof is formed from a separate piece of sheet metal. The car is rubber-stamped in bronze lettering, "MADE IN U.S.A./THE LIONEL CORPORATION/NEW YORK" on the frame underside. The car has one Type IIA-1 truck and one Type IIA-3 truck with nickel wheels riding on thick nickel axles, Bohn and Sullens Collections **35 50 25**

(H) Same as (G), but brown-maroon color, "822" stamped only on one end to the right of the door in serif lettering, two black painted Type IIA-1A trucks, Koff Collection (2 samples observed) **35 50 25**

(I) Same as (G), but two Type I-A trucks, Bohn Collection **35 50 25**

(J) Same as (G), but 25 vertical ribs embossed inward, red-brown body, "822" rubber-stamped in black 5/32" numbers at left of one end and "LIONEL/LINES/N.Y./MADE IN U.S.A.", rubber-stamped at right on same end, no stamping on bottom, Type IIA-I-A trucks, heavy crudely-flanged wheels, trucks mount 1-13/16" from frame ends, Kotil Collection **35 50 25**

(K) Same as (G), but "822" is 3/16" high, rubber-stamped on bottom in letters 2-1/8" long "MADE IN U.S.A./THE LIONEL CORPORATION/NEW YORK", later small folded frame, trucks mount 1-7/8" from end of frame, Kotil Collection **35 50 25**

(L) Same as (G), but one end stamped "822" only on right of car end, no four-line "Lionel Lines" stamping, rubber-stamped on bottom as in (K), but this lettering only 1-7/8" wide, trucks mount 1-7/16" from end of frame, Kotil Collection **35 50 25**

(M-R) Reserved for future listings

(S) 1926, maroon painted body, cupola, and small cupola roof, semi-gloss black painted main roof, body sides have outward ribbing, two arched window cut-outs with embossed frames; centered between windows is black rubber stamped fancy serif lettering within a black stamped double oval lettered on three lines, "NEW YORK/CENTRAL/LINES", with a very fancy "C", "822" in black rubber-stamped lettering on bottom right corners, ends have stamped door frames with cut-outs for windows, special stamped caboose frame Type 822-2, as opposed to Type 820-1 on other cars, painted semi-gloss black, with four step simulations on corners, two upraised end railing simulations, two coupler pockets pressed downward from frame to hold two early type nickel hook couplers from falling onto third rail, two slotted holes to fasten coupler ends, and embossed rod simulations on sides, lettering on bottom of frame appears yellow, may be discolored gold, "MADE IN U.S.A./THE LIONEL CORPORATION/NEW YORK", in three lines of serif lettering, two Type II-A-3 trucks, probably chemically blackened, with two small slotted depressions at top of each bolster bar intended for third rail roller insulation holding brackets, each truck is fastened by a nickel bolt through a hole in frame and has four nickel wheels with nickel backs on two thick nickel axles, Pauli Collection **40 55 25**

(T) 1920, same as (S), but body, cupola, and small cupola roof painted brown-maroon or very dark maroon, lettering identical except for car number "822" found only on one end in black serifs on right side of door, trucks are different and earlier Type II-A painted black with plain bolster bars, Koff Collection (2 cars observed) **35 50 25**

(U) 1925, same as (S), but gold rubber-stamped lettering in fancy serifs centered between windows on car sides, with gold "822" on bottom right hand corners of both sides, Koff Collection **35 50 25**

831 Flat Car, see second generation 800 Series

900 Ammunition Car, see early 800 Series

901 Gondola, see early 800 Series

902 Gondola, see second generation 800 Series

INTRODUCTION TO LIONEL LITHOGRAPHED FREIGHT CARS: THE RISE AND FALL OF THE IVES CORPORATION

In the 19th century, when railroads were beginning to pick up steam, so to speak, toy companies started to offer their own versions of the new-fangled, fascinating, fire-breathing machines that were huffing, whistling, hissing, and thundering across America. Early toys, like the engines they modeled, were crude. But as time passed and people became more familiar with trains, they preferred toys with more realistic detail. That presented a problem for manufacturers. It was hard enough to make a toy that even vaguely resembled a steam locomotive. The long, round boiler, the flaring stack, domes, cab, headlight, driving wheels - all of that required extra steps in production. Adding complex piping and still other detail would have priced such an intricate engine out of the market. Yet customers wanted detail, and any toy that could provide it would have a competitive edge.

Faced with this dilemma, toymakers devised an ingenious solution. They printed details on sheets of paper and pasted those sheets on their toys. A bare, rectangular piece of wood could become a passenger car, gaily colored, with people in the windows. Engineers and firemen could peer from the cabs of their engines, with a tantalizing glimpse of wonderfully complex levers, gauges, and valves visible through the cab windows. This method worked so well that it persisted even after crude wooden floor toys gave way to metal trains that rolled on tracks, propelled by sturdy clockwork motors or by that mysterious new force, electricity.

Manufacturers soon discovered that a more permanent process was necessary. Glue didn't adhere as well to smooth metal surfaces. It discolored the paper, and the paper flaked off or curled up easily. One company, the Ives Corporation of Bridgeport, Connecticut, began to use lithography during the first years of this century. Windows, doors, rivets, and other details were engraved on a metal plate, then printed on the sides and tops of locomotives and cars. The effect was quite striking, and Ives refined the technique. During the next twenty years, Ives would produce some of the world's finest model railroad lithography.

Unfortunately, World War I took its toll on Ives. Located in Bridgeport, Connecticut, away from big shipping centers, Ives' factory could not get enough raw material to produce its toys, including its trains. Furthermore, even though some toys were made, it was next to impossible to ship them to customers. Although Ives resumed production after the war, its cash reserves had been drained. In 1928, the firm declared bankruptcy, and it was sold at auction to raise funds to pay its debts.

Not surprisingly, this attracted the attention of Ives' two biggest competitors. Joshua Lionel Cowen of the Lionel Toy Corporation in New York City conferred with William O. Coleman of American Flyer in Chicago. Also reportedly in on the deal was A. C. Gilbert, head of the firm that manufactured Erector Sets and director of a Connecticut bank. A. C. Gilbert would become famous as the president of American Flyer, but that was still ten years into the future. In the corporate maneuvers surrounding the Ives auction, A. C. Gilbert served as a silent partner. When the auction was over, Ives lay in the hands of its archrivals. A thorough account of these proceedings has been published by Tom McComas and James Tuohy in Volume I of their series, **LIONEL: A COLLECTOR'S GUIDE AND HISTORY TO LIONEL TRAINS**, pages 63-66. They describe the aftermath of the auction in these poignant words:

"For a time Ives was jointly managed by Lionel and American Flyer, but in the fall of 1929 Joshua Cowen and W. O. Coleman held a business meeting. When it was over, Lionel was the sole owner of the Ives Corporation. A few days later, Harry Ives, who had been kept on as Ives' President after the auction, quietly gathered his belongings and walked out of his office. He never returned." (**LIONEL: A COLLECTOR'S GUIDE AND HISTORY, Volume I**, p. 65) *

From 1928 through 1930, Lionel and American Flyer kept Ives in business. They supplied trucks, bodies, and parts, so Ives trains from that era are a conglomeration of items from all three firms. That might have gone on for years, since profits from the Ives line went to its new owners. But the Depression forced a change. After W. O. Coleman withdrew, Joshua Cowen had all he could do trying to keep Lionel solvent. After the 1930 Ives line had been manufactured and shipped, the Bridgeport factory was closed (the building still stands today) and production moved to Lionel's factory in Irvington, New Jersey. Lionel offered Ives trains in 1931 and 1932 and published an Ives catalogue both years, but Lionel finished both years in the red. Its trains were priced too high for the times, yet Joshua Cowen refused to reduce cost by sacrificing quality. He did, however, reluctantly make use of Ives trains, transferring them to Lionel's catalogue.

The news arrived in Lionel's 1933 catalogue: "Lionel has bought the Ives Corporation." Ordinarily, that would be proclaimed in a banner headline. But it was printed without any fanfare, at the beginning of an illustrated list of new, inexpensive "Lionel-Ives" clockwork sets and electric sets. That name lasted only one year. In 1934, those trains were renamed "Lionel Jr."

That name change is interesting. It must have hurt Joshua Cowen to have seen his name on a low-priced line of train sets. He had prided himself on manufacturing top-notch, rugged, reliable trains. Even though a low-priced line was necessary to survive the Depression, it was a painful departure from traditional standards. The Lionel name belonged on big, burly bruisers like the twin-motor deluxe 408E and magnificent 21" long State cars, each six pounds of heavy sheet steel with brass window panels, full interior detailing, six-wheel trucks, and Lionel's renowned baked enamel finish. How could little low-priced sets live up to their Lionel lettering?

Having the Lionel name on those trains was unsettling enough. Adding Ives' name as well was still more jarring. Ives had been in business since 1868, 13 years before Joshua Lionel Cowen had even been born. Ives had built a commendable reputation with a variety of high-quality toys, especially its clockwork and electric trains. Even in its decline, Ives introduced legendary trains. The 1930 Ives catalogue, although published by Ives' new owner, Lionel, extols Ives' oil-less ball bearing electric motor and proclaims such mighty trains as Ives' NATIONAL LIMITED and the OLYMPIAN. On a little train set, Ives' name seemed just as much out of place as Lionel's. Renaming the line "Lionel Jr." softened the blow and restored a measure of dignity to both names.

There is a little landmark about those sets, though. After the stock market crash in 1929, Lionel had seen the need for a low-priced line. In 1930, the company published a flyer announcing the Winner Line, "for little brother", a group of seven sets. Four were headed by Ives clockwork steam locomotives; the other three, with electric-style engines. The Winner Line returned in 1932, in a four-page insert that came with the Lionel catalogue. But not until 1933, when their name was changed to "Lionel-Ives", were they deemed worthy to appear in the catalogue itself. That shows at least some respect for the Ives name. Indeed, Ives' influence did not end there. Supposedly, one stipulation of the takeover agreement was that the Ives name would always appear on some items. Apparently, this did not mean that the name was to have high visibility. The last item with the Ives name was the lowly 027 track clip!

Ives had been a leader in lithography, and Lionel made use of that throughout the Depression. It was far cheaper to print details on locomotives and cars than it would have been to add handrails, window frames, and other intricate parts by hand or even by machines. These little lithographed trains were small, but families could afford them. Tens of thousands of children were able to enjoy model railroading. They could speed along with passenger trains or lug freight through imaginary mountains. So popular were these trains that they became a permanent division on the Lionel Lines. In 1937, these sets were grouped as the 027 series. They ran on a light 027 Gauge track that formed a circle only 27" in diameter - perfect for smaller houses and apartments. This new lighter 3-rail track was adapted from a 2-rail track made for mechanically-operated trains.

*Also see **GREENBERG'S GUIDE TO IVES** by A. G. McDuffie (1984 publication)

They filled a need then, and new "027" sets have been offered each year to this day. *

Lionel's lithographed cars cover a wide range, from dinky four-wheelers to big uncatalogued cars, from realistic railroad cars to fanciful ones animated by Walt Disney's colorful cartoon characters. These spunky little trains provided a welcome, brightly colored gleam of fun and hope for many a family during the gloom of the Great Depression. Because of their light construction, the survival rate for these cars has been very low. Many "serious", somewhat stuffy collectors have raised an eyebrow in surprise at the increasing attention given to these cars as time takes its toll and they become more scarce and more desirable.

We will set criteria to describe the colors of these cars, though there are easier things to do in this world. The Train Collectors' Association (TCA) has compiled a color chart with standard descriptions so its members may at least attempt to agree when they describe the colors of their trains. Although the TCA chart does not attempt to cover the lithographed colors, we shall use TCA terms whenever possible throughout this section. The problem is that by this time, some of these lithographed cars have aged to a different shade of color. Furthermore, the same car can look different under different lighting conditions. But we shall highball bravely onward, using the following standards:

LAYMEN'S DESCRIPTIONS

Dark Blue
Medium Blue
Light Blue

TCA DESCRIPTIONS

Blue
Light Blue
Very Light Blue

Ives cars are not included in the four-wheel 1512 series; they are listed among the larger series.

Since lithographed cars, made by a special process, can be restored only with great difficulty, we have dropped that category from our prices here. The three prices listed apply to each item in good, very good, and excellent condition.

1512 Gondola

(A) 1933, blue sides and ends, lithographed ribs, rivets, and lettering, black block number (1512) inside orange rectangle on center of right side, "NEW YORK/CENTRAL/LINES" in white within black double oval, NYC herald on left side, "reporting marks" (capacity, load limit) across bottom above frame, frame painted semi-gloss black, extensively embossed with rivets, steps, indentations along middle of frame give the impression that steel beams support the car, two nickel late-style (Type II) round end hook couplers with oval ends, two raised sections under frame provide enough room for nickel wheels with nickel backs on two thin nickel axles, two lowered cutout sections of frame hold couplers supported by two 3/8" end slots, axles pass through frame sides, no journals, Bohn and Koff Collections **6 8 12**

(B) Circa 1936, same as (A), but very light blue sides and ends, color appears to be light green in fluorescent light, frame painted red, numbers in black sans-serif, black wheels with nickel backing, hook couplers with ears, "MADE IN U.S. OF AMERICA" embossed on bottom of frame, Koff, Bohn, and Kotil Collections **6 8 12**

(C) Circa 1937, same as (B), but red frame highlighted with gold; possible that frames were leftovers from Mickey Mouse production, Kotil comment **6 8 12**

(D) Circa 1931-32, same as (A), but Winner markings, probably across bottom above frame **6 8 12**

(E) Circa 1931-32, same as (D), but light blue **6 8 12**

1514 Box Car

(A) 1931-33, cream body, dark blue roof, orange doors and door guides, lithographed ribs and rivets, Erie herald on left side with "LIONEL" printed beneath herald in block lettering, "ERIE" inside black circle, circle surrounded by diamond, number (1514) inside gold rectangle near lower right corners, same frame, wheels, and couplers as 1512 Gondola (A). Door guides to left on one side and to right on other side **6 8 12**

(B) Same as (A), but gloss black frame, black oxide wheels with nickel backing, straight hook couplers, no "LIONEL" beneath Erie herald, brown doors and door guides match State car brown, Koff, Bohn, and Kotil Collections **6 9 15**

(C) 1934, same as (A), but orange roof **6 8 12**

(D) Circa 1931-32, same as (A), but "WINNER" instead of "LIONEL" road name **6 8 12**

(E) Same as (A), but light blue roof, tan doors and door guides, no "LIONEL" beneath Erie herald, Koff Collection **6 8 12**

(F) Same as (A), but blue roof, Erie herald and "LIONEL" on top left of one side and top right of other side, Baby Ruth Candy Bar advertising on opposite sides, lithographed ribs and rivets removed from center, orange rectangle with car number printed next to door, it can be covered when door is opened, "MADE IN/U.S./OF AMERICA" embossed on red painted frame, Bohn Collection **6 8 12**

1514 Box Car

(G) Same as (F), but brown doors and door guides match State car brown, Pauli and Kotil Collections **10 13 18**

(H) Same as (F), but terra cotta doors and door guides, Koff Collection **10 13 18**

(I) Same as (A), but black doors **7 9 13**

(J) Same as (F), but gold highlight on red frame **7 9 13**

(K) Same as (F), but black doors **7 9 13**

(L) Cream body, light blue roof with four embossed ribs, State car brown doors and guides, light red frame, "ERIE" inside black circle surrounded by diamond, "LIONEL" below "ERIE" logo and slightly to its right, "1514" inside gold rectangle on right, Baby Ruth litho on right, opposite side locations of these marks are reversed, door frames and doors over "ERIE" logo on both sides, late-style Type II hook couplers, Hoffman Collection **7 9 13**

(M) Same as (C), but "ERIE" and "BABY RUTH" reversed on opposite sides, Kotil Collection **7 9 13**

1515 Oil Tank Car

(A) 1933, aluminum body, lithographed rivets with "UNION TANK LINES, FUEL OIL", and number 1515 across tank, large center dome flanked by two smaller domes, two horizontal handrails, one along each side, two aluminum supports beneath body, same frame, wheels, and couplers as 1512 Gondola (A) **6 8 12**

(B) 1934, same as (A), but brass center dome, copper end domes and handrails, "SUNOCO" emblem at center of tank above handrail, "LIONEL LINES, MOTOR OIL", and number 1515 printed beneath handrail, Koff Collection **6 8 12**

(C) 1931-32, same as (B), but gloss black frame, hook coupler with ears, black wheels with nickel backing, no "LIONEL LINES", Bohn and Kotil Collections **6 8 12**

(D) 1931-32, same as (B), but "WINNER LINES" instead of "LIONEL LINES", Bohn Collection **6 8 12**

(E) Circa 1936, same as (B), but frame painted red, three nickel domes, hook couplers with ears, black wheels with nickel backing, two nickel handrails, Koff, Blackmar, Sattler, Kotil, and Bohn Collections **6 8 12**

(F) Circa 1937, same as (B), but gold highlight on red frame, nickel domes and handrails, blue Type B lithographed lettering; probable leftover Mickey Mouse circus frame production, Grams Collection **NRS**

---

*Except, of course, for 1943 and 1944, when no trains were produced.

1517 Caboose

(A) 1933, vermilion body, cream windows, end doors, and lettering, brown roof and cupola with red striping on cupola sides, "NEW YORK/ CENTRAL/LINES" in fancy serif lettering within double-oval NYC herald on side underneath off-center cupola, double rectangular number plates below herald, frame, wheels, and couplers as 1512 Gondola (A), Pauli, Bohn, Kotil, and Koff Collections **6 8 12**

(B) Same as (A), but "WINNER LINES" inside NYC herald **6 8 12**

(C) Same as (A), but light red roof and cupola, cream stripe on cupola, "LIONEL" printed beneath windows underneath cupola, "MADE IN U.S./OF AMERICA" embossed on bottom of red painted frame, Koff and Blackmar Collections **6 8 12**

(D) Same as (A), but light red roof and cupola, cream stripe on cupola, "LIONEL" printed beneath windows underneath cupola, "MADE IN U.S./OF AMERICA" embossed on bottom of red painted frame with gold highlights, Blackmar Collection **6 8 12**

(E) Same as (C), but "LIONEL" printed beneath windows opposite cupola, black nickel-backed wheels, one hook coupler with ears, Kotil Collection **6 8 12**

(G) Same as (A), but red roof and frame, Sattler and Kotil Collections **6 8 12**

THE MOUSE WITH THE ROAR OF A LION [EL]: THE MICKEY MOUSE SETS OF 1935

We have already described how, in 1934, Lionel had managed to pull itself out of its financial difficulties by offering the new streamlined Union Pacific M-10000 and its successors. Beautiful though the M-10000 was, the Great Depression had taught Lionel that something less expensive was needed, something that financially strapped families could afford. Perhaps inspired by a Walt Disney cartoon - "Mickey's Choo-Choo" Lionel designed a clockwork handcar with Mickey and Minnie pumping away. It could whip around its 27" circle of track ten times on a single winding. Although it was manufactured too late to be included in Lionel's 1934 catalogue, 253,000 were sold during that Christmas season. That was not enough to save the company on its own. Even if the entire retail price of $1.00 had been pure profit for Lionel, it would nevertheless have fallen $16,000 short of meeting Lionel's debts. But a folder packed with each handcar publicized Lionel's other trains, and the handcar's net profits - after deducting costs of manufacturing, shipping, and Disney's royalties - were welcome revenue in company coffers.

With the handcar's success, Lionel decided that Walt Disney's lovable little cartoon character could add "pizazz" to other clockwork sets. In 1935, Mickey received his own locomotive - a snappy red version (1508) of the New York Central's streamlined COMMODORE VANDERBILT, complete with a ringing bell, a handbrake, and a battery-powered headlight. Mickey stood right behind the engine, near the middle of an open red four-wheel Stoker Tender (1509), holding a coal scoop. Beneath him was a vertical rod. When that rod hit a special tie on a curved track section, it caused Mickey to bob back and forth as if he were shoveling coal. Mickey and his Commodore Vanderbilt engine headed a passenger set (1534) of two lithographed four-wheeled cars and a freight set (1533) with two lithographed four-wheeled freight cars, a tank and a caboose. For the traditional railroaders, Mickey also "fired" a red non-streamlined steam engine (1506) in a freight set (1532) comprised of a litho tank (1515) and a litho caboose (1517), which the catalogue claimed had sliding doors, but did not.

Of all these, the most expensive was the No. 1537 Passenger Outfit at $4.50. For that sum, a customer received a pair of switches and 16 track sections for a 35-1/2" x 44-1/2" layout complete with a grade crossing sign, a clock, a manually operated semaphore, 6 telegraph posts, and a station (1560) where passengers could board Mickey's passenger train, the Commodore Vanderbilt, Mickey's Stoker Tender, a Pullman (1811), an observation car (1812), and a baggage car (1813). The baggage car was available only in that outfit. The passenger set (1534) came with an observation car and two Pullmans instead of the baggage car. Now we come to the outfit that gets collectors excited. Like all these Mickey Mouse train sets, it was available only in 1935.

By far the gaudiest of Lionel's windup line was the Mickey Mouse Circus Train Outfit (1536, $2.00). A molded figure of Mickey, probably made of composition material, as a circus barker beckoned lucky owners into a gaily decorated Big Top, 20" long and 14" to the top of its flagpole. Also included were a gas station, a circus/Sunoco billboard, a "commissary auto" that looked more like a stake truck, and a picture of Mickey and Minnie rushing to see the show. All these accessories were printed on heavy cardboard and assembled by the owner. Hauled by Mickey's Commodore Vanderbilt, the circus train comprised three cars that resembled circus wagons. The dining car featured Mickey standing in one vestibule and Pluto sitting in the other. Between them, visible through three lithographed windows, Horace Horsecollar, Clarabelle Cow, and Minnie Mouse enjoyed a tasty meal. On the Band Car, wearing his maestro's uniform from his landmark color cartoon "The Band Concert," Mickey conducted his new, scrappy co-star, Donald Duck, and also the Three Little Pigs, with an imposing calliope between them. The final car, lettered MICKEY MOUSE CIRCUS, shows Minnie and Mickey tending animals in a cage. Perspective is somewhat lacking, though since the figures of Minnie and Mickey at each end are as large as the elephant in the center of the cage!

Beneath their colorful lithography, all three of these cars were identical, and none had numbers. For ready reference, we shall offer a brief description of each car and its value.

Circus Dining Car 1935, Mickey stands in one vestibule. Pluto sits in the other. Horsecollar, Clarabelle Cow, and Minnie Mouse, visible through three lithographed windows, enjoy a tasty meal. Red frame with gold indentations, two round end later-type hook couplers, four black wheels with nickel backs on two thin nickel axles attached to frame, same frame as 1512, 1514, 1515, 1517 series **35 50 75**

Mickey Mouse Band 1935, wearing his maestro's uniform from his landmark color cartoon, "The Band Concert", Mickey conducts his new, scrappy co-star, Donald Duck, and also the Three Little Pigs, with an imposing calliope in the center. Otherwise same as Circus Dining Car, Kotil Collection **35 50 75**

Mickey Mouse Circus 1935, Minnie at one end and Mickey at the other tend animals in a cage. Tigers prowl behind Minnie and chimps play behind Mickey. An elephant in the center is looking at Minnie, and no wonder. She and Mickey are as tall as the elephant! Otherwise same as Circus Dining Car **35 50 75**

INTRODUCTION TO LIONEL'S 1677-1682 LITHOGRAPHED SERIES

Our descriptions of Lionel's lithographed trains began with clockwork sets and their four-wheel cars, but it would be a mistake to assume that lithographed cars were forever consigned to the lowest, darkest, most disdained division of the Lionel Lines. Lithography, in Lionel's opinion, could not compare to the vaunted baked enamel finish relentlessly extolled in Lionel's catalogues, but it was far cheaper to print details using specially treated metal plates than it would have been to apply number plates, handrails, and other fine details by hand or by machine. Lithography enabled Lionel to manufacture good-looking, inexpensive trains that families, struggling in the grip of the Depression, could afford. In 1933, the lowest priced

Lionel-Ives clockwork set cost $1.50. For $5.75 and $7.50, customers could choose between three electric sets in the Lionel-Ives line. Lithographed cars for those trains were longer, more realistic, and rolled upon two four-wheel trucks. Although the smaller cars were last listed in Lionel's 1937 catalogue on page 46, the larger 1677-1682 series remained. In fact, they moved up in the world. In 1937, the Lionel Jr. name was dropped, and starter sets were displayed as "027" trains.

These eight-wheel lithographed cars were coupled to sleek black streamlined steamers, the 2-4-2 Commodore Vanderbilt (1689E) and the new four-wheel drive Pennsylvania "Torpedo" (1668E), which appeared in 1936. As the years rolled on, they turned up in other sets, and they even locked couplers with Lionel's enameled cars. Beginning in 1933, they were listed in every Lionel catalogue through 1942, the last catalogue of the prewar era.

Each of these cars can be found with two types of frames (Early and Late) and at least two colors. Colors, though, are open to discussion, since some differences are minor and others are caused by fading. The red gondola is easy to spot, but differences between its blue and light blue bodies are less obvious. Lettering could change as well, adding other variations. We shall list all the cars we have discovered, but we realize there may well be others. If you have one, please send us specific information. Cars with no journals are listed separately, since they were made for special orders and identified by an "X" printed in their boxes. Aggravating the situation, Lionel also applied an "X" to cabooses with two couplers and to other unusual cars like the 2812x Gondola with its low coupler height.

1677 IVES LITHOGRAPHED GONDOLA

TYPE I BODIES

(A) 1931-32, light blue sides and ends, simulated ribs and rivets, made by Lionel but lettered "IVES/R.R./LINES" in cream serif within black double oval on left side, number (1677) in black sans-serif lettering within dark cream-orange double oval on right, semi-gloss black painted early frame with embossed rivets, end steps and indentations, two 1/4" truck mounting holes, trucks secured by two eyelet rivets, two semicircular slots for truck tabs, two 5/8" end slots, two cut-out frame sections bent downward to accommodate two later-type nickel latch couplers with oval ends bent downward as retainers, two black Type III-A trucks with single ribs on bolsters, eight black wheels with nickel backs on four thin nickel axles, eight copper journals, Koff and Kotil Collections. We have listed this item because it is a Lionel product and shows the origin of this series. It is very difficult to find. **20 40 50**

(B) 1933-34, same as (A), but lettered "LIONEL/R.R./LINES", Koff Collection **20 40 50**

(C) Same as (A), but lettered "LIONEL/R.R./LINES" and nickel journals, Bohn and Sullens Collections **20 40 50**

(D) Same as (A), but lettered "LIONEL/R.R./LINES", no journals, numbered 1677X, this car is probably part of an uncatalogued set **5 10 15**

TYPE II BODIES

(E) 1939, dark red body, simulated ribs, rivets, and side panels, "LL (overscored serif lettering)/1677 (underscored serif lettering)/CU.FT.1848" (small block lettering) in first panel from left, "LIONEL" printed along both sides in large serif lettering, with one letter in each panel, "NEW 9-40" beneath "L" in second panel from left, "IL 40-6/IW 9-6/G-2" in block lettering inside last panel on right, semi-gloss black painted late frame with two deep depressions for two 1/4" truck mounting holes, trucks secured by two eyelet rivets, two unused 3/16" holes in the middle, several unused slots painted over, large 1-1/4" end opening punched from frame, considerably larger than small slots for latch couplers on previous cars, slots for ear body tabs, two 1936 Type III-D trucks with double ribbing on bolsters, shank extensions for two 1936 box couplers with two ribs on top, eight black wheels with nickel backs on thin nickel axles, nickel journals, Kotil Collection **5 10 15**

(F) Circa 1940, same as (E), but early frame, black journals, Koff Collection **5 10 15**

(G) Circa 1940, same as (E), but two 1939 trucks, Type III-F black journals **5 10 15**

(H) 1940, same as (E), but two 1940 trucks, Type III-J, with 1/8" rise on shank, simulated knuckle and lift pin atop box coupler, black journals **5 10 15**

(I) 1941, same as (E), but two 1941 trucks, Type III-G, with 1/8" drop on coupler shank, no simulated lift pin, omitted so box coupler could be moved partly beneath frame to enable cars to couple more closely, black journals, Pauli and Kotil Collections **5 12 20**

(J) 1940, same as (E), but early frame, two black Type III-B trucks with double ribs, two 1/8" holes on either side of 1/4" truck mounting holes on wide bolster, black journals, two latch couplers **5 10 15**

1678 Ives Lithographed Cattle Car

(A) 1931-32, dark pea green body, doors, and door guides, simulated wooden slats and number boards two brass door handles, orange roof, made by Lionel but lettered "IVES/R.R./LINES" in double oval symbol on top left side, number (1678) in gold block at bottom right side, same frame, trucks, couplers, and journals as 1677 Gondola (Type 1 Body A), very rare, Bohn comment **225 375 450**

(B) 1933, listed as Lionel-Ives Cattle Car in Lionel's 1933 catalogue, but not produced with Lionel or Lionel-Ives lettering. **Not manufactured**

(C) 1934-35, same as (A), but eight nickel journals, very rare, Bohn comment **225 375 450**

1679 Lionel R R Lines box car with lithographed "CURTIS/Baby Ruth B & R/America's favorite candy/five cents/accepted by the American Medical Association Committee on Foods". Black lettering, "Capacity 2500 cubic feet 110,000 pounds" in a handscript style lettering, orange door frame guide, orange door, yellow side black rivet detail, turquoise roof and black metal frame with no stamping on underside, trucks with long horizontal slot two rivets, nickel journals, coupler passes through frame slot and is held by a slot formed from the underframe.

TYPE I BODIES: Cream

(A) 1931-32, cream body, simulated ribs and rivets, dark blue roof, State car brown doors and door guides, two brass door handles, "IVES/R.R./LINES" within double oval (NYC) symbol on top left side, beneath symbol is gold rectangle with number (1679), beneath number is "MADE IN U.S.A." in block lettering, remainder of lettering consists of "reporting marks", "CAPACITY", "LENGTH", and five other smaller lines. * No. 1679's frame, trucks, couplers, and journals are the same as those on No. 1677 Gondola (Type I Body A) * **10 20 25**

(B) Same as (A), but cream body, simulated rivets and ribs, dark blue roof, State car brown doors and guides, "LIONEL/R.R./LINES" in double oval, "1679" in gold box with double black border below oval second panel from left has "CAPACITY/2500 CU.FT./110,000 LBS/" and at far right "1W 8-6 FT/1H 9-3 FT/LENGTH/OUTSIDE 32 FT/INSIDE 30 FT." "MADE IN U.S.A." below number on one side only, early black frame, nickel latch couplers bent down into frame punching, Type III-A trucks, black nickel-backed wheels, Kotil Collection **10 20 25**

(C) 1933, listed among Lionel-Ives electrical sets in Lionel's 1933 catalogue, but it was not produced with Lionel-Ives lettering **5 10 15**

(D) 1933-34, same as (A), but orange doors and door guides, "LIONEL/R.R./LINES" inside symbol **5 10 15**

(E) 1935, same as (D), but eight nickel journals **5 10 15**

(F) Same as (A), but no "MADE IN U.S.A." below number, Bohn Collection **10 20 25**

TYPE II BODIES: Cream with "BABY RUTH"

(G) Late 1935, cream Type II body with lithography on right side altered to accommodate Baby Ruth emblem plus Good Housekeeping and American Medical Association approvals, blue roof with matte (dull) finish, State car brown doors and door guides, eight nickel journals, same frame, trucks, and couplers as No. 1677 Gondola (Type I Body A), Pauli and Kotil Collections **5 10 15**

(H) 1936, same as (G), but light blue roof with matte finish, tan doors, and door guides, State car brown with a touch of orange, Pauli, Sattler, and Blackmar Collections **5 10 15**

This data told shippers how much room was available inside the car, how much it could carry, and how big it was. That saved shippers time and expense when loading.

(I) 1936, same as (G), but glossy light blue roof with a touch of green, tan doors and door guides, Pauli and Koff Collections **5 10 15**

(J) 1936, same as (G), but orange doors and door guides, gloss black frame, light blue roof, "MADE IN U.S.A." below number on one side only, Kotil Collection **5 10 15**

(Picture insert): Caption:

1679 Box Car, Type (J). Note door guides running the opposite way from (G)

(K) 1937, same as (G), but turquoise roof with matte finish, orange doors, brown door guides and nickel journals, Pauli and Bohn Collections **5 10 15**

(L) 1937, same as (G), but turquoise roof with matte finish, orange doors and door guides **5 10 15**

(M) 1937, same as (G), but very light blue roof with matte finish, orange doors and door guides **5 10 15**

(N) 1937, same as (G), but very light blue roof with matte finish, brown doors and door guides **5 10 15**

(O) 1938, same as (G), but turquoise-green roof with matte finish, some blue stripes or runs of ink, orange doors but yellow-orange door guides, same frame and couplers as No. 1677 Gondola (Type 1 Body A), two Type III-B trucks with double ribbing and two 1/8" holes on wide bolsters, two central holes hold trucks to frame with eyelet rivets. A few of these trucks were installed in 1937 and used in quantity after 1938, Pauli Collection **5 10 15**

(P) 1939, same as (O), but light green roof, orange door guides, Pauli and Koff Collections **5 10 15**

(Q) 1939, same as (O), but light green roof, State car brown doors and door guides, Koff Collection **5 10 15**

(R) Late 1939, same as (O), but very light blue roof, orange door guides, eight black journals, probably on Type III-B trucks **5 10 15**

(S) 1940, same as (P), but eight black journals **5 10 15**

TYPE III BODY: Yellow Body, Maroon Lithography and Lettering

(T) 1940, yellow body, new maroon lithography and lettering, maroon roof, "LIONEL LINES/No. 1679" within maroon borders on right side, reporting marks underneath in smaller block lettering, "CAPY. 12000/LD. LMT. 15000/LT.WT. 5000/NEW 4-31-39" (note impossible April date!), "CURTISS/Baby/Ruth/CANDY" on left side in serif lettering, "Baby/Ruth" much larger than "CURTISS/CANDY", orange doors and door guides, same frame and couplers as 1677 Gondola (Type 1 Body A), two Type III-B trucks as on Type II Body, eight nickel journals, Kotil Collection **5 10 15**

(U) 1940, same as (T), but eight black journals, Pauli, Kotil, Hoffman, and Koff Collections **5 10 15**

(V) 1940, same as (T), but brown roof, eight black journals **5 10 15**

(W) 1940, same as (T), but semi-gloss black painted late frame with two "deep-dish" depressions that raise car 1/4", in the center of each is a 1/4" truck mounting hole for an eyelet rivet, two unused 3/16" holes toward center, two 1-1/4" end openings where previous frames had smaller slots, two 1936 trucks, Type III-D, with double ribbing and two 1/8" holes on wide bolsters, straight shank extensions for 1936 box couplers with two ribs on top **5 10 15**

(X) 1939, same as (W), but eight black journals, Blackmar Collection **5 10 15**

(Y) 1940, same as (W), but two 1940 trucks, Type III-G, with long shank extensions having 1/4" rise for 1940 box couplers with simulated knuckles and lift pins, eight black journals **5 10 15**

(Z) 1941, same as (W), but two 1941 trucks, Type III-H, with short shank extensions having 1/8" drop to allow couplers to rest partially under car frame, enabling cars to couple together more closely, tight clearance beneath frame required removal of simulated lift pins, eight black journals, Pauli, Bohn, Kotil, and Koff Collections **5 10 15**

(AA) 1941, same as (Z), but roof and lettering are light maroon with a touch of orange-brown, unusual color, Koff Collection **5 10 15**

(BB) 1942, same as (Z), but black axles **5 10 15**

1679X Lithographed Box Car (Uncatalogued Special) To the best of our knowledge, the "X" indicates no journals. The "X" appears on the box, not on the car.

(A) 1936, cream Type II body, light blue roof, State car brown doors and door guides, same frame trucks, and couplers as 1677 Gondola (Type I Body A) except trucks have no journals **5 10 15**

(B) 1937, same as (A), but turquoise roof **5 10 15**

(C) 1939, same as (A), but very light blue roof, Pauli Collection **5 10 15**

(D) 1939, yellow Type III body, same frame, trucks, and couplers as 1679 Box Car (Type III Body D) except trucks have no journals **5 10 15**

(E) 1940, same as (D), but two 1940 trucks, Type III-G, without journals (see 1679, Type III Body F) **5 10 15**

(F) 1941, same as (D), but two 1941 trucks, Type III-H, without journals (see 1679, Type III Body G) **5 10 15**

(G) 1942, same as (F), but black axles **5 10 15**

1680 Ives Lithographed Oil Tank Car

TYPE I BODIES

(A) 1931-32, aluminum tank in matte finish with lithographed rivets, three copper domes, one copper handrail along each side, "IVES TANK LINES" in block lettering across tank above handrails, "FUEL OIL" on left side below handrails, number (1680) in block below handrails on right, two aluminum supports hold tank on frame, same frame, trucks, and couplers as 1677 Gondola (Type I Body A) **10 20 25**

(B) 1933, same as (A), but Sunoco decal over IVES name **20 30 40**

(C) 1933, same as (A), but "IVES TANK LINES" omitted **20 30 40**

(D) 1933, listed among Lionel-Ives electrical trains in Lionel's 1933 catalogue, but not produced with Lionel-Ives lettering.

TYPE II BODIES

(E) Late 1933, aluminum tank and tank supports, matte finish, nickel center dome, copper outer domes, handrails, and journals, "MOTOR OIL" on left side, number (1680) within double rectangle on right, "CPY. 12000 GALS." beneath number, same frame, trucks, and couplers as 1677 Gondola (Type I Body A) **5 10 15**

(F) Late 1933, same as (E), but yellow Sunoco emblem in middle of car above handrail, GAS above "SUNOCO" and "OILS" underneath, all three on yellow Sunoco diamond, red horizontal arrow points right **5 10 15**

(G) Late 1933, same as (F), but high-gloss finish **5 10 15**

(H) Early 1934, same as (G), but "LIONEL/LINES" centered below handrail, no Sunoco emblem, Blackmar Collection **5 10 15**

(I) Early 1934, same as (H), but matte finish **5 10 15**

(J) 1934, same as (I), but high-gloss finish **5 10 15**

(K) 1934, matte finish, Sunoco emblem and "LIONEL/LINES" on tank, blue lettering, nickel journals and handrails, Kotil Collection **5 10 15**

(L) 1935, same as (J), but all three domes are nickel **5 10 15**

(M) 1935, same as (L), but two nickel handrails, eight nickel journals, copper end domes **5 10 15**

(N) 1935, same as (M), but matte finish, Pauli Collection **5 10 15**

(O) 1935, same as (M), but Sunoco emblem **5 10 15**

(P) 1935, aluminum tank tinted yellow, perhaps due to age, three nickel domes, two copper handrails, Sunoco emblem but no "LIONEL/LINES", same frame, trucks, and couplers as 1677 Gondola (Type I Body A), eight nickel journals, Koff Collection **5 10 15**

(Q) Late 1935, same as (J), but nickel domes, handrails, and journals as "LIONEL LINES", Koff and Bohn Collections **5 10 15**

(R) 1936-38, same as (Q), but semi-gloss black painted late frame with two "deep-dish" depressions that raise car 1/4" and contains two 1/4" truck mounting holes, trucks secured with eyelet rivets, two unused 3/16" holes toward center, two 1-1/4" end openings punched from frame, considerably larger than small slots for latch couplers on previous cars, two black Type III-D trucks with long shank for 1936 box couplers which have two ribs on top, eight black wheels with nickel backs on four thin nickel axles, eight nickel journals **5 10 15**

(S) Square ends, 7-1/2" long, yellow "SUNOCO" emblem at upper right just below end domes, three nickel domes, two lines of data below "SUNOCO" emblem, "CAPY 10,000 GALS" and "BUILT 5-29", data on left reads as follows, "S.U.N.X. 1680/CAPY 100,000 LBS/LT.WT. 42,000/SHARON 5-29", "LIONEL LINES" below data at left in one line, four-wheel trucks, black journals, and thin axles, latch couplers, frame has 9/16" centered hole, I. D. Smith Collection **5 10 15**

(T) Same as (S), but low box couplers with simulated knuckles (3/4"), no 9/16" hole, extra hole to rear of truck mounting, painted gray tank ends, I. D. Smith Collection **5 10 15**

TYPE III BODIES

(U) 1939, orange tank, medium-gloss finish, lithographed rivets, three nickel domes, "SHELL" in hugh vermilion block lettering outlined in black above two nickel handrails, "PETROLEUM/PRODUCTS" in medium-sized block lettering on left below handrail, double rectangular number plate on right side below handrail with 1680 in medium-sized block numerals, "LIONEL/LINES" centered in larger block lettering, two yellow-orange supports, lighter shade than tank, hold tank on frame, semi-gloss black painted early frame with embossed rivets, end steps, and indentations, two 1/4" truck mounting holes secure trucks with eyelet rivets, semicircular slots for truck tabs, end slots, cut-out frame sections bent downward as retainers for two late (Type II) nickel latch couplers with oval ends bent downward to keep them in place, two Type III-B trucks with double ribbing and two 1/8" holes on wide bolsters. A few of these trucks were installed in 1937 and used in quantity after 1938. They have a total of eight black wheels with nickel backs on four thin nickel axles and eight nickel journals, Pauli, Kotil, and Koff Collections **10 15 20**

(V) 1940, same as (U), but eight black journals, Koff and Kotil Collections **10 15 20**

(W) 1939, same as (U), but late frame with two "deep-dish" depressions, two black Type III-I trucks with long shank for 1936 box couplers with two ribs on top, see Type II Body R **5 10 15**

(X) 1940, same as (U), but late frame as (W), above, two 1940 trucks, Type III-G, with long shank extensions having 1/8" rise for 1940 box couplers with simulated knuckles and lift pins, eight black journals, Griesbeck Collection **5 10 15**

(Y) Late 1940, same as (U), but aluminum tank and tank supports in matte finish, "LIONEL LINES" moved up from former position below handrails to replace SHELL lettering above them, eight black journals **10 15 20**

(Z) 1940, aluminum tank and tank supports, three nickel domes, two nickel handrails, high-gloss finish, far fewer lithographed rivets than previous bodies, "S.U.N.X. 1680" in large block lettering on left side above handrail, below handrail are printed "CAP'Y-100,000 LBS. LT. WT. 42,000 SHARON 5-29" in small block lettering, with "LIONEL LINES" centered beneath data, on right side, above handrail, "GAS/SUNOCO/OILS" is printed in block lettering within yellow Sunoco emblem, red horizontal Sunoco arrow points to right, beneath emblem and below handrail are reporting marks in small block lettering, "CAP'Y 10,000 GALS./SAFETY VALVES 25 LBS./TANK 60 LBS./TESTED 12-6-40/MARCUS HOOK, PA./SUN OIL COMPANY/BUILT 5-29, MADE IN U.S./OF AMERICA" centered on bottom of one side of car, same semi-gloss black painted early frame, later-type nickel latch couplers, and Type III-A trucks as 1677 Gondola (Type I Body A), eight black journals, unusual combination of late tank body and early frame, Koff and Hoffman Collections **5 10 15**

(AA) 1941, same as (Z), but late frame with two "deep-dish" depressions that raise car 1/4", in the center of each is a 1/4" truck mounting hole for an eyelet rivet, two unused 3/16" holes toward center, two 1-1/4' end openings punched from frame where early frame had smaller slots, two black 1941 Type III-H trucks with short shank extensions having 1/8" drop to allow couplers to fit beneath frame, tight clearance required removal of simulated lift pins from top of box coupler, short metal bar attached to back of box coupler to uncouple cars, couplers were not automatic, box rose and freed latch of mating coupler, Kotil Collection **5 10 15**

(BB) 1941, same as (AA), but four black axles, Koff and Kotil Collection **5 10 15**

(CC) Late 1941, same as (AA), but two copper handrails, two thin black axles on one truck, two thin nickel axles on the other. Interesting conglomeration of leftover parts, probably used because they were handy. On the cover of the 1941 catalogue, Lionel announced it was manufacturing precision instruments for the Navy. With production schedules getting tight, Lionel turned to its vast store of spare parts to save the time and expense of making new parts, Pauli Collection **10 20 25**

(DD) Early 1942, same as (AA), but light gray ends on tank; these ends intended for following car, Koff Collection **10 20 25**

(EE) 1942, same as (AA), but light gray tank with medium-gloss finish, two aluminum tank supports with matte finish, no handrails or handrail holes, all four thin axles and even eyelet rivets that secure trucks are black, Pauli, Kotil and Koff Collections **20 25 35**

(FF)Late 1942, same as (EE), but all black trim, domes, journals, and axles, tank supports may be light gray, not presently known to exist. Reader comments invited.

1680X Lithographed Oil Tank Car

Note: Not known to exist with Type I body

TYPE II BODY

(A) 1936, aluminum tank and tank supports with high-gloss finish, Sunoco emblem with block lettering centered above handrails, "LIONEL/LINES" in block lettering centered below handrails, "MOTOR OIL" in block lettering on left side below handrail, and, on one side, "MADE IN U.S.A." beneath it, number (1680) inside double rectangle on right side with "CPY. 12000 GALS" in small block lettering underneath, same semi-gloss black painted early frame, trucks, and couplers as 1677 Gondola (Type I Body A), no journals **5 10 15**

TYPE III BODY

(B) 1939, same as Type III Body (U), but no journals **10 15 20**

TYPE IV BODY

(C) 1941, same as Type IV Body (AA), but no journals, Blackmar Collection **10 15 20**

(D) 1942, no handrails, as Type IV Body (EE), no journals, either, pictured in TCA's **LIONEL TRAINS: STANDARD OF THE WORLD**, 1900-1943, p. 49 **10 20 25**

1682 Lithographed Caboose

TYPE I BODIES

(A) 1931-32, vermilion body, vermilion cupola sides, dark brown roof, cupola ends, and cupola roof, cream windows, white lettering, cream end doors, and number boards, lithographed ribs and rivets, "IVES/R.R./LINES" in serif lettering within double black (NYC) oval underneath cupola on both sides, number (1682) beneath oval in block lettering within long double rectangle, same frame, trucks, couplers, and copper journals as 1677 Gondola (Type I Body A), Bohn Collection **10 20 25**

TYPE II BODIES

(B) 1933-34, same as Type I body, but Type II body Ives lettering replaced by "LIONEL/R.R./LINES", Kotil Collection **10 15 20**

(C) 1935, same as (B), but eight nickel journals, Pauli Collection **10 25 30**

TYPE III BODIES

(D) 1936, light red body, roof, cupola ends, and cupola roof, light cream windows, lettering, end doors and number boards, light cream stripe on sides of cupola, lithographed ribs and rivets, same frame and trucks as 1677 Gondola (Type I Body A), only one coupler, eight nickel journals, Pauli and Koff Collections **15 25 35**

TYPE IV BODIES

(E) 1937-39, no stripe on cupola, Type III-B trucks, cupola matches light red body, otherwise identical to Type III body, including frame, Bohn and Kotil Collections **5 10 15**

(F) 1940, same as (E), but eight black journals, Type III-B trucks, Koff, Kotil and Hoffman Collections **5 10 15**

(G) 1936-39, same as (E), but late frame with two "deep-dish" depressions that raise car 1/4", in the center of each is a 1/4" truck mounting hole for an eyelet rivet, two unused 3/16" holes toward center, two 1-1/4" end openings punched from frame where previous frames had smaller (5/8") slots, two different black trucks, Type III-B has no coupler but it has double ribs and two 1/8" holes on its wide bolster, the other truck, Type III-D, has a long shank extension for a 1936 box coupler with two ribs on top. Both trucks have a total of eight black wheels with nickel backs on four thin nickel axles, eight nickel journals **5 10 15**

(H) 1940, two different trucks, as (G), but the coupler truck is Type III-G with a 1/8" rise on its long coupler shank, eight black journals, 1940 box coupler with a simulated knuckle and a lift pin on top, long vertical metal bar fastened to back of coupler, on later automatic couplers when pushed by rod protruding from solenoid, this bar opened box coupler and freed latch to mating coupler. However, although this bar is present, this car has no solenoid. **5 10 15**

(I) 1941, two different trucks, as (G) and (H), but the coupler truck is Type III-H with a 1/8" drop on its short coupler shank, 1941 box coupler rests partly under frame to enable cars to couple more closely and more realistically, tight clearance there required removal of simulated lift pin, eight black journals, Pauli, Kotil, and Koff Collections **5 10 15**

TYPE V BODIES

(J) 1940, tuscan body, roof, and cupola, terra-cotta windows and end doors, N.Y.C./1682 in white medium serif lettering centered on sides, "UNITED STATES/SAFETY APPLIANCES/STAND" in white small serif lettering on both sides beneath cupola, lithographed handrails and wooden slat construction, same semi-gloss black painted early frame as 1677 Gondola (Type I Body A), same later-type nickel latch coupler as Gondolas, but this caboose has only one coupler, two black Type III-B trucks with double ribs and a 1/8" hole on each side of a 1/4" truck mounting hole on wide bolster, eight black wheels with nickel backs on four thin nickel axles, eight black journals **10 15 20**

(K) 1940, same as (J), but late frame with two "deep-dish" depressions and two different trucks (Types III-B and III-G) as Type IV body (H), Bohn Collection **10 15 20**

(L) 1941, same as (K), but coupler truck is Type III-H, as Type IV body (I), Pauli, Kotil, Blackmar, and Koff Collections **15 20 25**

1682X Lithographed Caboose

Note: No versions of this car with Type I or II Bodies are known.

TYPE III BODY

(A) 1936, light red body, roof, cupola ends, and cupola roof, light cream windows, lettering, end doors, and number boards, light cream stripe on sides of cupola, lithographed ribs and rivets, "LIONEL/R.R./LINES" in serif lettering within double black (NYC) oval underneath cupola on both sides, number (1682) beneath oval in block lettering within long double rectangle, same frame, trucks, single coupler as 1677 Gondola (Type I Body A), no journals **10 20 30**

TYPE IV BODIES

(B) 1937-40, no stripe on cupola, cupola matches light red body, same frame, trucks, single coupler as 1677 Gondola (Type I Body A), no journals, Pauli Collection **5 10 15**

TYPE V BODY

(C) 1940, tuscan body, roof, and cupola, terra-cotta windows and end doors, N.Y.C./1682 in medium serif white lettering centered on sides, "UNITED STATES/SAFETY APPLIANCES/STAND" in small white serif lettering on both sides beneath cupola, lithographed handrails and lithographed wooden slat construction, same frame, single coupler as 1677 Gondola (Type I Body A), two black Type III-B trucks with double ribs and a 1/8" hole on each side of a 1/4" truck mounting hole on wide bolster, eight black wheels with nickel backs on four thin nickel axles, no journals **10 15 20**

(D) 1940, same as (C), but late frame with two "deep-dish" depressions and two different trucks (Types III-B and III-G) as 1682 Type IV body (H), no journals **10 15 20**

(E) 1941-42, same as (D), but coupler truck is Type III-H, as 1682 Type IV body (I), no journals **10 15 20**

THE IVES 1707 AND LIONEL 1717 SERIES LITHOGRAPHED CARS

Thanks to the harsh economic conditions of the Depression, the Lionel Corporation was running in the red. Although Lionel had prided itself on high-class, high-priced trains, hardly anyone could afford them any more. In previous sections, we described how Lionel made trains for those harsh times by turning to Ives' technology in lithography. Tradition dies hard, though, and one group of cars shows Lionel's attempt to adapt lithographed cars to standards of happier days.

Even after Lionel had taken over, Ives had offered a good-looking line of 9" freight and passenger cars. Following those designs, and adding a lithographed caboose to the line, Lionel introduced a new series in the 1932 Ives catalogue (the last Ives catalogue printed). An Ives 258 locomotive headed the entire series: 1707 Gondola, 1708 Cattle Car, 1709 Boxcar, and 1712 Caboose. All were 9-1/2" long, but they were cheaply constructed and they looked squat. Lionel was ambivalent about them. Although they were manufactured from 1932 through 1942, they were never shown in a consumer catalogue after their initial appearance. Yet they were listed in dealer catalogues and wholesale price lists.

After Lionel dissolved the Ives Corporation in 1933 and ceased producing Ives trains to conserve company resources, changes were made in this series. The cattle car was discontinued. The remaining cars were renumbered (Gondola 1717, Boxcar 1719, Caboose 1722) and LIONEL replaced IVES in the black oval heralds. Smaller, less expensive trucks were installed. After 1936, "deep-dish" frames raised the cars 1/4", and this new feature was reflected by an "X" following the car number on the box. They usually came in uncatalogued sets with a gray 249 locomotive. Since they weren't shown in Lionel's fabulously popular consumer catalogues, hardly anyone knew they were around. Consequently, fewer of these larger lithographed cars were made than their smaller, more publicized cousins. Collectors usually spurn these cars in favor of more glamorous trains but cars in this series are beginning to be valued as the unusual items they are.

1707 Ives Gondola, 1932, dark tan lithographed steel braces, yellow-orange lithographed wooden slats, "IVES" in cream rounded block lettering within block oval, reporting marks printed along bottom of car sides, gray painted interior, semi-gloss black painted early frame 9-1/2" long over center with two 1/4" truck mounting holes, two semicircular truck tab slots, two 1-1/4" end slots, and two slots near ends for early-type nickel latch couplers, round T-shaped tabs bent upwards secure each coupler to frame, both trucks fastened by combination of riveted studs, brass washers, and cotter pins, two black Type VI-A trucks with flat spreader bars, two triangular openings with long row of simulated rivets on each truck side frame, eight nickel wheels with nickel backs on four thick nickel axles, eight copper journals, Koff Collection **15 30 50**

1708 Ives Lithographed Cattle Car, 1932, light green lithographed wooden slats beneath lithographed metal braces, medium green simulated openings between slats, dark green painted roof, light brown doors and door guides, round brass handle on each door, brass ladder on each side at right end, "IVES" in white rounded block lettering within black oval on right side, number (1708) in same lettering in black oval on left side, same frame, trucks, and couplers as 1707 Gondola, very scarce and hard to find, Koff and Bohn Collections **100 250 350**

1709 Ives Lithographed Box Car, 1932, Stephen Girard green body with lithographed plates and rivets, separate roof painted medium light blue with a touch of green, two orange doors with matching door guides, brass or nickel center spreader bars under roof above doors, "IVES" in cream rounded block lettering within black oval on right side, number (1709) in same lettering black oval on left side, brass ladder on each side at right end, same frame, trucks, and couplers as 1707 Gondola **20 30 40**

1712 1932, orange body with lithographed rivets and plates, maroon painted roof and cupola, cream windows and end doors, nickel spreader bar with center slot, small offset hole, and four tabs under roof that fit slots in top of sides, "IVES" in cream rounded block lettering within black oval on right side, number (1712) in same lettering in black oval on left side, same frame, trucks, and couplers as 1707 Gondola, Koff Collection **20 30 40**

1717 Lionel Lithographed Gondola. This car was designed and manufactured by Lionel for its 1932 Ives line. In 1933 the car was redesigned for the Lionel line and offered in special uncatalogued sets through 1942. The following changes were made: "LIONEL" replaced "IVES" within the black oval centered on the car side. The designers retained the same cream rounded block lettering used with the Ives name; the number (1717) beneath oval in small black sans-serif lettering was smaller. The car was re-equipped with less expensive black Type III-A trucks, replacing the larger Type VI-A. Initially, the car came with copper journals and later-type nickel latch couplers, as did the 1677 Gondola (Type I Body A). Type III-A trucks have a single rib and two truck mounting holes on each bolster; there are small rectangular slots with round ends in side frames; the trucks rode on black wheels with nickel backs mounted on thin nickel finished axles.

(A) Circa 1933-34, copper journals **5 10 20**

(B) Same as (A), but nickel journals, Pauli, Bohn, and Kotil Collections **15 20 25**

(C) Same as (A), but black journals, latch couplers secured to car frame by half oval twist, Pauli Collection **10 15 25**

(D) Circa 1940, same as (A), but black journals, Type III-B trucks with double ribs and a 1/8" hole on each side of a 1/4" truck mounting hole on wide bolster, Koff Collection **10 15 25**

1717X Lionel Lithographed Gondola

(A) This car came in both an "X" and a plain version (described earlier). The "X" was on the box, but not on the car. This car had a semi-gloss black painted late frame, 9-1/2" long over centers, with two "deep-dish" depressions that raised the car height 1/4", in the center of each depression is a 1/4" truck mounting hole; there are two unused 3/16" holes toward the middle of the frame; two 1-1/2" end openings replace slots on the early frame; black Type III-D trucks with double ribs; each truck had two 1/8" holes and a stud on its wide bolster; the stud was riveted to the truck and because of the truck location it was necessary to provide nickel coupler shank extensions. These shank extensions were made with an unused 1/4" hole for alternative fastening. The truck studs were secured to the frame by nickel horseshoe clips. To make proper fit, Lionel engineers had to put two nickel washers between the truck and the car! The car had black finished 1936-style box couplers (with two ribs on top). These box couplers were fastened to their extension by close-fitting short nickel tabs on back of boxes. The car had black wheels with nickel backs which rode on thin nickel finished axles; the trucks were finished with nickel journals, Koff Collection **10 25 30**

(B) Circa 1940, same as (A), but black journals, Pauli Collection **10 25 35**

1719 Lionel Lithographed Box Car. This car was designed and manufactured by Lionel and was initially offered under the Ives name with an Ives number in 1932. In 1933, the car was redesigned and "LIONEL" replaced "IVES" in the oval on the right side. A new number, 1719, was located on the left side. The name and number were printed in the same cream block lettering as the Ives name and number had previously used. Under the Ives name, the car came with Type VI-A trucks; as a LIONEL issue it came with the less expensive Type III-A trucks.

(A) Circa 1933-34, copper journals, and later-type nickel latch couplers as 1717 Gondola (A) and 1677 Gondola (Type I Body A) **15 20 25**

(B) 1935-40, same as (A), but nickel ladders instead of brass, nickel journals, orange doors and guides, Kotil Collection **15 20 25**

(C) 1935-40, same as (A), but nickel ladders, brass door handles, orange doors, light peacock roof, light green sides, light green ends, nickel latch couplers, nickel journals, light brown door guides, Pauli and Bohn Collections **25 30 35**

(D) 1941-42, same as (A), but light Stephen Girard green body, separate roof painted new color, light blue, two nickel ladders, two early type nickel latch couplers with half-oval ends twisted to secure them to frame, two Type III-B trucks with double ribbing and 1/8" hole on each side of 1/4" truck mounting hole on wide bolster, small rectangular slots in side frames, black journals, trucks secured by two eyelet rivets, Pauli Collection **25 30 35**

(E) 1940, same as (A), but Type III-B trucks, black journals **15 20 25**

1719X Lionel Lithographed Box Car, 1942. "X" was printed after the number (1719) on the box but not on the car. It signified a semi-gloss black painted late frame with black Type III-D trucks with double ribs (for details, see 1717X Gondola (A), same light Stephen Girard green body, light blue separate roof, and nickel ladders as 1719 Box Car (D) **15 20 25**

1722 Lionel Lithographed Caboose

(A) 1933-34, designed and manufactured by Lionel with Ives lettering in 1932. Included among Lionel trains, though uncatalogued, through 1942 with the following changes: "LIONEL" replaced "IVES" in oval on right side, new number (1722) in oval on left side; name and number printed in same cream rounded block lettering as original Ives version; smaller, less expensive black Type III-A trucks replaced larger Type VI-A, only one early type nickel latch coupler with rounded "T" shaped tab bent upward to hold coupler to frame, same trucks, wheels, and copper journals as 1717 Gondola (A) and 1677 Gondola (Type I Body A) **15 20 25**

(B) 1935-40, same as (A), but nickel journals, Pauli and Bohn Collections **20 30 40**

(C) 1935-40, same as (A), but light red body, maroon roof, and nickel journals, Pauli Collection **25 35 45**

(D) 1940, same as (A), but light red body, Type III-B trucks with double ribbing and black journals, Koff Collection **15 20 25**

(E) 1941-42, same as (A), but orange-red body, Type III-B trucks with double ribbing and nickel journals, Koff Collection **20 30 40**

(F) 1941-42, same as (A), but orange-red body, Type III-B trucks with double ribbing, black journals **15 20 25**

1722X Lionel Lithographed Caboose

(A) 1939, although an "X" was printed on the box, it did not appear on the car. The "X" version came with a semi-gloss black painted late type frame with black painted Type III-D trucks with double ribs (for details, see 1717X Gondola (A)). This car has the same orange-red lithographed body as the 1722 Caboose **8 12 20**

(B) 1940, same as (A), but black journals **8 12 20**

THE 2650 SERIES: LIONEL'S AUTOMATIC COUPLER ADVENTURES

In 1935, Lionel was getting up steam. The vigorous publicity campaign the year before for the Union Pacific's new streamliner, the M-10000, had taken America by storm, since most people were eager for anything, any sign of hope, that the crushing grip of the Great Depression was easing.

The success of the M-10000 gradually transformed the Lionel Lines. Toylike trains began to give way to more realistic ones, though slowly. The cost of retooling all at once would have been prohibitive, indeed impossible. Besides, a whole new line of trains might not have sold well, since most people (most customers, that is) don't take well to drastic, abrupt changes.

However, a trend towards realism was inevitable. We have already seen how new die-casting techniques enabled Lionel to develop its famed scale series. This quest for realism also extended to the couplers on the cars. In its haste to develop a truly automatic coupler, Lionel made many mistakes, but finally did come up with a reliable coupler - just in time to discontinue it due to World War II!

The development of the automatic coupler is quite an interesting story. In the beginning, Lionel had used simple hook couplers. They worked, but it was necessary to lift the cars to couple them. To eliminate that, Louis Caruso, the brother of Mario Caruso, Lionel's secretary, treasurer, and factory manager, invented the "automatic" coupler. Protruding from the coupler was a latch with a triangular tip or key. When pushed into another coupler, a short metal bar or latch fell across the key and held it in place. That worked, too, but "automatic" was the wrong word. Diddling with those couplers could sorely test an operator's patience, language, and occasionally his (or her) religion as well. They didn't look like real couplers, either.

Lionel introduced a simpler, somewhat more realistic coupler in 1936. The key was retained, but instead of movable metal latch, a black box was mounted over the coupler. The box was hinged at the rear. When two couplers met, the box moved over the triangular key and fell into place behind it, locking the key in place. Box couplers worked much better than latch-type "automatic" couplers, and they had a big advantage. For the first time, cars could be coupled simply by backing one up to another. Without touching the trains, young engineers could couple cars and make up trains (except on curves) just like switching crews did on big railroads. Uncoupling, though, was still a manual operation. These box couplers could mate with the previous latch-type couplers.

Lionel took the next step in 1938. The first subtle hint was spread across the first two pages of the catalogue: "HEY FELLOWS - watch what happens now when you press a button!" Five black-and-white photos with blazing red banners announced that "MAGIC REMOTE CONTROLS" did incredible things "electrically: WHISTLING, REVERSING, UNCOUPLING, LOADING" (with Lionel's new 97 Coal Elevator), "UNLOADING" (with the 3659 Dump Car made for Coal Elevator). Remote-control couplers had arrived, but there were a few flaws that needed work.

Lionel Consumer Catalogue, 1938, pp. 2-3.

One flaw was that the couplers worked too well! Lionel had mounted a magnet at the front of the truck. When energized, the magnet attracted a metal plate fastened to the rear of the box coupler, raising the box and freeing the key of the mating coupler. To operators' dismay, the nickel contact shoe not only worked on remote control track sections, but it also worked when it touched the wide third rail on switches. It was most annoying to see a carefully assembled freight train disassemble itself as it went through the yard switches. Besides that, such haphazard uncoupling set the stage for a rear-end collision when the engine came around again. To keep engineers from the embarrassment of running into their own cabooses, Lionel added fiber (later on, bakelite) insulation to the contact shoe late in 1938. The following year, it became standard.

On the 2800 series of large freight cars, the magnetic coupler lasted into 1940, but on the 2650 series it was replaced with a solenoid in 1939, perhaps for more positive action. Solenoids were proven performers in Lionel's crossing gates, semaphores, and the tireless Automatic Gateman. Lionel sold so many cars of the 2600 series that the company could afford to experiment with them. However, one experiment didn't work. Due to a design flaw, the truck assembly had to be soldered in place, causing a weak bond. Lionel tried a spot weld instead, but trucks are still found with the front of the 1939 solenoid falling out. Late in the year, Lionel had more success with a third design: a nickel V-shaped yoke was placed on the back of the solenoid to keep it in place. It is visible from the back of the truck unless a third rail roller hides it.

Lionel offered an improved version of the 1939 solenoid-equipped box coupler in 1940, with a separate solenoid and a simulated coupler knuckle and lift pin on top of the box. The 2650 series also sported new, more realistic paint, rubber-stamping and decals.

The final improvements were brought about by grim preparations for World War II. Requested to reduce the amount of metal in its trains, Lionel was happy to comply: the 1941 coupler shank was shortened and lowered; the solenoid plunger was shortened and its thin end pointed; wider end openings were punched from frames; the new box coupler lost its simulated lift pin, allowing it to fit partially beneath the frame. Now the cars coupled more closely, more realistically. About an ounce of vital metal was saved on every 2650 Series car. The couplers worked better than ever. Lionel even introduced a new Sunoco Oil Car.

After Pearl Harbor, cutbacks became more drastic. Lionel offered one last hastily-assembled line in 1942, with a warning that "only an extremely limited number" of accessories were available (P. 23, 1942 catalogue). After the conclusion of the company's raid on its parts bins, production of trains ceased altogether until late 1945. An era had ended.

2620 Floodlight Car 1938—41:

(A) Early 1938, aluminum-painted die-cast searchlight head; large-headed screw-base bulb; black rubber wire to electrical contact button; round metal reflector, glass lens with round spring retainer; black die-cast yoke holding floodlight head, which is attached by two small nickel hex-nut bolts; four nickel handrails on sides; two Type IV nickel brakewheels which are mounted with stanchion and short shafts on right corners of car ends (as viewer faces ends). Light red painted Type 650-F frame with two dime-sized depressions containing two 1/4" truck mounting holes; two 7/8" end slots for truck-mounted couplers; special hole for floodlight yoke; rubber-stamped on frame bottom in black sans-serif lettering in four lines: "NO. 2620/MADE BY/THE LIONEL CORP./NEW YORK" (the sample observed had this lettering parallel to the frame ends, rather than to the frame sides). Round black washer on bottom riveted to yoke with spring beneath. Car has two different trucks. One is a Type III-E 1938 magnetic truck with a 1936-style box coupler possessing an extended tail on coupler boxes, a long coupler shank extension and a black bakelite base plate attached by screws. This plate has an eyelet rivet holding a fork-shaped brass spring, to which a plain nickel contact shoe is attached. The other truck is a Type III-ER which has a longer, larger base plate which is bent upward into a 1/2" bracket for a roller assembly. Trucks mounted to frame by riveted studs secured by washers. Black nickel-backed wheels on thin nickel axles; eight nickel journals, Pauli Collection **20 35 15**

(B) 1938, same as (A), but trucks have no nickel slider for operating magnet; plain copper truck shoes **18 30 12**

(C) Late 1938, same as (A), but contact shoes have maroon fiber insulators to keep trucks from accidental operation **18 30 12**

(D) Early 1939, same as (A), but brakewheels on left corner of car ends; Type 650-C frame with quarter-sized depressions; Type III-F and III-FR 1939 solenoid couplers (this sample had soldered solenoid assemblies. A nickel V-shaped yoke holds the solenoids of some of these trucks; see truck description); 1936-style box couplers have short black coupler tails; insulation on truck shoes; black journals; truck studs secured by horseshoe clips, Koff and Pauli Collections **20 35 18**

(E) Mid 1939, same as (D), but trucks are spot-welded instead of soldered (trucks must be removed from car to observe this) **20 35 18**

(F) 1939, same as (D), but V-shaped yokes attached to rear of solenoid assemblies on trucks **20 35 18**

(G) Late 1939, same as (F), but solenoid-coupler assemblies are black instead of nickel **20 30 12**

(H) Last 1939 production, same as (G), but small spring is spot-welded to long tail of coupler boxes **20 30 12**

(I) Early 1940, same as (H), but Type III-GX and III-GXR 1940-style solenoid couplers with insulated rivet contact, simulated lift pin and knuckle on top of coupler box, solenoid no longer riveted to black coupler shank extension, spot-welded springs on tail extensions, Koff Collection **15 30 10**

(J) 1940, same as (I), but no springs on coupler tail extensions (Type III-G and III-GR trucks) **18 30 12**

(K) 1941, light gray painted die-cast searchlight head, large head screw base bulb, black rubber wire to electrical contact button, round metal reflector inside, round glass lens, round spring lens retainer, black die-cast yoke holding floodlight head with two small nickel hex-nut bolts; four long nickel handrails on sides, two late one-piece nickel brakewheels, stands, and short connecting rods on right side of ends, facing ends; Light Red painted frame (Type 650-D) with two quarter-sized depressions containing two 1/4" truck mounting holes, two 1-1/8" end openings (widened for 1941 couplers), special hole for mounting black floodlight yoke; four lines of black vertical sans-serif rubber-stamped lettering on frame bottom which reads identically to (A). (This sample's rubber-stamped lettering is vertical, but the reverse of the usual vertical lettering. It is stamped at the top of the car rather than at the bottom.) Round black washer on bottom riveted to yoke with a spring beneath; one (Type III-H) truck, a 1941 solenoid type which has shortest shank of all automatic couplers with a drop of 1/8" on the short black coupler shank extension. The simulated lift-pin has been removed from the top of the coupler box. The box is recessed into the ends of the car, requiring the widening of the frame end openings. The thin end of the shortened solenoid plunger has been made into a point. The short tail of the 1936 box coupler has been restored and is nickel instead of the previous 1939 black. The metal base plate is identical to the 1940 coupler, except for a round nickel eyelet rivet which snaps in place to keep the solenoid plunger in place on truck without third rail rollers. The second truck (Type III-Hr) has third rail roller and is otherwise identical to first truck; both trucks have a total of eight black wheels with nickel backs on four thin nickel axles and eight black journals; trucks are fastened to frame by means of studs riveted to truck and to coupler shank extensions, two nickel horseshoe clips fasten over studs with a nickel washer beneath each, Pauli Collection **20 35 18**

(L) Same as (K), but brakewheels mounted on left corners of car ends as viewer faces ends, Koff Collection **20 35 18**

(M) Same as (K), but brakewheels mounted on right corners of car ends and floodlight head painted very light gray (92), Koff Collection **25 25 15**

2651 Flat, Log or Lumber Car 1938-41:

(A) Early 1938, four nickel stakes (two each side); two Type IV nickel brakewheels; catalogued as having removable lumber, either as one large piece with scribing or eight separate pieces; light green painted Type 650-F frame (color identical to 45-N watchman base) with two dime-sized depressions containing 1/4" truck mounting holes; two 7/8" openings for truck mounted couplers; black rubber-stamped sans-serif lettering in four horizontal lines on frame bottom: "NO. 2651/MADE BY/THE LIONEL CORPORATION/NEW YORK"; two Type III-E black 1938-style magnetic trucks with 1936-style box couplers and long coupler tails (see truck discussion); plain nickel contact shoes; trucks mounted to frame with studs secured by circular clips with nickel washers beneath each clip; black nickel-backed wheels on thin nickel axles; nickel journals. Price includes load, Koff and Pauli Collections **15 25 12**

(B) 1938, same as (A), but two 1938 Type III-E trucks with plain copper contact shoes on baseplates; probably factory error as to shoes, Pauli Collection **20 30 15**

(C) Late 1938, same as (A), but Type III-E trucks with maroon fiber insulation on contact shoes **20 30 15**

(D) Early 1939, same as (A), but Type 650-C frame with quarter-sized depressions; early black 1939 Type III-F trucks with soldered solenoid assemblies lacking retaining V-shaped yoke and short black coupler tails (see truck discussion); internal brass contact spring and shoe secured by copper eyelet; insulated contact shoes; trucks secured to frame with horseshoe clips atop nickel washers, Pauli Collection **25 30 15**

(E) Mid 1939, same as (D), but trucks are spot-welded instead of soldered (this cannot be seen without removing trucks) **20 25 15**

(F) Mid 1939, same as (D), but V-shaped retaining yoke at back of solenoid replaces soldering and spot welding **20 25 15**

(G) Late 1939, same as (F), but solenoid assemblies black instead of nickel **20 25 15**

(H) Last 1939 production, same as (G), but small spring spot-welded to coupler tails **20 25 15**

(I) Early 1940, same as (D), but Type III-GX black early 1940 trucks with solenoid assembly mounted within base fastened around axles by tab and slot arrangement; insulated bakelite contact shoes; long black coupler shank extensions with 1/8" rise; box coupler has simulated knuckle and lift pin; small springs spot-welded to long coupler tails; black journals **20 25 15**

(J) Same as (I), but springs removed from coupler tails **20 25 15**

(K) Same as (I), but Type 650-F frame with dime-sized depressions **20 25 15**

(L) Same as (K), but springs removed from coupler tails, Pauli and Koff Collections **25 30 15**

(M) 1941, four nickel stakes (two on each side); two late one-piece nickel brakewheels, stands, and short connecting rods on left hand side of ends as viewer faces ends; catalogued as having a "Load of Logs" (probably came with eight pieces of lumber); light green (45N watchman base) painted frame (Type 650-D) with quarter-sized truck depressions containing two 1/4" truck mounting holes and 1-1/8" end openings widened to accommodate coupler box which now is recessed partly under frame; four horizontal lines of black sans-serif lettering rubber-stamped on frame bottom as in (A); two black Type III-H trucks with free floating solenoids attached to axles by metal bases as in (I), but with shorter pointed solenoid plungers now secured by two snap-in eyelet rivet fasteners, short black coupler shank extensions have a 1/8" downward drop, resulting in the box coupler becoming recessed partly under widened car frame; simulated lift pin removed from 1940 box coupler design, leaving only a simulated knuckle on top. (Only by forcing the coupler shank to bend upward can this coupler be coupled to previously built cars, and it is all but impossible to hook it to a 1940 coupler — there is a full 1/4" difference in coupler height. However, this was the best working of all the automatic couplers and looked the best.) Both trucks have black wheels with nickel backs on thin nickel axles and black journals; trucks secured by horseshoe clips atop nickel washers **20 25 15**

(N) Same as (M), but brakewheels on right corners of ends as viewer faces ends, Pauli and Koff Collections **25 30 15**

(O) Same as (M), but axles, truck studs, horseshoe clips, washers, brakewheels and all other trim is black, not nickel. Reader comments invited **20 25 15**

2652 Lionel Gondola Car 1938-41:

(A) Early 1938, yellow painted sides and ends both inside and out; body embossed to simulate panels and extended ribs between them; two Type IV nickel brakewheels on left corners of car ends; second panel on body sides from each end is slotted to accept tabbed nickel plates which are gray on back (perhaps galvanized); left plate reads "LIONEL" in black serif letters and right plate reads "2652"; black Type 650-F semi-gloss frame with two dime-sized depressions containing 1/4" truck mounting holes; ends of frames have 7/8" openings for truck-mounted couplers; frame embossed "MADE IN/U.S.A." in two lines; Type IV-E black 1938 magnetic trucks with black 1936-style box couplers; long coupler tails (see truck and coupler discussions for full details); plain nickel contact shoes; trucks secured by circular clips atop nickel washers; black nickel-backed wheels, thin nickel axles and nickel journals; catalogued with two large wooden barrels inside, Pauli and Koff Collections **20 35 10**

(B) 1938, same as (A), but copper-colored contact shoes; possible factory error, Pauli Collection **30 40 15**

(C) Late 1938, same as (A), but fiber-insulated nickel contact shoes **20 35 10**

(D) Late 1938, same as (A), but brakewheels on right corners of car ends. Confirmation requested **20 35 10**

(E) Early 1939, same as (A), but Type 650-C frame with quarter-sized depressions; black Type III-F solenoid trucks with soldered coupler assemblies and no V-shaped yoke on solenoid; short black coupler tails and black coupler shank extensions; contact shoes are bakelite-insulated; black journals; trucks secured by horseshoe clips atop nickel washers **20 35 10**

(F) 1939, same as (F), but solenoid and coupler assembly spot-welded instead of soldered; cannot be observed unless trucks are removed from frame **20 35 10**

(G) 1939, same as (E), but nickel V-shaped yoke added to solenoid assembly to replace soldering and spot welding, Koff Collection **20 35 10**

(H) Late 1939, same as (G), but black coupler and solenoid assemblies instead of nickel, Pauli Collection **30 40 15**

(I) Last 1939 production, same as (G), but small springs spot-welded to coupler tails **20 35 10**

(J) Earliest 1940 production, burnt orange painted body, both inside and out; embossed body as in (A); Type IV nickel brakewheels on left corners of car ends; white rubber-stamped "LIONEL" on car sides in medium serif lettering; one letter per panel except first and last panels; first panel on left has white rubber-stamped serif lettering "LL/2652" in two lines over- and under-scored; "218000" stamped below in white sans-serif number; panel on extreme right has three data lines: "6-3/I.L 40 6/I.W. 10 2" in white sans-serif letters (note period missing after "L" in second line); Type 650-C frame as in (E); black 1939 Type III-F trucks as in (E); black nickel-backed wheels, thin nickel axles and black journals; trucks secured by horseshoe clips atop nickel washers, Koff Collection **20 35 10**

(K) Early 1940, same as (A), but black 1940 Type III-G trucks with solenoid assemblies mounted to axles by tabs; bakelite-insulated contact shoes; solenoid plugged by rectangular tabbed metal piece instead of V-shaped yoke; shank extension has 1/8" rise; simulated lift pin and knuckle atop coupler box; long black coupler tails; black journals; trucks secured by horseshoe clips atop nickel washers, Pauli Collection **20 35 10**

(L) Early 1940, same as (J), but black Type III-G trucks as in (K), springs spot-welded to coupler tails. This is the "normal" 1940 production car. It is probable that Lionel had a supply of 1938 yellow car bodies and mounted them on 1940-style trucks (K) before beginning the production run of this car, which is burnt orange. Catalogued as having a set of four large wooden barrels, Pauli and Koff Collections **25 40 10**

(M) 1940, same as (L), but no springs on coupler tails **20 35 10**

(N) Late 1941-early 1942, same as (J), but Type 650-D frame with quarter-sized depressions and 1-1/8" end openings to accommodate black Type III-H tracks with 1/8" drop on shank, bakelite-insulated contact shoes, shortened black coupler shank and removed lift pin on coupler box to allow box to recess into frame, Pauli Collection **30 40 10**

2653 Hopper: 1938-42, eight wheels, same as 653 but automatic box couplers, 6-1/2"

(A) Light green with nickel trim, plates and journals; magnetic type box couplers, 1938-39 **12 25 9**

(B) Light green with nickel trim and plates, black journals, solenoid type box couplers, 1939-40 **12 25 9**

(C) Black with nickel trim, no plates, white rubber-stamped lettering, large black and white "L" stamped on car, black journals, solenoid type small box couplers **12 40 11**

2654 Tank: 1938-42, eight wheels, same as 654 but automatic box couplers, 6-1/2"
(A) Aluminum body, "SUNOCO" decal, nickel trim, plates and journals and magnetic type box couplers, 1938-39 **12 25 9**
(B) Same as (A), but black journals **12 25 9**
(C) Orange body, nickel trim and plates, black journals, and solenoid type small box couplers, 1939-40 **11 25 9**
(D) Same as (C), but large box couplers **11 25 9**
(E) Orange body, red "SHELL" decal, no plates, decal lettering, black journals and solenoid type magnetic couplers, 1941-42 **12 25 10**
(F) Light gray, "SUNOCO" decal, decal lettering, no plates, blackened ladder and handrails, small box coupler, box journals **12 25 10**
(G) Same as (F), but nickel domes and ladders; rectangular stanchion holes, Kotil Collection **12 25 10**
(H) Orange body, red "SHELL" decal, nickel trim and plates ("LIONEL LINES" and "2654"), black journals, Type III trucks, Edmunds Collection **12 25 10**
(I) Aluminum body, "SUNOCO" decal at right, black frame and ladders, "S.U.N.X. 2654" and "CAP'Y 100,000 LBS. LT.WT. 42,000" on decal at left, "LIONEL LINES" below data, nine lines of data below "SUNOCO" decal at right, nickel handrails attached by cotter pins, aluminum domes, Type III-H 1941-style box couplers, black journals **12 25 9**

2655 Box: Eight wheels, same as 655 but automatic box couplers, 6-1/2"
(A) Cream body, maroon roof and door guides, nickel trim and journals, large box couplers with electromagnets, 1938, Kotil Collection **20 45 15**
(B) Cream body, tuscan roof and door guides, nickel trim and journals, large box couplers with solenoid mechanism, 1939, Kotil Collection **20 45 15**
(C) Cream body, tuscan roof and door guides, brown rubber-stamped "LIONEL LINES", "2655", and large brown Lionel "L". Small automatic box coupler with simulated knuckle, solenoid mechanism **25 55 20**
(D) Same as (C), but black rubber-stamped lettering instead of brown, Kotil Collection **25 55 20**
(E) Same as (A), but all-black trim, probably very late production. Reader comments requested, Claxton observation **NRS**

2656 Stock: Eight wheels, same as 656, but automatic box couplers, 6-1/2"
(A) Light gray body, red roof and door guides, gray doors, nickel trim and journals, large automatic box couplers, Sattler comment **27 60 25**
(B) Burnt orange body, tuscan roof, white rubber-stamped "LIONEL LINES" and "LL 2656", black journals, small automatic box couplers **40 80 35**
(C) Same as (B), but early larger box couplers and black lettering instead of white, Young Collection **40 80 35**
(D) Same as (A), but red doors. Confirmation requested, Ely comment **NRS**

2657 Caboose: 1940-41, eight wheels, same as 657, but one automatic box coupler, 6-1/2"
(A) Red body and roof, white windows, white rubber-stamped lettering, no plates, red painted trim, black journals, small automatic box solenoid coupler **10 20 8**
(B) Red body, brown roof and cupola, cream windows, rubber-stamped "LIONEL LINES" and "2657", no plates, red painted trim, black journals, large automatic box coupler **10 20 8**
(C) Red body and roof, cream windows, nickel trim and journals, large automatic box coupler **10 20 8**

2657X Same as 2657, but two automatic box couplers
(A) Same as 2657 (B), but small box couplers, Kotil Collection **10 20 9**
(B) Same as 2657 (C), but black journals. On these cars, the "X" is only on the box, not on the car itself, Kotil Collection **10 20 9**

2659 Dump: Eight wheels, same as 659, but automatic box couplers, 6-1/2"
(A) Green hopper, black frame, nickel trim, nickel journals, large automatic box couplers, rubber-stamped "No. 2659" **17 35 15**
(B) Same as (A), but black journals **17 35 15**
(C) Same as (B), but small box couplers, Kotil Collection **17 35 15**

2660 Crane: 1938-42, eight wheels, automatic box couplers, 6-1/2". (Note: There is no latch coupler version of this car)
(A) Pale yellow cab, red roof, green boom, black frame, nickel journals, large box couplers, 1938-40 **21 45 20**
(B) Same as (A), but black, journals, 1941-42 **25 50 20**
(C) Same as (B), but "LIONEL LINES", "2660" AND "L" are rubber-stamped on rear of cab, Blackmar and Kotil Collections **25 50 20**
(D) Same as (A), but nickel plate on cab rear, Kotil Collection **21 45 20**
(E) Same as (D), but black journals, Kotil Collection **21 45 20**

2677 Gondola: Eight wheels, lithographed; same as 1677 but automatic box coupler
(A) Red body, black frame, "LIONEL LINES" in white, black journals, small automatic box couplers and simulated knuckle **9 18 7**

2672 Caboose: Pennsylvania N5 style, brown body and roof, white rubber-stamped lettering "PENNSYLVANIA" and "477618", 6-3/8" long. Without window frames, steps and smokestack. Cupola end window not stamped out. Black journals, frame and trim, not illuminated, one automatic box coupler, 1942. (See 2757, premium version of 2672.) **10 25 10**

2677 Gondola. Note two different couplers — one has long tail and lift pin; the other (later) has neither. In the last stages of prewar production, such mixtures were common.

2679 Box: Eight wheels, lithographed; same as 1679, but automatic box couplers
(A) Yellow body, medium blue roof, orange door, "LIONEL LINES", "Baby Ruth" decal with candy, large automatic box couplers, nickel journals **9 20 8**
(B) Same as (A), but black journals **9 20 8**

2679 box car, Type (B). Note 1936-style box couplers.

(C) Yellow body, maroon roof, "Baby Ruth" lettering but no candy bar. Orange doors and door guides, black journals, large box couplers **9 20 8**
(D) Same as (C), but small automatic box couplers with simulated knuckles **9 20 8**

2679 box car, Type (D)

2680 Tank: 1938-42, eight wheels, lithographed; same as 1680, but automatic box couplers
(A) Aluminum, "SUNOCO" diamond herald, "MOTOR OIL" lower left; nickel journals, large automatic box couplers **9 20 8**
(B) Same as (A), but black journals **9 20 8**
(C) Orange, "SHELL", black journals, large automatic box couplers **9 20 8**
(D) Gray, "SUNOCO" diamond herald, upper right, "SUNX 2680" upper left, three nickel domes, black journals, small automatic box couplers with simulated knuckle **9 20 8**

2680 tank car, Type (D). Note absence of handrails and 1941 Type III-H recessed couplers.

(E) Aluminum, "SUNOCO" diamond herald in upper right, "SUNX 2680" in upper left, small automatic box couplers with simulated knuckle **9 20 8**

(F) Same as (D), but black domes, very late production, Claxton Collection **9 20 8**

2682 Caboose: 1938-42, eight wheels, lithographed; same as 1682, but one automatic box coupler

(A) Light red body and roof, cream windows, "LIONEL LINES", black journals, large automatic box coupler, Kotil Collection **8 20 5**

(B) Light red body and roof, cream windows, cream stripe through cupola, large automatic box coupler, Kotil Collection **8 20 5**

(C) Brown body and roof, white "N.Y.C." lettering, black journals, small automatic box coupler **8 20 7**

(D) Same as (A), but nickel journals and small box coupler, Kotil Collection **8 20 5**

(E) Same as (C), but large box coupler, Kotil Collection **8 20 5**

2682X Caboose: Same as 2682, but two automatic box couplers. Brown body and roof, white "N.Y.C." lettering, black journals, small automatic box couplers. The "X" does not appear on the car itself; it is only found on the box **8 20 8**

2717 Gondola: Eight wheels, lithographed car based on Ives design. Not catalogued, automatic box couplers, 9-1/2"

(A) Burnt orange and tan with nickel journals, 1938-39 **14 30 10**

(B) Same as (A), but black journals, 1940-42 **14 30 10**

2719 Box: Eight wheels, lithographed, based on Ives design, not catalogued, automatic box couplers, 9-1/2"

(A) Light peacock with blue roof, orange door and door guides, nickel journals, door knobs and ladders, 1938-39 **15 30 10**

(B) Same as (A), but black journals **15 30 10**

2722 Caboose: Eight wheels, lithographed car based on Ives design, not catalogued, automatic box couplers, 9-1/2"

(A) Orange-red with maroon roof, nickel journals, 1938-39 **14 30 10**

(B) Same as (A), but black journals, 1940-42 **14 30 10**

2755 Tank: 1941-42, eight wheels, scale detailed (not exactly scale), black die-cast frame, small automatic box couplers

(A) Gray with "SUNOCO" decal, lettered "S.U.N.X. 2755" **25 60 20**

(B) Same as (A), but aluminum tank **25 60 20**

2757 Caboose: 1941-42, PRR N5 type, with interior lights, attached red window frames, smoke stack, frosted windows, "PENNSYLVANIA" and "477618" rubber-stamped in white on tuscan body, with automatic box couplers at one end only, 6-3/4" **10 25 9**

2757X Caboose: 1941-42, same as 2757, but with automatic box couplers at both ends **11 25 9**

2758 Automobile Box: 1941-42, but with automatic box couplers at both ends **11 25**

2758 Automobile Box: 1941-42, tuscan body, rubber-stamped "PENNSYLVANIA", 9" **11 25 10**

2810 Crane: 1938-42, similar to 810, but with one automatic box coupler and one non-automatic box coupler. Non-automatic box coupler has long coupler shank designed to fit around control knob

(A) Yellow cab, red roof, bright green boom, nickel trim, aluminum or black control knobs, large box couplers, Peter Miller Collection **60 125 50**

(B) Same as (A), but two small automatic box couplers with simulated knuckles, small black knob for rotating cab and two larger black knobs. The smaller black knob allowed Lionel to use two automatic couplers, Peter Miller Collection **50 150 50**

2811 Flat: 1938-41, similar to 811, but with automatic box couplers

(A) Aluminum, black rubber-stamped "THE LIONEL LINES" on side, black stakes, eight logs **60 125 50**

(B) Same as (A), but later frame with deep-dish depressions in floor. This is the most rare of all the 800-2800 Series rubber-stamped cars, Henderson observation **NRS**

2812 Gondola: 1938-42, same as 812, but automatic box couplers

(A) Bright green, Blackmar Collection **18 40 15**

(B) Dark orange **18 40 15**

2812X Gondola: 1941-42, dark orange painted body with white rubber stamped lettering: "LIONEL LINES/2812/NEW 12-41" over- and underscored at one end. Reporting marks at other end as follows: "CAPY 10000/LD.LT. 10230/LT.WT. 6670/I.C. 33-6/I.W. 9-6/CU.FT. 810". Nickel brakewheels, with one-piece wheel soldered to staff. Disc underframe and trucks close to car ends. Solenoid-operated box couplers with plunger whose end is 7/8" from car and 9/16" high from rail. Coupler box has simulated knuckles on top surface. This car was catalogued 2812X to signify its lower coupler height, although actually numbered 2812. It is illustrated in this book with other late 800 and 2800 series cars, and its distinctive coupler height is readily apparent. Because of its low coupler height, the car was shown in 1941 with sets 841W, 843W (lettered "PENNSYLVANIA", though never made that way) and 859B. In 1942, the car is shown with sets 853W and 859B. This car may be scarce, since it was only offered for two years, Graves Collection **42 65 45**

2813 Stock: 1938-42, same as 812, but automatic box couplers

(A) Cream body, maroon roof and door guides, nickel trim, Sattler Collection **70 150 50**

(B) Same as (A), but light yellow body, Sattler Collection **70 150 50**

2814 Box: 1938-42, automatic box coupler. (See background on series No. 814)

(A) Pale yellow body, maroon roof, nickel plates with black lettering, maroon door guides, large automatic box couplers **70 150 50**

(B) Similar to (A), but catalogued as "2814X", Type III trucks closer to car ends, black oxidized journals **70 150 50**

(C) Orange body, brown roof, no plates, black rubber-stamped lettering, lowered dish in car frame, Type III trucks closer to car ends, black oxidized journals, black painted trim. Rare **250 400 200**

2814R Refrigerator: 1938-42

(A) White body, brown roof, no plates, rubber-stamped lettering, automatic box couplers, black journals, frame and trim. Extremely rare **200 300 100**

(B) White body, light blue roof, aluminum frame, nickel trim and plates which read "2814R", automatic box couplers, Type II trucks, Read and Kotil Collections **200 300 100**

(C) Same as (B), but black frame, Kotil Collection **200 300 100**

2815 Tank: 1938-42, similar to 815, but automatic box couplers

(A) Aluminum tank, black frame, nickel trim and plates, "SUNOCO" decal, large automatic box couplers, nickel journals **35 75 30**

2815 Tank car, Type (A). Note Type VI trucks with 1936-style box couplers.

(B) Orange tank, black frame, nickel trim and plates, red "SHELL" decals, large automatic box couplers **45 100 40**

(C) Same as (B), but decal lettering rather than nickel plates, black painted trim, small automatic box couplers **50 100 45**

(D) Orange tank, black frame, no "SHELL" decal, decal lettering rather than nickel-plated, black painted trim, small automatic box couplers **50 110 45**

2816 Hopper: 1935-42, similar to 816, but automatic couplers

(A) Black, white rubber-stamped lettering, small automatic box couplers with simulated knuckle, Type III trucks with black journals **85 150 60**

(B) Red, nickel plates and trim, automatic box couplers **30 65 30**

2816 Hopper, Type (B). Note oversized side wheel and 1936-style box couplers.

2817 Caboose: 1936-42, but with automatic box couplers

(A) Light red body and roof, aluminum trim with nickel plates **20 50 25**

(B) Light red body, tuscan roof and white trim with nickel plates **50 100 35**

(C) Flat red body, tuscan roof, black frame, white window inserts, white rubber-stamped lettering, red enameled observation railing, small automatic box coupler with simulated knuckle **50 100 35**

2820 Floodlight: 1938-42, similar to 820 but automatic box couplers

(A) Green base; nickel, stamped searchlights, nickel handrails, brakewheels and journals, rubber-stamped "THE LIONEL LINES", large automatic box coupler **45 100 40**

(B) Green base, gray, die-cast searchlights, nickel handrails, brakewheels and black journals, white rubber-stamped "THE LIONEL LINES", small automatic box coupler with simulated knuckle couplers **70 150 60**

2954 Box: 1940-42, in scale series, same as 715, but with automatic box couplers and tinplate trucks **90 200 75**

2955 Tank: 1940-42, in scale series, same as 715, but with automatic box couplers and tinplate trucks

(A) Lettered "SHELL" **90 200 75**

(B) Lettered "SUNOCO". Much scarcer than (A), Sattler Collection **NRS**

2956 Hopper: 1940-42, in scale series, same as 715, but with automatic box couplers and tinplate trucks **140 300 120**

2957 Caboose: 1940-42, in scale series, same as 715, but with automatic box couplers and tinplate trucks **120 250 100**

3651 Lumber: 1939-42, matches 2650 series, eight wheels, operating car with dump motion with logs and bin, automatic coupler. (Note: There is no latch coupler version of this car.)

(A) Black with nickel stakes, brakewheels, black journals, small box with solenoid type coupler, 6-1/2" **10 25 9**

(B) Same as (A), but earlier large box couplers with solenoid couplers, Sattler and Kotil Collections **10 25 9**

3652 Operating Gondola: 1939-42, eight wheels, with bin, dumps eight wooden barrels, box couplers, 6-1/2"

(A) Yellow body, black frame, black rubber-stamped "LIONEL", nickel brakewheels, black journals, small box coupler, Blackmar Collection **17 35 12**

(B) Same as (A), but with nickel journals **17 35 12**

(C) Same as (A), but large box couplers **17 35 12**

(D) Same as (A), but red rubber-stamped "LIONEL", Blackmar Collection **20 40 15**

(E) Same as (A), but large 1936-style coupler boxes and bakelite insulation on contact shoes. This car predates (A), Hoffman Collection **17 35 15**

(F) Yellow body, black frame, two nickel plates instead of rubber-stamping. Left plate reads: "LIONEL" and right plate reads "3652". Large automatic box couplers, nickel Type IV brakewheels and black journals. This car represents the earliest stage of production, Blackmar, Claxton, Kotil and Sattler Collections **17 35 15**

3659 Operating Dump: 1939-42, matches 2650 series, hopper tilts, large automatic box couplers, 6-1/2"

(A) Black frame and end unit, red hopper **11 25 12**

(B) Black frame and end unit, bright green hopper, catalogued in 1938 as part of set, previously reported as not manufactured, Aziz Collection. **NRS**

(C) Same as (A), but small operating box couplers, Kotil Collection **11 25 12**

3811 Lumber-dump: 1939-42, matches 2810 series, eight wheels, operating lumber-dump (with lumber), black, no lettering, nickel stakes and brakewheel, automatic box couplers, 8-7/8" **22 50 20**

3814 Merchandise: 1939-42, matches 2810 series, (see 814 for series details). Operating car which "delivers" black or red merchandise packages

(A) Tuscan body and roof, black frame and painted trim, white rubber-stamped lettering, small automatic box couplers with simulated knuckle, brown and white large "l", Type III trucks, black journals, 1941-42 **70 125 65**

(B) Tuscan body and roof, black frame, white decal lettering, large automatic box couplers; red, white and blue large "L", Type II trucks, nickel journals and trim, 1939-40 **65 100 55**

3814 Merchandise Car, Type (C). Note loading hatch and 1936-style box couplers. Brakewheels only have one stanchion.

3859 Dump: 1938-42, matches 2810 series, eight wheels, black operating car whose hopper dumps coal, automatic box couplers and embossed number on frame

(A) Black frame with red bin, Blackmar Collection **20 50 20**

(B) Same as (A), but Type III trucks and later dished-out frame, Blackmar Collection **20 50 20**

Chapter VI

0 AND 0-27 GAUGE PASSENGER CARS

Gd Exc Rst

529 Pullman, 1926-32, four wheels; window, door, name plate is one-piece insert. Latch couplers, with twist ends. Usually with oiling instruction labels; stamped "529 PULLMAN 529", 6-1/2", Ely comment

	Gd	Exc	Rst
(A) Olive green body and roof, maroon trim, one spring embossed over axle on frame, gold lettering	8	20	8
(B) Same as (A), but two springs over axles	8	20	8
(C) Olive green body and roof, red trim, no journals, gold lettering	8	20	8
(D) Same as (C), but nickel journals	8	20	8
(E) Olive green body and roof, orange trim, nickel journals, flat frame ends (not rounded), olive green lettering	8	20	8
(F) Maroon frame with squared ends, terra-cotta body and roof, cream trim, gold lettering, nickel journals	8	20	8
(G) Same as (F), but black lettering	8	20	8
(H) Same as (G), but copper journals	8	20	8

530 Pullman 1926-32, four wheels; window, door, name plate is one-piece stamping inserted in matching body. Latch coupler with twist ends; usually with oiling instruction labels, rubber-stamped "530 OBSERVATION 530" beneath windows, blue speckled celluloid in upper window section, Ely comment

	Gd	Exc	Rst
(A) Matches 529 (A)	8	20	8
(B) Matches 529 (B)	8	20	8
(C) Matches 529 (C)	8	20	8
(D) Matches 529 (D)	8	20	8
(E) Matches 529 (E)	8	20	8
(F) Matches 529 (F)	8	20	8
(G) Matches 529 (G)	8	20	8
(H) Matches 529 (H)	8	20	8

600 Pullman, Early 1915-23, four wheels, seven windows and two doors, each with window on each side; steps, hook couplers, gold rubber-stamped "NEW YORK CENTRAL LINES" above windows, "PULLMAN" within elaborate scrollwork beneath windows, black frame, 5-1/2", gold stripe under window, Ely comment

	Gd	Exc	Rst
(A) Dark green	10	20	10
(B) Maroon	10	20	10
(C) Brown	10	20	10
(D) Dark brown	10	20	10

600 Pullman, Late 1933-42, six three-part windows and two doors on each side, single stamped piece forms windows, doors, name and number plates for each side, one-piece stamped roof, one interior light, 4 single step units, stamped handrails on both sides of each door, fishbelly with embossed air-tanks, removable roof with spring latches, twist end latch couplers or manual box couplers, rubber-stamped "600 PULLMAN 600" on side below window, four-wheel trucks

	Gd	Exc	Rst
(A) Light red body and roof, ivory windows, doors, name and number boards, red fishbelly, frosted windows, latch or non-automatic box couplers, nickel journals	37	75	25
(B) Light gray body, red roof and fishbelly, ivory doors, windows, name and number boards, copper journals, latch couplers	35	75	25
(C) Light blue body, aluminum roof and windows, doors, name and number boards, fishbelly, nickel handrails, latch coupler	50	100	40

601 Pullman, Early 1915-23, seven one-part windows and two doors on each side formed from a one-piece stamping, windows have a slight rounding at top, four-wheel trucks; windows and door wood lithographed, gold rubber-stamped "NEW YORK CENTRAL LINES" above windows, and "PULLMAN" beneath windows, "601" on one end. Dark green body and roof, hook or combination latch couplers, 7" long. Early versions embossed "LIONEL MFG CO." on underside — 8 20 8

601 Observation, Late Type (C)

601 Observation, Late 1933-42, matches 600 Pullman Late. (See 600 Pullman, Late, for background.) Six three-part windows, one door on each side; windows, door, name and number boards stamped from one piece; observation deck with red, aluminum or nickel railings; rubber-stamped "601 OBSERVATION 601" on side below window

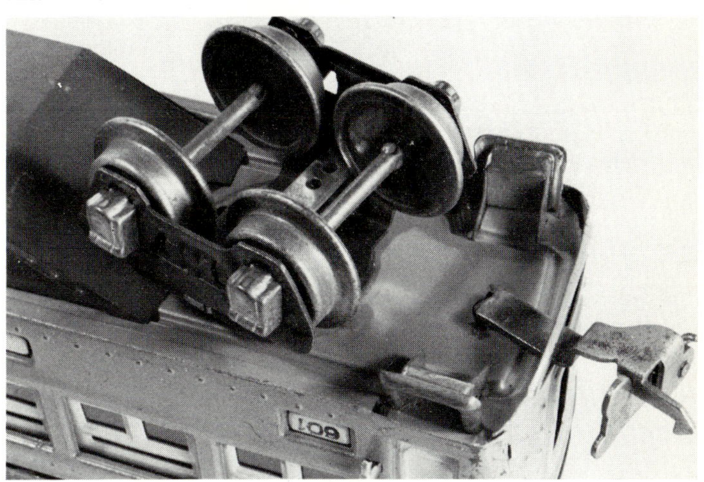

601 Underside Detail

	Gd	Exc	Rst
(A) Light red body and roof, ivory insert, red observation railing, frosted window, latch or box coupler	40	80	35
(B) Same as (A), but aluminum railing	40	80	35
(C) Light gray body, red roof, ivory trim, copper journals, latch couplers	35	75	30
(D) Light blue body, aluminum roof and trim and blue railing, nickel trim, usually latch couplers	50	100	40
(E) Same as (D), but aluminum railing	50	100	40

Comparison of 601 with its automatic coupler 2601 revision. Note difference in platform base.

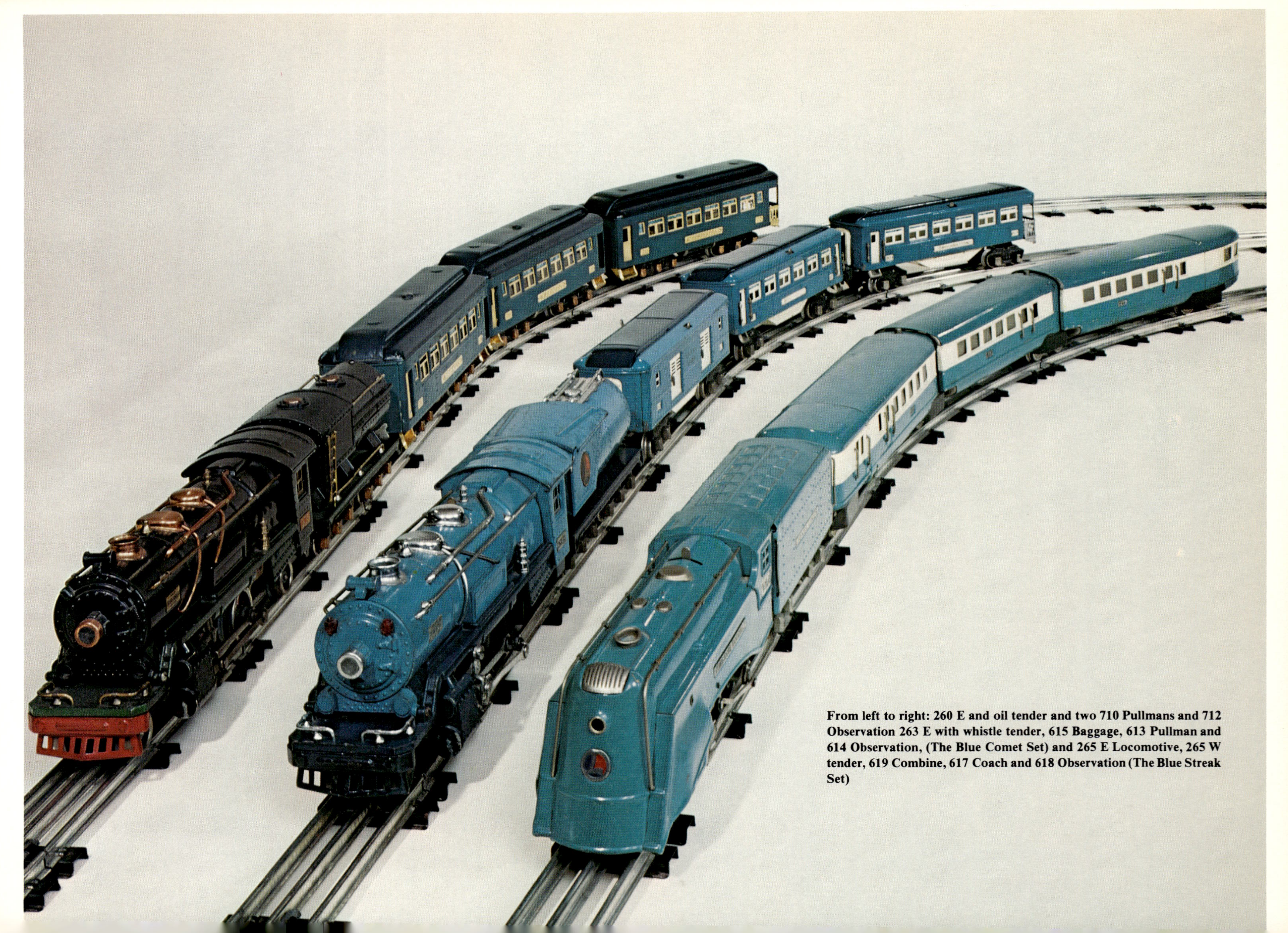

From left to right: 260 E and oil tender and two 710 Pullmans and 712 Observation 263 E with whistle tender, 615 Baggage, 613 Pullman and 614 Observation, (The Blue Comet Set) and 265 E Locomotive, 265 W tender, 619 Combine, 617 Coach and 618 Observation (The Blue Streak Set)

602 Baggage, Early 1915-23, two baggage doors on each side, four-wheel trucks, gold rubber-stamped "NEW YORK CENTRAL LINES" above doors and "UNITED STATES RAILWAY POST OFFICE" between doors and "602" at each end on the sides; hook or combination latch couplers between doors, "602" on one end

(A) Dark green body and roof, wood lithographed doors	8	20	8
(B) Yellow-orange body and roof, wood lithographed doors	15	30	15

602 (B) Baggage Car.

602 Baggage, Late 1933-42, matches 600 Pullman, Late. (See 600 Pullman, Late, for background.) Rubber-stamped in black "THE LIONEL LINES" between doors. Two small baggage windows and two doors that open on each side; "602" appears on number boards on the side near each end, 9" long

(A) Light red body and roof, ivory trim, latch or box coupler	40	80	35
(B) Light gray body, red roof and fishbelly, ivory trim, copper journals, latch coupler, brass door knobs	35	75	30
(C) Light blue body, aluminum roof and trim, usually latch coupler	50	90	45
(D) Same as (C), but one light and nickel journals, I. D. Smith Collection	50	90	45

603 Pullman, Early, eight wheels

(A) Early, 1922, uncatalogued, same as 601, with seven one-piece windows on each side, matches Early 602; yellow-orange body and roof and wood grained doors, rubber-stamped "NEW YORK CENTRAL LINES", 7" long **10 25 10**

603 Pullman, Later, eight wheels

(B) Later version, 1920-25, different body from 603 (A), without rubber-stamped road name, with five three-part windows, with or without interior lights, white celluloid in upper window section, hook or combination latch couplers, 6-1/2" long

(C) Orange body and roof, wood-grained trim	15	35	15
(D) Same as (C), but maroon doors and trim	15	35	15

603 Pullman, Latest 1931-36, eight wheels, 7-1/2" long, 5 three-part windows and two doors on each side. It differs from 603 immediately above in that the windows, doors, number boards and letter boards are a one-piece stamping that fits into matching openings on the coach side and is a contrasting color to body. The roof is a one-piece stamping. This same body was used for the matching 604 Observation, and two other matching sets; 607, 608 and 609, 611. The different numbers reflect differences between the three sets. 603 and 604 were not lighted but had journals and airtanks; 609 and 611 each had one interior light, but had neither journals nor airtanks. All 603s are rubber-stamped "THE LIONEL LINES" above windows, have latch couplers, and are lettered "603 PULLMAN 603" beneath windows

(J) Light red body and roof, white trim, red underbelly instead of tanks, "RED COMET", 1935-36	20	40	15
(K) Red body, black roof, cream trim	10	25	15
(L) Yellow-orange body, terra-cotta roof and cream trim	10	25	15
(M) Stephen Girard green body, dark green roof, cream trim	10	25	15
(N) Maroon body and roof, cream trim, "MACY SPECIAL"	20	75	15

604 Pullman, Later 1920-25, matches 603 Pullman, Later, 603 (C) and 603 (D), 6-1/4" long

(C) Orange body and roof, wood-grained trim	25	50	25
(D) Orange body and roof, maroon trim	25	50	25

604 Observation, Later, 1920-25, matches 603 Pullman, Later 603 (C) and (D), 6-1/4" long, lettered "OBSERVATION" below windows, Hahn Collection **25 50 25**

604 Observation, Latest, 1931-36, matches 603 Latest, (J)-(N). Brass railing, 7-1/2" long

(J) Light red body and roof, white trim, red underbelly instead of tanks, part of Red Comet train, 1935-36	20	50	15
(K) Red body, black roof, cream trim	15	35	15
(L) Yellow-orange body, terra-cotta roof and cream trim	15	35	15
(M) Stephen Girard green body, dark green roof, cream trim	15	35	15
(N) Maroon body and roof, cream trim, "MACY SPECIAL," brass plate on railing lettered "MACY SPECIAL"	20	90	15

605 Pullman, 1925-32, large, 10-1/4" long cars with six three-part windows, two lavatory windows, and two operating doors on each side. Three-piece roof construction, interior benches, separate stampings for windows and doors, operating doors & brass steps, latch couplers, large four-wheel trucks, rubber-stampings; (A) through (H) catalogued with only the 251 from 1925-29; from 1930-32 with the 251 and with the orange or gray 4 and from 1931-32 with the 251, 4 or 254 — the cars matched the engine's color. Red versions had low trucks; gray versions had high trucks, Kotil observation

(A) Gray body and roof with maroon trim, rubber-stamped "NEW YORK CENTRAL LINES"	50	100	45
(B) Same as (A), but reads "THE LIONEL LINES"	50	100	45
(C) Same as (A), but with apple green clerestory	50	100	45
(D) Same as (B), but with apple green clerestory	50	100	45
(E) Same as (A), but with red trim, uncatalogued 1930-32	50	100	45
(F) Same as (B), but with red trim, uncatalogued 1930-32	50	100	45
(G) Red body and roof with ivory trim, rubber-stamped "LIONEL LINES"	100	150	45
(H) Same as (G), but reads "ILLINOIS CENTRAL"	150	200	45
(I) Orange body and roof with cream trim, rubber-stamped "LIONEL LINES"	100	150	45
(J) Same as (I), but reads "ILLINOIS CENTRAL"	175	250	45
(K) Olive green body, roof and doors with red trim, uncatalogued, 1931, with long or short door windows, rubber-stamped "THE LIONEL LINES"	100	150	45
(L) Same as (K), but reads "ILLINOIS CENTRAL"	175	250	45
(M) Same as (A), but "ILLINOIS CENTRAL," Kotil Collection	50	100	45

606 Observation 1925-32, matches 605

(A) Matches 605 (A)	50	100	45
(B) Matches 605 (B)	50	100	45
(C) Matches 605 (C)	50	100	45
(D) Matches 605 (D)	50	100	45
(E) Matches 605 (E)	50	100	45
(F) Matches 605 (F)	50	100	45
(G) Matches 605 (G)	100	150	45
(H) Matches 605 (H)	150	200	45
(I) Matches 605 (I)	100	150	45
(J) Matches 605 (J)	100	150	45
(K) Matches 605 (K)	100	150	45
(L) Matches 605 (L)	175	250	45
(M) Matches 605 (M), Kotil Collection	50	100	45

607 Pullman 1926-27, same body as 603 Latest, (See 603 Latest for background.), 5 three-part windows and two doors on each side; windows, doors, number and letter boards are one-piece stampings on each side, one-piece roof stamping, no attached steps, airtanks, interior light, inside benches, 7-1/2" long

(A) Peacock body and roof, orange trim, rubber-stamped "THE LIONEL LINES"	15	35	15
(B) Same as (A), but reads "ILLINOIS CENTRAL"	30	54	15
(C) Stephen Girard green body, dark green roof with cream trim, rubber-stamped "THE LIONEL LINES"	20	40	15
(D) Red body and roof, cream trim, rubber-stamped "THE LIONEL LINES"	25	55	15
(E) Same as (C), but has fishbelly instead of airtanks, Blackmar Collection	20	40	15

608 Observation 1926-37, matches 607. (See 603 Pullman, Latest, for background)

(A) Same as 607 (A)	15	35	15
(B) Same as 607 (B)	30	65	15
(C) Same as 607 (C), but with brass observation railings	20	40	15

254 E (A)
610
610
612

253 (I)
610
610
612

253 (H)
610
610
612
cars repainted

253
607
607
608

252 (A)
607
608

1560
184
208

(D) Same as 607 (C), but with aluminum painted observation railings 20 40 15
(E) Same as 607 (D) 25 55 15

609 Pullman 1937, uncatalogued, same body as 603 Pullman, Latest. (See 603 Pullman, Latest, for background.) Rubber-stamped "THE LIONEL LINES" over window, "609 PULLMAN 609" under window; blue body and aluminum roof and trim, lighted, no journals, latch coupler, no airtanks 20 50 15

610 Pullman, Early 1915-25, six three-part windows, hook or combination coupler, no added trim or name plates, gold rubber-stamped "NEW YORK CENTRAL LINES" above windows, "PULLMAN" below windows, four-wheel trucks, 8-1/2" long
(A) Dark green body and roof, maroon doors, mottled green celluloid in windows, 1915-23 20 50 15
(B) Same as (A), but wood-grained doors 20 50 15
(C) Same as (A), but with red celluloid in upper windows 20 50 15
(D) Same as (B), with red celluloid in upper windows 20 50 15
(E) Maroon body and roof, dark green door, with mottled green celluloid, 1923-25 25 55 15
(F) Mojave body and roof with maroon door and mottled green celluloid, 1923-25 25 55 15
(G) Same as (F), but with wood-grained door, 1923-25 25 55 15

610 Pullman, Late, 1926-30, 8 large single pane windows and 2 doors on each side, one-piece stamping includes 8 windows, 2 doors, and name and number boards for each side, interior benches, no brass steps, fixed doors, latch couplers, large 4 wheel trucks, interior light, rubber-stamped "THE LIONEL LINES" above windows and "610 PULLMAN 610" below windows except as noted, 8-3/4" long
(A) Olive green body and roof with maroon trim 20 50 25
(B) Same as (A), but red trim 20 50 25
(C) Same as (A), but orange trim 20 50 25
(D) Mojave body and roof, maroon trim 20 50 25
(E) Same as (D), but rubber-stamped "NEW YORK CENTRAL LINES" 20 50 25
(F) Terra-cotta body, maroon roof, cream trim; 1933, uncatalogued 20 50 15
(G) Pea green body and roof with orange trim 30 75 25
(H) Same as (G), but with white window shades 30 75 25
(I) Light blue body and aluminum roof and trim with scroll lettering, 1936-37 65 170 25
(J) Light red body, aluminum window and name and number inserts, aluminum roof, rubber-stamped "THE LIONEL LINES" in serif lettering above windows, Kotil Collection 20 50 25
(K) Same as (J), but sans-serif lettering, Kotil Collection 20 50 25

611 Observation 1937, uncatalogued, matches 609. (See 603 Pullman, Latest for background.) 20 50 15

612 Observation, Early 1915-25, matches 610 Pullman, Early
(A) Matches 610 (A) 25 50 20
(B) Matches 610 (B) 25 50 20
(C) Matches 610 (C) 25 50 20
(D) Matches 610 (D) 25 50 20
(E) Matches 610 (E) 25 60 20
(F) Matches 610 (F) 25 60 20
(G) Matches 610 (G) 25 60 20

612 Observation, Late 1926-30, matches 610 Pullman, Late
(A) Matches 610 (A) 20 50 25
(B) Matches 610 (B) 20 50 25
(C) Matches 610 (C) 20 50 25
(D) Matches 610 (D) 20 50 25
(E) Matches 610 (E) 25 55 25
(F) Matches 610 (F) 25 55 25
(G) Matches 610 (G) 30 75 25
(H) Matches 610 (H) 30 75 25
(I) Matches 610 (I) 30 75 25
(J) Matches 610 (J), Kotil Collection 20 50 25
(K) Matches 610 (K), Kotil Collection 20 50 25

613 Pullman 1931-40, three-part windows and two doors on each side, one-piece stamping for each side provides windows, doors, name and number boards; fixed doors, underbelly with embossed airtanks painted same contrasting color as window/door/board insert; brass single step units; light fixture, large stamped handrails on both sides of each door, removable roof with spring latches, latch couplers (early) or non-automatic box couplers (later). Rubber-stamped "THE LIONEL LINES" above windows and "613 PULLMAN" beneath windows on boards, two-piece roof construction, 10-1/4" long
(A) Terra-cotta body and maroon and terra-cotta roof, cream windows, doors, underbelly and vestibules, brass trim, and steps, copper journals, latch couplers 125 250 80
(B) Light red body, light red and aluminum roof, aluminum trim, nickel journals, latch couplers 125 250 80
(C) Same as (B), but manual box couplers 125 250 80
(D) Blue body, blue and dark blue roof, ivory windows, doors, boards and underbelly, nickel trim, latch couplers. Cars known as "0 Gauge Blue Comet" and are highly desired. (See next entry for another version.) 60 125 50
(E) Same as (D), but non-automatic box couplers 60 125 50

614 Observation 1931-40, matches 613, 10-1/8" long, and rubber-stamped "614 OBSERVATION 614" beneath windows, brass or aluminum painted observation railing
(A) Matches 613 (A) 60 125 50
(B) Matches 613 (B) 200 350 100
(C) Matches 613 (C) 200 350 100
(D) Matches 613 (D) 115 200 100
(E) Matches 613 (E) 115 200 100

615 Baggage 1933-40, matches 613, 10-1/4" long, rubber-stamped "LIONEL LINES" on two lines in car center between doors, and "615" on two number boards on each side
(A) Matches 613 (A) 60 125 50
(B) Matches 613 (B) 200 350 100
(C) Matches 613 (C) 200 350 100
(D) Matches 613 (D) 115 200 100
(E) Matches 613 (E) 115 200 100

617 Coach 1935-41, came with either "Flying Yankee," No. 616, or "Blue Streak," No. 265 sets. Early versions have four doors, later models two doors, frosted windows, connects with lighted vestibule unit, nickel trim, price includes vestibule
(A) Blue Streak, blue coach with white band through windows 30 70 18
(B) Flying Yankee, chrome sides, gunmetal skirts 20 50 18
(C) Flying Yankee, chrome sides, chrome skirts 20 50 18

618 Observation 1935-41, came with either "Flying Yankee," No. 616, or "Blue Streak," No. 265, sets. Frosted windows, lighted vestibule units, nickel trim, price includes vestibule
(A) Blue Streak, blue observation with white band through windows 30 70 18
(B) Flying Yankee, chrome sides, gunmetal skirts and tail 20 50 18
(C) Flying Yankee, chrome sides, skirts and tail 20 50 18

619 Combine
(A) Blue with white window band; came only with "Blue Streak" set, Sattler Collection 85 200 75
(B) All-chrome version; came only with No. 279E set catalogued only in 1935 on page 12, Kotil and Sattler Collections 85 200 75

629 Pullman 1924-32, same as 529; four rounded windows, single stamping for contrasting trim, four-wheel except as noted, no mottled green celluloid in windows (early), latch couplers (except early ones with hook couplers), no trim; journal boxes only on later cars, 6-1/2", Ely comment
(A) Dark green body and roof, maroon trim, no window inserts, gold lettering, hook couplers 10 25 10
(B) Orange body and roof, peacock trim, rubber-stamped gold lettering, hook couplers, very early production 15 25 12
(C) Same as (B), but frame has two springs embossed over axle, not one 15 25 12
(D) Red body, cream trim, gold rubber-stamped lettering, latch couplers and nickel journals, Kotil Collection 8 20 8
(E) Same as (D), but copper journals 8 20 8
(F) Same as (E), but black rubber-stamped lettering 8 20 8
(G) Same (F), but light red body and roof 8 20 8

630 Observation 1926-31, matches 629 Pullman
(A) Matches 629 (A) 10 25 10
(B) Matches 629 (B) 15 25 12
(C) Matches 629 (C) 15 25 12

619

617

637

617

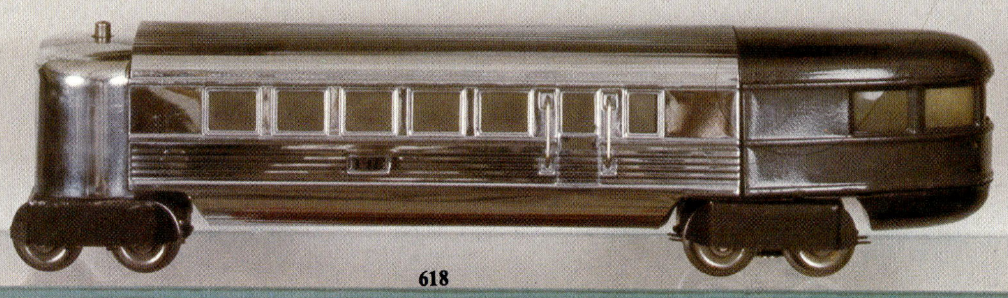
618

603 (J)

(D) Matches 629 (D) **8 20 8**
(E) Matches 629 (E) **8 20 8**
(F) Matches 629 (F) **8 20 8**
(G) Matches 629 (G) **8 25 8**

637 Coach 1936-39, part of "City of Denver" set, see 636 locomotive for background **35 75 45**

638 Observation 19036-39, part of "City of Denver" set, see 636 locomotive for background **35 75 45**

702 Baggage 1917-21, same as 602, but in gray for armored set only, no trim, name plates or lettering, two four-wheel trucks, 7" **90 200 75**

710 Pullman 1924-34, 3-piece roof construction, interior benches, interior lights, four-wheel or six-wheel trucks, separate stampings for six paired windows and doors, nickel journals, operating doors, brass steps, latch couplers, rubber-stamped "THE LIONEL LINES" and "710" except as noted, 11-1/2"
(A) Red body and roof, ivory trim and doors, 1930-32 (usually with red 251 in uncatalogued set), four-wheel trucks, copper or nickel journals **120 220 90**
(B) Same as (A), but with Stephen Girard green operating doors, 1930-32 (usually with 260E), speckled blue celluloid in upper windows and end windows **100 175 70**
(C) Orange body and roof, dark olive green trim, with four-wheel trucks, 1928-29 (with orange 256) **70 150 55**
(D) Same as (C), but with six-wheel trucks **80 160 60**
(E) Orange body and roof, with maroon doors and brown window inserts, four-wheel trucks, 1924-27, "NEW YORK CENTRAL" **100 175 70**
(F) Same as (E), but reading "ILLINOIS CENTRAL" **150 300 100**
(G) Same as (E), but with six-wheel trucks **100 175 70**
(H) Same as (F), but with six-wheel trucks **100 175 70**
(I) Same as (E), but with wood grained doors **100 175 70**
(J) Same as (F), but with wood grained doors **100 175 70**
(K) Same as (A), but with six-wheel trucks **100 175 70**
(L) Medium blue body, dark blue roof, cream trim and doors, six-wheel trucks, copper journals, brass steps, blue-mottled celluloid in windows, 1933-34 **150 275 120**
(M) Orange body, dark olive green trim, green frame, rubber-stamped "NEW YORK CENTRAL," came with 260 loco, Kotil Collection **100 175 70**

712 Observation 1924-34, matches 710, 11-1/2"
(A) Matches 710 (A) **120 220 90**
(B) Matches 710 (B) **100 175 70**
(C) Matches 710 (C) **70 150 55**
(D) Matches 710 (D) **80 160 60**
(E) Matches 710 (E) **100 175 70**
(F) Matches 710 (F) **150 300 100**
(G) Matches 710 (G) **100 175 70**
(H) Matches 710 (H) **100 175 70**
(I) Matches 710 (I) **100 175 70**
(J) Matches 710 (J) **100 175 70**
(K) Reserved for confirmation of match for 710 (K)
(L) Reserved for confirmation of match for 710 (L)
(M) Matches 710 (M) **150 275 120**

753 Coach 1936-41, part of articulated streamliner set, "UNION PACIFIC", City of Portland, frosted celluloid windows. Came with 752 Locomotive and 754 Observation
(A) Yellow sides, brown roof and belly **60 125 50**
(B) Aluminum sides, roof and belly **60 125 50**

754 Observation 1936-41, part of articulated streamliner set "UNION PACIFIC," City of Portland, frosted celluloid windows. Came with 752 Locomotive and 753 Coach
(A) Yellow sides, brown roof and belly **35 75 30**
(B) Aluminum sides, roof and belly **35 75 30**

782 Combine 1935-41, part of articulated streamliner set, Hiawatha, with 250E, 783 and 784. Lettered "THE MILWAUKEE ROAD" above windows and "782 LIONEL LINES 782" below windows; gray roof, orange sides and maroon belly. Die-cast belly replacements available. Price for car only **165 350 150**

783 Coach 1935-41, part of articulated streamliner set, Hiawatha, with 250 E, 782, 784. Lettered "THE MILWAUKEE ROAD" above windows and "783 LIONEL LINES 783" below windows, gray roof, orange sides and maroon underbody. Price for car only **165 350 150**

784 Observation 1935-41, part of articulated streamliner set, Hiawatha, with 250 E, 782, 783. Lettered "THE MILWAUKEE ROAD" above windows and "784 LIONEL LINES 784" below windows, gray roof, orange sides and maroon underbody. Price for car only **165 350 150**

792 Combine 1937-41, part of articulated streamliner set, Rail Chief with 700E, 793 and 794. Lettered "792 LIONEL LINES 792" below windows. Maroon roof, red sides, maroon underbelly. Replacements for die-cast underbelly available. The car is coupled to the next car in the train through a vestibule. The vestibule has four wheels and a lighting pickup. The Combine is coupled to the tender with a scale coupler matching that on the 700T tender. Note that Hiawatha cars can be repainted in Rail Chief colors. However, Rail Chief car wheels have scale flanges, Hiawatha cars do not. Price for car only **180 400 150**

793 Coach 1937-41, matches 792, see 792 for background. Lettered "793 LIONEL LINES 793". Price for car only **180 400 150**

794 Observation 1937-41, matches 792, see 792 for background. Lettered "794 LIONEL LINES 794". Price for car only **180 400 150**

1001 Pullman Catalogued in 1930, Winner Flyer, but not manufactured **Not Manufactured**

1011 Pullman 1931-32, four wheels, lithographed hook couplers, sets only, 6"
(A) Light orange, cream door and windows, green roof, reads "WINNER LINES" **8 20 7**
(B) Same as (A), but dark orange body **8 20 7**

1019 Observation 1931-32, four-wheel, matches 1011 lithographed, body, one hook coupler, brass railing, sets only, 6"
(A) Light orange, cream windows, green roof, "WINNER LINES" **8 20 7**
(B) Same as (A), but dark orange body **8 20 7**

1020 Baggage 1931-32, four wheels, lithographed body, hook couplers, two doors; matches 1011, sets only, 6"
(A) Light orange, cream doors, green roof, "WINNER LINES" **8 20 7**
(B) Same as (A), but dark orange **8 20 7**

1542 Coach, catalogued 1935, but not made **Not Manufactured**

1543 Observation, catalogued 1935, but not made **Not Manufactured**

1630 Pullman, 1938-42, seven three-part windows, one-piece stamping provides window frames, two doors and name and number boards, one-piece roof, not illuminated, interior longitudinal benches, no steps, fishbelly, latch couplers, black lettered boards "1630 PULLMAN 1630" on each side below windows, 9-1/2" long, similar to 2630 which has electric couplers
(A) Blue sides, aluminum windows, doors, boards, fishbelly and roof **15 25 12**
(B) Blue sides, light gray windows, doors, boards, fishbelly and roof **15 25 12**
(C) Same as (B), but non-automatic box couplers, Kotil Collection **15 25 12**

1631 Observation 1938-42, matches 1630, observation deck with aluminum painted railing and lettered "1631 OBSERVATION 1631"
(A) Blue sides, aluminum windows, doors, boards, fishbelly and roof **15 25 12**
(B) Blue sides, light gray windows, doors, boards, fishbelly and roof **15 25 12**
(C) Same as (B), but gray painted observation railing, Kotil Collection **15 25 12**

1673 Coach 1936-37, streamlined coach with vestibule so as to appear articulated, red painted stamped steel, two four-wheel trucks, coupling through vestibule. Came with 1588 Locomotive, 1599T Tender, 1674 Pullman and 1675 Observation, nickel plates with black lettering "LIONEL LINES," seven windows plus doors with windows on each side, no window material, no numbers on car, not illuminated **8 20 8**

1674 Pullman 1936-37, matches 1673, see 1673 for background **8 20 8**

1675 Observation 1936-37, matches 1673, see 1673 for background **8 20 8**

710 (K) 710 (E) 712 (E)

710 (L) 605 606 (I)

610 Late 610 Late 612 Late

610 Early 610 Early 612 Early

1685-1687 Passenger Cars

These cars were based on Ives designs and incorporated removable roofs with spring latches. However, the doors do not open and the cars do not have steps. They were never catalogued by Lionel, but were used with a variety of special promotional sets for large buyers.

1685 Passenger Car

(A) 1933, six-wheel trucks, with copper journals, gray body, maroon roof, black rubber-stamped lettering "LIONEL LINES", latch couplers, brass trim **140 300 100**

(B) Four-wheel trucks, red body, yellow doors and trim, maroon roof, gold rubber-stamped lettering "LIONEL LINES", latch couplers, 1934 **85 175 75**

(C) Four-wheel trucks, deep red body, cream doors and trim, maroon roof, gold rubber-stamped lettering "LIONEL LINES", latch couplers, 1935-36 **100 190 75**

(D) Four-wheel trucks, blue body, silver inserts and roof, nickel trim, block style, rubber-stamped lettering "LIONEL LINES", latch couplers, 1935-36 **100 190 75**

(E) Four-wheel trucks, vermilion body, cream inserts, maroon roof, rubber-stamped lettering "LIONEL LINES", latch couplers, 1936-37 **100 190 75**

1686 Baggage

(A) Matches 1685 (A) **140 300 100**

(B) Matches 1685 (B) **85 175 75**

(C) Matches 1685 (C) **100 190 75**

(D) Matches 1685 (D) **110 200 75**

(E) Matches 1685 (E) **100 190 75**

1687 Observation

(A) Matches 1685 (A) **140 300 100**

(B) Matches 1685 (B) **85 175 75**

(C) Matches 1685 (C) **100 190 75**

(D) Matches 1685 (D) **110 200 75**

(E) Matches 1685 (E) **100 190 75**

1690 Pullman: Eight wheels, twist end, latch couplers, belly unless noted

(A) Dark red body, brown roof, yellow windows, upper window sections punched out, brass handrails, copper journals, 1933-34 **8 15 7**

(B) Same as (A), but brass journals **8 15 3**

(C) Dark red body, brown roof, yellow windows, solid upper window section, nickel handrails and journals, 1935 **8 15 3**

(D) Dark red body and roof, cream windows, red solid upper window section with black speckles, nickel handrails and journals, 1936-39 **8 15 3**

(E) Same as (D), but without belly and handrails **8 15 4**

(F) Same as (D), but black journals and without belly and handrails **8 15 4**

1691 Observation

(A) Red sides with yellow window trim. This car differs from the 1693 in that the upper window panel is punched out; in addition, the car has a black painted fishbelly beneath the frame and (unlike the 1693) both the frame and the sides are painted the same color. Car has yellow doors, probably brass door handrails and yellow lettering "1690 LIONEL LINES 1690". Fishbelly has airtank embossed on side; type III black finished trucks with long slot and copper journals. The red ends from this 1691 Observation were subsequently used on the 1693. **8 15 7**

1691 Observation, type (A)

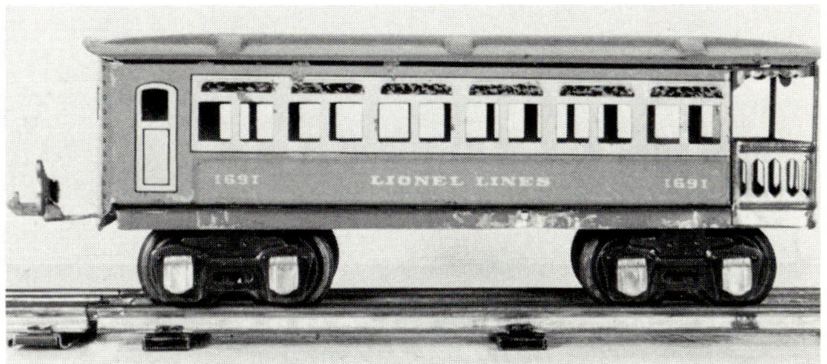

1691 Observation, type (B)

(B) Orange-red body with yellow windows and yellow lettering, solid upper horizontal window painted red and black above two punched windows. The red frame is a different color from the red-orange sides. Type III black painted trucks with long slots, nickel journals, no lettering on underside. This variety lacks the handrails on the doors found in (A). This paint scheme differs from the blue and green paint scheme found on the blue 1692 cars, and it also differs from (A). It also lacks the fishbelly found on (A). **8 15 7**

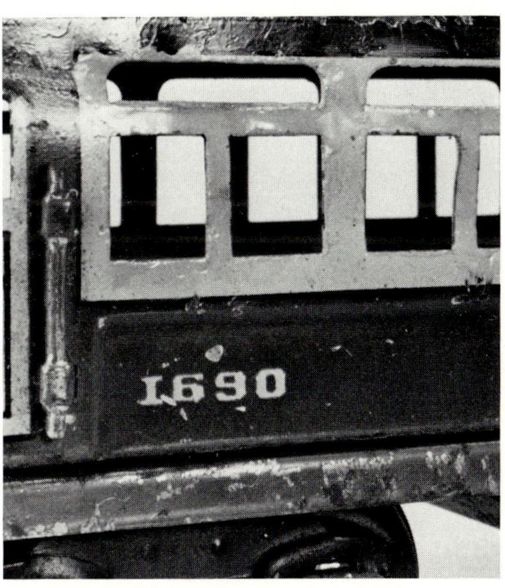

Two versions of the 1690 Pullman. Note the absence of handrails and solid upper windows in the left car. Fishbelly also absent on this car.

224
2224 W
2640
2640
2641

1689 (A)
1689 T
1630
1630
1631

289 E
1688 T
1703
1701
1702

1668 E (A)
1689 T
1679
1680
1682

229
1688 T
2654
2651
2657

261
257 T
529
530

1692 Passenger car, greenish-blue sides with embossed yellow window frames and sides; nickel-finished door handrails. The doors have a black line on the inside of the door on the lower door panel. Sides are serif-lettered "1692 LIONEL LINES 1692". Medium blue base, latch couplers, nickel journals on black finished Type III trucks with long slots. The windows and doors on the car ends are punched out and outlined in black. The latch couplers are supported by a slot through the frame end. **8 20 8**

1693 Observation, generally matches 1692, but the upper window panels have a solid painted blue and black pattern. The rear end of the observation is red with a yellow door and a large yellow observation window. A brass railing encloses the platform. Over the observation deck is a red and blue awning with black separation stripes and two simulated red lights. The cars have no rubber-stamping on the bottom. For this car, Lionel used a single piece of stamped brass to form the rear wall of the car and the brass railing. Consequently, the inside of the car is brass and the inside of the brass railing is red! Riley Collection **8 20 8**

1701 Coach 1935-37, streamlined design with vestibules, cars connect through vestibules, two four-wheel trucks under each car, fluted chrome sides and roof, light red band along lower edge, six windows and door with window on each side, black lettered "LIONEL LINES" on side beneath window, 9" long **10 25 8**

1702 Observation 1935, matches 1701 **10 25 8**

1811 Pullman 1933-37, 4 wheels, lithographed body and frame, hook couplers, no journals, 6"

(A) Peacock body, orange roof, black frame, cream windows, "PULLMAN", "LIONEL LINES" **10 20 7**

(B) Light red body, roof and frame; cream windows, "PULLMAN" and "LIONEL LINES" **10 20 7**

(C) Gray body, red and gray roof, red frame **10 20 7**

1812 Observation 1933-37, 4 wheels, lithographed body and frames, hook couplers, no journals, matches 1811, 6"

(A) Matches 1811 (A) **8 20 7**

(B) Matches 1811 (B) **8 25 7**

(C) Matches 1811 (C) **10 30 7**

1813 Baggage, matches 1811 and 1812 with two doors on each side

(A) Matches 1811 (A) **8 20 7**

(B) Matches 1811 (B) **8 20 7**

1817 Coach 1935-37, streamlined design with vestibules, cars connect through vestibules, two four-wheel trucks under each car, fluted chrome sides and roof, orange or red band, Came with 1816 or 1816W Power Car and 1818 Observation, black lettered "LIONEL LINES" on side below windows, six windows and door with windows on each side

(A) Orange band **8 20 8**

(B) Red band **8 20 8**

1818 Observation 1935-37, matches 1817

(A) Orange band and orange tail **8 20 8**

(B) Red band and tail **8 20 8**

2600 Pullman 1938-42, same as 600 Pullman, Late but with electric box couplers and lettered "2600 PULLMAN 2600" on sides, only light red body and roof, ivory windows, doors, name and number boards, red fishbelly, frosted windows and nickel journals **45 100 40**

2601 Observation 1938-42, same as 2601 Observation, Late, but with electric box couplers and lettered "2601 OBSERVATION 2601" on sides, only in one paint scheme with two different railings

(A) Light red body and roof, ivory insert, red observation railing, frosted windows **45 100 40**

(B) Same as (A), but aluminum railing **45 100 40**

2602 Baggage 1938-42, same as 602 Baggage, Late, but with electric box couplers and lettered "THE LIONEL LINES" between doors. Two small baggage windows and two doors that open each side, "2602" appears on number boards on the side near each end, 9" long, light red body and roof and ivory trim **45 100 40**

2613 Pullman 1938-42, same as 613, but with electric box couplers and lettered "2613 PULLMAN 2613"

(A) Blue body, blue and dark blue roof, ivory windows, doors, boards and underbelly, nickel trim. Cars known as "0 Gauge Blue Comet" and are highly desired **180 325 100**

(B) State green body, State green and green roof, ivory windows, doors, boards; dark green underbelly **90 200 80**

2614 Observation 1938-42, same as 614 but with electric box couplers and lettered "2614 OBSERVATION 2614"

(A) Blue body, blue and dark blue roof, ivory windows, doors, boards and underbelly, nickel trim. Cars known as "0 Gauge Blue Comet" and are highly desired **180 325 100**

(B) Same as (A), but aluminum observation railing **90 200 80**

(C) State green body, State green and green roof, ivory windows, doors, boards; dark green underbelly, State green observation railing **90 200 80**

(D) Same as (C), but aluminum observation railing **90 200 80**

2615 Baggage 1938-42, same as 615, but with electric box couplers and lettered "2615" on number boards on each side

(A) Matches 2613 (A) **180 325 100**

(B) Matches 2613 (B) **90 200 80**

2623 Pullman Bakelite tuscan painted body, scale detail, interior light, six-wheel tinplate trucks, opening doors, automatic box couplers, undercarriage detail, 1941-42, 14-1/4" long

(A) Tuscan, white lettered "2623 IRVINGTON 2623", Sattler Collection **100 225 100**

(B) Tuscan, white lettered "2623 MANHATTAN 2623", uncatalogued but more common than (A), Sattler Collection **90 200 80**

(C) Pullman green body, no lettering or numbers, automatic box couplers, uncatalogued. Possibly produced postwar with knuckle couplers, Ely comment, but confirmation of this is needed. Very rare car. Sattler Collection. **NRS**

2624 Pullman, same as 2623 (B), but rubber-stamped "2624", 1941-42, catalogued. Rare **700 1500 500**

2624 Observation, catalogued in 1941-42, "MANHATTAN", but never made **Not Manufactured**

2630 Pullman 1938-42, seven three-part windows, one-piece stamping supplies window frames, two doors and name and number boards, one-piece roof, not illuminated, interior longitudinal benches; no steps, fishbelly, electrically-operated box couplers, black lettered board "2630 PULLMAN 2630" on each side below windows, 9-1/2" long. Same as 1630 but with electric couplers

(A) Blue sides, aluminum windows, doors, boards, fishbelly and roof **12 30 12**

(B) Blue sides, light gray windows, doors, boards, fishbelly and roof **12 30 12**

2631 Observation 1938-42, matches 2630 but observation deck has aluminum painted railing and is lettered "2631 OBSERVATION 2631". Same as 1631 but with electric couplers

(A) Blue sides; aluminum windows, doors, boards, fishbelly and roof **12 30 12**

(B) Blue sides, light gray windows, doors, boards, fishbelly and roof **12 30 12**

2640 Pullman 2938-42, same as 2630, but with lights and letterd "2640 PULLMAN 2640"

(A) Light blue body; one-piece window, door, board insert painted aluminum, aluminum roof and fishbelly **20 35 20**

(B) State green body, one-piece window, door, board insert painted cream, dark green roof **12 30 12**

2641 Observation 1938-42, matches 2631, but with lights and lettered "2641 OBSERVATION 2641" **12 30 12**

2642 Pullman 1941-42, same as 2630, but with lights and lettered "2642 PULLMAN 2642"

(A) Tuscan body, one-piece window, door, board insert painted 92 gray, tuscan roof and fishbelly **12 30 12**

2643 Observation 2941-42, matches 2631, but with lights and lettered "2643 OBSERVATION 2643"

(A) Tuscan body, one-piece window, door, board insert painted 92 gray, tuscan roof and fishbelly **12 30 12**

IVES
1694
1696
1695
1697
262
262 T
1686
1685
1687
249 E
265 W
1686
1685
1687
249 E
265 W
1686
1685
1687
249
265 T
1717
1717
1722
IVES
1651
1690

262 (A)
262 T
615
613
614

262 (B)
262 T
602
600
601

238 E
265 T
602
600
601

226 E
2226 W
2615
2613
2614

225 E
2235W
2602
2600
2601

1695
615
1686
2613
1685
2614
1685
601
1687
2601

Chapter VII
ACCESSORIES

In background, two 155 Freight Sheds, 94 High Tension Towers, five 444 Roundhouse Sections, 200 Turntable. In foreground, on left 195 Lionel Terrace with 189, 184 and 191 buildings, 435 Power Station and 126 Station.

By Rev. Robert E. Pauli

Year after year, Lionel offered an impressive array of rugged, reliable trains. A vast variety of stations, signals, bridges, street lights, tunnels, and miniature houses beckoned enterprising pioneers to open their wallets and construct a mighty railroad. Yet a layout from that era may seem strangely static, even if every flagpost, scenic plot, and station platform is properly positioned. Sidings and yard tracks may bustle with cars, but when the switcher leaves and the freight train rumbles out of town, there is no action. Railroads serve shippers. Straining freight handlers wrestle crates in and out of boxcars; lumbermen muscle logs on flatcars; miners laboring deep in the earth fill hopper cars with ton after ton of coal, nature's "black diamonds". Loading, hauling, using big machinery — all of that happened only in operators' imaginations on the Lionel Lines. It did, that is, until the success of the Union Pacific streamliner, the M-10000, inspired more realism. It's easy to assume that the quest for realism influenced Lionel trains. However, it took another turn as well. At that time it was remarkable, though by now the products it spawned are so intimately linked with toy trains that people take them for granted. Lionel's search for realistic action turned to the world just beyond the trains, the world of coal and lumber, the world of fascinating machinery, the world that railroads served. Lionel's Engineering Department brought that world to toy train layouts with new and wonderful items — remote control operating accessories.

"The most unusual model railroad accessory ever conceived" made its debut on page 31 of Lionel's 1935 catalogue — the same one that introduced the Hiawatha and Lionel's new motor-driven whistle, "the greatest invention that ever contributed to the realism of model railroading", as the catalogue modestly put it. That new accessory — the Automatic Gateman — marked a great step forward for Lionel. For the first time, a moving miniature man animated Lionel layouts. As a train approached he dashed out of his shack to warn motorists to stop, just like a real watchman. After the train had passed, he whipped back inside. Children loved it. What fun it was to see an adult at their command for a change! This ingenious accessory also made use of Lionel's remarkable talent for remote lighting. Real watchmen had lighted lanterns, but mounting a bulb in the Gateman's hand would have been too fragile and probably too expensive. Instead, a bulb was hidden beneath the base, with an unobtrusive hole directly above it. When the gateman rushed out, swinging his red translucent plastic lantern, it caught the light from the bulb below it and glowed.

Remote lighting would be used in other ways. Lionel's beautiful scale and semi-scale Pennsylvania B6 0-6-0 switcher had a raised headlight, like its prototype. Lionel did not want wires or an oversized bulb to mar its appearance, so a bulb was

Left to right across back: 921 Scenic Park including 921 C Center Section, 189 Villa, 191, 184, 189, 191, 184, 189 and partially shown 191. In foreground: 438 Signal Tower, 911 Country Estate with 191 Villa.

mounted in the smokebox and a clear plastic bar carried the light to the headlight. Fiber optics in 1939! A variation of the gateman's lantern would be used on Lionel's postwar 252 Crossing Gate — the automatic gate that made watchmen obsolete. A vertical bulb was installed in the base behind a square opening. When the gate came down, a clear plastic bar on the gate lined up with the bulb and carried its light to two tiny red lanterns. Lionel also used less sophisticated methods, such as adding two red lenses on observation cars that were illuminated by bulbs inside the car (though these were not effective).

In 1937, Lionel offered a new accessory: Automatic, Illuminated Double Arm Crossing Gates (47) that faced each other on a simulated approach to a grade crossing. Listed on the same page as the Automatic Gateman, those gates were probably inspired by Lionel's stalwart Automatic Crossing Gate (77N), one of Lionel's earliest accessories. As yet, though, there was no actual contact with the train. Miniature motorists were well protected, but freight cars were still loaded and unloaded by hand.

That changed in 1938, when Lionel unveiled its new Electric Remote Control Coal Elevator (97) and the Electrically Operated Remote Control Dump Cars (3659 for 027 Gauge and 3859 for 0 Gauge with Remote Control couplers) to go with it. Coal could be dumped into a bin in back of the elevator. From there, an endless chain with buckets carried it into the "loft". An electrically-operated gate opened to load a waiting car. Lionel sold a whole 0 Gauge set with this elevator (225E, 2225W Tender, three 3659 Dump Cars, and 2657 Caboose) so operators could enjoy the sheer pleasure of loading and unloading coal without touching it even once.

In 1939, freight cars started to get into the act. Besides the 3811 Remote Control Log Car, Lionel introduced three new cars. The 3652 Gondola opened one side to let a dozen barrels roll out of the car. The 3814 Merchandise Car ejected twelve miniature cases. The 3859 Dump Car tilted its hopper to allow sand or gravel to fall into a trackside bin.

Three new accessories joined the series in 1940: the 164 Log Loader and its 3651 Log Dump Car ("Lumber Car" in the catalogue) and 313 Bascule Bridge and the 165 Triple-Action Magnetic Crane. The Log Loader followed the pattern set by the Coal Elevator. Logs were dumped into a bin, raised by stakes on two parallel chains, and released into a waiting car from a bin on the other side. The Bascule Bridge, modeled after drawbridges in the New York City area, opened to let imaginary ships pass. Some operators used this bridge on aisles that provided access to their layouts. Besides providing a realistic touch, the bridge also offered a safety feature. When properly wired to the track, it cut off current and stopped approaching trains when it was open. The Triple-Action Crane raised and lowered its block and tackle, revolved in a complete circle, and picked up steel scrap with a realistic electromagnet, like cranes in scrap yards. "THIS IS THE END of make-believe", the catalogue announced. "Never again will freight trains run back and forth around the pike, forcing imagination to make all the pick-ups and deliveries. This is real railroading." (p. 44). There was a paradox there, and the catalogue made it an advantage: "By a great stroke of genius Lionel engineers have created rolling stock which does what no real railroad car is able to do: unload by electric, remote control." (p. 44). Although World War II curtailed further developments of these sheet metal marvels, after the war they blossomed into Lionel's fun-filled array of fascinating accessories.

See if you can find the pieces we like. From left to right, starting at the rear, two 437 Signal Towers in late colors, numerous 94 High Tension Towers, three sections of the 444 Roundhouse, several 300 Hell Gate Bridges in early colors, 440 Signal Bridge, 911 Country Estate with 191 Villa, a 913 Landscaped Bungalow with 184 Bungalow, a 912 Suburban Home with 189 Villa, a 205 Merchandise Container, a 437 Signal Tower, six 155 Freight Sheds in late colors and a 92 Floodlight Tower.

Gd Exc Rst

No Number Whistle Demonstrator Box and Track: special dealer promotional device to demonstrate Lionel's whistle in 1935. Painted light yellow plywood box, 18" long, 4" wide, 4-1/4" high, "A REAL WHISTLE BY LIONEL" in red painted art deco letters on box side, 0 Gauge track mounted atop box and rubber roadbed, wooden "bumper" at right end, two wires (apparently for whistle contacts) soldered to track, rectangular opening to right of lettering, large opening on rear box wall shaped like T lying sideways. Reader comments on this interesting device invited. Anderson Collection **NRS**

2 Countershafting Structure: With 3 pulleys, 11-1/2" long, 4" wide, 7-1/2" high, 1904-11 **NRS**

013 0 Gauge Distant Control switch and Panel Board Set; included one pair of 012 switches and one 439 illuminated panel board. See 012 entry in Chapter X and 439 entry in this Chapter for values.

20 Direct Current Reducer: With off-on switch and train speed regulator, 1906 **NRS**

20 Crossing: box shows picture c. 1920 "All Aboard" with boy (Joshua Lionel Cowen's son, Lawrence) stretching over 402 Broadway set with Nos. 15, 17 and 19 passenger cars. Reader comments on values requested.

(A) Gunmetal base with green enameled center block, brass plate reads "No. 20 CROSSING" **NRS**

(B) Green base with red-brown fiber block in center, oval fiber "LIONEL" plate on outside, c. 1928 **NRS**

(C) Sheet metal base, small square center, no plate, usually rubber-stamped "LIONEL" **NRS**

(D) Same as (B), but Bakelite center block, c. 1933 **NRS**

(E) Black base with red fiber center block, 1934 **NRS**

23 Bumper: Standard Gauge, three-rail, steel frame type, 1906-33 **3 6 2**

023 Bumper: 0 Gauge, red or black with spring plunger, 1915-33 **2 5 2**

24 Railway Station: Two doors on one side, projecting bay, 11" x 7-1/2" x 8", 1906 **200 400 175**

25 Illuminated Bumper: Standard Gauge, die-cast type, 1927-42 **3 9 3**

25 Open Railway Station: Two sections, one with fence only, for one side of track; other with four pillars and roof for other side of track; one miniature figure, 11" wide, 11" long, 8" high, 1906 **NRS**

025 Illuminated Bumper: 0 Gauge, 1928-42

(A) Cream, 1928-33 **3 8 2**

(B) Semi-gloss black, 1934-42 **3 8 2**

26 Passenger Foot Bridge: With two semaphores on bridge and two miniature fixtures, 24" long, 17" high, 1906 **50 100 —**

27 Lighting Set: For car interiors, five feet of flexible cord, three bulbs (3-1/2 volt), sockets and contacts, for batteries or reduced direct current, 1911-23 **7 15 —**

28 Station: Large, double station, with leaded glass dome spanning tracks. Consists of two 27 stations plus leaded dome resting on triangular supports. Overall size given in catalogue is 18-1/2" x 22-1/2" x 11" which is the same as the Ives 123 Double Station with glass dome. The cuts in the Ives 1910 catalogue are very similar to those shown in the Lionel catalogues for 1909-12 **500 1000 450**

32 Miniature Figures: For trolley or Pullman cars, dozen figures, 1909-18 **— 75 —**

35 Boulevard Lamp: Aluminum or 92 gray, 6-1/8" high, clear/opalescent lamp, 1940. Has die-cast trunk, milk colored plastic chimney, plastic "thorny" painted cap and finial "35" and Lionel Corp. information embossed on bottom* **10 25 10**

043 Bild-A-Motor Gear Set, for 0 Gauge, 1929 **30 50 25**

43 Bild-A-Motor Gear Set 1929, fits Standard motor **30 50 25**

43 Mechanical Boat: 17" long, red, white and beige, 1933-36, 1939-41. Pleasure boat, admiralty flag, two man crew **170 350 175**

No. 43 and 44 Lionel Boats

44 Mechanical Boat: 17" long, green, white and brown, 1935-36. Racer with large exposed motor, two man crew **90 400 125**

45 Automatic Gateman: Red roof and white sides, 1935-36, for Standard Gauge **10 25 8**

45N Automatic Gateman: Red roof, cream sides, green base, 1937-42* **10 25 8**

045 Automatic Gateman: 0 Gauge; red roof, white sides, green base, 1935-36 **10 25 8**

46 Automatic, Illuminated, Single Arm Crossing Gate: Green and cream base, 1939-42 **15 35 10**

47 Automatic, Illuminated, Double Arm Crossing Gate: Green (512) base, light red gate body and ivory road, 1937-42 **35 75 30**

48W Whistle Station: Two-tone red lithographed roof, lithographed cream-yellow walls and vermilion base, 5-1/2" x 3-3/4", 1937-42 **10 20 8**

The 48W Whistle Station. Note the vented ends near the roof to allow the whistle sound to escape and the fiber whistle button below the end window. Photo by Bartelt

The roof of the 48W Whistle Station slides off to allow access to the whistle casing. Photo by Bartelt

49 Lionel Airport: Lithographed, 58" diameter circular cardboard base for pylon, 1937-39 **60 150 –**

50 Remote Control Airplane: Red, 1936, with pylon and controls **60 150 –**

51 Lionel Airport: 1936, 1938, lithographed cardboard square for use with 50 **60 150 –**

52 Lamp Post: Die-cast, opalescent globe, aluminum, 10-1/4" and 10-1/2" high, 1933-41 **15 35 15**

53 Lamp Post: Aluminum, gray, or light mojave, opalescent globe, has "53-1" cast on base bottom, 8-7/8" or 8-1/2" high, 1931-42 **12 30 10**

54 Lamp Post: Double light, rubber-stamped "54" on base bottom, 9-1/2", 1929-35 **15 35 15**

55 Remote Control Airplane: Red and silver with pylon and control. Does not include cardboard base, 1937-39 **120 250 100**

56 Lamp Post: "Gaslight", 7-3/4", "Lionel #56" or "56" rubber-stamped on bottom, 1924-49

(A) Green **15 25 10**

(B) Gray, 1939 **15 25 10**

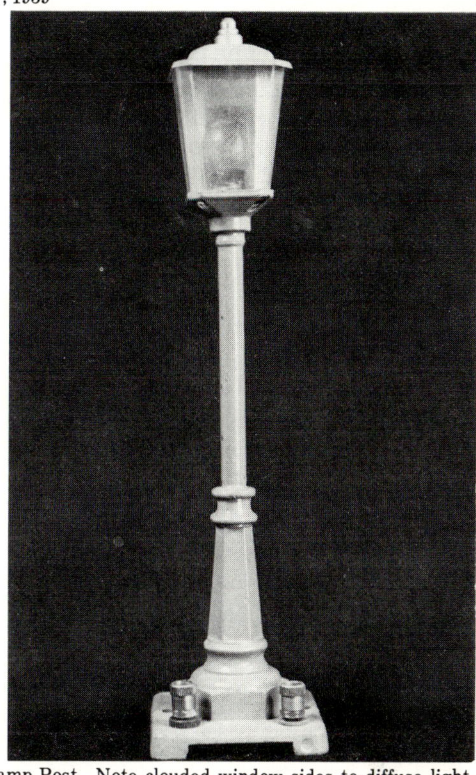

56 (A) Lamp Post. Note clouded window sides to diffuse light. Photo by Bartelt

57 Lamp Post: "Broadway", square top, 1922-42, 7-1/2". Base die-cast, stem rolled sheet metal, "Lionel #57" usually stamped on base. Variations occur in street names, printing color — black or silver — and in stampings — hot or rubber-stamped.

(A) 9E Orange, "Broadway" on two panels and "Main" on two panels in serif lettering **18 40 20**

(B) Same as (A), but sans-serif lettering **18 40 20**

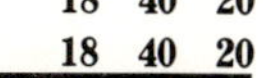

(C) 9E Orange, "Broadway" on one panel, "42nd Street" on second panel, "Fifth Avenue" on third panel, "21st Street" on fourth panel. All in sans-serif lettering. **22 60 20**

(D) Yellow, numbered 2013 and made for American Flyer by Lionel. Came with American Flyer box. "Broadway" on two panels, "Main" on two panels; serif lettering. Hacker and Koff Collections **18 40 20**

*Continued in postwar period.

Left: 57 (B) with sans-serif lettering. Right: 57 (A) with serif lettering. Photo by Bartelt

(C) "Broadway" on one panel, "42nd Street" on second panel, "5th Avenue" on third panel, "21st Street" on fourth panel, 9E orange post, top, base. Very rare **40 65 30**

(D) Same as (A), but all serif lettering, Koff Collection **18 40 20**

(E) Yellow, numbered 2013 and made for American Flyer by Lionel. Came with American Flyer box. "Broadway" and "Main Street" is serif lettering. Identical to (B) except for color, Hacker and Koff Collections **30 60 25**

(F) Same as (B), but serif lettering **18 40 20**

NOTE: The 57 Lamp Post is reputed to exist in gray, but confirmation is lacking. Reader comments are invited.

58 Lamp Post: Gooseneck, 7-3/8"; some rubber-stamped "Lionel #58" on bottom; late ones have "58-19" embossed on bottom. Lamp embossed "The Lionel Corporation New York" on base, 1922-50

An early peacock 58 lamp post with its original box. Photo by Bartelt

(A) Maroon **10 25 8**
(B) Peacock, 1935-39 **10 25 8**
(C) Cream, 1940-50 **10 25 8**

59 Lamp Post: A smaller version of the 61; 8-3/4" tall, catalogued 1920-36; cast-iron base; "LIONEL #59" sometimes rubber-stamped in black on underside of base

(A) Dark green, Koff Collection **9 25 10**
(B) Light green, Koff Collection **9 25 10**
(D) Olive green, Koff Collection **9 25 10**

Examine this comparison of a 58 early (left) in peacock and a 58 late (right) in cream. The bulb is not the only difference! The inside lattice work on the cream version ends closer to the shade and has one less point. The knurled parts of the poles at the "C"-shaped lattice work also differ in shape. Photo by Bartelt

60 Telegraph Post
(A) Peacock base and post, open lattice work, maroon crossarms, brass cap **2 6 2**

060 Telegraph Post: Early open lattice work
(A) 9E Orange post, maroon crossarm, brass cap **2 6 2**
(B) Green post, brass cap, red crossarm **2 6 2**
(C) Same as (B) but without lattice work (late) **2 6 2**
(D) Same as (B) but without lattice work, with black cap **2 6 2**

61 Lamp Post: Lionel's first, 12-3/4", 1914-36. Early: cast-iron base, 2-3/8" x 2-1/4". Later: 2-1/4" square base, "Lionel #61" sometimes rubber-stamped on bottom. Maroon, mojave, dark green or olive **12 30 10**

62 Semaphore: Manual; yellow and green or red base, green or yellow post, red crossarm, not lighted, 8-3/4" high, 1920-32 **10 25 10**

63 Lamp Post: Double globes; die-cast, tapered, long stem topped by crossarm and fancy sockets; no i.d. on bottom, aluminum, 12-3/4", 1933-42 **10 25 10**

63 Semaphore: One arm, mechanically operated, not lighted, 14", 1915-21 **10 25 10**

64 Semaphore: Two arms, mechanically operated, not lighted, 14", 1915-21 **12 30 10**

64 Highway Lamp Post: Die-cast base and bracket, formed sheet metal arm, 0 Gauge, special bulb required, 512 green, 6-3/4", 1940-42 **11 25 10**

65 Semaphore: One signal arm with one electric light enclosed by lantern, arm controlled manually by lever, 14" high with finial on top, 1915-26 **11 25 10**

65 Whistle Controller, 1935 only: Black painted small metal box with three buttons and four terminals. Provided with whistle tenders which were available for separate sale as well as with sets which had whistle tenders. **2 3 1**

66 Whistle Controller, 1936-39: Black painted metal box 3-3/8" long x 2-3/4" wide x 2-7/8" high. Top of box has three red buttons and four terminal posts. Black-bordered metal plate embossed with rather vague directions in black lettering: "Connect These 2 Posts To Transformer" and "Connect These 2 Posts To Track". Bottom half of plate explains functions of whistle and directional buttons. Plates on 65 and 67 identical except for number. Inside the box are two galvanized L-shaped mounting brackets. The upper parts of both brackets have asbestos-insulated turns of fine wire around them. The DC rectifier disk is built of two black painted squares of metal sandwiched around two round washer-type disks, all connected by a large bolt and nut through the center. The square plate shows that Lionel did some subcontracting: lettering stamped around the edges reads "MAL-

LORY/TYPE 65/MADE IN U.S.A./PAT. 1649741 ET AL." A small "R" is also stamped in the upper right corner. The other bracket holds a small square transformer coil with maroon laminated wire turns. The construction is quite different from the postwar 167 whistle and direction controllers, with their copper-oxide rectifier disks, LaVoie Collection **2 3 1**

66 Semaphore: Two signal arms with two electric lights enclosed by lanterns, arms controlled manually by two levers, 14" high with finial on top, 1915-26 **11 30 12**

67 Whistle Controller, 1936-39: Black painted small metal box; essentially similar to 65 and 66. We do not know how these three whistle controllers differ electrically. Readers are asked to compare the inside electrical arrangements of their 65 and 67 controllers with the description of the 66 above and write to us about any differences they find. **2 3 1**

67 Lamp Post, 1915-32 **20 60 20**

068 Crossing, 1927-42: Close to pea green; square base, punched out truss-type girder shaft, (6-7/16" tall), with brass cap. Brass diamond sign, with black lettering: "LOOK OUT FOR LOCOMOTIVE" and "RAILROAD CROSSING" across center. Usually black rubber-stamped on bottom: "LIONEL #068" in two lines. This is one of only a few accessories where there are significant differences between the 0 and Standard Gauge versions. It came with most 0 Gauge sets from 1927 through 1933. Readers are asked to comment on values.

(A) Large sans-serif lettering variety "LOOK" 9/16" long, Herzog Collection **1 2 1**

(B) Small serif lettering variety, "LOOK" 11/16" long, Herzog Collection **1 2 1**

(C) Large serif lettering variety, "LOOK" 11/16" long, Herzog Collection. Note that the serifs are very small on this variety compared with (B). **1 2 1**

(D) Red rectangular base, yellow painted stamped-out girder with brass cap, white painted steel diamond with black lettering "RAILROAD CROSSING" and "LOOK OUT FOR ENGINE" and "DANGER" in center. This was apparently made for Lionel by Hafner. This product is shown in a mid or late 1930s Hafner Catalogue as part of No. 1200 accessory set. 1 The diamond appears to have been made from an Ives die owned by Lionel. This catalogue announces "SOLE EXPORTERS LIONEL CORPORATION". 2 **1 2 1**

68 Crossing, 1920-39, for Standard Gauge **1 2 1**

069, 69, 69N Electric Warning Signals: 069 and 69, 1921-35; 69N, 1936-42. This was the first track-actuated electric accessory made by Lionel. It was introduced in an off year, 1921; apparently it rapidly became a major sales item and consequently led to a whole series of track actuated accessories. The device utilized a very simple and ingenious Lionel innovation — a special piece of track with an insulated outside rail. (We have requested the patent information to provide more background.) The lockon (the power connection) to the track was installed from the insulated rail side. Consequently, the accessory received half of its circuit from the center rail which was powered whenever the train was operated. The other half of the circuit came from the normally dead outside rail of the special track. The rail would have power only when the train came through and carried the power from the non-insulated outside rail on one side through the wheels and axles to the insulated rail on the lockon side.

Left: The Ives crossing sign. Right: The likely Lionel produced Hafner sign which apparently used old Ives diamond die and lettering. Photo by Bartelt

Lionel offered two versions — the 069 for 0 Gauge track and the 69 for Standard. To the best of our knowledge, the accessory units were identical. What differed was the track piece that came with the accessory. In the case of 069, a special piece of 0 Gauge track with insulated outside rail was furnished, and for 69 a special piece of Standard Gauge track with insulated outside rail was included. For the continuation of this story, see next entry.

Carrying two versions of the same accessory was more costly than having one version. Furthermore (and probably more important), the duality created customer confusion. Hence, in 1936 Lionel introduced the 41 track contactor to operate this accessory with both 0 and Standard Gauge track. Lionel called the new version 69N. It was offered through 1942. Lionel also introduced "N" versions to replace the previous 0 and Standard versions for 82 and 082 Automatic Semaphores, 80 and 080 Automatic Semaphores 440 and 0440 Twin Signal Bridges and the 77 and 077 Automatic Crossing Gates. However, Lionel did not introduce the N version of the 45 Gateman until 1937.

The sound produced by the 69 Electric Warning Signal leaves something to be desired, especially when compared with the Marx version.

At the present time, we are listing the color varieties that we have observed. We expect this list to be incomplete. We also know that dating is a problem and ask your assistance.

(A) Maroon base and girder, brass cap; nickel-finished bell mechanism mounted on rear of unit; left bell has small half-moon opening; adjusting screw. Rectangular box on base has P-shaped slot for use with 62 semaphore; brass diamond with red etched outline paralleling inside and outside edges; red lettering with very small serifs: "RAILROAD CROSSING" and "LOOK OUT FOR LOCOMOTIVE"; black rubber-stamped on bottom in two lines "LIONEL #069", Herzog Collection **11 25 10**

(B) Maroon base and girder, brass cap, bell mechanism not present; brass diamond with black etched line outlining inside and outside edges; heavy black etched serif lettering: "LOOK OUT FOR LOCOMOTIVE" and RAILROAD CROSSING" across center. Black rubber-stamped on bottom in two lines "LIONEL #069", Herzog Collection **11 25 10**

(C) Dark olive green (as in 33 loco) base and girder; cap apparently missing; bell mechanism not present and apparently missing; brass diamond with black etched line outlining inside and outside edges; heavy black etched serif lettering "LOOK OUT FOR LOCOMOTIVE" and "RAILROAD CROSSING" across center; black rubber-stamped on bottom in two lines "LIONEL #069", Herzog and Edmunds Collections **11 25 10**

(D) Light red (as in late 517 caboose) base and girder; nickel-finished mechanism mounted on front on example observed. Nickel-finished diamond warning sign with black outlining, black sans-serif lettering "RAILROAD CROSSING" with highly stylized "R"s and "S"s. No rubber-stamping on bottom. This is a late unit because of the paint color and aluminum sign. We

---

1 This Hafner catalogue is available as a reproduction from Greenberg Publishing Co.

2 Among collectors, it has been rumored for many years that Lionel and Hafner made an agreement whereby Lionel would end the production of mechanical trains in exchange for handling the overseas distribution of the Hafner line and for Hafner's agreement not to make electrically powered trains. (In Vol. I of their series, McComas and Tuohy say that the rumor is false, but it persists.) In any case, Hafner was selling products made by Lionel and Lionel was distributing Hafner products overseas.

A Selection Of Lionel Accessories
300 (B) Bridge (late colors)
80 Semaphore
840 Power Station
90 Flag
438 (B) Signal Tower
437 Signal Switch Tower
911 Country Estate
94 Tower
35
58
64
116 Station with 550 Miniature Railroad Figures
440 Signal Bridge
LIONELVILLE
92 Floodlight
76
060

suspect that the bell mechanism was originally mounted on the rear and ask reader comments. **11 25 10**

70 Outfit, 1921- , 2 No. 62, 1 No. 59, 1 No. 68 **25 75 30**

071 Set of 6 no. 060 Telephone Poles, 0 Gauge, terra-cotta, 1929-42 **20 50 —**

71 Telegraph Poles **20 50 20**

NOTE: There were three different accessories which used the number 76:

76/076 Block Signals, 1923-28: Olive green painted stamped rectangular base and metal girder, two nickeled lamp bases, two nickeled lamp housings with red and green celluloid lenses, brass finial on pole top. Three screw terminals on base with rubber-stamped lettering "A", "B", etc. The unit came with two special track sections with insulated outside rails (0 for the 076 and Standard for the 76). Lockons provided power from the outside rails only when the train was on that particular section. The center rail connection is continuous. The bulb wired to the occupied section would light. The lockons were labeled with letters that correspond to the letters on the signal's base. **15 35 15**

76/076 Crossing Signal: With stamped rectangular metal post, truss-type post similar to that illustrated with the 060, stamped steel crossbar with two bulbs and lamp heads. Lamp heads are same as those used on the switches. The 0 Gauge and Standard Gauge revisions are believed to be identical except for the special track piece and connector that came with each.

(A) White painted unit with black lamp heads, numbered "#76" on underside of base, Koff Collection **NRS**

(B) Mojave painted unit with black lamp heads, numbered "#076" on underside of base, Koff Collection **NRS**

76 Warning Bell and Shack, 1939-45: Two-part red painted pressed steel base with two screw terminals. Silver painted warning post with black simulated bell approximately half-dollar size. One-piece die-cast sign painted off-white with black raised lettering. Off-white painted steel building with orange painted roof and orange painted window inserts on each side. Inside the building, there is a bell mechanism with a solenoid similar to that found on a modern E-unit and a large, silver-dollar size bell housing mounted on a black metal frame. Silver label on tool box lid lettered on blue, "No. 76/WARNING BELL AND SHACK/MADE IN THE U.S. OF AMERICA/THE LIONEL CORP./NEW YORK". This unit was based on the 45 Automatic Gateman building. However, it included a new type of crossing sign with a die-cast crossarm instead of the stamped brass sign which came with the 45. **NRS**

This is the 76 warning bell and shack. The black bell on the signpost is strictly cosmetic — the real bell is inside the shack! Similar construction to 45N gateman, but roof has no chimney and slot for gateman is not present.

77/077/77N Automatic Crossing Gate, 1923-39: This accessory, one of Lionel's most popular (judging from the number that are found and its long run) was introduced with little fanfare. This is curious, since the low-keyed 1921 introduction of the 69/069 had resulted in such market success. We would expect that Lionel would very aggressively and strongly promote such a promising new product.

The 0 Gauge version came with a special 0 Gauge track piece with insulated outside rail and the Standard Gauge version with a special Standard Gauge version with a special Standard Gauge track piece with insulated outside rail. Other than the track differences and differences on the plate, the pieces are identical. The first three versions are unlighted, Edmunds comment.

(A) 1923: Black painted stamped steel base and mechanism box, nickeled cover on mechanism box, black painted stamped steel gate with white paper insert. This version has not yet been verified. Brass plate. **15 30 15**

(B) Same as (A), but with circular area near gate end with red printed paper label "STOP", 1924. Brass plate. **15 30 15**

(C) 1927-30: Green enameled base, maroon (or terra-cotta) painted mechanism box with nickeled lid, green painted stamped metal gate with paper insert and circular area near end for "STOP" warning. (This has not been verified.) (Also illustrated in the Lionel 1928 Catalogue, pages 26 and 35; 1939, p. 31 and 1930, p. 35.) Brass plate on base. **15 30 15**

(D) 1931-34: Green enameled base, terra-cotta (or maroon) painted mechanism box with nickeled lid, green painted stamped metal gate with paper insert and red bulb located adjacent to circular area near gate end. This innovation was very casually mentioned in the text (see Lionel Catalogue, 1931, page 39) **15 30 15**

(E) 1935: Black enameled base, red painted mechanism box with black painted lid, black painted stamped metal gate with paper insert and red bulb located to illuminate circular area near end. (Illustrated in Lionel 1935 Catalogue, page 31.) Brass plate on base. **15 30 15**

(F) 1936-39: Same color scheme as 1935, but change in name on brass plate to "No. 77N". This version did not come with the 0 or Standard Gauge insulated track. Rather, a No. 41 contactor was included. **15 30 15**

78/078 Train Control Block Signal

(A) Dark red base with Standard Gauge lettering (78) and numbering on back control panel, Koff Collection **20 50 20**

(B) Orange base with 0 Gauge (078) lettering and numbering on back control panel, Koff Collection **20 50 20**

79 Flashing Railroad Signal, 11-1/2", 1928-42: Early color cream, later aluminum, 1928-40 **20 50 20**

80 Electrically Controlled Semaphore: Standard Gauge, orange base, 1926-35 **25 60 25**

080 Semaphore: Same as 80, but for 0 Gauge trains **25 60 25**

80N Semaphore: Same as 80, but for either 0 or Standard, 1936-42 **25 60 25**

80 Racing Automobile: Eight sections of track, 36" diameter with auto, driver and starting post, 1912-16 **600 1100 450**

81 Racing Automobile: Eight sections of track, 30" diameter with auto, driver and starting post, 1912-16 **600 1100 450**

82 Train Control Semaphore: Standard Gauge, double block base, yellow and green, 1927-35 **30 65 25**

082 Semaphore: Same as 82, but for 0 Gauge, 15", 1927-35 **35 75 35**

82N Semaphore: Same as 82, but for either 0 or Standard, 1936-42 **35 75 25**

83 Traffic and Crossing Signal, 6-1/4"

(A) Tan base, 1927-34 **35 75 30**

(B) Red base, 1935-42 **35 75 30**

84 Two Racing Automobiles: Eight sections of curved track 36" diameter, 8 sections of curved track 30" diameter, driver and starting posts, 1912-16 **1200 2200 1100**

84 Semaphore: Electrically lighted, Standard Gauge, 15", yellow and green, 1927-32 **30 65 25**

084 Semaphore: Same as 84, but for 0 Gauge trains, 1928-32 **305 675 25**

85 Telegraph Pole: With track connector, Standard Gauge, orange, 1929-42, 9" high **4 10 4**

85 Two Racing Automobiles: With drivers, 8 sections curved track 36" diameter, 8 sections curved track 30" diameter, 8 sections straight track, and starting post, 1912-16 **1200 2200 1100**

86 Set of Telegraph Poles: Standard Gauge, orange, 9" high, box included for excellent, 1929-42 **45 100 40**

87 Railroad Crossing Signal: 6-3/4", large round head with celluloid disk. Base is black rubber-stamped "CAUTION/DRIVE/SLOWLY" in three lines on three sides; embossed "MADE BY/THE LIONEL CORPORATION/NEW YORK" on fourth side. Drum-shaped head painted to match base. Celluloid insert on each side with orange or red bulls-eye and black crescent, lettered "RAILROAD CROSSING". This piece is very hard to find in excellent condition because the die-cast base deteriorates. A bimetallic strip wound with copper wire acts as a thermostat, opening and closing to produce a blinking effect. Catalogue shows painted black shade

atop red part of light face, but this is absent from production, Edmunds comment

(A) Orange base, 1927-34 **35 75 30**

(B) Green base, cream body **35 75 30**

(C) Light tan base, orange central square pillar, Clement Collection **40 80 20**

88 Direction Controller, 1933-42 **1 3**

89 Flag Pole: 14", ivory, rectangular base, 1923-34 **8 20 8**

90 Flag Pole: 14-3/4", ivory, fits on ornamental green base with miniature grass plot, 1927-42 **15 35 13**

91 Circuit Breaker: Brown with red light, 1930-42 **7 15 5**

092 Illuminated Signal Tower: Terra-cotta body, maroon trim, green roof, 5" x 4" x 5-1/2", 1923-27 **40 85 35**

92 Floodlight Tower: With two bulbs, 1931-42

(A) Green tower, orange base, 1931-34 **70 150 60**

(B) Red base, aluminum tower, 1935-42 **70 150 60**

93 Water Tower, 9", 1931-42

(A) Maroon base, burnt orange legs, pea green tank and tube, brass spout, 1932-34 **12 30 10**

(B) Vermilion base, aluminum legs, tank and tube, black spout, "LIONEL TRAINS" decal, 1935-32 **15 35 12**

94 High Tension Tower, with porcelain insulators and 25' of copper wire, 24" 1932-42

(A) Gray, 1932 **70 150 60**

(B) Red base, 1935-42 **70 150 60**

Reproductions have been made by Williams Reproductions and are stamped "WRL". Value of reproductions **— 30 —**

96 Remote Control Elevator: With endless-chain buckets, hand-operated, 1938-40 **70 150 60**

97 Coal Elevator: Similar to 96 but with motor-driven conveyor buckets, coal included, 1938-42

(A) Black base and legs, lift works are aluminum, 1685 cream house, vermilion ladder, window and roof **70 150 60**

(B) Same as (A), but aluminum legs, Edmunds Collection **70 150 60**

097 Telegraph Set: 0 Gauge, 1-068, 6-096 poles **35 60 —**

98 Coal bunker, 1938-40: Apparently, Lionel didn't know what to call this accessory. The 1940 catalogue calls it an "elevated coal storage bunker". The packing box is labeled "No. 98 COAL TIPPLE". The tag on the unit's base is stamped "NO. 98 COAL HOUSE". At least as far as the name is concerned, this confusion would seem to justify the old adage, "A camel is a horse which was designed by a committee." Brueckl Collection **90 200 80**

99 Color Light Train Control: For Standard Gauge trains

(A) Black base, 1932-34 **30 75 25**

(B) Red base, 1935 **30 75 25**

099 Control, same as 99, but for 0 Gauge, 1932-35 **30 75 25**

99N Control, same as 99, but for 0 or Standard, 1936-42 **30 75 25**

100 Bridge Approach: Sections, 2, Standard Gauge **10 25 10**

101 Bridge: Single Span and Two Approaches, Standard Gauge, 1920-31 **15 40 14**

102 Two Bridge Spans, Two Approach Sections, Standard Gauge, 1920-31 **25 60 20**

103 Three Bridge Spans, Two Approach Sections, Standard Gauge, 1920-31 **45 100 40**

103 Bridge, 1913-16 **10 25 10**

104 Bridge, Center Span, Standard, 14", 1920-31 **5 10 5**

104 Tunnel, 13 x 9 x 9", 1909-14 **30 75 30**

105 Two Bridge Approach Sections, 0 Gauge, 1920-31 **5 10 5**

105 Bridge, 6 x 6", 1911-14 **10 25 10**

106 Bridge Span, Two Approach Sections, 0 Gauge, 1920-31 **10 20 10**

108 Two Bridge Spans, Two Approach Sections 0 Gauge, 1920-31 **20 50 15**

109 3 Bridge Spans, 2 approximately 1920-31 **25 60 25**

109 Tunnel: 25" x 12-1/2" x 14", 1913-14 **17 35 15**

110 Bridge Span: 0 Gauge, 1920-31 **5 10 5**

111 Assortment of 50 Bulbs: 12 and 18 volts, 1920-31 **— 100 —**

112 Single Window Station: No outside light bracket, cream, 1931-35 **80 175 75**

113 Station: Same as 112, but with outside light bracket, cream, 1931-34 **95 200 85**

114 Double Window Station: With two outside light brackets, 19-3/4" x 9-1/2" x 9", cream sides, mojave base and trim, 1931-34 **450 1000 400**

115 Illuminated Single Window Station: 13-3/4" x 9-1/4" x 9" high

(A) Vermilion base, window trim, roof and skylight; ivory walls, aluminum outside lights, 1935-42 **70 150 60**

(B) Dark cream building, green trim, mojave base **100 200 90**

116 Double Window Station: Same as 114, but with train stop control, 19-3/4" x 9-1/2" x 9" high, "Lionel City", 2 removable grilled skylights

(A) Cream sides, green trim, mojave base, 1935-36 **450 1000 400**

(B) White sides, red trim, red base, 1937-42 **450 1000 400**

117 Station: Same as 115, but with train stop control, but no outside light, 1936-42 **75 150 70**

The 117 Station. The 115 was identical, but had two lights adjacent to the doors. Photo by Bartelt

118 0 Gauge Tunnel: Hotel on side

(A) 10" long, 1915-20 **20 40 20**

(B) 8" long, 7-1/4" wide, 7" high, sheet steel, 1922-32 **7 15 8**

118L Tunnel: Same as 118 (B), but lighted, 1926 **9 20 10**

119 0 and Standard Tunnel

(A) 16", 1915-19 **10 20 10**

(B) 12", 1920-42 **7 15 10**

119L Tunnel: Same as 119 (B), but lighted, 1927-33 **9 20 19**

The 119L lighted tunnel. Note binding posts at near base of portal. This one has a single snow-capped peak. Photo by Bartelt

120 0 and Standard Tunnel

(A) 20", 1915-21 **20 40 20**

(B) 17", 1922-27 **18 35 18**

120L Tunnel: Same as 120 (B), but lighted, 1927-42 **17 35 15**

Compare this 120L tunnel with the 119L. It is longer and has two snow-capped peaks. Note also the higher bridge and lower, smaller hotel. It is rubber-stamped inside, just as its 119L counterpart. Photo by Bartelt

121 Station
(A) 14" x 10" x 9", 1909-16 **125 350 110**
(B) New model, 13-1/2" x 9" x 13", 1917 **80 200 75**

121X Station: Lighted, 1917-19, made for Lionel by Schoenhut **80 200 60**

121 Station: New model, light gray base, cream trim, pea green windows, door and roof, brass signs, semi-dull State brown walls, no arrival signs, 13-1/2" x 9" x 13", 1920-26 **45 100 40**

122 Station
(A) Same as 121, but with center light, 1920-30 **45 100 45**
(B) Gray speckled base, salmon sides, cream-buff building and window trim, pea green roof, green window frames, wood-grained doors, two brass signs with black lettering: "LIONEL CITY" and "WAITING ROOM", Petruzzio Collection **45 100 45**

123 Station: Same as 121, but with 110 volt bulb, 1920-23 **45 100 45**

123 Tunnel, House and Trees: 0 Gauge, 18-1/2" x 16-1/4", 1933-42 **25 60 20**

124 Station: Similar to 121, but with three lights (two exterior lights with brackets), 1920-30, 1933-36
(A) Dark gray base, cream trim, pea green windows and roof, red doors, burnt orange walls, brass outside lights and trim, black card stock arrival signs **45 100 45**
(B) Same as (A), except tan base **45 100 45**
(C) Same as (A), except pea green base, red roof, cream trim, 1935 **100 200 90**
(D) Same as (A), but pea green doors, cast metal lights and no card stock arrival signs, Hundertmark Collection **45 100 45**

The 124 Station is a very nice addition to one's layout. This is Type (A). Note the fancy lights, the brass signs and the embossed brickwork. Photo by Bartelt

125 Track Template, 1928 **1 3 –**

125 Station: "LIONELVILLE", red brick lithographed sides, two sets of arched doors on each long side, arched window between doors, green roof with two brick lithographed chimneys, dark mojave base, not lighted, 1923-25. The older Lionel lithographed buildings prior to about 1930 were varnished. **80 200 75**

126 Station: "LIONELVILLE", same as 125, but with interior light, 1923-36. Reader comments on values requested.
(A) Dark gray base, bright red brick lithographed sides, mojave front and back doors with dark green frames, brass ticket window between front doors, small white windows on back ends. Brass plates: "LIONELVILLE" on front, "EXPRESS" on left, and "BAGGAGE" on right; maroon end doors with green frames and white window pane inserts. Green roof (same color as 438 tower struts), red lithographed chimneys, Koff Collection **25 50 30**
(B) Light gray base, bright red lithographed ends, orange-red brick lithographed front and back walls, light green front and back doors with dark green frames, brass ticket window between front doors, same signs as (A), same end doors and small windows as (A), interior lamp with brass shade and ground screw terminal mounted on steel spreader bar. Same green roof and chimneys as (A), Koff Collection **25 50 30**
(C) Red enamel sides. More information requested **NRS**
(D) Mojave base, red crackle sides, green doors (same color as 438 signal tower struts), light cream door frames and small windows; brass ticket window on front, brass plates: "LIONELVILLE" on front, "EXPRESS" on right, "BAGGAGE" on left; interior lamp with brass shade and two terminals mounted on steel spreader bar. Green roof (same color as doors) with red lithographed chimneys, Koff Collection **25 50 30**

127 Station: "LIONELTOWN", 8-1/2" long x 4-1/4" wide x 5" high, for 0 Gauge, with interior lighting fixture, 1923-36
(A) Mustard sides, green windows, maroon door and roof, dark gray base **35 75 30**
(B) White sides, green window trim, gloss red roof, cream base **40 90 35**

The 127 "LIONELTOWN" station, Type (B). The large arched windows are a nice touch, even though they make the station seem smaller than it is. Photo by Bartelt

128 Station and Terrace: Terrace includes flowerbeds, flag, stairways, and electric lamps on railing. Came with three different stations: 124, 113, 115
(A) 124 station and terrace, 1928-30 **500 1100 450**
(B) 113 station and terrace, 1931-36 **500 1100 450**
(C) 115 station and terrace, 1937-42 **500 1100 450**

129 Terrace: With flowerbeds, flag, stairway and electric lamps on railing, 1928-42. (Excellent condition requires all landscaping) **450 900 400**

130 Tunnel: Metal construction
(A) 17" long, 12" wide, and 11" high, with portal 6-1/2" wide and 8" high; with mountain road and Swiss chalet. Same as 120 tunnel, but illuminated, 1920 **120 250 100**
(B) 1926 only: Very large metal tunnel designed for an 0 Gauge curve, 26" long x 23" wide x 14-1/2" high; four miniature houses, snow-covered peak, portals are 4-1/2" wide and 5-1/2" high. See next entry for 130L. Reader confirmation requested **120 250 100**

238 Locomotive, with tender, 602 Baggage, 600 Pullman, 601 Observation

93 Water Tower

115 Station

58 Lamp Post

442 Landscaped Diner

4 Locomotive, two 610 Pullmans, 612 Observation

262E Locomotive with tender 615 Baggage, 613 Pullman, 614 Observation

130L Tunnel:
(A) 1927 only: Same as 130 (B) above, but with illumination. Reader confirmation requested **120 250 100**
(B) 1928-33: Same as (A), but different dimensions: 24" long, 18-1/2" wide, still 14-1/2" high. Portals are 5" wide and 6-1/2" high. Reader confirmation requested **120 250 100**

131 Corner Display: Part of large Lionel display units, 1924-28 **70 200 70**

132 Corner Grass Plot: Part of large Lionel display units, 1924-28 **70 200 70**

133 Heart Shape Grass Plot: Part of large Lionel display units, 1924-28 **70 200 70**

134 Oval Shaped Grass Plot: Part of large Lionel display units, 1924-28 **70 200 70**

134 "LIONEL CITY", with two elaborate exterior brackets. Same as 124, but with different colors and automatic train control, 1937-42
(A) Brown sides, cream trim, red roof, green base, cream chimneys **140 300 125**

135 Circular Grass Plot: Part of large Lionel display units, 1924-28 **70 200 70**

136 Large Elevation: Part of large Lionel display units, 1924-28 **NRS**

136 Station: Same as 126, but has automatic stop control. Green base (same color as 512), 10-1/8" x 7-1/8"; three connection terminals, structure 8-1/4" long x 5-1/2" wide x 4-1/2" high. Two sets of arched-top double doors, white door frames, cream walls and red rectangular door at each end with six-pane window and white frame. Two six-pane windows with white frames are on the rear station wall, and two six-pane white-framed windows are on each end. Red four-sided ribbed roof with two red dormers having four-paned arched windows; two yellow chimneys. Lighted with lamp socket mounted on automatic stop control unit, Hahn observations
(A) Brass plates: "BAGGAGE" at left end, "EXPRESS" at right end and "LIONELVILLE" on front, Hahn and Koff Collections **55 75 50**
(B) Same as (A), but plates are nickel, Hahn and Koff Collections **60 85 50**

137 Station: Same as 127, but with automatic stop control, tan base, pea green frames, cream windows and doors, ivory walls and chimney, vermilion roof, nickel sign, "LIONELTOWN", 1937-42 **40 85 45**

140L Tunnel: Standard, illuminated, 37" x 24-1/2" x 20" high, for curved track, sheet steel, 1927-32 **190 400 200**

152 Automatic Crossing Gate: Double arm, red base, 1940-42 (Excellent condition must include contactor) **9 20 8**

153 Automatic Block Signal: 9", green base, red and green lights, aluminum post, orange ladder, semi-gloss black light fixtures, 1940-42 (Excellent must include 153C contactor). This was also made for many years after World War II. **7 15 8**

154 Automatic Highway Signal: Two red flashing lights, 1940-42 (Excellent must include contactor). This was also made for many years after World War II. **7 15 8**

155 Freight Shed: Illuminated, with two lights, 18" long, 8-1/4" wide and 11" high
(A) Yellow base, burnt orange floor, pea green posts, maroon roof with yellow underside, three brass finials, brass number plate, 1930-39 **90 200 80**
(B) White base, terra-cotta floor, aluminum posts, gray roof trimmed in red, 1940-42 **120 250 100**

156 Station: Platform illuminated
(A) Vermilion roof, nickel roof caps, green base, aluminum posts, black plastic fence with four lithographed signs, 1939-40 **12 25 10**

157 Hand Truck: 3/4" long, red, 1930-32 **15 30 10**

158 Set of two 156 Platforms and one 136 Station, 1940-42 (Excellent includes original box) **75 150 60**

159 Block Control Actuator: Operates two trains on one track: one contactor, lockon and two fiber pins, 1940 **10 25 10**

161 Baggage Truck: 4-1/2" long, green, 1930-32 **20 50 20**

162 Dump Truck: Red and gray, 4-1/2" long, 1930-32 **22 50 20**

163 Freight Station Set: Two 157 hand trucks, one 162 dump truck and one 160 baggage truck, 1930-42 (Excellent includes original box) **90 200 80**

164 Automatic Log Loader: Green base, vermilion roof, cream post, nickel roof caps, 1940-42 **70 150 60**

165 Magnetic Crane: Green bakelite base, aluminum or gray structure, cream house, vermilion roof and ladder, medium green boom, Cutler-Hammer magnet, 1940-42
(A) At the boom top, the line slides over a molded plastic cylinder. Hole for cord knot immediately beneath cylinder and another small hole below first; nickeled inside magnet casing, aluminum-finished structure, shiny base, Lemieux Collection **70 150 60**
(B) At the boom top, the line slides over a metal pulley. There is only the hole for the cord knot. Blued inside magnet casing, gray painted structure, dull base, Lemieux Collection **70 150 60**

167 Whistle Controller: Whistle and train direction, 1940-42 **1 3 1**

167X Whistle Controller: 00, 1940-42 **1 3 1**

169 Controller: Two button, reversing and uncoupling, 1940-42 **1 3 1**

170 Direct Current Reducer: 220 volts, 1914-38 **2 4 2**

171 DC to AC Inverter: 115 volts, 1936-42 **2 4 2**

172 DC to AC Inverter: 220 volts, 1939-42 **2 4 2**

184 Bungalow: 4-3/4" x 23/4" x 4", 1923-32, illuminated
(A) White, lithographed sides, red brick foundation, green lithographed roof **17 40 18**
(B) White enamel sides, dark green roof, white chimney, came only with set No. 186-187 **25 40 18**
(C) White enamel sides, dark green roof, white chimney, came only with set No. 186-187 **25 40 18**
(D) Cream enamel sides, orange roof, white chimney, came only with set No. 186-187 **25 40 18**

185 Bungalow: Same as 184, but not illuminated, 1923-24
(A) White, lithographed sides, red brick foundation, green lithographed roof **17 40 15**
(B) White enamel sides, dark green roof, white chimney, came only with set No. 186-187 **20 45 20**
(C) White enamel sides, dark green roof, white chimney, came only with set No. 186-187 **20 45 20**
(D) Cream enamel sides, orange roof, white chimney, came only with set No. 186-187 **20 45 20**

186 Set of 5 185 Bungalows: 1923-32 (Excellent condition required original box) **140 300 100**

186 Automatic Log Loader Outfit: Log loader, car, bin and uncoupling piece, 1940-41 (Add $100 to excellent for original box) **100 200 100**

187 Set of 5 185 Bungalows: 1923-24 (Excellent includes original box) **140 300 100**

188 Coal Elevator: 0 Gauge car and track set, 1938-41 (Add $75.00 to Excellent for original box) **90 200 80**

189 Villa: Two story with attic, illuminated, 5-1/2" x 4-7/8" x 5-3/8"
(A) White sides, peacock roof, red enameled chimney **45 100 40**
(B) White sides, gray roof, red lithographed chimney **45 100 40**
(C) Dark tan base, 1685 cream first floor windows and dormers, ivory doors and other windows, terra-cotta chimney **45 100 40**

191 Villa: Largest house in series, 7-1/8" long, 5-1/8" wide, 5-1/4" high, two story plus attic and sun porch
(A) Dark tan base, white porch and windows, red brick lithographed walls, pea green roof and dormer, dark green porch rails **45 100 40**
(B) Same as (A), but crackle red walls and dormers and brass rails on porches **45 100 40**
(C) Red lithographed brick, white trim, dark green roof **45 100 40**
(D) Cream sides, red roof, only came with plots **45 100 40**
(E) Same as (A), no dormer on roof, uncatalogued, came with plots **45 100 40**

The 191 Villa, Type (E). This is the uncatalogued version without the roof dormers. Some of these villas were modeled upon the real homes of Lionel executives. According to Ron Hollander in his fine book "All Aboard". This one was modeled upon the residence of Louis Caruso, the inventor of the latch coupler. Photo by Bartelt

193 Automatic Accessory Set, 1 No. 76, 1 No. 78, 1 No. 80, 1 No. 77, 1 No. 69, 5 No. 28, etc. (Add $50 to Excellent for boxed set) 1927-29 **140 300 120**

194 Accessory Set: Same as 193, but Standard Gauge, 1927-29 (Add $50 to Excellent for boxed set) **140 300 120**

195 Terrace: Includes: one 191 villa, one 189 villa, one 184 bungalow, one 90 flagpole and flag, two 56 lamp posts, 1927-30 **275 600 275**

196 Accessory Set: Includes: one 127 station, six 60 telegraph poles, one 62 semaphore, one 68 warning signal, two 58 lamp posts, 1927 (Excellent condition requires original box) **75 150 70**

200 Turntable: 17", green and tan, 1928-33 **75 150 70**

205 Merchandise Containers: Set of three, LCL (Less than Carload Lots), green 3-1/2" x 3" x 4", 1930-38 **125 250 110**

206 Sack of Coal: Approximately 1/2 lb., 1938-42* **5 15 —**

208 Tool Set: Includes pick, shovel, axe, rake, hoe, sledge; in enameled metal chest with brass handle, 1934-42 **30 75 30**

209 Wooden Barrels: Set of four open-center barrels, 2-1/8" high, 1934-42 **4 10 4**

0209 Barrels: Set of six open-center wooden barrels, 1-3/8" high, 1934-42* **4 10 4**

217 Three-Car Lighting Set: With three 14-volt bulbs to be used on reduced alternating current, 1914-23 **NRS**

270 Lighting Set: Two 8-volt bulbs with three feet of flexible cord and sockets. To be used on batteries or reduced D.C., 1915-23 **NRS**

270 Bridge: Single-span, 0 Gauge, 10" long, 1931-42

(A) Maroon **12 20 10**

(B) Vermilion, nickel sign "LIONEL", 1942 **12 20 10**

(C) Cherry red painted sheet metal; yellow decal with green "LIONEL" in green oval line instead of metal plate; slots for plate not present. This is a puzzling piece. It could represent very early or very late production — or even very early postwar production. Reader comments are invited. Luftkopf Collection **NRS**

271 Lighting Set: Same as 270, but with two 14-volt bulbs to be used on reduced A.C., 1915-23 **NRS**

271 Two 270 Bridge Spans: 20" long, 1931-33; 1935-40 **15 40 20**

272 Three 270 Bridge Spans: 30" long, 1931-33; 1935-40 **25 60 20**

280 Single Bridge: Standard Gauge, 14" long

(A) Gray with green portals and walks, 1931-35 **10 25 10**

(B) Green, 1936-42 **10 25 10**

281 Bridge Spans: Two 280 spans, 28" long

(A) Gray, 1931-33 **15 35 13**

(B) Green, 1935-40 **15 35 13**

282 Bridge Spans: Three 280 spans, 42" long

(A) Gray, 1931-33 **15 30 15**

(B) Green, 1935-40 **15 30 15**

300 Hell Gate Bridge: 28-3/4" x 11" x 10-1/2"

(A) Cream towers, green trusses, orange base **350 850 300**

(B) Ivory towers, aluminum trusses, red base **350 1100 300**

THE HELL GATE BRIDGE: PROTOTYPE AND MODEL

By William Meyer

Perhaps the reason why Lionel's Hell Gate Bridge looked so awesome as an accessory is that the prototype itself is quite a remarkable piece of engineering. The East River Arch Bridge (its proper name) was designed by Gustav Lindenthal. It is a massive steel arch structure with a clear span of 977 feet 6 inches and a clearance of 135 feet above high water. It acquired its nickname because of the vicious currents stemming from the confluence of the East and Harlem Rivers under the bridge.

The bridge was opened to rail traffic on April 1, 1917, creating a direct rail route to New England. For about a year, all trains were pulled by steam locomotives over the bridge. In late 1918, an 11,000 volt AC catenary system was installed over the four-track bridge line for the Pennsylvania Railroad's fast passenger trains. In 1927, the catenary was extended so that freight service could be electrified as well. The bridge took five years to build and cost 27 million dollars, the equivalent of a quarter of a billion dollars today.

Lionel produced its model of the Hell Gate Bridge in 1928. Although it was not scaled to the exact length of the bridge, it was certainly big — two and a half feet long and a foot high. It was never provided with approach piers, as was the prototype, but Standard and 0 Gauge trains certainly looked great passing through its piers and span. The 0 Gauge trains were more amenable to the true proportions of the bridge.

This bridge has become one of the most highly prized accessories ever produced by the Lionel Corporation. Even a battered copy will sell quickly for several hundred dollars, and the later silver, ivory and red version is especially prized. To reproduce this accessory today would incur astronomical manufacturing and retailing costs. If there were ever an accessory typifying the Golden Age of Lionel, this is the one.

For further details of Lionel's model, see Ron Hollander, **All Aboard! The Story of Joshua Lionel Cowen & His Lionel Train Company** (New York: Workman Publishing Co., 1981), pp. 96-99.

308 Five Signs: Whistle and yard-limit posts, no trespassing sign and two different crossing warnings. Enameled white steel with black lettering, 1940-42* **6 15 5**

313 Bascule Bridge: Electrically-operated, green base, light green bridge, building with cream walls, orange windows, vermilion roof, no door, 1940-42* **140 300 175**

314 Girder Bridge: Single span, scale, 10" long, aluminum, 1940-42 **6 15 5**

315 Trestle Bridge: Illuminated, 24-1/2" long, silver, 1940-42* **15 35 10**

435 Power Station: 1926-38, similar to 436 Power Station but modestly smaller, base 7-1/2" x 6", building 5-3/4" x 4-1/2" x 5" high. Used with transformers A or B

(A) Light green base, ivory sides, white windows, red window frames, State brown cornice and roof, red skylight, red stack base, aluminum stack **60 125 50**

(B) Gray base, terra-cotta sides, cream windows, green window frames, light cream cornice and roof, green skylight, mojave stack base, red stack **60 125 50**

(C) Same as (A), but cream sides, red door frame, white doors, brass black-lettered "POWER STATION" plate over door, mustard cornices, Weisblum Collection **60 125 50**

This is a 435 Power Station like variety (B), but the base and roof colors look different. We need help from readers in identifying this variety. Photo by Bartelt

436 Power Station, 1927-37: Similar to 435 Power Station but modestly larger, base 9-1/8" x 7-5/8", building 7" x 5-1/2" x 5-7/8" high to cornice

(A) Gray base, terra-cotta sides, light green windows, dark green window frames, maroon door, dark green door frame, dirty yellow cornice and roof, light green skylight, dark gray stack base, bright red stack **60 125 50**

(B) Gray base, burnt orange walls, orange windows, pea green window frames, red doors, medium green door frame, cream cornice and roof, pea green skylight, mojave chimney base, red chimney **60 125 50**

(C) Gray base, burnt orange walls, cream windows, pea green window frames, red doors, medium green door frame, light cream cornice and roof, pea green skylight, mojave chimney base, red chimney **60 125 50**

(D) Same as (C), but pea green windows and dark green window frames; maroon door and green door frame, dark mojave shade base and green ventilator, Weisblum Collection **60 125 50**

(E) Green base, same as 45 Gateman, cream walls, white windows and doors, red windows and door frames, mustard roof cornices, red skylight and chimney base, aluminum chimney; brass plates over doors at each end with black sans-serif "POWER STATION"; block rubber-stamping on underside of base in five lines: "NO. 436 POWER STATION/MADE BY/THE LIONEL CORPORATION/NEW YORK/U.S. OF AMERICA", Riley and Koff Collections **60 175 50**

437 Switch-Signal Tower: 10-1/4" x 8-3/8" x 8-7/8" high, 1926-37, illuminated, with knife switches on rear

(A) Mojave base, burnt orange lower wall, ivory band between floors, shell orange upper wall, peacock windows, red door, vermilion trim under dormer, pea green roof, red chimney **125 250 100**

(B) Mojave base, burnt orange lower wall, ivory band between floors, orange windows, upper cream walls, red door, peacock roof **125 250 100**

(C) Red base, entire wall in yellow, green windows, red doors, orange roof. Rare **250 425 200**

438 Signal Tower: Base 6" x 4-3/4" x 12" high, 1927-39; switches on back except for 1927

(A) Mojave base, pea green legs, cream upper base, orange house walls, red doors and roof, white windows, lithographed brick chimney, brass ladders and number plate **140 300 100**

(B) Gray base, aluminum legs, gray upper base, ivory house walls, red doors and roof, red windows, ivory chimney, red ladders and nickel number plate **170 350 125**

439 Panel Board: 8-3/16" x 7-3/16", 1928-42

(A) Crackle red frame, white marble-finish panel board; brass switches, meter rims, lamp hood, i.d. and number plates; black bakelite handle ends with small L on each side of switches, 1928-34, 1936-42 **35 75 30**

(B) Same as (A), but black panel, 1935 **35 75 30**

440C Panel Board: Used as controller for 440N Signal Bridge; similar to 430 Board, but has track controller. Red frame, black panel board; nickel switches, meter rims, light hood, i.d. and number plates, switches with same black handles as 439 **35 75 30**

440N Signal Bridge: 1932-42, large bridge spans two Standard Gauge tracks with two multi-light black signal units, includes illuminated panel board, 20-1/2" wide by 14" high

(A) Red die-cast base, aluminum painted trusses - vertical and horizontal; red walkway across top **120 250 100**

(B) Terra-cotta die-cast base, mojave vertical and horizontal trusses, maroon walkway across top **120 250 100**

0440 Signal Bridge: 1932-42, same a 440N, but with 0 Gauge track connectors

(A) Red die-cast base, aluminum painted bridge unit **120 250 100**

(B) Terra-cotta base, mojave trusses, maroon walkway, McLaren Collection **120 250 110**

441 Weighing Station: 1932-36, for Standard Gauge only, green base, cream building with die-cast scale and weights; double doors on back of lighted building, 29-1/2" long, 4-3/4" high, 9-1/2" wide **225 500 200**

442 Landscape Diner: 1938-42, ivory building, red doors, window frames and roof; name and number boards are red with silver lettering. Williams Reproductions has manufactured a building that is quite similar. **60 150 50**

444 Roundhouse: 1932-35, very large building, 24" wide in back and 8-3/4" wide in front. A number of sections could be put together, Lionel recommended four. Terra-cotta sides, cream trim bands, pea green roof and maroon windows; each section is lighted and has two green roof grills. Most valuable of all accessories. Price for one section **1100 2500 1000**

444-18 Clip: 1933, for holding roundhouse sections together **NRS**

455 Electric Range: 1930, 1932-33, green legs, cream oven and stove sides, two stove top heating units, two units in oven with one for broiling and one for baking, thermometer on oven door, four controls and master switch, pilot light, five cooking utensils, 25" wide, 11" deep, 33" high **135 300 140**

500 Dealer Display: 1927-28, pine bushes **NRS**

501 Dealer Display: 1927-28, small pine trees **NRS**

502 Dealer Display: 1927-28, medium pine trees **NRS**

503 Dealer Display: 1927-28, large pine trees **NRS**

504 Dealer Display: 1924-28, rose bushes **NRS**

505 Dealer Display: 1924-28, oak trees **NRS**

506 Dealer Display: 1924-28, platform with composition board, completely painted and wired, two sections **NRS**

507 Dealer Display: 1924-28, platform similar to 506, but three sections **NRS**

508 Dealer Display: 1924-28, sky background, two composition board sections **NRS**

509 Dealer Display: 1924-28, mountains on composition board **NRS**

510 Dealer Display: 1924-28, canna bushes **NRS**

550 Miniature Railroad Figures: 1932-36, set of six includes engineer, conductor, porter with removable footstool, a male passenger, female passenger, Red Cap with removable luggage. Each 3" high. Price for set, although figures were also available separately (see next six entries) **95 200 80**

551 Engineer: 1932, figure 3" high **10 25 7**

552 Conductor: 1932, figure 3" high **10 25 7**

553 Porter: 1932, figure with removable footstool, 3" high **10 25 7**

554 Male Passenger: 1932, figure 3" high **10 25 7**

555 Female Passenger: 1932, figure 3" high **10 25 7**

556 Red Cap: 1932, figure with removable luggage, 3" high **10 25 7**

840 Industrial Power Station: 1928-40, largest single-unit accessory ever built by Lionel, 26" wide, 21-1/2" deep, and 18" high. Separate green base, two sets of cream steps mount on base, dark mojave floor attached to building which fits into green base, building with cream sides, many multi-paned green windows, orange bands around building at first and second floor levels, two orange roof grates, one for each wing, orange roof, three smokestacks in one unit with word "LIONEL" fastened across them, red sheet metal water tower, side panel with six knife switches, can hold two transformers, interior light with larger socket bulb. Prices quoted require all accessories listed above. Replacement grates, steps, and smokestack units with signs have been made and not marked. **1200 2400 1000**

910 Grove of Trees: 1932-42, base 16" x 8-3/4", eleven trees **70 150 70**

911 Country Estate: Illuminated and landscaped, includes: 191 villa, shrubbery and trees, base 16" x 8", 1932-42. House colors vary, come in red, yellow and light cream

(A) Cream house comes with dark tan base, cream dormers, white front porch walls, pea green windows and doors, brass porch railings, red roof and cream chimney **140 300 125**

912 Suburban Home: Illuminated, includes 189 villa with trees and shrubbery, base 16" x 8"

(A) Base dark tan, walls, first floor windows and dormers 1685 cream, doors and other windows ivory, terra-cotta chimney **140 300 125**

913 Landscaped Bungalow: Illuminated base 16" x 8-3/4", trees and flowering bushes, removable roof

(A) White lithographed walls, orange windows, painted pea green roof, red chimney; walls and roof not varnished (whereas 184 lithographed bungalows are varnished), 1940-42 **90 200 80**

914 Park Landscape: With centerpiece, cedars, two grass plots, flowering bushes, and pale yellow or light cream base, 1932-35 **90 200 80**

915 Large Tunnel: Standard Gauge, mountain, trees and five houses on mountainside, constructed of molded felt on wooded base, 65" x 28-1/2" 23-1/2", tunnel openings 6-1/4" x 7-3/4", 1932, 1934-35 **100 250 100**

916 Curved Tunnel: 0 Gauge with trees and three houses on hillside

(A) 37" x 30-1/2", tunnel openings, 1932 **70 150 60**

(B) 29-1/4" x 24" x 13-1/2", 1933-42 **90 150 60**

917 Scenic Hillside: Two red-roofed houses and trees, 34" x 9-1/2" 15", 1932-36 **90 200 80**

918 Scenic Hillside: Same as 917, but one house 30" x 9-1/2" x 10", 1932-36 **90 200 80**

919 Park Grass: 8 oz. bag, 1932-42* **7 15 —**

920 Village: Two end-sections, 57" x 31-1/2" x 10", four villas and two bungalows, buildings illuminated, 1932-33 **600 1500 500**

921 Scenic Park: Three sections, same as 920 with 921C center section added, 85" x 31-1/2" x 10", 1932-33 **1000 2500 1000**

921C Park Center: Section of 921, two villas and one bungalow 28" x 31-1/2" x 10", 1932-33 **400 1000 400**

922 Terrace: Illuminated lamp terrace, flowering shrubs, green grass, 156 lamp post, 7-3/4" high, gray base 13" x 3-3/4", 1932-36 **80 200 75**

923 Tunnel: 0 Gauge, curved, 40-1/4" x 14-1/4" x 23", portals 7-3/4" x 8-1/2", felt composition with wooden base, 1933-42 **70 200 70**

924 Curved Tunnel: Same as 916, but for 0-72

(A) 29-1/4" x 30-1/2" x 13-1/2", portals 4-3/4" x 5-1/8", felt composition with wooden base, 1935 **65 160 60**

(B) 30-1/8" x 21-1/4" x 12-1/4", portals 4-3/4" x 5-1/8", 1936-42 **50 125 45**

925 Lubricant: Two ounces, nozzle-tube of train lubricant, 1935-42* **1 2 —**

927 Ornamental Flag Plot: Silk flag fitted with cord for raising and lowering, 14-3/4" high, color variations of base; pale yellow, light cream, 1937-42 **25 50 30**

1012 Winner Station: Removable roof with inside transformer, 1932 **10 25 13**

1022 Curved Tunnel: For Lionel Jr. outfits. Same as 123, but without house and trees, 1935-42 **7 15 7**

1023 Tunnel: Straight, 1934-42; felt composition, 0 Gauge, 14-3/8" long x 10-3/4" wide x 8-1/2" high; portals 4-1/4" wide x 5-7/8" high **10 15 7**

1025 Bumper: 1940-42; illuminated; black die-cast body, nickel metal cage protects large red screw-base bulb; came with a straight piece of 027 track **4 7 2**

1027 Junior Transformer Station: 5-1/2" x 3-3/4" x 3-3/4", red roof, yellow sides, green base, 1934 **9 20 10**

1045 Operating Watchman: 7" high, 1938-50

(A) Vermilion base, aluminum post, brass sign, nickel cap and black uniform **10 25 10**

(B) Green base **10 25 10**

1560 Mechanical Station: Red roof, 5-1/2" long, 1933-37 **12 20 10**

1569 Mechanical Accessory Set: Eight pieces; four telegraph poles, one semaphore, one railroad sign, one railroad gate, one clock, 1933-37 **12 30 11**

Chapter VIII

LIONEL 2 7/8 INCH GAUGE

by James M. Sattler

Less is known among collectors about Lionel 2-7/8" gauge cars and accessories than any other category or era of Lionel's years of production. This lack of information and knowledge is due primarily to the paucity of documentation of these items and to the extremely limited number of original 2-7/8" gauge items which have survived and come to the attention of toy train historians.

Actual production of Lionel 2-7/8" gauge cars and accessories was minute when compared to any later period of production, and it is doubtful that any person is still living who has first hand knowledge of exactly what, when, how, and how many of each item was produced. No production records or other contemporaneous documents have yet turned up to aid in the examination of the earliest period of Lionel production other than a few catalouges. The only known Catalogues which show and describe 2-7/8" gauge cars and accessories are the recently discovered 1902 and the more well-known 1903, 1904, and 1905 Lionel Catalogues. The 1906 Catalogue which introduced Standard Gauge does not mention or describe any 2-7/8" gauge item, and therefore it can reasonably be assumed that actual production of 2-7/8" gauge cars and accessories ceased sometime in 1905.

The 1902-1905 Lionel Catalogues, together with the few surviving original specimens of the cars and accessories, form the primary research materials relating to the commencement and subsequent developments of Lionel's earliest days of production, and they also afford some very interesting insights into Lionel's and America's turn-of-the-century history.

The 1902 Catalogue, for example, states:
"The goods described herein are offered for sale to the general public for the second year, although they have been in use for a long time by mechanical institutions for demonstrating purposes, as they give a thorough insight into the workings of the electric cars now so universally used. We received so many inquiries from the students and their friends for duplicate outfits that we decided to manufacture them in larger quantities, thereby reducing their cost and enabling us to offer them at a popular price."

Similarly, the 1903 and 1904 Catalogues state that the goods described "are offered for sale to the general public for the third year", and for the "fourth year", respectively, and the 1905 Catalogue states that Lionel had been constructing its goods "For the past five years." The recent discovery of a 1902 Catalogue shows that it follows similar patterns to those of its better-known 1903 versions.

Since no earlier Catalogues are known to exist, the commencement date of 2 7/8" gauge production as 1901 must be deduced from the later Catalogue statements and other sources.

The generally-accepted view is that the production era of Lionel 2-7/8" gauge "Electric Miniature Cars" was the five-year period from 1901 through 1905.

The first published work generally available to train collectors which mentions Lionel 2-7/8" gauge trains is "Riding The Tinplate Rails" by Louis H. Hertz which was published in 1944 almost 40 years after production of these items ceased. Hertz states that "Actually, it was in 1901 that Joshua Lionel Cowen, then twenty-one years of age, who had already proved himself inventive in the electrical field, founded the original Lionel Mfg. Co. and made his first trains." Hertz also found that in 1937 when Lionel stock was placed on the open market, the company stated in a report filed with the Securities and Exchange Commission that the company had started business in 1901.

The conclusion that 1901 represents the commencement date of Lionel production is somewhat at variance with the 1902 Catalogue statement that although the goods were being offered for sale to the general public for the second year, "they have been in use for a long time . . . ". For many later years the Lionel Catalogues used the advertising slogan "STANDARD OF THE WORLD" followed, for example, in the 1917 Catalogue by "FOR 17 YEARS" and in the 1920 Catalogue by "FOR TWENTY YEARS". If these numbers of years are counted backwards beginning with the year of the catalogue, the year of 1901 consistently results as the first year. However, in the 1923 and many later Catalogues, the advertising slogan was changed to "STANDARD OF THE WORLD SINCE 1900" and this slogan was also printed on the contemporaneous train set boxes. It might be said that the latter slogan is technically correct because if 1901 was the first year of production, then the goods had been made "since 1900". The actual commencement date of Lionel's 2-7/8" gauge production may never be known for certain unless reliable documentation is found.

As far as the Catalogues are concerned, it would be unwise in the extreme to blindly accept as true and accurate all of the statements found in Lionel Catalogues.

The Lionel 2-7/8" gauge cars and equipment were amazingly advanced in view of subsequent developments in model railroading.

Lionel began its train production with two rail tracks and with one side of the wheels and axles insulated from the other. Although manually operated, all powered units had a reversing mechanism, the details of which varied over the years of production. All units, whether powered or trailers, had cast-iron frames and working coil springs.

The track was comprised of two strips of tinplated steel inserted into slots or grooves cut in wooden ties. The track was supplied only in straight sections which had to be bent to form curves. The earliest track was composed of straight strips 1/16" thick and 3/8" wide and of two different lengths of approximately 11" and 13" each. When the unequal lengths of rail were curved they would form a complete circle of eight sections having a diameter of approximately 34 inches.

The ties supplied with the earliest track were red-stained pieces of wood 4"wide, 1" thick, and 1/2" high with slots or grooves cut in one side 2-7/8" apart to admit the steel rails. Each section of the earliest track was supplied with five ties, two of which had plates of brass which fit into the slots or grooves and bent outward to lay flat against the top surface of the tie and these brass plates were held in place by a single brass brad. The brass plates allowed the electrical contact to be made between the ends of the adjoining steel rails. The other

No. 300

2⅞ Gauge Trolley

with Converse body

three ties without the brass plates were to be spaced equally between the two end ties. The 1902 Catalogue suggested that: "A complete circle may also be formed, but it is not prudent to do so, as the continual friction on the wheels rounding the curve consumes a great deal more battery current than when car is run straight or slightly curved." This suggestion was eliminated in the later Catalogues.

The 1903 Catalogue indicated a change in the track and stated that the steel rails would be supplied with "offsets" which consisted of an L-shaped bend in one end of each rail and a hook-shaped bend in the other end. The sections of track, each one foot long, were joined by sliding the L-shaped end of one rail into the hook-shaped end of the adjoining rail. The ties supplied with the 1903 and later "offset" rails were reduced in size to 1/2" square and 4" long, and five ties were also supplied for each two-rail section of track. Interestingly, the 1905 Catalogue announced that the track was "Improved 1905" however, the accompanying illustration is identical to that shown in the 1903 and 1904 Catalogues, and the description is identical to that in the 1904 Catalogue. The later and smaller ties were also stained red.

In addition to the track, Lionel offered a No. 320 "Switch and Signal", a No. 330 ninety-degree "Crossing", a No. 340 "Suspension Bridge", (the design of which changed in 1903), a No. 350 terminal track "Bumper" (the design of which changed between 1902 and 1904), and a No. 380 set of "Elevated Pillars". Power was supplied either by a set of dry cell batteries (Catalogue No. 301) A "Plunge Battery" (Catalogue No. 302) consisting of four glass jars, each containing a carbon cylinder and pencil-shaped zinc, a 9" x 12" x 8" wooden box to keep the jars from touching, and a 3-pound supply of electric sand to be added to three quarts of water to charge the four cells which were to be wired in series, and an alternative power source utilized direct electric current through an outfit (Catalogue No. 370 in 1902 and 1903 only) of two glass jars, lead plates, a mixture of sulphuric acid and water, and a light bulb.

All powered units and all trailers had only four wheels. A realistic model, for the time, of link and pin-type couplers was used with a fiber link and metal pins which passed through holes in the coupler pockets and through corresponding holes in the fiber links. Original fiber links and pins are usually missing when an occasional 2-7/8" gauge item is found. 2-7/8 gauge cars and accessories are definitely among the most difficult to acquire of all collectible train-related items.

As described in the accompanying list, there are at least twenty-four significantly different versions of 2-7/8" gauge rolling stock. In addition, when minor variations are considered, such as types of wheels (either hollow brass or cast-iron), lettering variations (such as paint color differences or the presence or absence of design trim on the destination boards of the 300 and 309 cars), the presence or absence of coupler pockets (on the Wooden Gondolas and the 300 and 309 cars), cast knobs or wire handles on the controllers, and the presence or absence of trolley poles (on the 300 and 1000 cars), there are well over thirty different collectible variations of rolling stock.

It should be understood, however, that some of the twenty-four significant versions described in the list may not have been made. To the author's knowledge, no examples of a 100 Electric Locomotive as a "trailer", of the 100 Electric Locomotive or the 400 Trailer in nickel or of the motorized versions of the 200 Electric Express or the 500 Electric Derrick Car in light green presently exist in the hands of collectors. Original examples of the remaining items described in the list presently reside in collections. The author has nine of the remaining nineteen pieces in his personal collection. Needless to say, he would like to have more.

WOODEN GONDOLAS

The generally accepted view is that the first item of 2-7/8" gauge production was the uncatalogued motorized wooden gondola produced in 1901 or earlier. Two distinct variations of the motorized wooden gondola have been found. The first has a red-stained finish and mortised and tenoned corners and lacks any steps, handrails, or coupler pockets. Because of the rather primitive construction features of this version, it is believed to be the earliest 2-7/8" gauge item ever produced, and the generally accepted production date is 1901 or possibly earlier.

The second variation is similar; however, it has a natural brown-stained finish and brass corner braces as opposed to mortised and tenoned corners. It also appears with steps, handrails, and a coupler pocket. This variation is described exactly in the recently discovered 1902 Catalogue, although the cut illustrating this item incorrectly shows the words "Electric Express" in a darkened circle. All original examples found to date of both versions of the wooden gondola bear the words "Electric Express" in a straight gold line 5-1/2" long on each side.

One of the most overworked, and in many cases misused, words commonly heard in train collecting is "rare." As applied to the wooden gondola, however, there is hardly another adjective that fairly or more accurately can be used. All versions of the Lionel wooden gondola are among the rarest items confronted in train collecting.

No. 100 Electric Locomotives

The first model of a locomotive ever made by Lionel was the No. 100 Electric Locomotive. The No. 100, which always bore the designation "No. 5" on its sides and ends, was modeled after the 1,800 horse power electric locomotives which hauled trains through the Camden-Waverly tunnel section under the City of Baltimore, as a part of the Baltimore and Ohio Railroad. The prototype had four articulated sets of wheels, which Lionel reduced to two. The Lionel model, like all powered 2-7/8" gauge items, had an electric motor which was entirely below floor level.

Although the Catalogues all state that the "Actual size" of the No. 100 is "12 inches long", in fact the overall length of the No. 100 is 10-1/2". A longer measurement could only be derived by also including the two fully-extended fiber link couplers.

The No. 100 is occasionally found with a light green body and roof and a black frame. The 1903 Catalogue states that "All parts are japanned and lettered in harmonious colors." The term "japanned" means to give a coat of "japan" which in turn refers to a type of varnish or lacquer having a hard, brilliant finish, and it most commonly refers to a black coating used on metal and fixed by heating. The light green finish on the early locomotives is definitely and distinctly of a different type of finish than that which appears on maroon and black examples. The light green finish chips easily, and when the finish chips or flakes off the shiny, tinned metal underneath is readily visible.

The 1904 and 1905 Catalogues changed the word "japanned" to "enameled", and consequently it is reasonable to assume that the light green models were of 1903 or possibly earlier production, while the maroon and black versions followed the Catalogue language change. Therefore, the maroon and black versions can be fairly dated as 1904 or later production. At least

The Sattler Collection
ELECTRIC EXPRESS.
No. 1
No. 2
No. 500 (A)
B. & O.
No. 5.
METROPOLITAN.
EXPRESS
No. 100 (A)
No. 100 (B)
No. 800
No. 1000 (B)
No. 1000 (A)
No. 300

one No. 100 has been found with gold-colored paper stickers on both sides stamped "C & St. L" on the left sides of the center door and "No. 5" on the right sides.

There is a significant difference in the manner by which the bodies are held to the frames in the light green and the maroon and black versions. The light green locomotives have two 1/2" holes in the bottom of the floor through which a portion of the cast-iron frame passes to hold the body to the frame. In the maroon and black versions these holes are not present and the body is fastened to the cast-iron frame by means of two screws with square nuts on the inside of the body. The reversing switches are also very different, and in this regard there is a curiosity which arises out of the Catalogue illustrations. The 1904 and 1905 Catalogues both contain an illustration of the underside of a car which "represents the mechanism contained in all our motor cars". The 1903 Catalogues do not contain such an illustration. The reversing switch shown in the 1904 and 1905 illustrations is identical to that found on the light green locomotives; however, the maroon and black locomotives have a reversing switch which is circular and concentric. As is the case in the prewar and postwar eras, the Catalogues cannot be take as accurate in all instances, and in this particular case it ma well be that the 1904 and 1905 Catalogues used an illustration o a 1903 or earlier mechanism.

The 1904 and 1905 Catalogues also describe a "Special Show Window Display" outfit with a nickel-plated No. 100 Electric Locomotive with all working parts constructed of phosphor-bronze. No example of a nickel-plated No. 100 is known to exist.

The light green electric locomotives are in the same category, as far as scarcity is concerned, as the wooden gondolas. If a nickel-plated No. 100 should turn up, it would be more rare than the light green version. Relatively speaking, the maroon and black versions are "common". The Catalogues do not show, and no one has yet found, a No. 100 locomotive in a non-motorized version.

No. 200 and No. 400 Steel Gondolas

In 1903 Lionel replaced the wooden gondola with a steel version. The earliest steel gondolas had two ribs on each side and were "japanned" in light green to match the light green No. 100. These gondolas were also lettered "B. & O." and it appears that the same stamp was used both on the No. 100 locomotives and the No. 200 gondolas.

Beginning with the 1904 Catalogue, the steel gondola was shown with "Lake Shore" lettering and all examples with "LAKE SHORE" lettering found to date have been enameled in maroon with gold trim and lettering. The 1904 and 1905 Catalogues also list a deluxe nickel-plated steel gondola as a non-motorized "Trailer" with the "Special Show Window Display" outfit. No examples of the nickeled versions have been found to date.

While at least one light green steel gondola has been found as in the "Trailer" version, no motorized version is known to exist. As in the case of the No. 100 locomotives, the maroon and black versions of the No. 200 and No. 400 steel gondolas are seen much more often than their light green counterparts.

No. 300 and No. 309 Open Trolleys

Another early production item, possibly contemporaneous with the wooden Gondolas, is the No. 300 Electric Trolley Car. This item, catalogued in 1902, 1903, 1904, and 1905, used a body supplied by Morton E. Converse & Co. to which was added a Lionel cast frame, motor, and controller.* The bodies were also used and sold by the Converse company in a trackless pull toy version, but when found their painting and lettering is usually much different than the Lionel versions, although the Author has examined one original converse trolley painted in the same colors and configured as the Lionel versions.

All examples of the No. 300 found to date have been generally similar in maroon, pea green, and cream paint colors, lettering, and trim; however, variations are found in the color of the lettering on the destination boards and in the presence or absence of design trim on the destination boards. The lettering on the destination boards appears either in red or in black on white reversible boards. The black lettering versions also have a design on both sides of the lettering. Some examples have been found with a stamped steel reversible trolley pole, but most do not have the pole.

Beginning in 1904 and continuing in 1905, a No. 309 Electric Trolley Trailer was illustrated and described in the Catalogues which was the same as the No. 300 but without a motor. It appears that coupler pockets were added to the post-1904 versions.

Both the No. 300 and the No. 309 are difficult to find, with the No. 309 being the more difficult of the two.

No. 500 and No. 600 Derrick Cars

One of the most intriguing cars and certainly the piece with the greatest "play value", is the derrick car.

The No. 500 is a motorized version which has a manually-operated drum to which is attached a metal chain and a cast-iron hook. The No. 600 was identical except for the absence of the motor and the controller.

The derrick cars were only catalogued in 1903 and 1904, and are among the most difficult to find of all the 2-7/8" gauge pieces. Due to the height of the derrick car boom, it appears that its introduction in 1903 was responsible for a change in design of the No. 340 Suspension Bridge from a clearance height of about 10" as shown in the 1902 Catalogue to about 14" as shown in the 1903 to 1905 Catalogues. The design change was to eliminate the two upper straight horizontal members at both top ends of the bridge and to substitute two arched members which would allow for more than sufficient clearance for the derrick car boom which rose a total of 11" above the height of the track. Interestingly, the No. 300 Electric Trolley Cars which have been found with trolley poles, also rise exactly 11" above the height of the track, and it is possible that such cars with poles may represent only 1903 and later production, because only the 1903 and later Suspension Bridges would allow the trolley poles to pass under the top members of the bridges. The catalogues are of no assistance to such a determination because none of the catalogue illustrations shows a No. 300 Electric Trolley Car with a trolley pole. Although the No. 600 Derrick Trailer is known to exist in both light green and maroon and black versions, the motorized No. 500 Electric Derrick is only known to exist in maroon and black.

No. 800 and No. 900 Box Cars

This car is sometimes called the "Jail Car" because of the bars in the windows. It is the only 2-7/8" gauge item with opening doors. All known examples are maroon and black with "Metropolitan Express" in gold on both sides.

*These trolleys have an aluminum stamped Lionel emblem tacked to their underside.

No. 100
Electric Locomotive

No. 1000 and No. 1050 Passenger Cars

The No. 1000 and No. 1050 Passenger Cars are only shown in the 1905 Catalogue. These "late production" items are found most often with either "Metropolitan St. R. R. Co." or "Maryland St. Ry. Co." lettering, although at least one example with "Philadelphia R. T. Co." lettering is known.

The colors are the familiar maroon and black, with variations of the maroon running almost to red.

At least one example has been found with a 6-1/2" brass trolley pole painted black which is mounted on a swiveling and sprung base. No Lionel identification appears anywhere on these cars.

Conclusion

Because of their extreme scarcity, 2- 7/8" gauge pieces are seldom seen even by seasoned train collectors. No known collection has more than 9 different original pieces. Many long-time train collectors who have been knowledgeable about Lionel train production for more than thirty years have never had the opportunity to acquire a single piece. Moreover, the vast majority of Lionel train collectors have never even seen an original piece of 2-7/8" gauge other than in photographs; and interestingly, most collectors display little or no interest in 2-7/8" gauge.

In car collecting, the same is true of the Duesenberg. The lack of interest in the Lionel 2-7/8" gauge may well stem from the fact that during their lifetime most train collectors will never have the chance to acquire a 2-7/8" gauge item. But, like the Duesenberg, the inability to own one has not had a dampening effect upon the prices at which these items infrequently change hands. The fact of the matter is, however, that it is usually only the most experienced collectors who are interested in and who are willing to make the financial commitment required to acquire specimens of the earliest, and certainly the most unique, of all Lionel trains.

Because of the great scarcity of 2-7/8" trains and the small number of active collectors who often communicate one with the other, sales of 2-7/8" gauge items usually are conducted privately and are only rarely offered for public sale.

Reproductions of some of the 2-7/8" cars were made from 1957 to 1961 by McCoy Manufacturing Company of Kent, Washington. None of the McCoy reproductions were made with motors, and none of them were embossed in the floor bottoms with the name "Lionel Mfg. Co." All of the McCoy reproductions were rubber-stamped in gold on the underside with either "REPRODUCTION BY McCOY" or "McCOY'S OF KENT". This rubber-stamping can easily be removed.

The cast portions of the McCoy reproductions were made using original Lionel 2-7/8" gauge parts as patterns and they were die-cast in "white metal" (sometimes called "zamac") and are subject to deterioration and crumbling. The McCoy reproductions are very faithful to their Lionel counterparts in most respects, however, the dimensions of the cast portions are slightly smaller than Lionel originals due to a shrinkage factor in the die-castings. The paint colors and the size, style, and color of the lettering and numbering of the McCoy reproductions differ considerably from the Lionel originals.

McCoy made approximately 100 sets of 2-7/8" gauge cars and each set consisted of one each of: a B & O No. 5 locomotive, a steel "Lake Shore" gondola, a derrick car, a "Metropolitan Street" box or "jail" car, and a passenger trailer car (sometimes referred to as a 2-7/8" gauge "closed end trolley"). Each set sold for $300.00 and, when available, individual cars were sold for $60.00 each.

In addition to the cars in the sets, McCoy also made wood bottoms, side frames, wheels, and axles which were installed on about 20 to 25 original Converse pull toy bodies to simulate the Lionel No. 309 non-motorized "Electric Trolley Trailer". It is not known whether these items were marked as reproductions. McCoy also made one "Metropolitan Street" box or "jail" car body entirely of copper and brass which was installed on the standard frame and given by McCoy to veteran train collector Russ Hafdahl for his birthday in 1961. This particular item is now in the author's collection.

Due to their age and relatively early appearance in train collecting, the McCoy 2-7/8" gauge reproductions are highly prized and command significant prices today.

James Cohen of Trumbull, Connecticut has made approximately 200 non-motorized 2-7/8" gauge car reproductions and plans to make more. To date he has reproduced the No. 400 steel gondolas in both the green "B & O" and the maroon and black "Lake Shore" versions, the maroon and black No. 900 box or "jail" car, the No. 600 derrick cars in both the green and maroon and black versions, and the No. 1050 passenger car trailers in all three of the known Lionel lettering variations. Cohen made a prototype No. 100 "B. & O." locomotive in 1977, and plans to make more copies. He has also made the No. 400 steel gondola in nickel-plated brass and the No. 600 derrick cars with nickel-plated brass bottoms with black painted booms.

All of Cohen's original tooling for the 2-7/8" gauge cars came from McCoy, but due to difficulties with the shrinkage factor in the "white metal" die-castings, Cohen had new patterns made to have the cast portions made of cast-iron. Therefore, except for some very early examples, most of the Cohen reproductions differ from the McCoy reproductions in that the cast portions are made of cast-iron rather than die-cast "white metal", and the dimensions of the cast portions of Cohen's more recent reproductions are more accurate to the Lionel originals than the McCoy reproductions. The paint colors and lettering of the Cohen reproductions also differ slightly from the Lionel originals. Most of the Cohen reproductions bear a gold rubber-stamping on the underside which reads:

REPRODUCTION BY
JAMES COHEN
69 STEMWAY ROAD
TRUMBULL, CONN. 06611

and none have been embossed by Cohen with "Lionel Mfg. Co." in the floors.

The Cohen reproductions are also faithful reproductions in most respects to the original Lionel cars, but having been made in recent years they usually appear to be much shinier and cleaner than either the now over twenty-two-year-old McCoy reproductions or the Lionel originals, although the author has seen examples of the Cohen reproductions which have been "weathered" to create an appearance very similar to original Lionel specimens.

Great care should be exercised to avoid paying the price of a Lionel original for an unmarked (and/or fradulently embossed) McCoy or Cohen reproduction. The absence of a motor and the absence of the embossing of "Lionel Mfg. Co." in the floors are the two easiest, although not always reliable, ways to tell an original from a reproduction. Although all Cohen reproductions made up to the present time have been made without motors, Cohen is in the process of making reproduction motors for

2-7/8" gauge cars. Depending upon the accuracy of such motors, either a McCoy or Cohen reproduction could be motorized to appear like a Lionel original. Cohen also plans to reproduce the following 2-7/8" gauge track and accessories: Sectional Track, Switch and Signal, Crossing, Suspension Bridge, Track Bumper, and Elevated Pillars.

Both the No. 800 and No. 900 are among the more commonly seen 2-7/8" gauge items, with the No. 900 being the scarcer of the two. **Gd VG Exc**

100* Not catalogued, believed to be manufactured in 1901, wooden gondola, 14-1/2" long, 4-1/2" wide, and 4-1/8" high, red stained finish, mortised and tenoned corners, metal tag attached to underside with two brads which reads: "MFG. BY LIONEL MFG. CO. NEW YORK", motorized, cast-iron frame 11-5/8" long and 1-7/8" high, either hollow or brass or cast-iron wheels 2" in diameter, round journals, cast knob on controller, no steps, no coupler pocket. Reportedly, the earliest example of these cars are initialed by Joshua Lionel Cowen himself. "Electric Express" in gold 5-1/4" long on both sides **NRS**

200 Wooden gondola, catalogued 1902 only, 14-1/2" long, 4-1/2" wide, and 4-1/8" high, natural brown stained finish, brass corner braces and brass handrails and steps, metal tag attached to underside with two brads which reads: "MFG. BY LIONEL MFG. CO. NEW YORK", motorized, cast-iron frame 11-5/8" long and 1-7/8" high, cast-iron wheels 2" in diameter, round journals, cast knob on controller, coupler pocket on controller, "Electric Express" in gold 5-1/4" long on both sides **NRS**

100(A) Electric Locomotive, catalogued 1903, 1904, and 1905. Catalogues do not show or describe colors and so the light green version cannot be conclusively dated, but the light green versions are believed to be the earliest. $6.00 in some 1903 Catalogues, $7.00 in all others, steel reproduction of 1,800 horse power electric locomotives used by the B.& O.R.R. for hauling trains through the tunnels of Baltimore, 10-1/2" long, 4-1/4" wide, and 6-5/8" high, light green body and roof with black painted cast-iron frame and gold painted trim on controller, motorized, hollow brass wheels 2" in diameter, rectangular journals, wire handle on controller, coupler pockets on both ends, "LIONEL MFG.CO. N.Y." stamped in floor bottom readable from underside, cast-iron frame passes through two 1/2" diameter holes in floor bottom and attaches to floor bottom without screws, reversing switch has tabs, "B. & O." in gold 2" long on left of both sides, "No. 5" in gold 1-3/8" long on right of both sides and on both ends **NRS**

100(B) Electric Locomotive, see 100 (A) for Catalogue and Catalogue price information. Description same as 100(A) but with cast-iron wheels 2" in diameter and with maroon body and black roof and frame, cast-iron frame attaches to floor bottom by means of two screws with nuts on inside on floor bottom, no 1/2" holes in floor bottom, reversing switch is circular without tabs, many differences in motor and in the manner in which wires connect from motor to reversing switch, lettering same as 100(A) **1500 2000 3000**

100(C) Electric Locomotive, uncatalogued. Description same as 100 (A), except that gold paper stickers appear on both sides with "C & St. L" to left of center door and "No. 5" to right of center door. **NRS**

100(D) Electric Locomotive, catalogued 1904-05. $25.00 for set, not catalogued individually. Description same as 100(A), but all parts and nickeled and polished, motor mechanism is constructed throughout of phosphor-bronze, catalogued only as a component of "Special Show Window Display", lettering unkown **NRS**

200(A) Electric Express, catalogued 1903 for $6.00, steel gondoloa, 12-1/4" long, 4-1/2" wide, and 4-1/8" high, light green with black painted cast-iron frame 11" long and 1-7/8" high, two ribs on each side, one-piece gold painted handrails and steps at each corner, motorized, cast-iron wheels 2" in diameter, rectangular journals, cast knob handle on controller, coupler pockets on both ends, "B. & O." in gold on both sides (Note: 1903 Catalogue shows other lettering on sides of car with "CAPACITY 80,000" on left side and "WEIGHT 35,000" on right side but as found no such lettering is present) **2000 2500 3000**

200(B) Electric Express, catalogued 1904-05 for $6.00, steel gondola, 12-1/4" long, 4-1/2" wide, and 4-1/8" high, maroon with gold edge trim and black painted cast-iron frame 11" long and 1-7/8" high, no ribs on sides, inner portions of gondola body and underside are painted a flat reddish brown that is not as glossy or as maroon as exterior portions of gondola body (the same flat paint also appears as an undercoat on the exterior portions of gondola body), one-piece gold painted handrails and steps at each corner, motorized, cast-iron wheels 2" in diameter, rectangular journals, wire handle on controller, coupler pockets on both ends, "LIONEL MFG. CO. N.Y." stamped in floor bottom readable from underside, "Lake Shore" in gold 3-1/4" in gold 3-1/4" long on both sides, "CAPACITY 80,000 LBS." in gold on left lower corners on both sides, "WEIGHT 35000 LBS." in gold on lower right corners on both sides (Note: no comma appears in "35000" but a comma does appear in "80,000") **1200 1500 2000**

300 Electric Trolley Car, catalogued 1903-05. $7.00 in 1903-04, $8.00 in 1903 other Catalogue and in 1905, Steel Open Trolley Car, 16-1/2" long, 5" wide and 8-1/8" high, maroon, pea green, and cream with yellow design trim, 4-1/2" long destination boards on top of each side which are reversible, six cream seats with red back design trim which are reversible, wood subframe 15" long and 3-3/4" wide, black painted cast-iron frame 11" long and 1-7/8" high, no steps or handrails, motorized, either hollow brass or cast-iron wheels 2" in diameter, rectangular journals, wire handle on controller, no coupler pockets, found with or without 6" stamped steel trolley pole which is attached to a wire which protrudes through roof and subroof and into metal frame (but not through wood subframe). No Lionel identification appears anywhere, "CITY HALL PARK" and "175" in yellow on both ends 3-1/2" long, "UNION DEPOT" and "CITY HALL PARK" in red and white reversible destination boards with no designs on either side (Note: some examples have same lettering in black on white reversible destination boards with a design on both sides.) **1700 2200 2800**

309 Electric Trolley Trailer, 1904-05, $3.25 in 1904, $3.75 in 1905 Catalogue. Description same as 300, but without motor and known to exist only with cast-iron wheels 2" in diameter, lettering same as 300 **1700 2200 2500**

400(A) Express Trailer Car, 1903, $2.25 and $2.50 in distributor Catalogue. Description same as 200(A) Electric Express, but without motor, lettering same as 200(A) **NRS**

400(B) Express Trail Car, 1903, $2.25 and $2.50 in distributor Catalogue. Description same as 200(B), but without motor, lettering same as 200(B) **1000 1200 1700**

400(C) Trailer, 1904-05, sold only as set for $25. Description same as 200(B), but all parts are nickeled and polished, motor mechanism is constructed throughout of phosphor-bronze, catalogued only as a component of "Special Show Window Display", lettering unknown **NRS**

500(A) Electric Derrick Car, 1903-04, $7.00 in 1903-04, $8.00 in distributor 1903 Catalogue, Steel Derrick Car, 14-1/2" long, 4-1/2" wide, and 10-7/8" high , cast-iron derrick 8-1/2" high, light green with gold trim and black painted cast-iron frame 11" long and 1-7/8" high, no handrails or steps, motorized, cast-iron wheels 2" in diameter, rectangular journals, wire handle on controller, coupler pockets on both ends, no lettering **NRS**

500(B) Electric Derrick Car, 1903-04, $7.00 in 1903-04, $8.00 in other 1903 Catalogue. Description same as 500(A), but painted maroon with gold trim, no lettering **2000 3000 3500**

---

*In the 1902 Catalogue the first item shown and described is the No. 300 "ELECTRIC TROLLEY CAR" and the second item is the NO. 200 hard wood "ELECTRIC EXPRESS". The No. 100 does not appear in the 1902 Catalogue. However, since there are two distinct variations of the hard wood gondola, the first being "uncatalogued" (so long as aa 1901 or earlier catalogue does not appear), and being finished in Red with mortised and tenoned corners, and the second variation being the now "catalogued" version (i.e., in the recently-discovered 1902 Catalogue) which is finished in Brown with brass corner plates, handrails, and steps as described on page 5 of the 1902 Catalogue, I submit that documentation will eventually surface which will indicate that (1) the first 2-7/8" gauge car manufactured by Lionel was the first variation of the hard wood gondola and (2) the first variation of the hard wood gondola was assigned the number "100". I also submit that, with the changes in the color and construction of the hard wood gondola as described in the 1902 Catalogue, the subsequent number "200" was logically assigned to that second variation. I further submit that due to the discontinuance of the hard wood gondola in 1903 in favor of the steel gondola, the then-unused catalogue number "100" was re-assigned to the then-new B. & O. No. 5 "ELECTRIC LOCOMOTIVE".

600(A) Derrick Trailer, $3.25 in 1903-04, $4.00 in distributor 1903 Catalogue. Description same as 500 (A), but without motor and with "LIONEL MFG. CO." stamped in bottom of car body readable from top, no lettering **2500 3500 4000**

600(B) Derrick, Catalogue dates and prices same as 600(A). Description same as 500(B), but without motor, no lettering **2000 3000 3500**

800 Box Car, catalogued 1904 and 05. Catalogue price $7.00, Steel Box Car (sometimes called the "Jail Car" because of the bars on the windows), 14-1/2" long, 4" wide, 7-1/8" high, maroon with black roof and black painted cast-iron frame 11" long and 1-7/8" high, gold painted bars in windows, opening doors with gold painted door knobs, one piece gold painted handrails and steps, motorized, cast-iron wheels 2" in diameter, rectangular journals, wire handle on controller, coupler pockets on both ends of car, no Lionel identification on car, inner portions of car body are painted a flat reddish brown that is not as glossy or as maroon as exterior portions of car body (the same flat paint also appears as an undercoat on the exterior portions of car body), "METROPOLITAN" in gold 2-3/8" long on left side of door on both sides of car, "EXPRESS" in gold 1-3/4" long on right side of door on both sides of car **1100 1500 2000**

900 Box Trail Car, catalogued 1904-05, sold for $3.25. Description same as 800, but without motor, lettering same as 800 **1000 1500 2000**

1000(A) Passenger Car, catalogued 1905 at $7.00, steel closed sided passenger cars, 14-3/4" long, 4-1/2" wide and 7-1/4" high (excluding trolley pole), maroon with black roof and black painted cast-iron frame 11" long, motorized, cast-iron wheels 2" in diameter, rectangular journals, wire handle on controller, coupler pockets on both ends, found with or without 6-1/2" sprung trolley pole made of brass and painted black, no Lionel identification appears anywhere, "METROPOLITAN St. R.R. Co." in gold 7-3/4" long on both sides and "416" in gold 3/4" long on both ends **2000 2500 3000**

1000(B) Passenger Car, years and price not catalogued. Description same as 1000(A), "MARYLAND ST. RY. Co." in gold 7" long on both sides and "BROADWAY" in gold 2-3/4" long on both ends **1500 2000 2500**

1050(A) Passenger Car Trailer, 1905 catalogued sold for $3.25. Description same as 1000(A), but without motor, lettering same as 1000(A) **2000 2500 3000**

1050(B) Passenger Car Trailer, years and prices not catalogued. Description same as 1000(B), but without motor, lettering same as 1000(B) **2000 2500 3000**

1050(C) Passenger Car Trailer, years and prices not catalogued. Description same as 1050(A), but in brighter red with black roof and black painted frame, "PHILADELPHIA, R.T. CO." in gold on both sides **2000 2500 3000**

Batteries, Track and Accessories

301 Batteries, 1903-05, set of 4 for $1.20, dry cell battery with wire and directions for connecting (early 1903 Catalogue shows "Everbest Dry Cell" batteries, early 1904 Catalogue states that "Eastern dry cell No. 3" would be supplied, early 1905 Catalogue states that "Climax Dry Cell" would be supplied) **NRS**

302 Plunge Battery, catalogued in 1902 only. Price of complete battery, with full charge $2.50, consisting of four glass jars, each containing a carbon cylinder and pencil-shaped zinc, and a wooden box measuring 9" x 12" x 8". The jars were charged with three pounds of "electric sand" which was added to three quarts of water to make a full charge for the four cells. The cells were connected in series — that is, the carbon of one to the zinc of the other. The jars had to be kept apart, and the wooden box was supplied to hold the four jars apart so they would not touch. **NRS**

303 Carbon Cylinders, catalogued in 1902 only. Price per cylinder $.25. **NRS**

304 Composite Zincs, catalogued in 1902 only. Price each $.07. **NRS**

305 Electric Sand, catalogued in 1902 only. Price of 3-pound can $.50. **NRS**

306 Glass Jars, catalogued in 1902 only. Price per jar $.125. **NRS**

310 The Track, 1902 and earlier, Steel tin-plated rails and wooden ties, rails are straight unbent strips of tin-plated steel 3/8" high, 1/16" thick and 13-3/8" long, ties are red stained pieces of wood 4" wide, 1" thick and 1/2" high and grooved to admit the insertion of the rails, the grooves are 2-7/8" apart, some ties have plates of brass which fit into the grooves and are bent outward to cover the outside portions of the ties and are held in place by a single brass brad, these brass plates allow the electrical contact to be made by the ends of the adjoining rails, rails were only supplied in equal length straight sections and had to be bent (with the inside rails cut shorter) to make curved sections. Two rails and fine ties comprised one complete section of track. Two of the fine ties have brass plates. **NRS**

310 The Track, 1903-05, 24 rails and 60 ties for $1.50, steel tin-plated rails and wooden ties, rails are straight strips of tin-plated steel 3/8" high, 1/16" thick and about 12" long with one end bent into an L-shape offset and the other end bent into a hook or a hoop shape to accept insertion of the L-shaped end of an adjoining section, ties are unstained and unpainted pieces of wood 4" wide, 1/2" thick and 1/2" high and grooved to admit the insertion of the rails, the grooves are 2-7/8" apart, the offsets on the ends of the rails had to be turned outward and the five ties per two sections of rails were used, the sections were joined by sliding the L-shaped end of one into the hook shaped end of the other, rails were supplied in two different lengths with the shorter length used on the inside of a curve, a complete circle was formed by using 8 sections of track, the 1905 Catalogue states that "The Track" was "Improved 1905", however, the track illustrated and described in the 1905 Catalogue is identical to that illustrated and described in the 1903 and 1904 Catalogues. Two rails and five ties comprised one complete section of track. **NRS**

320 Switch and Signal, 1902-05, $1.50, turnout 17-1/2" long, 8" high, and 4-1/2" wide, lever which shifts the track changes the signal at the same time, signal discs are red and white, signal is cast-iron **NRS**

330 Crossing, 1902-05, $.50, 90 degree crossover, cross-rails mounted on a base 6" square **NRS**

340 Suspension Bridge, 1902, $1.50, suspension-type bridge, 24" long, 10" high, 6" wide, braces are cast-iron with wooden end and center ties, the end top members are straight and allow clearance of only cars under 10" in overall height. **NRS**

340 Suspension Bridge, 1903-05, $1.50, suspension-type bridge, 24" long, 14" high, 6" wide, braces are cast-iron with wooden end and center ties the end top members are arched to allow high clearance for cars to pass through bridge **NRS**

350 Bumper, 1902, only $.50, terminal track bumper (without spring), 4" long, 4" high, and 3" wide, supplied with one tie to be inserted between the joints of the last two sections of the track instead of a tie with a brass plate to cut off the current before the car strikes the bumper to lessen the impact. **NRS**

350 Bumper, 1903-05, $.50, terminal track bumper, spring loaded, 4" long, 4" high, and 3" wide, supplied with one tie which was used to cut off track current to lessen the impact from a car striking the bumper **20 35 50**

370 Jars and Plates, 1902-03, $.50 in 1920, $.60 in 1903, outfit consisting of two glass jars 2" by 1-1/4" by 3-1/2" and lead plates 1" wide and 1/16" thick supplied for the purpose of utilizing direct electric current to operate powered items, jars were to be filled with water and sulfuric acid and connected in series to a 110-volt current and a 32 candle-power lamp bulb **NRS**

380 Elevated Pillars, 1904-05, 12 pillars for $2.00, cast-iron posts 8-1/2" high with 6" wide bases supplied with screws and washers for attaching wooden ties to posts for elevation of trackwork, including switches, bridges, crossings, and bumpers **30 50 75**

700 Special Show Window Display, 1903-05, $25.00, outfit consisting of No. 100 Electric Locomotive and No. 400 Trailer, both items nickeled and polished, mechanism is constructed of phosphor-bronze, supplied with No. 340 Suspension Bridge and 24 feet of track **NRS**

912
911
913
912
0077
0075
0047
0074
004TW
0046
004E
0045
0044
0027
003T
0025
003E
0017
0024
0016
002TW
0015
002E
001TW
0014
0015
0017
001E
092 Tower

00 Gauge

Chapter IX
00 GAUGE EQUIPMENT

by Robert S. Friedman, D.D.S.

The year was 1938, and Lionel needed a new steam locomotive to match the success of the 0 Gauge 700E Scale Hudson it had brought out the previous year. The new engine was to be yet another Hudson, but a smaller size duplicate of the 700E Scale Hudson. The 00 Hudson was built to a scale of 5/32nds to the foot as opposed to the 8/32nds of the 0 Gauge Hudson.

To quote the 1938 Lionel catalog: "Visualize the great 0 Gauge scale model Lionel Hudson reduced to 5/8ths its size and you will have the new Lionel 00 Gauge locomotive - for the 00 model has been made from exactly the same blueprints, reduced to scale 15-1/4" in length . . . . Nothing has been overlooked - nothing left undone!"

The engine and tender, which were manufactured from 1938 to 1942, were produced in four different versions. There were two super detailed versions, one for three-rail track and one for two-rail track, as well as a less detailed or modified version of each. The two-rail versions were designed to run on Lionel's solid T-rail two-rail track, which had a 48" diameter curve. This track looked far more realistic than the tubular three rail track with its 27 inch diameter curve.

The four cars that accompanied the new 00 Hudson were all die-cast metal. They were a box car, a hopper, a tank car and a caboose. The 00 Hudson was a Lionel original, but the cars unfortunately were not. The four Lionel cars were copies of the same cars made by the Scalecraft Company of Chicago. Lionel had copied the Scalecraft cars which came as kits and had slightly changed the ladders and trucks and made small modifications to the castings. Scalecraft had a patent on the truck suspension; consequently, Lionel had to pay Scalecraft a royalty because of this. When the Lionel and Scalecraft cars are placed next to one another, it is difficult to see the differences. The accompanying photographs will illustrate the difficulties.

Other companies offered 00 equipment at the time, but none had as direct a relationship with Lionel as did Scalecraft. Some of these other companies were Nason, Famoco, Star Lines, Amity, Kemtron and many more.

My knowledge of Lionel 00 has come from searching out the various publications which have run articles about Lionel 00, questioning people at train meets and stores who had information about 00 and by carefully examining my own collection over and over again. The information presented by me in this chapter is as accurate and documented as I could make it. Surely someone of you reading this chapter will have some new or different information than that which you see here. Please be kind enough to send it along so that we may all share it in future editions.

Knowingly or unknowingly, many fine people have greatly contributed to my knowledge of 00. To name a few, if I may: William J. Krone and George J. Adamson for their fine articles in the TCA Quarterlies; Don Shaw of "The Train Station"; Tom McComas and James Tuohy for the 00 chapter in Vol. III of their series; Carl Shaw of Madison Hardware; and two fine collectors and runners of 00; Tony Cavanna and George E. Jones. To Bruce Greenberg, a special thanks for allowing me the pleasure of updating this chapter for his book.

Gd Exc Rst

Presentation set

001 Presentation Set, 1938, consists of loco numbered 5342 (we are not certain as to which one), 0014 yellow Lionel Lines box car, 0015 silver Sunoco tank car, 0016 gray Southern Pacific hopper and 0017 Pennsylvania caboose. This set was contained within a dark brown leather-covered wooden case 20-1/2" long, 15-1/4" wide and 2" thick. The case lid is hinged to the bottom of the case at rear. Inside the case are die-cut hard cardboard dividers 1/4" thick suspended at points to allow rolling stock to be held in place. The lid and sides have compartments to hold track - six straight on each side and twelve curved across lid. The case interior is lined with red velvet material; there is gold lettering inside the lid. The case also has a leather carrying handle. A matching transformer case with a leather carrying strap, 3-3/4" wide, 4-3/4" deep and 5-1/2" high, holds a 1040 transformer. This set was probably made by Lionel for special presentations and awards ceremonies as a public relations device. As such, there are probably very few sets of this nature still intact today. Exter Collection **NRS**

Engines and Tenders

00 Engines and tenders came in both super detailed and modified versions. The super detailed locomotive has; boiler turret caps, booster steam pipes, a feedwater pump, flag stanchions on the pilot, a front coupler, full valve gear, headlight number boards, complete piping, a power reverse cylinder and a turbo generator. The modified locomotive has none of the above.

The super detailed coal tender has; four corner rails, one handrail, four stanchions and an air brake cylinder. The modified coal tender has none of the above. **NRS**

001 Steam locomotive, 1938-1942, 4-6-4, Hudson prototype, black boiler and frame, 9" long, rubber-stamped "5342" in silver below cab window. Came with 12-wheel New York Central tender, 6-1/2" long. Locomotive and tender are super-detailed, for use on three rail track, catalogued as 001.

(A) Locomotive with miniature drawbar pin and chain. Came with 001W whistle tender. Neither locomotive nor tender are stamped 001, 1938 only. **120 225 110**

(B) Same as (A), but with 001T tender without whistle, 1938 only. **120 225 110**

(C) Miniature drawbar pin and chain replaced by spring loaded pin without chain, 001 stamped on inside of cab roof as well as 001W stamped on bottom of tender with whistle, 1939-1942. **120 225 110**

(D) Same as (C), but with 001T stamped on bottom of tender without whistle, 1939-1942. **120 225 110**

002 Steam locomotive, 1939-1942, 4-6-4, Hudson prototype, black boiler and frame, 9" long, rubber-stamped "5342" in silver below cab window and "002" on inside of cab roof. Came with 12-wheel New York Central tender stamped "002W" or "002T" on bottom, 6-1/2" long. Locomotive and tender are modified, for use on three rail track.

(A) Locomotive with 002W tender with whistle. **100 200 95**

(B) Locomotive with 002T tender without whistle. **100 200 95**

Two-Rail Engines and Tenders

Lionel 00 engines of the 001 and 002 series were designed to run on conventional tubular three rail track, while the 003 and 004 engines were designed to run on T-rail two rail track. In order for this to be accomplished, the following changes in design of the running gear had to be made: the locomotive center double pickup was removed; the trucks were insulated, and the left side drivers were made of bakelite with metal rims. The tender single center pickup was removed, the right side wheels of the tender trucks were insulated, and the trucks themselves were insulated from the tender body. The electrical connections between the locomotive and the tender were accomplished by a plug from the tender to a jack on the brush plate and then to the E-unit. The other connection was by way of the tender drawbar and the spring-loaded pin of the locomotive. The two-rail cars, as well as the kit cars, came with all the wheels insulated and could be run on either two or three rail track.

003 Steam locomotive, 1939-1942, 4-6-4, Hudson prototype, black boiler and frame, 9" long, rubber-stamped "5342" in silver below cab window and "003" on inside of cab roof. Came with 12-wheel New York Central tender stamped "003W" or "003T" on bottom, 6-1/2" long. Locomotive and tender are super-detailed, for use on two-rail track.

(A) Locomotive with 003W tender with whistle **130 275 100**

(B) Locomotive with 003T tender without whistle **120 250 95**

004 Steam locomotive, 1939-1942, 4-6-4, Hudson prototype, black boiler and frame, 9" long, rubber-stamped "5342" in silver below cab window and "004" on inside of cab roof. Came with 12-wheel New York Central tender stamped "004W" or "004T" on bottom, 6-1/2" long. Locomotive and tender are modified, for use on two-rail track.

(A) Locomotive with 004W tender with whistle **120 245 110**

(B) Locomotive with 004T tender without whistle **110 225 100**

0081K Locomotive and tender kits. Catalogued 1938. Existence not verified **NRS**

0081KW Locomotive and whistle tender kits. Catalogued 1938. Existence not verified **NRS**

NOTE: The 00 tenders had one other feature of interest, which was that the tone chamber was an integral part of the body casting and could not be replaced separately. If the field or casting were defective, the entire tender had to be returned for repair.

00 BOX CARS

Top: Scalecraft's B & LE box car.
Bottom: Lionel's 0014(B) Pennsylvania box car. Lionel's steps at the corners are slightly smaller than Scalecraft's. Lionel's wheels are larger. Note that the Lionel catwalk protrudes slightly beyond the roof, while the Scalecraft's catwalk ends are flush with the car ends.

Super detailed box cars have an air brake cylinder under the frame. Modified box cars do not have the air brake cylinder.

0014 Box car, 1938-1942, 6-7/8", super detailed, three rail

(A) Yellow body, maroon catwalk and door guides, black ladders, black decal lettering "LIONEL LINES 0014", and a red and blue Lionel "L" emblem, 1938 only **25 50 20**

(B) Tuscan body and catwalk, may have black ladders, white decal lettering "PENNSYLVANIA 0014", 1939-1942 **25 50 20**

0024 Box car, 1939-1942, 6-7/8", tuscan body and catwalk, may have black ladders, white decal lettering "PENNSYLVANIA 0024", modified, three rail. **25 50 20**

0044 Box car, 1939-1942, 6-7/8", tuscan body and catwalk, may have black ladders, white decal lettering "PENNSYLVANIA 0044", super detailed, insulated wheels for two-rail operation. **25 50 20**

0044K Box car, 1939-1942, 6-7/8", same as 0044 but in unpainted kit, may have been factory painted with gray primer. **50 100 40**

0074 Box car, 1939-1942, 6-7/8", tuscan body and catwalk, may have black ladders, white decal lettering "PENNSYLVANIA 0074", modified, insulated wheels for two-rail operation **25 50 20**

00 HOPPER CARS

Super detailed hopper cars have an air brake cylinder on top of the frame. Modified hopper cars were not manufactured.

Lionel's 0046(A) car (bottom) shows several differences from its Scalecraft counterpart (top). Note the air brake cylinder at left on frame. Lionel's bay doors are much closer to the car center. Also note the double row rivet patterns on the Lionel car.

0016 Hopper car, 1938-1942, 5-1/2", super detailed, three rail

(A) Gray hopper, black decal lettering "SP 0016" and a round "SOUTHERN PACIFIC LINES" emblem, 1938 only, uncatalogued **25 55 20**

(B) Gray hopper, black decal lettering, "LIONEL LINES 124947", and a red and blue Lionel "L" emblem, catalogued 1938 **Not Manufactured**

(C) Black hopper, white decal lettering "SP 0016" and a round "SOUTHERN PACIFIC LINES" emblem, 1939-1942 **35 65 30**

(D) Black hopper, white decal lettering, "READING" plus six digits, catalogued 1941, but existence not verified **NRS**

0046 Hopper car, 1939-1942, 5-1/2", super-detailed, insulated wheels for two rail operation

(A) Black hopper, white decal lettering, "SP 0046" and a round "SOUTHERN PACIFIC LINES" emblem **25 50 20**

(B) Same as 0016(D), but for two-rail operation **25 50 20**

0046K Hopper car, 1939-1942, 5-1/2"

(A) Same as 0046(A), but in unpainted kit, may have been factory painted with gray primer **40 75 35**

(B) Same as 0046(B), but in unpainted kit, may have been factory painted with gray primer **NRS**

00 TANK CARS

Super detailed tank cars have an air brake cylinder under the frame. Modified tank cars do not have the air brake cylinder.

The Scalecraft tank car shown above differs from the Lionel car in its dome, absence of steps, and brake cylinder design.

The Lionel tank car shown above differs from the Scalecraft version in dome and brake cylinder detail as well as including steps.

0015 Tank car, 1938-1942, 5-3/4", super detailed, three-rail operation
(A) Silver tank, black frame with no number stamp on bottom, black decal lettering "THE SUN OIL CO.", "S.O.C.X. 0015", plus a small Sunoco herald at the opposite end, 1938 only, uncatalogued **25 50 20**
(B) Silver tank, black frame, black decal lettering "LIONEL LINES 601614" and Sunoco style herald, catalogued 1938 **Not Manufactured**
(C) Black tank, black frame with 0015 silver stamped on bottom, white decal lettering "SHELL", "S.E.P.X. 8126", 1939-40, 1942 **25 50 20**
(D) Silver tank, black frame with 0015 silver stamped on bottom, black decal lettering "S.U.N.X. 2599" and large Sunoco herald, 1941-42 **25 50 20**
(E) Black tank, black frame, white decal lettering "S.U.N.X. 0015" and Sunoco herald, catalogued 1941, but existence not verified **NRS**

0025 Tank car, 1939-1942, 5-3/4", modified, three-rail operation
(A) Black tank, black frame, silver stamped "0025" on bottom, white decal lettering "SHELL, S.E.P.X. 8126", three-rail, 1939-40, 1942 **25 50 20**
(B) Silver tank, black frame with 0025 silver stamped on bottom, black decal lettering "S.U.N.X. 2599" and large Sunoco Herald, 1941-42 **25 50 20**

0045 Tank car, 1939-1942, 5-3/4", super detailed, insulated wheels for two-rail operation
(A) Black tank, black frame with 0045 silver stamped on bottom, white decal lettering "SHELL, S.E.P.X. 8126", 1939-40, 1942 **25 50 20**
(B) Silver tank, black frame with 0045 silver stamped on bottom, black decal lettering "S.U.N.X. 2599" and large Sunoco herald, 1941-42 **25 50 20**
(C) Same as 0015(E), but for two-rail operation **25 50 20**

0045K Tank car, 1939-1942, 5-3/4"
(A) Same as 0045(A), but in unpainted kit, may have been factory painted with gray primer, no number on frame **50 100 40**
(B) Same as 0045(C), but in unpainted kit, may have been factory painted with gray primer, no number on frame, catalogued 1941, but existence not verified **NRS**

0075 Tank car, 1939-1942, 5-3/4", modified, insulated wheels for two-rail operation
(A) Black tank, black frame with 0075 silver stamped on bottom, white decal lettering "SHELL, S.E.P.X. 8126", 1939-40, 1942 **25 50 20**
(B) Silver tank, black frame with 0075 silver stamped on bottom, black decal lettering "S.U.N.X. 2599" and large Sunoco herald, 1941-42 **25 50 20**
(C) Gray tank, color may have been primer of kit cars, black frame with 0075 silver stamped on bottom, white decal lettering "SHELL S.E.P.X. 8126", 1942 only, uncatalogued **25 50 20**

00 CABOOSES

The super detailed caboose has a stove pipe with hood on the roof and a drain pipe under the frame. The modified caboose has none of these details.

0017 Caboose, 1938-1942, 4-5/8", super detailed, three-rail operation
(A) Red body, maroon catwalk, white decal lettering "PENNSYLVANIA 0017", manufactured 1938 only, but catalogued as 0047 in 1940. The red color of the 1938 caboose is lighter than that of all the following years **25 50 20**
(B) Red body and catwalk, white decal lettering "N.Y.C. 0017", 1939-1942 **25 50 20**
(C) Red body and catwalk, black decal lettering "LIONEL LINES 477626", catalogued 1938 **Not Manufactured**

Lionel's 0017(A) caboose differs in many respects from its Scalecraft counterpart (top). The brakewheels differ in design and placement. Lionel's version has a battery box as well as a drain pipe. The rivet detail on the sides didn't help Lionel's lettering!

0027 Caboose, 1939-1942, 4-5/8", modified, three-rail operation, red body and catwalk, white decal lettering "N.Y.C. 0027" **25 50 20**

0047 Caboose, 1939-1942, 4-5/8", super detailed, insulated wheels for two-rail operation
(A) Red body, maroon catwalk, white decal lettering "PENNSYLVANIA 0047", catalogued 1940, but existence not verified. **NRS**
(B) Red body and catwalk, white decal lettering "N.Y.C. 0047" **25 50 20**

0047K Caboose, 1939-1942, 4-5/8"
(A) Same as 0047 (A), but in unpainted kit, may have been factory painted with gray primer, catalogued 1940, but existence not verified **NRS**
(B) Same as 0047(B), but in unpainted kit, may have been factory painted with gray primer **50 100 40**

0077 Caboose, 1939-1942, 4-5/8", modified, insulated wheels for two-rail operation, red body and catwalk, white decal lettering "N.Y.C. 0074" **25 50 20**

00 TRACK, SWITCHES AND CROSSOVER

		Gd	Exc
	Two-Rail Track: 48" circle		
0031	Curved Track, 1939-42	2	3
0032	Straight Track, 1939-42	2	3
0034	Connection Curved Track, 1939-42	2	3
0061	Curved Track, 1938	1	2
0062	Straight Track, 1938	1	2
0063	1/2 Curved Track, 1938-42	2	3
0064	Connection Curved Track, 1938	2	3
0065	1/2 Straight Track, 1938-42	2	3
0066	5/6 Straight Track, 1938-42	1	2
	Three-Rail Track: 27" circle		
0051	Curved Track, 1939-42	1	2
0053	Straight Track, 1939-42	2	2
0054	Connection Curved Track, 1939-42	2	3
0070	90 degree Crossover, 1938-42	3	5
0072	Remote Control Switches, 1938-42	30	60

Two-Rail Track - 48" circle

Chapter X

CROSSOVERS, SWITCHES, UNCOUPLING UNITS, POWER SUPPLIES, MOTORS, AND TRACK

CROSSOVERS, SWITCHES AND UNCOUPLING UNITS

Note: For 00 Gauge equipment, see Châpter IX. **Gd Exc Rst**

011 Distant Control, Non-Derailing Switches (pair) 0 Gauge
(A) Green base, 1933 **20 40 20**
(B) Black base, 1934-37 **20 40 20**

012 Remote Control Switches, 1927-33 (pair) 0 Gauge **12 30 10**

013 0 Gauge Distant Control Switch and Panel Board Set - 1 pair 012 switches, one 439 Illuminated panel board **55 125 50**

20 90 degree Crossover Standard Gauge
(A) Open base version with small center square with small center square without enameled center, 1909-13 **2 5 3**

(B) Open base version with small center square with small center square with enameled center, 1914-26 **2 5 3**

(C) Closed base version with green enamel, 1927-32 **2 5 3**

(D) Closed base version with black enamel, 1927-32 **2 5 3**

20X 45 degree Crossover Standard Gauge, 16-1/2 x 9", green base, 1928-32 **3 7 2**

020 90 degree Crossover 0 Gauge
(A) Tin Base, 1915-26 **2 5 –**
(B) Green enamel base, 1927-33 **2 5 –**
(C) Black enamel base, 1934-42 **2 5 –**

020X 45 degree Crossover 0 Gauge, 11-1/2 x 6"
(A) Tin base, 1917-26 **3 7 –**
(B) Green base, 1927-33 **3 7 –**
(C) Black base, 1934-42 **3 7 –**

21 90 degree Three-Rail Crossover 8", Standard Gauge, 1906 **7 15 –**

21 Lighted Lantern Switches Standard Gauge, right and left hand, 1915-25 **10 20 10**

021 Lighted Lantern Switches 0 Gauge
(A) Right and left hand, green base, 1915-22 **8 20 8**
(B) Improved with fiber strip at cross points, 1923-33 **8 20 8**
(C) Black base, 1934-37 **8 20 8**

22 Manual Three-Rail Switch and Signal right and left hand, Standard Gauge, 1906-25, with signal discs **10 25 15**

022 Manual Switches
(A) 0 Gauge right and left hand, 1915-22 **15 30 15**
(B) Improved with fiber strip at cross points, 1923-37 **15 30 15**

022 Remote Switches with controllers and plugs **25 50 20**

042 Manual Switches (pair) 0 Gauge, 1938-42 **15 30 15**

210 Illuminated Lantern Switch Standard Gauge
(A) Green base, 1926 (pair) **10 25 12**
(B) Black base, 1934-42 (pair) **10 25 12**

220 Lantern Switch Same as 210, not lighted, for Standard Gauge, 1926 (pair) **10 25 12**

222 Electric Distant Control Illuminated Switches Standard Gauge, 1926-32 (pair) **20 40 20**
(A) Non-Derailment feature, 1931 only **20 40 20**

223 Distant Control Switch Same as 222, but with non-derailing switches (pair)
(A) Green base with fiber insert, 1932-33 **20 45 20**
(B) Black base, 1934-42 (pair) **20 45 20**

225 Distant Control Switch and Panel Board Set Includes one pair 222 distant control switches (right and left) and one 439 illuminated panel board, Standard Gauge, 1929-32 **65 135 60**

711 0-72 Switches 1935-42, remote control with two die-cast controllers for tubular track with a diameter of 72", non-derailing feature. Note that replacement switch lanterns are available (price quoted includes switch lanterns and controllers) **75 150 75**

720 0-72 Crossing 1935-42, 90 degree with black base for tubular track **7 15 7**

721 0-72 Switches 1935-42, manual for tubular, 72" diameter track **45 100 45**

730 0-72 Crossing 1935-42, 90 degree with black base for solid T-rail track **9 20 9**

731 0-72 Switches 1935-42, remote control for solid T-rail, 72" diameter track **85 175 75**

1021 0-27 Crossover, Winner, 90 degree, 0-27, 1934-42 **1 2 1**

1024 0-27 Manual Switches 1937-42, hand-operated switches, 9-1/8" long x 5-1/8" wide, not illuminated, (pair) **2 5 4**

1121 0-27 Remote Control Switches 1937-42, remote control for 0-27 track, with illuminated controller, switches (pair). Prewar control boxes were metal and had integral red painted levers. Postwar boxes were bakelite and the levers were attached to the base instead of the box cover. The prewar mechanism box on the switches was square metal with celluloid light indicator inserts. Its postwar equivalent had a rounded plastic box with rubber light indicator inserts. LaVoie comments **10 20 10**

1550 0-27 Windup Switch 1933-37, pair of manually-operated switches; two rails spaced the same as outside rails of 0-27 track (pair) **2 5 4**

1555 0-27 Windup Crossover 1933-37, 90 degree, for two-rail windup track, two rails spaced the same as outside rails of 0-27 track **1 2 1**

MOTORS, TRANSFORMERS AND RHEOSTATS

Motors

Gd Exc Rst

A Lionel Miniature Motor 2-7/8 x 2-7/8 x 2-1/4", 1904 **50 100 50**
B New Departure Motor 3-1/4 x 3 x 2", 1906-16 **50 100 50**
C New Departure Motor wound to run on single or double cell, 1906-16 **50 100 50**
D New Departure Motor reversing device, cut-off switch, 1906-14 **50 100 50**
E New Departure Motor two-speeds, 1906-14 **50 100 50**
F New Departure Motor two-speeds, reversible, 1906-14 **50 100 50**
G Battery Fan Motor 1909-14 **50 100 –**
K Power Motor for sewing machines, 1904-06 **50 100 –**
L Power Motor for sewing machines, 1905 **50 100 –**
M Battery Motor peerless, one-speed, one direction, 1915-20 **30 75 –**
R Battery Motor peerless, operates backward and forward, 1915-20 **30 75 30**
Y Battery Motor peerless, three-speeds, operates backward and forward, 1915-20 **30 75 30**
1 Bild-A-Motor Three-speed reversible motor, 5-1/2 x 3 x 3", red base and trim on main pulley wheel, nickel plated motor sides, converts to O motor, 1928-31 **60 125 50**
2 Bild-A-Motor Three-speed reversible motor, 7 x 3-5/8 x 4", converts to Standard motor, 1928-31 **60 125 50**

Transformers

Transformers are usually bought to operate trains and related items. Hence, if a transformer is not operating it has little if any value. (If a transformer is repairable, after it is repaired it will yield the values indicated). Several of the larger models, V and Z, have some minimal value - even if completely burned out - for knobs and nuts. In the listing that follows, we report only Good and Excellent conditions and require that the transformer be in operating condition to yield the price indicated. We have only listed transformers for 110-120 volts, 50-60 cycle current, since the others have little if any practical use.

A Click-type Rheostat
(A) Early, 40 watts, 1921-31 **1 2 –**
(B) Late, 60 watts, 1931-37 **1 3 –**

B Click-type Rheostat
(A) First, 50 watts, 1916-17 **1 2 –**
(B) Early, 75 watts, 1917-21 **1 3 –**
(C) Late, 50 watts, 1921-31 **1 2 –**
(D) Latest, 75 watts, 1931-38 **1 3 –**

K Click-type Rheostat
(A) Early, 150 watts, 1913-17 **2 5 –**
(B) Middle, 200 watts, 1917-21 **4 8 –**
(C) Late, 150 watts, 1921-38 **2 5 –**

L Click-type Rheostat
(A) Early, no rheostat, 75 watts, 1913-16 **1 2 –**
(B) Late, click-type rheostat, 50 watts, 1933-38 **1 2 –**

N Click-type Rheostat, 50 watts, 1941-42 **1 2 –**

Q Click-type Rheostat
(A) Early, no rheostat, 50 watts, 1914-15 **1 2 –**
(B) Late, dial-type rheostat, 75watts, 1938-42 **4 8 –**

R Dial-type Rheostat, 100 watts, 1938-42 **5 9 –**

S Click-type Rheostat
(A) 50 watts, 1914-17 **1 2 –**
(B) Later production, dial-type rheostat, 80 watts, 1938-42, whistle and reversing controls, also made postwar, Diamond Collection **4 8 –**

T Click-type Rheostat
(A) Early, 75 watts, 1914-17 **1 3 –**

(B) Middle, 150 watts, 1917-21 2 5 —
(C) Late, 110 watts, 1921-22 2 4 —
(D) Latest, 100 watts, 1922-28 2 5 —
U Click-type Rheostat "ALADDIN", 50 watts, 1932-33 1 2 —
V Dial-type Rheostat, 150 watts, 1938-42* 15 30 —
W (A) Early, click-type Rheostat, "ALADDIN", 75 watts, 1932-33 1 3 —
(B) Late, click-type Rheostat, 75 watts, 1938-42 1 3 —
Z Dial-type Rheostat, 250 watts, 1938-42* 20 50 —
106 Click-type Rheostat, 1911-14 3 9 —
1017 Transformer in lithographed tin station, 1932-33 15 40 —
1027 Transformer in lithographed tin station, 1933-34 15 40 —
1029 Lever-type Rheostat, 25 watts, 1935-39 1 2 —

1030 Lever-type Rheostat, built in whistle control, 40 watts, 1935-38 2 3 —
1037 Lever-type Rheostat, 40 watts, 1940-42* 1 2 —
1039 Lever-type Rheostat, 35 watts, 1937-40 1 2 —
1040 Lever-type Rheostat, built in whistle control, 60 watts, 1937-39 2 6 —
1041 Lever-type Rheostat, built in whistle control, 60 watts, 1939-42* 2 6 —

Rheostats

81 Controlling Rheostat 1927-33:
Lionel's "Multi-Volt transformers" did not produce a continuous variable voltage output. Rather, when the voltage was increased (or decreased), a momentary current interruption occurred. This was not a problem until 1926, since Lionel's locomotives rolled freely and a short current interruption was barely noticeable if the engine was highballing (as was usually the case). However, in 1926 Lionel introduced the pendulum reverse unit to compete with Ives' automatic reversing unit. The Lionel design was such that a momentary interruption caused the locomotive to abruptly change direction with humorous or disastrous consequences. Consequently, Lionel needed a device to vary the transformer voltage without interrupting the current flow.
Lionel already had a potential candidate for the job, the No. 88 Battery Rheostat. With some structural changes (and possibly some change in the wire resistance), Lionel created a continuous variable voltage output by linking the rebuilt 88 (now an 81) with its transformers. The 81 consists of resistance wire wound around a ceramic core. One end of the resistance wire is connected to the unit frame. (This arrangement has implications for current draw and current waste. Transformer output was dissipated in heat!) The balance of the circuit was completed through a spring steel slide which ran along the top side of the coil. The spring steel slide is connected by an on/off switch to two bars which ground into the frame. The unit has a black stamped steel frame with two terminal posts. A green painted stamped steel cover is tabbed and screwed to the black steel frame. An embossed brass plate is affixed to the top of the green steel cover. Weisblum Collection 1 3 5
88 Battery Rheostat, 1915-27 1 3 —
95 Controlling Rheostat, 1934-42, this unit is the same as the 81 controlling rheostat above, but it substitutes a red push button for the fiber on/off toggle of the 81. This change probably relates to the introduction of the modern three-position E-units in Lionel trains about this time (1933). A momentary current interruption would be very useful for sequencing the reversing unit. Weisblum Collection 1 3 5
107 Direct Current Reducer, four porcelain tubes mounted on a steel base 8" x 10" and 3/4" thick. The tubes were protected and ventilated by a perforated, asbestos-lined steel cover. A sliding lever regulates the voltage. Four porcelain supports with screws were supplied so that the reducer could be fastened to a wall or table. For 110 volts. Weisblum Collection NRS
108 Battery Rheostat, 1912 only NRS

TRACK, TRACK BEDS, LOCKONS, CONTACTORS AND TRIPS

Straight Standard track comes in three types: Type 1 - three narrow width ties, about 1906-20; Type 2 - three wide ties, about 1920-30 and Type 3 - four ties, 1930-40.

Curved track comes in three types: Type 1 - four narrow ties, 1906-24; Type 2 - four wide ties, 1925 - 30 and Type 3 - five ties, 1930-42. ("Leading 0s" are shown but not used in indexing.)

For 00 Gauge track sections, see Chapter IX.

C Three-rail, Curved Track, Standard, 1906-42 .50 1 —
1/2 C Three-rail, Curved Track, Half-Section Standard Gauge, 1906-42 .50 1 —
CC Curved with battery connections, Standard Gauge, 1915-22 .75 1.50 —
MS Mechanical Straight Track 9" long, 1933-38 .30 .50 —
MWC Mechanical Curved Track 27" diameter, 1933-38 .30 .50 —
OC 0 Gauge Curved 1915-42 .25 .50 —
1/2 OC 0 Gauge Half-Section, Curved 1934-42 .25 .50 —
OCC Curved Track with battery connection, 0 Gauge, 1915-22 .25 .50 —
OCS Insulated Curved Track 0 Gauge, 10" long, 1934-42 .25 .50 —
OSS Insulated Straight Track, 0 Gauge, 1934-42 .25 .50 —
OTC Lockon 0 Gauge, 1923-36 .25 .50 —
RCS Remote Control Track Set 0 Gauge, 1938-42 1.50 3 —
S Three-rail, Straight Standard Gauge, 1906-42 .50 1 —
1/2 S Three-rail, Straight Half-piece Standard Gauge, 1906-42 .50 1 —
SC Straight with battery connections, Standard Gauge, 1915-22 .50 1 —
SCS Insulated Curved Standard Gauge, 1934-42 .50 1 —
SS Special Track for train operated accessories, 1923-42 .50 1 —
STC Lockon Standard Gauge, 1923-36 .25 .50 —
UTC Lockon for use with 0 or Standard Gauge, 1937-42 .25 .50 —
30 Silent Track Bed (curved) Standard Gauge, 1931-37 2 5 —
030 Silent Track Bed (curved) 0 Gauge, 1931-39 2 5 —
31 Silent Track Bed (straight) Standard Gauge, 1931-37 2 5 —
32 Silent Track Bed for 90 degree crossing, 1931-37 2 5 —
33 Silent Track Bed for 45 degree crossing, Standard Gauge, 1931-37 2 5 —
033 Silent Track Bed for 45 degree crossing, 0 Gauge, 1931-39 2 5 —
34 Silent Track for switches, Standard Gauge, 1931-37 2 5 —
034 Silent Track Bed for switches, 0 Gauge, 1931-39 2 5 —
41 Accessory Contactor 1936-42 1 2 —
60 Automatic Trip fits on side of track to reverse trains, 1906-12 2 5 —
62 Automatic Reversing Trip 1914 2 5 —
760 Tubular Curved Track. Sixteen sections of 0-72" in diameter, (price for set of 16 sections) Note that a completely compatible version of this track is being made and sold by A. Kriswalus of Endicott, New York (and others). Kriswalus' track has a slightly different tie and is currently priced at about $35 for sixteen pieces 25 35 25
761 0-72 Curved 1934-42, one piece of 0-72 tubular curved track .50 1.50 .50
762 0-72 Straight 1934-42, one piece of 14-3/8" 0-72 tubular curved track .50 1.50 1
762 0-72 Insulated Straight 1934-42, same as 762 but with one insulated outside rail to operate various accessories on as the train passes over it. Came with lockon. 2 3 2
771 0-72 Curved 1935-42, one section of 0-72 solid T-rail curved track with screws, wrench, nuts and fishplates for assembly; 16 sections form a circle 72" in diameter 2 4 2
772 0-72 Straight 1935-42, one section of 0-72 solid T-rail straight with screws, wrench, nuts and fishplates for assembly; matches 771 2 4 2
773 0-72 Fishplate Outfit 1936-42, 100 screws, 100 nuts, 50 fishplates, and wrench 25 30 —
773 Solid, T-rail, Fishplate Outfit, 100 bolts, 100 nuts, 50 fishplates and wrench, 1936-42 25 30 —
1013 0-27 Curved Track 1932-42, one section of 0-27 tubular track, forms circle with diameter of approximately 27". First called "Winner", then "Lionel-Ives", and "Lionel, Jr." and finally 0-27 .10 .25 —
1018 0-27 Straight Track 1932-42, 9" long, one section of 0-27 tubular straight track, mates with 1013 (see 1013 for background) .10 .25 —
1019 Remote Control Track 1938-42, mates with 0-27 track, five-rail straight section for uncoupling and unloading rolling stock, with two button controller. (Note that insulation from the four conductor wire is often badly decayed. Replacement for conductor wire is available.) 1 2 1

*Continued into postwar production.

PREWAR LIONEL PAPER

Listed by year. Within individual years, listed by variations. Many different reproductions have been made of the early catalogues. We believe that the following listing will grow substantially over the next few years.

Gd Exc

1902

Catalogue: 16 pages plus covers in 3-1/2" x 6-1/4" vertical format. Cover is light green paper printed with red ink. Text is black ink on white paper. Front cover reads "Miniature Electric Cars with full accessories for Window Display and Holiday Gifts". Cover portrays Converse trolley on track. Company address is 24 and 26 Murray Street. Items offered are 300 trolley, 200 powered gondola, Electric Express 300 unpowered gondola.

(A) Original. One known copy. **NRS**

(B) Reproduction by E. A. Basse, Jr. 1 3

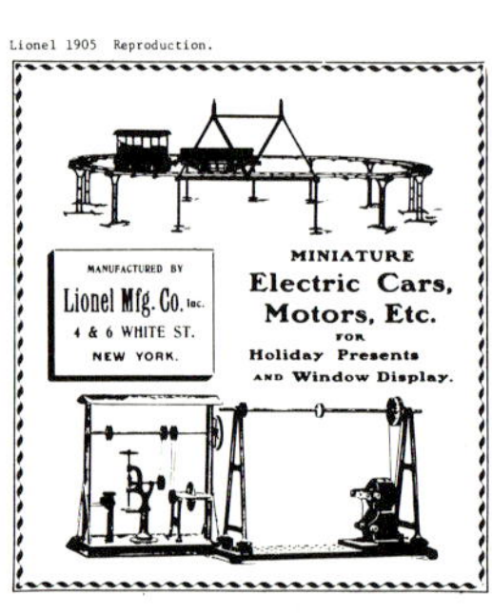

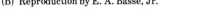

Reproductions of 1903 Type I on left and 1905 on right

1903

Type I: 6" x 9" vertical format. Cover reads "Electrical Novelties and Appliances for Boys, Ewing-Merkle Electric Co., Saint Louis, Mo. U.S.A." Cover shows portrait of young boy, dressed in cap and scarf, speaking into telephone. In Lionel's earliest years, it was apparently customary for large electrical supply houses like this one to promote Lionel products with their own names. See 1910 and 1912 entries for other examples. This is the only one in which the name "LIONEL" does not appear on the cover. Products shown: B&O tunnel loco, Derrick motorless trailer unit, glass wet cell jars and batteries. 16 pages

(A) Original **NRS**

(B) 1977 reproduction by Greenberg Publishing Company on plain paper 2 4

(C) White paper reproduction by William Vagell on semi-translucent paper 2 3

Type II: 6-1/4" x 3-1/2" horizontal format, same legends as 1902 predecessor and 24-26 Murray Street address. Lionel "lion" logo added to upper left corner. Cover shows 100 B&O locomotive and 600 Derrick trailer. Also shown in catalogue: 200 powered and 400 trailer gondolas, 300 Converse trolley track and varied accessories. 20 pages.

(A) Original **NRS**

(B) Reproduction by Greenberg Publishing Company 2 4

(C) Reproduction by William Vagell 2 3

(D) Reproduction by Don LaSpaluto with light gray cover stock and without reproduction notice 2 4

1904

Catalogue: 6" x 6-1/2" square format. Cover legend reverses order of "Holiday Presents" and "Window Display" (see introduction). Black print on white paper. Cover shows products within diagonal stripe running downhill. Countershafting apparatus in lower left corner; directly above it is legend "Manufactured By/Lionel Mfg. Co. Inc./4 & 6 White St./New York". inside black border. New products: "Special Show Window Display", 300 and 3090 trolley and trailer, 800 and 900 Box Car and trailer, Type A and K miniature motors and No. 2 countershafting apparatus. 12 pages.

(A) Original **NRS**

(B) Reproduction by Greenberg Publishing Company 2 4

(C) Reproduction by William Vagell with blue and black cover 2 3

(D) Reproduction by Don LaSpaluto. Some may not be marked as reproductions 2 4

(E) 1959 reproduction by Train Collector's Association. "VALLEE BROS. ELECT. CO." in place of "MANUFACTURED BY LIONEL MFG. CO. INC." 1 2

1905

Catalogue: 6" x 6" square format. Black ink on white paper. Cover has same wording as 1904 catalogue, but pictures differ. 100 locomotive pulling 400 trailer gondola passes through 340 suspension bridge on its way around an oval of track supported by 380 elevated pillars. Below the lettering, the No. 2 countershafting apparatus is shown powering an unidentified set of toy saws and drills mounted on a platform. New products: 1000 and 1050 passenger car and trailer, a "new improved 1905" track and a Type L power motor. 12 pages. This is the last catalogue showing 2-7/8" Gauge equipment.

(B) Reproduction by Greenberg Publishing Company with heavy blue index stock cover 2 4

(C) Reproduction by Greenberg Publishing Company with regular weight paper printed cover 2 4

(D) Reproduction by William Vagell on translucent paper 1 3

(E) Reproduction by Don LaSpaluto on coated stock without reproduction notice 2 4

1906

Catalogue: 4-1/2" by 6-1/2" horizontal format, 24 pages plus covers, black ink. Features completely new line of three-rail Standard Gauge trains. Front cover shows elevated trackage leading to ornate Victorian-style train station. In upper left corner is large sign with legend, "Look Out/for the/Third Rail". Lower right corner shows White Street address and Chicago sales office address.

(A) Original **NRS**

(B) Reproduction by Greenberg Publishing Company, black ink on plain white paper 2 4

(C) Reproduction by William Vagell, blue ink on cover, translucent paper 1 3

(D) Reproduction by Don LaSpaluto, may or may not be marked 2 4

1907

Catalogue: supposedly 6" x 9" format, 28 pages. No other details are available, and confirming evidence of this catalogue has yet to surface.

1908

Catalogue: supposedly 6" x 9" format, 28 pages. Purported to show 5 and 6 locomotives and the 16 ballast car, the 17 caboose and the 29 day coach. Reliable evidence for this catalogue's existence is lacking.

1909

Catalogue: 6" x 9" format, 32 pages plus covers. Cover is tan with black ink. Text is printed in black ink on white paper. Front cover: Lion logo in upper left and right corners; between them is legend "Standard Of The World". Center of cover: "LIONEL" in heavy black type above "Miniature Electric Trains/and/New Departure Battery Motors". Lower right has dealer's name and address. At lower left: "As superior to any on the/market as the telephone/is to the speaking tube" in three lines. Featured 1, 2, 3, 4, 8 and 9 trolleys, 10 Series freight cars and 29 day coach.

(A) Original NRS

(B) Reproduction by Greenberg Publishing Company on plain white paper marked "REPRODUCTION" on rear cover and in some gutters between pages 2 4

(C) Reproduction by William Vagell on translucent paper 1 3

(D) Reproduction by Don LaSpaluto with tan colored cover, some rubber-stamped "ORIGINAL REPRINT" in red on rear cover 2 4

1910

Type I: Catalogue, 28 pages plus covers, 8" x 10" vertical format, black ink on white paper. Front cover: lion logo in all four corners. At top: "Standard of the World". Date below upper right logo. "LIONEL" in heavy boldface type. "Miniature Electric Trains and/New Departure Battery Motors" in two lines underscored by heavy double line. Lower half of catalogue cover has space for dealer name, in this case "Anderson Light & Specialty Co./known as/LA SALLE LIGHT STORE/140 N. La Salle St./CHICAGO OPPOSITE NEW CITY HALL". Introduction on page 1 shows new address for Lionel Manufacturing Company: 381-383 Broadway. Next three pages detail motor and frame construction, track details, body construction and patent lists. Extensive line of trolleys. Contains 5, 5 Special, 6 and 7 steam locomotives, 10 Series freight cars, 1910, 1911 and 1912 electric locomotives and 18, 19 and 190 passenger cars.

(A) Original NRS

(B) 1976 reproduction by Greenberg Publishing Company on plain paper 2 4

Type II: Same contents as Type I above, but front cover has picture of Lionel factory at bottom center instead of dealer address.

(A) Original NRS

(B) Reproduction by William Vagell on translucent paper 1 3

Type III: Same contents as Type I, but cover is wrap-around multi-colored cover showing five rows of trains and sets. "The Lionel Mfg. Co." runs vertically along the right cover border, and "381 Broadway, New York" runs vertically along the left cover border.

(A) Original NRS

1911

Type I: Catalogue, 32 white text pages with black ink plus tan covers with black ink, 8" x 10" vertical format, pulp. Same general design as 1910 Type I but dealer name replaced by "Preserve This Book" and description of contents followed by bolder print: "DO NOT MISPLACE THIS BOOK." Lionel address at bottom center between two lion logos. First pages show five photos of Lionel Manufacturing Co. factory.

(A) Original NRS

Type II: Same contents as Type I but with multi-color wraparound cover.

(A) Original NRS

Type III: Same as Type I but space below double horizontal line, lists store name following "FOR SALE BY". Only known example lists: "MARYLAND ELECTRICAL SUPPLY CO., JOSEPH A. BECKER, Prop." Red ink for numbers on page 4.

(A) Original, Weisblum Collection NRS

(B) Reproduction by Greenberg Publishing Company 2 4

1912 LIONEL CATALOGUE REPRODUCTION

"Standard of the World"

LIONEL

Miniature Electric Trains and
New Departure Battery Motors

FOR SALE BY

Maryland Electrical Supply Co.

400 N. EUTAW ST.

BALTIMORE
MD.

Reproduction of 1912 Type I.

1912

Type I: Catalogue, 36 white text pages with black ink, plus red ink on page 4, gray vellum cover with black ink, 8" x 10" vertical format. Lion logo in four corners of the front cover. Cover lettering: "Standard of the World/Lionel/Miniature Electric Trains and New Departure Battery Motors" followed by a double horizontal line. Then "FOR SALE BY/Maryland Electrical Supply Co." Text page 1 shows four interior factory views plus exterior facade. "FACTORY NEW HAVEN, CONN." Racing cars are offered on pages 16 and 17. Pages 34-36 are devoted to "DIRECTIONS".

(A) Original, Weisblum Collection NRS

(B) Reproduction by Greenberg Publishing Company with tan cover stock, black ink on white-coated text pages and red ink on page 4 2 4

Type II: Same as Type I but with different cover lettering. "DIRECTIONS/FOR THE USE AND CARE OF/LIONEL ELECTRIC TOYS/ARE GIVEN ON PAGES 34, 35 & 36".

(A) Original NRS

(B) 1955 reproduction by J. C. Andrews and W. H. Kitchelt, Jr. in reduced size of 6-1/2" wide by 8-1/2" high NRS

(C) 1966 printing of (B) by Train Collector's Association 2 4

(D) Reproduction with gray cover and red ink and only 24 text pages. Pages were deleted without notice as were page numbers. Rubber-stamped on rear inside cover "REPRINT AS IS/NOVEMBER 1972". We would like to learn who published this reprint. 1 2

Type III: Color wrap-around cover. Text pages probably the same as Type I. More information requested.

(A) Original NRS

1913

Type I: Catalogue, 36 white text pages with black ink, and gray vellum cover with black ink and lion logos in four corners, 8" x 10" vertical format; text page 1 shows four interior factory views plus exterior facade. On page 2 "the manufacture of electric toys thirteen years ago..."

(A) Original NRS

Type II: Catalogue, 6" wide x 6-3/4" high, 16 pages including cover. Cover is lettered "LIONEL ELECTRIC TOYS" with red "L, E and T" and "ARE STANDARD OF THE WORLD". A boy and girl are playing on the floor with an elaborate double tracked railway. Page 2: "the manufacture of electric toys thirteen years ago..." Left center fold, page 8 shows 33, 38, 53 and 42 locomotives.

(A) Original NRS

(B) Reproduction by Greenberg Publishing Company in black ink only, on plain white paper. On top of front cover lettered: "LIONEL 1913 CATALOGUE REPRODUCTION" 2 4

(C) Reproduction by Don LaSpaluto with blue and red outside covers. Coated stock pages. Some not marked as reproductions. 2 4

(D) Reproduction in black ink only on translucent paper by William Vagell. Marked as reproduction as a reprint on page 2. 1 3

1914

Type I: Catalogue, 32 white text pages with black ink and gray vellum cover with black ink; 8" x 10" vertical format; text page 2 "the manufacture of electric toys fourteen years ago".

(A) Original NRS

Type II: Catalogue, same cover as 1913 Type II, 6" wide and 6-3/4" high, 16 pages including cover. Cover and text are printed in green and black with "L, E and T" on front cover in green, light green screen behind cover image, and green text copy. Interior halftones are printed in black.

(A) Original, Weisblum Collection NRS

(B) Reproduction by William Vagell in black with green and black front cover, translucent paper 1 3

Type III: Apparently exactly the same as Type II, but text is printed in brown ink and images are in orange ink.

(A) Original NRS

(B) Reproduction by Jerry Rubenstein 2 4

(C) Remaining Rubenstein reproductions were sold to Greenberg Publishing Company and rubber-stamped: "1975 REPRODUCTION GREENBERG PUBLISHING CO..." 2 4

1915

Consumer catalogue: 10" x 7" horizontal format, 40 pages including cover and color insert but pages numbered only to 38. Printed in black and orange ink with orange used as a highlight primarily for headings. The center image on the front cover shows a 42 electric locomotive with two cars; four line drawings flank the center image. This catalogue introduces "A LITTLE TRIP THROUGH MY FACTORY" for the first time. The tour includes an extremely slanted comparison of Lionel and Ives production. The catalogue also contains the first catalogue photograph of J. Lionel Cowen. "250,000 Boys Now Operating Them" on all but front cover and centerfold. Page 2: "For fifteen years I have been making boys happy..." Page 24: "LIONEL FREIGHT CARS. PRICE LIST..." The catalogue center fold was printed in color on heavier stock showing the 42 locomotive with 19, 18 and 190 cars on a Meccano bridge.

(A) Original, Weisblum Collection **NRS**

(B) Reproduction; believed to be Type I, but all black ink. Details requested **NRS**

Type II: Exactly the same as Type I, but the old price of $32.50 for outfit 421 on the left center fold page is overprinted with a red line and a new price of $40.00.

(A) Original, Weisblum Collection **NRS**

1916

Type I: Consumer catalogue, 10" x 17" horizontal format, 40 pages including cover and color insert but pages numbered only to 30. Printed in black and orange ink with orange used primarily as a highlight for headings. This catalogue is very similar to 1915 Type I, but has "LIONEL FREIGHT CARS. PRICE LIST..." on page 23, and "LIONEL PULLMAN CARS..." price list on page 25. It does have "250,000 BOYS..." on all but front cover and center fold. 1-3/8" diameter red label on front cover: "IMPORTANT/All prices in this/Catalogue are withdrawn./See enclosed sheet/for revised figures." Enclosed in the catalogue is a 10" wide x 7" high "SCHEDULE A" with new 1916 price list. On this sheet Cowen blames "Old Mister War" for the price increases on his entire line.

(A) Original, Weisblum Collection **NRS**

Type II: Reportedly same as Type I, but with "For sixteen years I have been making boys happy" on page 2, with new higher prices compared to Type I and "260,000 BOYS..." on all but front cover and center fold, without separate "SCHEDULE A" and without red cover sticker. Verification requested.

Type III: reportedly 6" x 9" folder with 16 pages; more details and verification requested.

1917

Type I: consumer catalogue, 40 text pages with pages 17-24 in full color and balance black ink only; front cover is printed in red and black with white block with ornate red and black lettering: "LIONEL ELECTRIC TRAINS/& Multivolt Transformers". Below is a picture of Lawrence Cowen, Joshua Cowen's son, posing as the "Happy Lionel Boy" operating a 420 passenger set. Plant pictures are on the inside and semaphores are portrayed on the back cover. Introduces 0 Gauge series. Text page 1 "STANDARD of the WORLD for 17 YEARS" with page entirely in black. Text page 2: "Seventeen Years Ago I Started To Make"; pages 3-19, 22-40, back covers with heading "Over 300,000 Boys Are Now Operating Them."

(A) Original, Weisblum Collection **NRS**

Type II: Consumer catalogue, similar to Type I, but without extra color 4 page wraparound cover and text page 1 has "LIONEL" and "TRAINS" in red and black lettering. Type III has most other pages with red headings.

(A) Original, Fitchett Collection **NRS**

(B) 1971 reproduction by Greenberg Publishing Company as all black catalogue bound by a staple at the edge rather than through the center fold as in the original. Picture quality is modest at best **1 2**

(C) 1977 reproduction by Greenberg Publishing Company as all black catalogue bound by a staple through edge. Much better picture quality than (B) **3 6**

Type III: Consumer folder, 6" x 9" vertical format, 8 pages on each side, unfolds to 24" x 15" horizontal format, black and red ink on coated stock with red ink used only for headings and outlines. Side 1: front cover with Lawrence Cowen with arms spread wide over 42 passenger set. Cover lettering: "1917/CATALOGUE OF/LIONEL/ELECTRIC/TOY TRAINS/And Multivolt Transformers". Upper left panel with transformer chart with B, S, T, and K transformers. Side 2 lower center right panel with illustration of 121 and 121X station as well as tunnel.

(A) Original **NRS**

(B) 1967 Gordon Reproduction **1 2**

Type IV: Consumer folder, similar to Type III, but significant differences: front lettering: "1917/CATALOGUE OF/LIONEL/ELECTRIC/TOYS". Front panel is outlined by solid red rule. Side 1 upper left panel with transformer chart with S, T, and K transformers. Side 2 lower, center right panel with illustration of tunnel only.

(A) Original, Weisblum Collection **NRS**

(B) Reproduction on coated stock by Greenberg Publishing Company. Extremely close match to original but with extra outlining added around panel. Reproduction printed by Collins Lithography, Baltimore **2 4**

Directions for Operating...: 4-1/2" wide x 5" high, 20 pages, black ink on white paper, "The Lionel Manufacturing Co./48 East 21st Street New York City" on page 1. Operating instructions, lubrication points, voltage specifications, packed with each train set.

(A) Original, Weisblum Collection **5 10**

(B) Reproduction by Greenberg Publishing Company **1 2**

1918

Consumer folder: 6" x 9" vertical format, 8 pages on each side, unfolds to 24" wide x 18" high, black and red ink on coated stock with red ink used only for headings and outlines. Side 1: front cover panel with boy (Lawrence Cowen) with arms spread wide over a 42 set. Cover panel is outlined with a thin red rule enclosed in a triangular rule. Lettering: "LIONEL/ELECTRIC/TOY TRAINS/And Multivolt Transformers/SOLD BY/MANUFACTURED AND GUARANTEED BY/The Lionel Manufacturing Company, 48-52 East 21st Street, New York". Side 1 upper left panel with transformer chart with B, T and K transformers. Side 1 lower center left panel: 'PLAY WAR!" Shows armored loco and armored loco with two sets. Side 2 lower center right panel without illustrations of tunnels or station. (Compare with 1917 folders.) Side 2, lower right edge: "NOTE - All locomotives...equipped with 3-1/2" volt bulbs".

(A) Original, Weisblum Collection **NRS**

(B) Reproduction on coated stock by Greenberg Publishing Company. Extremely close match to original including imperfections caused by original's wear and tear on folds. Example of imperfection is Side 2, lower right panel "Battery". Printed by Collins Lithography, Baltimore **2 4**

(C) 1955 black and white reduced size reproduction by Andrews et al. 18-1/2" wide x 29" high **1 2**

Type I: Directions for Operating..., 16 pages, black ink on white paper, "The Lionel Manufacturing Co./48 East 21st Street New York City" on page 1. Page 3: "Standard Gauge brushes are known as No./74./Price...Per pair $.25".

(A) Original, Weisblum Collection **4 8**

(B) Reproduction by Greenberg Publishing Company **1 2**

Type II: Directions for Operating, 16 pages, black ink on white paper, "THE LIONEL CORPORATION/48 East 21st Street, New York City". Bohn comment

(A) Original **4 8**

Consumer catalogue, probably 40 pages, 10" x 8" horizontal format. We suspect that this catalogue exists but have no confirmed reports.

1919

Consumer folder: 6" x 9" vertical format, 8 pages on each side, unfolds to 24" wide x 18" high, black and red ink on coated stock with red ink used only for headings and borders. Side 1: front cover with Lionel Cowen with boy (Lawrence Cowen) with arms spread wide over 42 set. Cover is outlined with a thin red rule enclosed in a triangular rule. Lettering: "LIONEL/ELECTRIC/TOY TRAINS/And Multivolt Transformers/SOLD BY/MANUFACTURED AND GUARANTEED BY/THE LIONEL CORPORATION/48-52 East 21st Street, New York". Note change of company name compared to 1918 Consumer folder. Side 1 lower center left panel shows Standard Gauge 5 and 51, and 6 and 7 locomotives. (Compare with 1918 folder.) Side 2 lower right corner panel shows illustration of single tunnel. (Compare with 1917 and 1918 folders.) New listing of Lionel 158 locomotive on Side 2, lower left corner. Price of 420 and 421 outfits in Canada is

$77.55 and $85.70 respectively.

(A) Original, Weisblum Collection **NRS**

(B) Reproduction by Greenberg Publishing Company 2 4

NET PRICE SHEET: "Effective February 18, 1919", 4 page folder, 7" wide x 10-1/2" wide; black and red ink on coated stock with red ink used only for border rule and headings. Announces new 158 locomotive (Outfit 159) and 'BUILD-A-LOCO". The 158 was produced but the "BUILD-A-LOCO" was not produced until 1928. It also announced the discontinuation of the 53.

(A) Original **NRS**

(B) 1971 reproduction by Max Knoecklein 1 2

Type I: Directions for Operating Lionel Electric Toy Trains...16 stapled pages including covers, 4-9/16" wide x 5-1/8" high, shows sliding shoe Standard Gauge motor on page 4 and on page 5 shows four dry cells wired in series and labeled "LIONEL MFG CO. DRY BATTERY". The product is undated but by inference we have dated it late 1918. The inference is based on the prices of the B, T, and K transformers shown on page 13 and priced respectively at $4.25, $6.75 and $8.00. These prices are shown in the February 18, 1919 trade price list (Reproduced by Knoecklein). The address shown for shipping goods for repair is: "603 to 619 SOUTH 21st ST. IRVINGTON, N.J." The company name and address is shown as "THE LIONEL CORPORATION 48 East 21st Street, New York City", Weaver and Bohn comments

(A) Original, Weaver Collection **NRS**

Type II: Directions for Operating Lionel Electric Trains...16 pages including covers, 4-9/16" wide x 5-1/8" high shows sliding shoe Standard Gauge motor on page 4 and on page 5 shows four dry cells wired in series and labeled "LIONEL MFG. CO. DRY BATTERY". The product is undated and exactly similar to 1919 Directions (A) except for the prices shown for the B, T, and K transformers on page 13 of $6.25, $9.75 and $11.25 respectively. Another 1919 publication, a black and red folder entitled "LIONEL ELECTRIC TOY TRAINS and Multivolt Transformers" shows "East of Missouri River" prices of $6.35, $9.65 and $11.30 respectively. Since this catalogue evidently was originally published later in 1919 our best hypothesis is that this Directions (B) pamphlet is also 1919 but later in the year than the pamphlet cited earlier, Bohn comment.

(A) Original **NRS**

AN APOLOGY: 11" x 17" page and 6" x 9" Apology folder with 16 pages are listed on page 142 as 1919 on **LIONEL TRAINS: Standard of the World edited by Donald Fraley.** Our reading of both sheet and folder suggests 1920 based on the Side 1 text of the 11" x 17" sheet: "A Twenty Year Record/Lionel Trains have been on the market for twenty years..." The 16 page folder cites the sheet as accompanying it on Side 1, lower left panel "...there you will also find explained the cause of my not being able to send you the big Lionel Catalog..."

1920

AN APOLOGY: 11" x 17" page printed both sides in red and black with red used only for headings and borders. Came with 16 page 6" x 9" folder. (See next item.) There is some question about the dating of this item. See 1919 listing for explanation. Side 1 shows 156 passenger set on top and carries the explanation of how a New York printers' strike prevented the printing of the "wonderful big Xmas catalogue". The text is a real piece of advertising bravura which captures the essence of Joshua Lionel Cowen's excellence as a salesman. It is appropriately signed "J. LIONEL COWEN/friend of the boys". The second side of this sheet provides detailed drawings and explanations of the Standard and 0 Gauge chassis and motors.

(A) Original **NRS**

(B) Reproduction in black and red on coated stock by Greenberg Publishing Company shows wear and tear of original with one damaged line of type on Side 1 1 2

(C) Reproduction in black only on translucent paper by William Vagell but not marked. The picture reproductions are poor .50 1

Consumer apology folder: 6" x 9" vertical format, 8 pages on each side, unfolds to 24" wide x 18" high, black and red ink on coated stock with red ink used only for headings and borders. Side 1: front cover panel: boy (Lawrence Cowen) with arms spread wide over a 42 set. Cover panel is outlined with a thin red rule enclosed in a triangular rule. Lettering: "LIONEL/ELECTRIC/TOY TRAINS/And Multivolt Transformers/SOLD BY/MANUFACTURED AND GUARANTEED BY/THE LIONEL CORPORATION/48-52 East 21st Street, New York". Side 1, lower left panel contains a message to "BOYS" to see the enclosed 11" x 17" Apology sheet; side 2 lower right center panel shows illustration of single tunnel. The 1920 16 page folder appears identical to the 1919 except for the message to the boys. The likely explanation is that the 1919 type and cuts were rerun when the 1920 printers' strike prevented the new 1920 catalogue from being produced. Reader comments invited.

(A) Original **NRS**

(B) Reproduction by Greenberg Publishing Company in black and red ink on coated stock 2 4

(C) Reproduction by William Vagell as two 11" x 17" sheets reduced in size from the original. The 11" x 17" sheet side with the front folder panel is printed on red and black; the second side is black only. The second 11" x 17" sheet is printed in black ink only on translucent paper 1 2

Consumer catalogue: 10" wide x 6-3/4" high, 46 pages plus unnumbered front cover. Gray front cover with white rectangular block with red and black lettering "LIONEL ELECTRIC TOY TRAINS & Mutlivolt Transformers", boy with arms spread over 42 set. We have only examined the TCA reproduction and do not have access to an original for details of the use of color. It is likely that the inside front cover showing a claimed 120,000 square foot plant was in color. Text page 1 shows in red ink "STANDARD of the WORLD FOR TWENTY YEARS" and Uncle Sam holding a boy and a girl and a rhyme urging "Buy Toys Made in U.S.A." This text was probably in response to the expected resumption of German toy imports with the war's end. Page 2 "...Trip Thru My Factory". (Note condensed spelling of through.) Most text pages carry heading "Standard of the World for 20 Years...500,000 Boys Enjoying Them" except for inserts 36a-36h. It is highly likely that many if not most sets were in color. Reproduction illustrations on pages 18 and 19 appear to be translations of original color printing into reproduction black and white images. Reader comments invited.

The TCA reproduction insert pages 36a-36h is headed "New Lionel Numbers for Nineteen Twenty" on page 36-a but pages 36-b - 36-h all have heading "Standard of the World for 21 years...550,000 Boys Enjoying Them". The full color reproduction insert implies issuance for the 1921 season. It is therefore possible that the 1920 TCA reproduction is actually a 1921 consumer catalogue which was constructed from the strike delayed 1920 catalogue updated with the 1921 insert. It is also possible that Cowen was hedging his bets and making a late 1920 catalogue also available in 1921. The insert shows the new 603 Pullman and 604 Observation in dull orange with brown window inserts and doors. These cars are not shown in the 16 page 6" x 9" 1920 folder. Weisblum comments. Reader comments invited.

(A) Original **NRS**

(B) 1969 reproduction by TCA. See comments above. 5 12

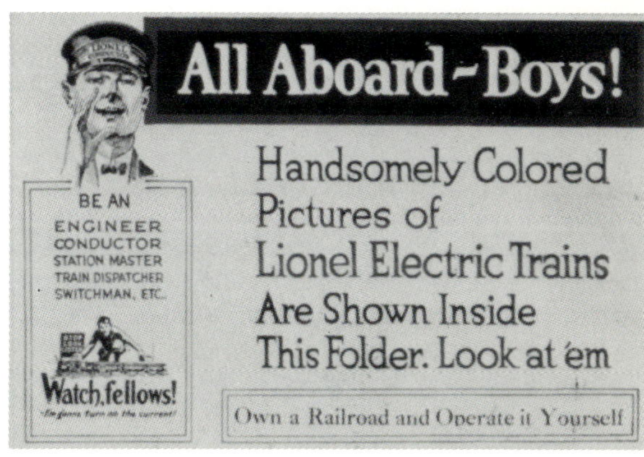

Reproduction of 1920 large consumer folder

Large consumer folder: 32 panels 7" wide x 5" high with 16 panels on each side, opens to 40-1/2" wide and 20" sheet, full color. Front cover panel, side 1, black rectangle with white lettering "All Aboard - Boys!" and to left of rectangle there is a boy wearing conductor cap. Beneath the boy is black lettering: "BE AN/ENGINEER/CONDUCTOR/STATION MASTER/TRAIN DISPATCHER/SWITCHMAN, ETC." Below these words is Lionel boy with arms spread over 42 set and words "Watch Fellows!" Upper left panel, side 1, red words: "STANDARD of the WORLD/FOR TWENTY YEARS" and in black "TWENTY YEARS AGO I STARTED TO MAKE LIONEL ELECTRIC TRAINS". And "...over 550,000 sets are in daily use..." New stations and bridges shown on side 1, lower left side. Also new 62 Semaphore, new 60 Telegraph Post and new 65 Railroad Warning Sign are shown on right center lower panel. On side 2, lower right panel, the same "120,000 Square Feet" factory is shown in color. This is the same image shown in black and white in the 1920 46 page catalogue.

(A) Original. Caution in purchasing originals is highly recommended. See (B) **NRS**

(B) 1976 full color reproduction by House of Heeg. Very small reproduction notice appears on lower left corner of side 1 **10 18**

1921

Large consumer folder: 32 panels, 7" wide x 5" high with 16 panels on each side, opens to 40-1/2" wide x 18" high sheet. Front cover panel somewhat similar to 1920 folder but with "LIONEL ELECTRIC TOY TRAINS" inside orange rectangular box replaced "All Aboard - Boys!" Center of panel has boy with arms stretched over 42 set. Upper left panel on side 1 "STANDARD of the WORLD FOR TWENTY-ONE YEARS". Side 1, lower left panel shows new 69 and 069 Warning Signal. Side 2, lower center left panels shows new 71 Telegraph Post outfit and 70 Semaphore-Lamp Signal Outfit.

(A) Original, Weisblum Collection **NRS**

(B) Reproduction has not been made!

1 Greenberg Publishing will produce this item once there is sufficient reader interest. Estimated price is $20.00.

DIRECTIONS: "This Book Tells/HOW TO GET THE MOST FUN/Out of LIONEL ELECTRIC TOY TRAINS". 5-7/16" wide x 8-5/8" high, 12 stapled pages including covers, Page 3: Voltage obtainable from LIONEL "MULTI-VOLT" TRANSFORMERS, Types A, B, T, and K. Centerfold shows a chart for "PROPER LAMP RENEWALS" both for battery and house current operation. The Outfit Numbers shown date the booklet as 1920-1921. However, the rear page shows the new 069 and 69 Electric Warning Signals introduced in 1921, Weaver Collection. There is a 1921 edition which differs from this one only in type style. Bohn comment

(A) Original, Weaver Collection **2 4**

1922

Consumer catalogue: 10" wide x 6-3/4" high, 40 pages including covers, gray front cover with white rectangular block containing: "LIONEL ELECTRIC TRAINS..." Boy with arms stretched over 42 set. "Standard of the World for 22 years...Over Two Million Happy Users" as heading for most pages. Lionel claimed 500,000 users by 1920, 550,000 users by 1921 and this copy claims 2,000,000 by 1922. 1921 must have been a great year!

(A) Original, Weisblum Collection **35 90**

(B) 1974 black and white reproduction by Bruce Greenberg with full color front cover and "1922" added to the cover. The original catalogue was printed in color. Printed by Bendix Field Engineering, Columbia, Maryland from negatives prepared by Photo Offset Service. Reproduction logo is on lower left corner of inside front cover **3 6**

(C) 1976 full color reproduction by House of Heeg. The House of Heeg was the Pittsburgh area partnership of Robert Schnitzer and Frank Heeg. "REPRODUCTION" appears on the lower left corner of all even pages except the rear cover. **8 15**

TRADE PRICE SHEET: "MARCH 1st, 1922". Prices were reduced from 1921 reflecting the national business downturn. 7" wide x 10-9/16" high, four pages, black ink on white paper.

(A) Original **NRS**

(B) 1971 reproduction by Max Knoecklein **1 2**

1923

Consumer Catalogue: 48 pages including covers; 10" x 7" horizontal format; four-color picture measuring 5" x 5" dominates center of cover; background is light blue-gray; two black-print drawings of train scenes flank center picture; "Lionel Electric Toy Trains" logo in red and black on bottom. The center picture is highly significant. It shows a man in his easy chair captivated by his son's trains, which appear to cover the whole living room floor and vanish into the parlor. The man's newspaper, symbolic of the "real world" falls carelessly to the floor. This father-son theme, appearing on a catalogue cover for the first time, would be trumpeted ceaselessly in years to come. Content: pages 4 and 5 show amusing - and phony! - comparisons with "inferior" makes. The "other" passenger car appears to have been blown up by a firecracker. Rear cover has four-color somewhat fanciful picture of gigantic Irvington factory. The 402 and 380 locomotives are shown for the first time. All trains are illustrated in full color.

(A) Original **35 30**

(B) 1974 black and white reproduction by Bruce C. Greenberg, printed at Bendix Field Engineering, Columbia, Maryland; color front cover only with "1923" added for identification. The cover was printed on heavier stock than inside pages. **3 6**

(C) 1975 full color reproduction by House of Heeg, Pittsburgh. The remaining inventory and negatives were purchased by Greenberg Publishing Company. The inventory has been sold out; however, the negatives were used in printing Greenberg's Lionel Catalogues: Volume I. **8 15**

1924

Consumer catalogue: 44 pages including covers; 10-1/2" x 8" horizontal format, four-color cover, "LIONEL ELECTRIC TOY TRAINS" logo at top. The entire remaining cover has a four-color portrait which is one of the great Lionel masterpieces of advertising art. Two boys, dressed immaculately in coats and ties, mischieviously cheer on a speeding passenger express pulled by a 402 electric as it chases the terrified family dog down the track. This triumvirate of boy, dog, and train would reappear (in somewhat less perilous circumstances for the dog). Contents: the comparisons with other "inferior" makes are gone (see Ron Hollander, **All Aboard!**, pp. 56-59, for an amusing background story about the disappearance). Factory pictures are on the rear cover. LaVoie comment

(A) Original **35 75**

(B) 1971-2 black and white reproduction by Bruce C. Greenberg in Galesburg, Illinois. 11" x 8-1/2" pages bound by staples on left edges. Fair to good reproductions of train images **1 2**

(C) 1974 black and white reproduction with full color cover only by Bruce C. Greenberg. "1924" added for identification to the front cover. The cover is printed on heavier stock than inside pages. Printed by Bendix Field Engineering, Columbia, Maryland from negatives supplied by Photo Offset Service, Baltimore **3 6**

(D) 1975 full color reproduction by House of Heeg, Pittsburgh. The negatives were purchased by Greenberg Publishing Company and used in printing Greenberg's Lionel Catalogues: Volume 1. **8 15**

Miniature consumer folder: 6 panels each, 3-5/16" wide x 6-1/4" high, printed in orange and black duotones. Front panel: "BOYS - YOUR LIONEL TRAIN IS HERE." with space for store name below. Second side with three panels shows a single image — the 1924 image of the two boys with train and retreating dog PLUS the continuation of the picture story. Note the track to the left of the 78 Signal on the left side of the cover. On the folder the track continues with another train being urged on by another boy to a potential collision unless the Signal stops the train in time! Weisblum comment.

(A) Original with store name: "GOLDENBERG BROTHERS/717 NORTH GAY STREET/Baltimore, Maryland". Weisblum Collection **7 15**

1925

Consumer catalogue: 44 pages including covers, 10-1/2" x 8" horizontal format, four-color cover on white. Lionel logo at top changed to read "LIONEL ELECTRIC TRAINS/Model Railroad Accessories/Multivolt Transformers"; red and black paint on light brown. Cover painting, signed by Walter Beach Humphrey, has a Norman Rockwell "Americana" quality to it. A well-dressed boy runs a big 402 passenger express while his curious, but fearful, terrier looks on. (At least the dog is not running away!) In the background, both boy and dog sit in the cab of a real NYC S-class electric locomotive. The artist is suggesting that the boy imagines himself in the real loco cab while operating his Lionel trains! Complete scenic railroads are offered on pages 42-43. Factory pictures are on rear cover.

(A) Original, Prendergast Collection **35 80**

(B) 1971-2 black and white 11" x 8-1/2" reproduction by Bruce Greenberg in Galesburg, Illinois. Bound by a staple along left edge. Original supplied by Rev. Robert Prendergast **1 2**

(C) 1974 black and white reproduction with full color front cover only by

Bruce Greenberg. Printed by Bendix Field Engineering, Columbia, Maryland from negatives made by Photo Offset Service, Baltimore. "1925" added to front cover to aid identification 3 6

(D) 1975 reproduction in full color by Robert Schnitzer and Frank Heeg (House of Heeg). Negatives were purchased by Greenberg Publishing Company and used in printing Greenberg's Lionel Catalogues: Volume I 8 15

Miniature folder: We believe this exists but have not been able to locate one to describe. Reader assistance requested.

DIRECTIONS FOR THE USE AND CARE OF LIONEL ELECTRIC TRAINS: 5-1/4" wide x 8" high, 12 stapled pages, black ink on white paper. No dates appear in the pamphlet. We have dated it based on a diagram on page 7 showing the later Super Motor with small gears on the wheels and the listing on page 12 of 337, 338, 339 and 341 which were first offered in 1925. Service Dept. is 605 South 21st St., Irvington, N.J., Bohn Collection.

1926

Consumer catalogue: 48 pages including covers, 10-1/2" x 8" horizontal format, four-color cover. Cover painting, again signed by Humphrey, shows a boy operating an elaborate railroad using levers behind a power station. This time, his terrier looks as interested in the trains as he does. The 402 again pulls a fast passenger express, but the freight cars are the new 200 Series freights, introduced this year. The 219 crane dominates the spur siding. Electric locomotive reversing is introduced on page 3. On page 17, a boy is shown using a rheostat control to reverse a locomotive. Electric switches are introduced on page 39. Factory pictures are on a rear cover, and a Newark, N.J. warehouse address has been added.

(A) Original 35 80

(B) 1969 black and white reproduction by Richard Rex. Reproduction logo is on the top left corner of page 2 3 6

(C) 1974 black and white reproduction with full color front cover only by Bruce Greenberg. Reproduction logo is on the top left corner of page 2. Printed by Bendix Field Engineering, Columbia, Maryland with negatives prepared by Photo Offset Service, Baltimore 3 6

(D) 1975 full color reproduction by Robert Schnitzer and Frank Heeg (House of Heeg). The negatives were purchased by Greenberg Publishing Company and used in printing Greenberg's Lionel Catalogues: Volume I 8 15

Miniature folder: orange and black duotone, unfolded size: 21" wide x 5-3/4" high. Folds to 5-3/4" wide x 3" high and shows a miniature image of 1926 catalogue front cover. A white block on the front cover was provided for the store name. Features new 437 Tower, 436 and 435 power stations as well as numerous sets. The folder offered the larger consumer catalogue for $.10. Weisblum comment.

(A) Original, Weisblum Collection 3 10

DIRECTIONS FOR THE USE AND CARE OF LIONEL TRAINS: 12 stapled pages, 5-1/4" wide x 8" high, black ink on white paper. Dating based on page 12 parts list which includes Standard Gauge 211, 712, 213, 214, 215, 216, 217, 218, 219, 428, 429 and 430 cars. It also included 0 Gauge cars: 811, 812, 813, 814, 815 and 817 cars. These were all first issued in 1916. It did not include 816 (1927), but this could be an early 1927 issue, Bohn comment.

(A) Original, Weisblum Collection 1 2

1927

Consumer catalogue: 46 pages including covers, 11-1/2" x 8-1/2" format, four color cover. Cover has Lionel rectangular logo in red and black on light blue-gray background. Entire cover dominated by ballast-eye view portrait of new dual-motored 408E in mojave color. Also introduced are 500 freight series for Standard Gauge and 800 and 810 series 0 Gauge freights. Magnificent center fold-out shows 409E "Lionel Limited" passenger set: 408E locomotive pulls 418, 419, 431 and 490 passenger cars. Train is portrayed in brown against a dramatic black background. The center fold ink coverage was only possible because of development in printing technology. The back cover shows two factory complexes. Value of original 35 80

(A) 1974 black and white reproduction with full color front cover by Bruce C. Greenberg. "1927" added to the cover for identification. Cover stock is heavier than inside pages. Reproduction logo on page 2 center bottom. 600 copies printed by Bendix Field Engineering, Columbia, Maryland from negatives made by Photo Offset Service, Baltimore 3 6

(B) 1975 full color reproduction by House of Heeg. The negatives were purchased by Greenberg Publishing Company and used in printing Greenberg's Lionel Catalogues: Volume I. 8 15

Miniature folder: orange and green duotone, unfolded size 21" wide x 5-3/4" high. Folds to 5-3/4" wide x 3-1/2". Side 1 has front panel with miniature version of 1927 consumer catalogue 408 image with 78 Signal and 82 Semaphore. Panel provides block for store name and address. Other panels show new 83 Traffic Blinker and 87 Crossing Signal and other accessories as well as eight sets.

(A) Original with "STONE & THOMAS/Wheeling, W.Va." as listed store **NRS**

(B) 1976 reproduction of (A) by House of Heeg. This item is still available from Greenberg Publishing Company or Iron Horse Productions. 1 2

DIRECTIONS FOR THE USE AND CARE OF LIONEL ELECTRIC TRAINS: "IS IT NOT A FACT..." with very elaborate "I", 12 pages, 5-1/8" wide x 8" high, black ink on white paper. Dating based on page 12 list which is similar to that for 1926 DIRECTIONS and to page 11 Lamp Renewal chart. The chart lists the following new accessories which were introduced in 1927: 82, 84, 83, 87 and 438. We have therefore dated the booklet as 1927.

(A) Original, Weisblum Collection 1 2

Reproduction of 1928

1928

Consumer catalogue: 46 pages including covers, 11" x 8-1/2" horizontal format, four-color cover. Cover has Lionel rectangular logo in red and black type on cream background edged in orange. Catalogue is dated "1928" in right lower side of rectangle. Cover painting signed by Fernando E. Ciavatti shows two boys using a peacock and red 219 crane to load lumber onto a 211 flat car. Page 13 explains new "Bild-A-Loco" outfits number 4, 9E and 381E. The "Lionel Limited" 408E-powered fold-out is repeated. Page 42 introduces the 300 "Hell Gate" bridge. Page 40 shows the new 200 turntable. Rear cover introduces the 840 Power Station, probably Lionel's most magnificent accessory.

(A) Original **40 80**

(B) 1974 black and white reproduction with full color front cover by Bruce Greenberg. Cover stock is heavier than inside pages. Reproduction logo is on page 2, lower right corner. 600 copies printed by Bendix Field Engineering, Columbia, Maryland from negatives made by Photo Offset Service, Baltimore 3 6

(C) 1975 full color reproduction by Robert E. Schnitzer and Frank E. Heeg. The negatives were purchased by Greenberg Publishing Company and used in printing Greenberg's Lionel Catalogues: Volume I. 8 15

Miniature folder: orange and green duotone, 32 pages, 7-7/8" wide x 5-5/8" high. This catalogue has a different format from those used in 1924-1927. It also differs from its predecessors in that its front cover shows 12 boys and 1 girl rather than reproducing a miniature version of the consumer catalogue front cover. Pages 2 and 3 of the Miniature catalogue are slightly modified reductions of pages 2 and 3 of the consumer catalogue.

(A) Original 10 25

Type I: DIRECTIONS FOR THE USE AND CARE OF LIONEL ELECTRIC TRAINS. 16 stapled pages, 7" wide x 10-1/4" high (possibly the original was smaller in size), black ink on white paper; dating based on page 12, Price List of Parts, 516 (1928) and 816 (1927) are listed for the first time. 437 (1926) is added to the Lamp Chart on page 15. Bottom of page 1: "Manufactured and Guaranteed by/THE LIONEL CORPORATION/15-17-19 EAST 26th STREET NEW YORK". 1927 directions do not have street address at the bottom of the page.

(A) Original 2 5

(B) T.T.O.S. reprint; rubber-stamped "A T.T.O.S./REPRINT" on rear cover 1 2

Type 2: DIRECTIONS FOR THE USE AND CARE OF LIONEL ELECTRIC TRAINS. 16 stapled pages, 5-1/4 wide x 8" high, black ink on white paper; similar to Type I but smaller in size with changes in text. Page 1: "IS IT NOT A FACT" with "I" in white inside a block with fine black lines. Inside "IMPORTANT" block address is: "Service Department, The Lionel Corporation, 605 South 21st Street, Irvington, New Jersey". Adds 437 signal tower lamp replacement. Type I has "Sager Place" address.

(A) Original, Bohn Collection 2 5

1929

Consumer catalogue: 46 pages including covers, 11-1/2" x 8-1/2" format, four-color cover edged in yellow on white. Some paper collectors consider this catalogue to be the best one ever produced by Lionel; others favor 1928. In any case originals are highly prized. Cover painting shows speeding steam and electric trains hurtling toward viewer against a dark blue background. A smiling boy towers over them from behind. Page 8 introduces several new 0 Gauge electric locomotives. Page 9 shows new 267 passenger outfit, and page 17 shows its 349 Standard Gauge counterpart. Pages 18 and 19 show the 390 steam engine and sets pulled by it. Center foldout now shows two classic sets: the 409E "Deluxe Express" pulled by a 408E electric loco and the new 411E "Transcontinental Limited", which has the new 412, 413, 414 and 416 "State" passenger cars pulled by a 381E electric locomotive. Page 36 shows the 128 station and its matching 129 terrace.

(A) Original, Weisblum Collection 50 125

(B) 1968 black and white reproduction with full color front cover by Lester T. Gordon. Still available from Gordon 3 6

(C) 1973 full color reproduction by Max Knoecklein. Still available from M. Knoecklein 10 20

(D) The catalogue is also reprinted in full color in Greenberg's Lionel Catalogues: Volume I.

Miniature catalogue: red and blue duotone, 32 pages, 7-5/8" wide x 5-3/4" high. This catalogue has an unusual page layout being composed of sheets of paper 3-1/2" wide x 5-3/4" high. Many of the Miniature catalogue pages are miniature versions of the consumer catalogue.

(A) Original, Weisblum Collection 10 20

DIRECTIONS FOR THE USE AND CARE OF LIONEL TRAINS, 16 stapled pages, 6" wide x 9" high, black ink on white paper, first reference to 402E and 408E, Bohn Collection 2 5

1930

Consumer catalogue: 48 pages including covers; 11-1/2" x 8-1/2" horizontal format, four-color front cover. Cover is an excellent example of the "art deco" motif of Thirties popular art; it is signed by Ciavatti and shows a highly stylized "Lionel Electric Trains/Model Railroad Accessories" in red and black on top of cover with no rectangle or borders. Cover painting shows busy yard scene with pink toned Hell Gate Bridge and Power Station in background. Two electric passenger trains head towards viewer; one is headed by an orange tinted 381 while a smoking steam engine awaits clearance on siding. Sky and clouds are highly abstracted in dark blue and white. A village is portrayed at the left. All pages of this catalogue have a half-inch red lower border. Page 9 introduces the 260E 0 Gauge steam loco. Many sets are now hauled by steam locomotives rather than electrics. Page 26 introduces the Standard Gauge "Blue Comet" set. Pages 30-31 introduce new accessories and the 810 0 Gauge crane car. Back cover introduces Lionel electric stove for girls. Value of original 35 100

(A) 1974 black and white reproduction with full color front cover by Bruce C. Greenberg 3 6

(B) 1974 full color reproduction by Iron Horse Productions. IHP notice on lower rear cover and on page 2 8 15

Miniature folder: full color, folded size 3-1/2" wide x 6-1/8" high, opens to 14" wide x 12-1/4" high. Front panel shows 390 Blue Comet loco with green flags and green pilot marker lamps. Rear panel shows electric range.

(A) Original 10 30

(B) T.T.O.S. reproduction. Marked "A GENUINE/T.T.O.S./REPRINT" on front panel 2 4

"Winner" Lines folder: 4 pages, 11-1/2" x 8-1/2"; plain gray cover with black "art deco" lettering; "WINNER TOY/CORPORATION" separated by heavy black line at upper left; text on cover reads "ANNOUNCING/A COMPLETE ELECTRIC TRAIN/AND TRANSFORMER/TO RETAIL AT/$3.95". Winner passenger train with 1000 electric loco shown inside.

(A) Original 10 25

Miniature folder: front panel is 3-7/16" wide x 6-1/4" high; folder opens to 13-7/8" wide x 12-3/8" high; full color, front panel shows 390E.

(A) Original 10 25

(B) Reproduction by T.T.O.S. 2 4

DIRECTIONS FOR THE USE AND CARE OF LIONEL TRAINS, 16 stapled pages, 6" wide x 9" high, adds 91 circuit breaker, Bohn Collection 2 5

LIONEL MAGAZINE: More details needed. Reportedly, very scarce and expensive.

1931

Consumer catalogue: 52 pages including covers; 11-1/2" x 8-1/2" horizontal format, four-color front cover on white. Radical change in cover layout; top of cover shows white and black sans-serif lettering within red rectangle: "LIONEL ELECTRIC TRAINS/The Trains That Railroad Men Buy For Their Boys". Cover shows engineer holding 400E loco for two boys dressed in white suits (looking as if they've just stepped out of a boys' choir). In the background is the gigantic valve gear and one driver of a New York Central 4-6-4 Hudson loco. At lower right is a red rectangle containing the black-printed legend "Just Like Mine" Says Bob Butterfield, Engineer of the 20th Century Limited. (See Page 3)". The first two pages contain sepia photos and testimonials from railroad men. Contents introduce several steam locos, including the huge 400E. There is a noticeable increase in the appeal to realism in this catalogue. Page 46 introduces the non-derailing 222 and 012 remote control switches. Page 48 shows new "silent track bed". Rear cover introduces issues of **The Lionel Magazine**, published every other month.

(A) Original 50 100

(B) 1973 black and white reproduction with color front cover by Bruce C. Greenberg. No reproduction markings 3 6

(C) 1975 full color reproduction by Iron Horse Productions. Marked as reproductions in gutter between pages 8 15

IT'S FUN TO BUILD YOUR OWN RAILROAD: 4 pages, 8-7/16" wide x 11" high, black and light orange ink on white paper, light orange ink used only for the border. Shows 9" x 16" Standard Gauge and 5-1/2" x 6" 0 Gauge Railroad. Shows new 94 High Tension Tower, new 99 Automatic Train Control (3 light head), and lists new 223 Standard non-derailing switches. Also shows many other accessory items. Weisblum comment.

(A) Original, Weisblum Collection 6 15

WINNER SALES FOLDER: 11-1/8" high x 8-1/2" wide but opens to 14-1/4" high. Four pages, black ink on white paper. Gives firm name and address as "WINNER TOY CORPORATION/15 EAST 26th STREET/NEW YORK CITY" but does not indicate that Winner has any relation with Lionel. Shows sets 1000, 1001, 1002 and 1003.

(A) Original, Weisblum Collection 13 25

Miniature folder: folded size, 2-13/16" wide x 5-3/4" high, unfolded 17-1/2" wide x 11-1/2" high, red and yellow front panel, "Oh Boy! HAVE THE FUN OF YOUR LIFE with LIONEL..." Shows new 396E Blue Comet set with 400E locomotive, new silent track bed, and the new **Lionel Magazine**. Weisblum Collection

(A) Original 7 25

INSTRUCTION BOOKLET/FOR THE USE AND CARE OF LIONEL: 6" wide x 9" high, 12 stapled pages, black ink on white paper. First use of "INSTRUCTION BOOKLET" in title, 92 Floodlight shown on page 10, "BILD-A-LOCO" motor on page 11. Quantity and date code, bottom of page 15 "8-3-110M". **Lionel Magazine** advertised on rear cover. Weisblum and Bohn Collections 2 7

1932

Consumer catalogue: 52 pages including covers; 11-1/2" x 8-1/2" format; four-color front cover has same logo as 1931 against robins'-egg blue background. Picture shows young boy in the cab of a thundering locomotive; this engine has been identified by Rev. Philip Smith as Reading G-1sa Pacific 134. Blue area with red border contains black print: "A Boy's Dream Come True". Red circle contains "$.10/A/COPY". Page 3 carries heading: "Take Your Dad Into Partnership - Make Him Your Pal". The "Pennsylvania Limited", pulled by a 392E steam loco, is introduced on page 23. It is outdone by the "20th Century Limited" shown on page 25. On page 24, the Milwaukee "Olympian" is introduced. Many new signaling accessories are introduced on pages 30-31. Miniature railroad figures appear for the first time on page 35. On page 47, a new 455 Roundhouse and a 441 Weighing Scale are introduced. The Lionel 455 electric range now appears on page 51, with the ironic line, "There's lots of fun in playing housewife." The rear cover is devoted to membership in the Lionel Engineer's Club.

Type I: As described above.

(A) Original 20 65

(B) 1975 full color reproduction by Greenberg Publishing Company, date added to lower right hand block by publisher 7 15

Type II: as above but with four page Winner insert included.

(A) Original 25 75

(B)1974 black and white reproduction with full color front cover on heavy stock by Bruce Greenberg 3 6

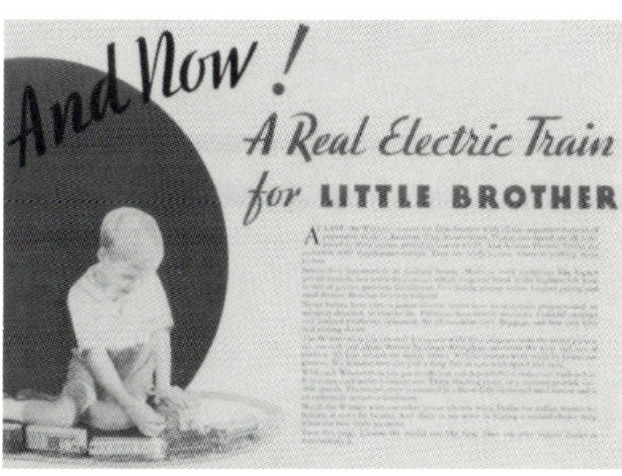

Reproduction of Winner consumer folder

WINNER consumer folder: 4 pages, 11-1/2" wide x 8-1/2" high; front cover is black and orange on gray background. Legend: "And Now! A Real Electric Train/For LITTLE BROTHER". Boy plays with Winner train against half-circle orange background.

(A) Original 5 15

(B) 1974 black and white reproduction by Greenberg Publishing Company 1 2

(C) Orange and black reproduction by Les Gordon 1 2

1933

Consumer catalogue: 52 pages including covers; 11-1/4" x 8-3/8" format; four-color front cover shows boy atop pedestrian bridge waving to engineer in a Pennsylvania K-4s Pacific steam loco 3759. Same logo as 1931 against red rectangle; zig-zag line lightning bolt added to emphasize "electric". Page 1 advertises Lionel radio program "True Railroad Adventures". Page 3 introduces the "Chugger" steam loco sound. Pages 1 to 10 done in monotone green on white paper; pages 11-42 are in color and pages 43-50 are in monotone. Pages 12-15 introduce the inexpensive Lionel-Ives mechanized and electric trains. Lionel downplays this tremendously significant development. Rear cover shows new Lionel speedboat.

Type I: As described above 30 75

Type II: Same as Type I, but National Recovery Act price increase information inserted in red-bordered block on page 11 and Pennsylvania Limited lettering and Keystone emblem added to page 24 30 75

(A) 1971 Xerox type reproduction by Bruce C. Greenberg, printed in Galesburg, Illinois at the Knox College Printing shop from an original lent by Rev. Robert Prendergast. Press run of 100 copies. Does not have a reproduction logo 1 2

(B) 1974 black and white reproduction by Bruce C. Greenberg. Printed in Columbia, Maryland by Bendix Field Engineering. Press run of 600 3 6

(C) 1975 full color reproduction by Greenberg Publishing Company. Printed by Barton and Cotton, Baltimore, Maryland. Reproduction logo on page 2 and at the bottom of some pages. Press run of 3000. The color separations were used in 1982 in producing Greenberg's Lionel Catalogues: Volume II. 1 2

1934

Consumer catalogue: 36 pages including covers, smaller 11-1/2" x 7-1/2" format. Same logo as 1931 in red rectangle; black and white lettering at top of page. Four-color cover shows father and son looking at Union Pacific M-10000 and steam freight passing through signal bridge against a navy blue background. Pages 8 and 9 show the re-named Ives electric sets as "Lionel Jr." Page 13 introduces the streamlined M-10000 and 072 Model Maker's Track. Mechanical trains and boats are described on pages 34-35. Back cover gives details of the **Lionel Magazine** and the Lionel Engineer's Club.

Type I: As described above

(A) Original; LIONEL TRAINS along top of cover 25 75

(B) 1971 Xerox type reproduction by Bruce C. Greenberg from original lent by Robert Prendergast. Printed at Knox College Print Shop, Galesburg, Illinois 1 1

(C) 1974 black and white reproduction with full color front cover by Bruce C. Greenberg. Reproduction information appears on page 2 in the upper left hand corner. The cover stock is heavier than the text pages and "1934" was added by the publisher to the upper right hand corner. 3 6

(D) 1975 full color reproduction by Greenberg Publishing Company. Reproduction information appears on the upper right hand corner of page 2 as well as on pages 4, 9, 12, 16, 17, 29, 32, 35. Date was added to the cover by the publisher. The negatives for this reproduction were used in printing Greenberg's Lionel Catalogues: Volume II. 7 15

Type II: Same as Type I, but logo and red rectangle at bottom of page. Reported but not confirmed. Reader comments invited.

English consumer catalogue: 9" wide x 6" high, 16 pages, black ink on white-coated stock; cover shows father and son constructing Standard Gauge layout. Railroad rolling stock and accessories are described by their English names.

(A) Original NRS

(B) 1970 reproduction by Max Knoecklein 2 4

1935

Consumer catalogue: 44 pages; 11-1/4" x 8-3/8" format. Four-color front cover shows "LIONEL TRAINS" in large block letters at top. An engineer points to a real Milwaukee Hiawatha loco as a boy holds his Lionel model up to compare it. At left in white is legend, "Announcing/The First/MODEL RAILROAD WHISTLE". Page 4 introduced the new DC-triggered whistle. Page 5 shows the new 0 Gauge Commodore Vanderbilt and Hiawatha streamlined steam locos. Great proliferation of 0 Gauge and decline of Standard Gauge is very evident in this catalogue. On page 18, the Standard "Washington Special" uses former Ives passenger cars. Automatic Gateman appears for the first time on page 31. Mickey Mouse circus train shown on page 40, as well as Santa and Mickey Mouse handcars. Other Mickey Mouse mechanical sets on page 42, and a second Lionel boat is on page 43. Rear cover devoted to the **Lionel Magazine** and the Lionel Engineer's Club.

Type I: One train set, 1535, on page 412, caption "With Brilliant Chromium Finish" beneath the locomotive, three red lines at the bottom and three at the top of page 4.

(A) Original, Prendergast Collection 30 100

(B) 1974 black and white reproduction by Bruce C. Greenberg with color front cover. There is a gray screen background on all other pages. Cover stock is the same weight as interior pages. No reproduction notice. 600 copies printed. Printed in Mason City, Illinois 3 6

Type II: One train on page 41, no caption beneath locomotive. Three red lines at the bottom and at the top of page 4.

(A) Original, Weisblum Collection 30 100

Type III: Three train sets on page 41: 1535, 1521 and 1523, red lines are missing from the top and bottom of page 4.

(A) Original 30 100

(B) 1975 full color reproduction by Iron Horse Productions. Reproduction logo found in center gutter 7 15

Instructions FOR ASSEMBLING AND OPERATING: 6" wide x 9" high, 32

pages plus covers, orange cover stock with blue ink, "STREAMLINER INSTRUCTIONS" for Flying Yankee and Union Pacific on page 19; advertisement for Lionel Engineer's Club on page 32.
(A) No date or quantity on page 32. Weisblum Collection 2 4
(B) "100M-8-35" on page 32, Weisblum Collection 2 4

REPLACEMENT PARTS FOR LIONEL TRAINS: 9" wide x 6" high, 32 pages including covers, black ink on white paper, rear cover lower right corner: "FORM NO...5M-11-35".
(A) Original, Weisblum Collection 3 7

At Last a Real Railroad Whistle: 4 pages, 8-1/2" wide x 11" high, red and black ink, shows 0 Gauge streamline trains, new automatic gateman, invites readers to write for 1935 consumer catalogues.
(A) Original NRS
(B) 1977 reproduction by T.T.O.S. Reprint notice on bottom of page 2 1 2

1936

Consumer catalogue: 11-1/4" x 8-1/2" format, 48 pages including covers. Four-color cover increases Lionel's appeal to realism. It shows large "LIONEL" white letters bordered in red against a blue-gray blueprint background. Precision instruments lie atop the full-page locomotive blueprint, and die-cast steam engine, the Pennsylvania "Torpedo" and a New York Central Hudson (a harbinger of what is to come in 1937) dominate the left and center of the cover. Pages 2 and 3 explain whistle and automatic reversing. Page 14 set is captioned "City of Denver", and rust-colored blocks next to Standard Gauge sets on page 20 are blank with no prices. Pennsylvania "Torpedo" introduced on page 5. Lionel Jr. trains are on pages 8-9. "Flying Yankee" streamliner introduced on page 12. Eight Standard Gauge sets remain. Solid "T" rails (Model Builder's Track) introduced on page 26. Page 43 relates details of magazine **The Model Engineer**. Mechanical trains, now with whistles, are on pages 45-46. Rear cover introduces Lionel airplane.

Type I: Page 14 "the LIONEL Union Pacific CITY OF DENVER" above train; page 20: blocks to left of locomotive are blank; page 3: "This catalogue is effective July 1, 1936..."
(A) Original, J. Smith Collection 50 100

Type II: page 14: "the/LIONEL/Union Pacific/CITY OF DENVER" above train; page 2: blocks to left of locomotives are numbered "No. 371W/WHISTLER/$32.50" and "No. 366W/WHISTLER/$30.00", page 3: "This catalog is effective July 1, 1936..."
(A) Original 30 75
(B) 1974 black and white reproduction with color front cover by Bruce C. Greenberg. Reproduction identification on page 2; cover stock is heavier weight paper than interior pages; date added to front cover by publisher 3 6

Type II: Page 14: "the/LIONEL/Union Pacific/OVERLAND" above train set; page 20: blocks to left of locomotives have set numbers and prices; page 33: 46 Automatic Grade Crossing does not appear.
(A) Original, Weisblum Collection 25 75
(B) 1974 full color reproduction by Greenberg Publishing Company. Date added to cover by publisher. The negatives were also used in producing Greenberg's Lionel Catalogues: Volume II. 7 15

Type IV: page 14: "the LIONEL Union Pacific OVERLAND" above train set; page 20: blocks to left of locomotives have set numbers and prices; page 33: Automatic Grade Crossing is present.
(A) Original 25 75

English consumer: 24 pages, 9-7/8" wide x 6-15/16" high, shows Hiawatha on cover and list address "LIONEL SERVICE DEPT./35/36, ALDERMANBURY, LONDON, E.C.2." Trains are priced in pounds, shillings, and pence with English rolling stock names. We do not know in what colors the catalogue was printed as we have only a Xerox-type copy. Shows several devices not appearing in U.S. version: a special transformer and a rotary convertor for changing DC current to AC. Foster Collection 20 60

INSTRUCTIONS for Assembling/and Operating: 32 pages plus covers, 6" wide x 8-7/8" high. Light blue cover stock printed in blue ink on front outside cover only. Page 32 at bottom: "PRINTED IN U.S. OF AMERICA-97M-8-36". Page 32 also carries introductory subscription offer for **Model Engineer**. Weisblum Collection 3 7

Model Engineer: a Lionel sponsored magazine apparently introduced in 1937. Its name changed to **Model Builder** in 1938. Reader comments and descriptions requested.

1937

Consumer catalogue: 11-1/4" x 8-3/8" format, 48 pages including covers. Front cover shows "LIONEL" in white lettering against rust background in upper right corner. To the left and beneath "LIONEL" are white outlines of locomotives against terra-cotta background. Entire remainder of cover has front 3/4 view of 5344 Hudson scale steam engine. Pages 2-3 give details of "Dispatcher Control". Pages 4 and 5 introduce 700EW Scale Hudson loco. Page 9 introduces 1668E PRR "Torpedo" six-driver 027 engine. Catalogue clearly divided into 027, 0, 072, and Standard sections. New 1121 switches for 027 shown on page 11 and page 30. The 636W City of Denver shown on page 16. The 763E Hudson appears on page 22; the magazine is on page 47, and the airplane is on page 48, the back cover. There are several different versions of this catalogue. We would appreciate reader assistance with the descriptions.

Type I: Page 39: white background, page 22: caption on the left bottom side of the page: "...through worn gears..."
(A) Original, Weisblum Collection 20 60
(B) 1975 full color reproduction by Greenberg Publishing Company. "1937" added to the upper right corner of the front cover. The negatives for this reproduction were used in printing Greenberg's Lionel Catalogues: Volume II. 7 15

LIONEL ADVANCE CATALOG/COMPLETE PRICE LIST/1937 DEALER DISPLAYS: 10-1/8" wide x 7-1/2" high, 28 pages, black ink on off-white stock. Includes dealer displays: 930 Accessory Stand, 7 Display, 3 plane mural (each 4" x 13") Lionel Trains conductor. Also shows net (dealer cost) price for 1100 Mickey Mouse, dozen $7.50; 1105 Santa Claus, dozen $7.20 and 1107 Donald Duck, dozen $8.40.
(A) Original, Weisblum Collection 50 100

INSTRUCTIONS FOR ASSEMBLING/AND OPERATING: 32 pages plus covers, 5-7/8" wide x 8-5/8" high. Light tan cover stock printed in brown ink on front outside cover only. Page 32 at bottom on right: "No. 267E-1-100X-1-8-37". Compared to 1936 book printing quantities rose from 97,000 to 100,000, a reflection of slowly returning prosperity. Page 32 also offers subscriptions to **Model Builder** which replaced **Model Engineer**. We would appreciate a reader comparison of annual text charges in these instruction booklets. Weisblum Collection 3 7

LIONEL TRACK LAYOUTS: 8-1/2" wide x 5-1/2" high, 24 pages, black and blue ink on white paper; cover shows boiler front of 5344 surrounded by a circle of track.
(A) Original, Weisblum and I. D. Smith Collections 3 7

LIONEL HUDSON 5344 J-1E: 8" wide x 5-3/8" high, 16 pages printed in blue and black ink on white paper, introduces scale Hudson.
(A) Original, Weisblum Collection 5 10
(B) Reproduction 2 5

Model Builder: bimonthly magazine in 1937 that was successor to **Model Engineer**. Reader comments describing the issues would be appreciated.

LIONEL TRAINS: 10-1/2" wide x 7-1/2" high, 24 pages, black ink on pulp paper which has yellowed and dried out. Slightly reduced size and substantially edited version of consumer catalogue.
(A) Original, Weisblum Collection 3 7
(B) T.T.O.S. reproduction on coated stock, lettered "A GENUINE/T.T.O.S./REPRINT" on lower right front cover 2 4

1938

Consumer catalogue: 11-1/2" x 8-1/2" format, 52 pages including covers; front cover has very large "LIONEL" in red and white against sky blue background. An array of 0 Gauge locomotives emerges from between the letters, while the Lionel plane executes a loop above them. On the most common version, prices are printed for each entry. Pages 2 and 3 illustrate new electric remote controls for uncoupling new automatic box couplers, loading and unloading. Pages 6 and 7 introduce 00 Gauge. Page 4 shows new 1664E locomotive. Also new in 0 Gauge are 1666E, 224E, 225E and 226E. Pages 21 and 22 include special tear-out note from son to father, a classic example of Lionel's marketing prowess. Center foldout for accessories and track layout plans. New 97 coal elevator and 3659-3859 automatic coal cars on page 39. Electric couplers on passenger cars described on page 40.

Automatic flagman introduced on page 45. Lionel airplane on rear cover.

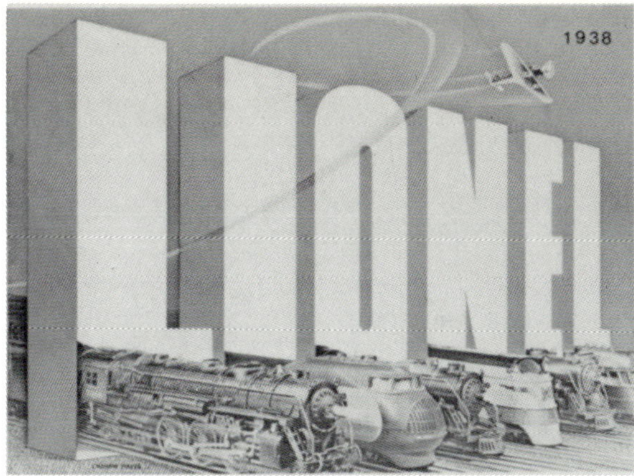

Reproduction of 1938 with date added to cover.

Type I: As described above.
(A) Original, Weisblum Collection 20 50
(B) 1974 black and white reproduction with full color front cover by Bruce Greenberg. Cover is printed on heavier stock and has date added to the cover for user identification. Reproduction logo on inside front cover. 600 copies. Printed by Bendix Field Engineering, Columbia, Maryland. Subsequently 100 copies were used in a special hardback book: **Lionel Catalogue Reproductions: 1938-1942** by Greenberg Publishing Company. Price for a single catalogue only 3 6
(B) 1975 full color reproduction by Greenberg Publishing Company. Date added to cover. Negatives subsequently used in printing Greenberg's Lionel Catalogues: Volume II. Price only for single catalogue 7 15

Type II: Same as Type I, but with new page "CANADIAN RETAIL PRICE LIST 1938" glued to inside rear cover. Weisblum Collection 25 60

Type III: Same as Type I but with 6-15/16" wide x 3-7/16" high white paper insert "NOTICE OF CHANGE IN PRICES" glued to inside rear cover. Weisblum Collection 25 60

INSTRUCTIONS FOR/Assembling LIONEL NO. 700KW: 24 pages, (although numbered only to 22), 7" wide x 9-1/2" high, black ink on white paper, inside front cover at bottom: "Form No. 700K-75X-7-38".
(A) Original, Weisblum Collection 3 9
(B) 1977 reproduction by Greenberg Publishing Company, 6-11/16" wide x 9-7/16" high. Reproduction notices on front and rear covers 2 2.50
(C) Reproduction by Harry Gordon, 7" wide x 9-1/2" high, marked "REPRINT" on front cover 2 2.50
(D) Reproduction by Dan Moss, 5-1/2" wide x 8-1/2" high, marked "Reprint by/Dan Moss" with rubber-stamp on rear cover 1 2
(E) Reproduction by Bruce Greenberg, 5-1/2" wide x 8-1/2" high 1 2

HOW TO BUILD A MODEL RAILROAD: 32 pages plus covers, 5-15/16" wide x 9" high, orange cover stock printed with blue ink on both outside front and rear covers. This marks the first use of this famous Lionel color scheme on an instruction booklet. This booklet also has a different name from those immediately before and after it, as well as the booklet that follows. Lower rear cover: "1B-100M-10-38". Weisblum and I. D. Smith Collections 3 7

Instructions FOR ASSEMBLING/AND OPERATING: 32 pages plus covers but text pages numbered 3-33 (with 34 as unnumbered). 5-13/16" wide x 8-5/8" high, gray cover stock printed with blue ink on front outside cover only. Page 34 lower right corner: "Part No. 267E-1-110X-10-36-TT". We assume that 110X stands for 110,000 copies. We do not know what "TT" represents. Weisblum Collection 3 7

1939

Consumer catalogue: 52 pages including covers, 10-3/4" x 8-3/8" format; front cover in red with large gunmetal blue rectangle bordered by white line. "BUILT BY/LIONEL" in white inside rectangle. Designe patterned after steam locomotive builder's plate. Lower right part of cover shows 700E Hudson in three-quarter, fireman's side view. -Use of electric remote control couplers universal except in lowest-price 027 series sets. Scale and semi-scale 708, 227 and 228 locos appear on pages 20 and 21. Scale Hudson kit shown on page 25. New two-rail 00 sets introduced on pages 26-29. Standard Gauge sets appear for the last time on pages 30-31. Dial-type rheostat transformers introduced on pages 36 and 37. Rear cover gives details of free "Locoscope" with subscription to **Model Builder** magazine.

Type I: on page 49 captions beneath 56 and 57 lamp posts illustrations are reversed.
(A) Original, Weisblum Collection 25 60
(B) 1973 Xerox type black and white reproduction by Bruce Greenberg 1 2
(C) 1974 black and white reproduction with full color front cover printed on heavier stock by Bruce Greenberg. No reproduction logo but "1939" added by publisher to upper right hand corner of front cover. Printed by Bendix Field Engineering, Columbia, Maryland. Press run, 600 31 62
(D) 1975 full color reproduction by Greenberg Publishing Company. Date on cover added; slightly reduced in size from original. Color separations and printing by Barton and Cotton, Baltimore 7 15

Type II: Captions on page 49 are corrected.
(A) Original 30 75

INSTRUCTIONS/FOR ASSEMBLING AND OPERATING/LIONEL TRAINS: 5-15/16" wide x 8-7/8" high, 40 pages plus covers, gold cover stock printed with brown ink on front outside cover only, white text pages with black ink; lower right side of page 40: "Form No. 267E-1-75X 10-39 TT".
(A) Original, Weisblum Collection 2 5

1940

Consumer catalogue: 52 pages including covers, 10-3/4" x 8-3/8" format; front cover in red with large gunmetal blue rectangle bordered by white line. "BUILT BY/LIONEL" in white inside rectangle. Design patterned after steam locomotive builder's plate. Lower right part of cover shows 700E Hudson in three-quarter, fireman's side view. Use of electric remote control couplers universal except in lowest priced 027 series sets. Scale and semi-scale 708, 227 and 228 locos appear on pages 20 and 21. Scale Hudson kit shown on page 25. New two-rail 00 sets introduced on pages 26-29. Standard Gauge sets appear for the last time on pages 30-31. Dial-type rheostat transformers introduced on pages 36 and 37. Rear cover gives details of free "Locoscope" with subscription to **Model Builder** magazine. 53. The 313 Bascule Bridge appears for the first time on page 56. The back cover shows an old 5 locomotive against the legend "40 YEARS of Leadership!"

Type I: With all white "LIONEL" letters on cover; page 20 caption beneath bottom train set describes 2651 lumber car as automatic unloading. The car did not have this feature.
(A) Original, Weisblum Collection 50 100

Type II: Red "LIONEL" letters edged in white on front cover; same caption error on page 20 as Type I.
(A) Original, Weisblum Collection 25 75
(B) 1975 full color reproduction by Greenberg Publishing Company. Color separations and printing by Barton and Cotton, Baltimore, Maryland. Reproduced slightly smaller than original; date on cover added by publisher; reproduction logo on page 64 9 15

Type III: Red "LIONEL" letters edged in white on front cover; caption error corrected by removing caption.
(A) Original, Weisblum Collection 25 75
(B) 1975 black and white reproduction with full color front cover by Bruce Greenberg. Date on cover added by publisher. Printed by Bendix Field Engineering, Columbia, Maryland; press run of 600. 100 copies of 1940 were used in producing limited edition book **LIONEL CATALOGUE REPRODUCTIONS: 1938-1942** by Greenberg Publishing Company 3 6

Advance Catalogue: Same as Type I consumer catalogue but printed on heavy stock with metal spiral binding and heavy cloth covered board covers. Contains additional pages 65-80 with dealer displays and pricing information. Weisblum Collection 75 150

Instructions FOR ASSEMBLING AND OPERATING: 48 pages plus covers, 5-9/16" wide x 8-9/16" high. Light tan cover stock printed in brown ink on front outside cover only. Unnumbered page 2 lists three Lionel addresses: Irvington, Chicago and San Francisco. Page 5 carries copyright notice and 1940 date. Pages 43-48 list "APPROVED SERVICE STATIONS". Reprinted in 40-page edition in 1942, I. D. Smith comment. Weisblum Collection 3 7

1941

Consumer catalogue: 11-1/4" x 7-3/8" format; 64 pages including covers. Front cover: medium blue background, stripes at top in red-white-red pattern, single row of small white stars, large "LIONEL" in ribbed light yellow letters. Appeals to patriotism increased as World War II loomed. Below "LIONEL" in red in one line: "ELECTRIC TRAINS FOR THE YOUTH OF AMERICA". Lower left shows mid to front boiler of 700E Hudson; lower right has Navy shield in white rectangle and legend below it: "PRECISION INSTRUMENTS/for the/UNITED STATES NAVY". First six pages extol realistic operation; page 3 has pictures of real layouts. New 2642-2643 passenger cars in set 838W on page 15. New 2758, 2755 and 2757 freight cars in set 865B on page 17. Set 846W on page 19 shows new "Irvington" and "Manhattan" passenger cars. "Teledyne Couplers" explained on page 24. 165 Gantry Crane appears on page 55. Chem-Lab Chemistry sets are introduced on pages 61 through 63. Rear cover devoted to **Model Builder** magazine and 192-page **Handbook For Model Builders.**

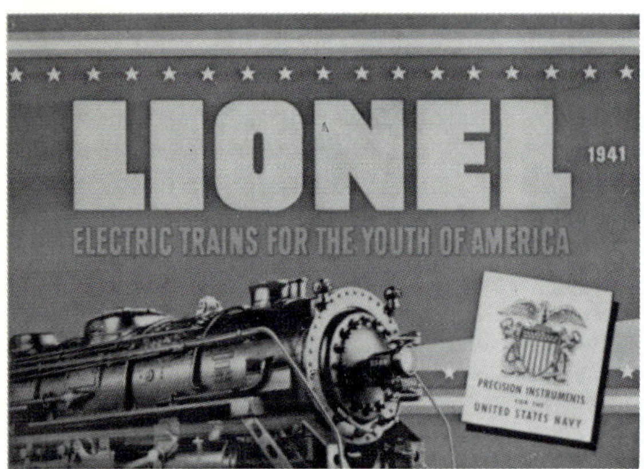

Reproduction of 1941 with date added to cover.

Type I: As described above
(A) Original, Weisblum and I. D. Smith Collections 25 75
(B) 1974 black and white reproduction by Bruce Greenberg with full color front cover printed on heavier stock. Date added to the cover to aid user identification. Printed by Bendix Field Engineering, Columbia, Maryland. 600 were printed and 100 of these were used in LIONEL CATALOGUE REPRODUCTIONS: 1938-42, a limited edition hardback. 2 6
(C) 1975 full color reproduction by Greenberg Publishing Company; reproduction logo on page 2, date added to cover; color separation negatives and printing by Barton and Cotton, Baltimore; press run of 3000. Negatives subsequently used in printing Greenberg's Lionel Catalogues: Volume II 7 15

Type II: Same as Type I, but yellow "LIONEL" letters are edged in black. Reported but not confirmed. Reader reports requested.

LIONEL CHEM-LAB: 8-1/2" wide x 11" high, 4 pages, red and black ink on heavy white coated stock. Brochure intended for dealers, rear cover reports: "A NATION-WIDE/ADVERTISING/CAMPAIGN/PLUS STORE HELPS". Weisblum Collection 5 15

1942

Consumer catalogue: 11" x 8-1/2" format; 32 pages including covers. Front cover has red, white and blue American flag design with white "LIONEL TRAINS" lettering where stars would be on blue field. The 700E Hudson goes across entire lower third of cover. Page 2 details Lionel's war contracts for the Navy - "LIONEL GOES TO SEA" in white on blue banner at top of page. On page 3 in small agate type, consumer is told that many trains will be in short supply due to exigencies of national defense. Train sets greatly reduced throughout catalogue. Chem-Lab sets from pages 29-31. Rear cover offers free scale 0 Gauge engine house with subscription to **Model Builder** magazine. (This locomotive shed was modeled after the PRR engine house in Mt. Carbon, PA.) Value of original 10 30

Type I: As described above
(A) 1974 black and white reproduction with full color front cover by Bruce Greenberg. Cover printed on heavier stock; date added to lower right cover. Reproduction logo inside front cover, lower left corner. 600 copies printed by Bendix Field Engineering. 2 6
(B) 1983 full color reproduction as part of Greenberg's Lionel Catalogues: Volume II. This was not published separately.

1943

LIONEL Wonder Book OF RAILROADING: 48 pages plus cover, not paginated, 8-3/8" wide x 11-3/8" high, color front and rear cover with drawing of 5344 front end. Consumer planning book, trains not offered for sale in this book. Contents also include "WILL TRAINS OF THE FUTURE LOOK LIKE THIS?" "WHAT MAKES A LOCOMOTIVE GO?" "LANGUAGE OF THE RAILS" "100,000 FOR A MODEL" "ALBUM OF ENGINE PORTRAITS". It also includes pictures of the Lionel showroom layout which included an 840 power house and 129 terrace. Bryan Collection 5 15

1944

LIONEL RAILROAD Planning Book: 6-1/16" x 9", four-color front cover, red and black interior pages, 40 pages plus covers; illustrates prewar equipment in layout settings, designed to keep children interested in trains during production hiatus of World War II, copyright 1944, Piker Collection 2 5

Two Standard Gauge billboards from the Larry Battley Collection. The billboards are printed on heavy card stock and measure 6-1/4" from the base to the top of "General Outdoor Adv. Co." on the top. The width of the sign itself (not including the foliage at the bottom) is 9-1/4". We do not know when these were made nor how they were distributed.

Reading locomotive 134 taken by Harold K. Vollrath on May 9, 1940. Photograph courtesy of Mr. Vollrath.

THE UNUSUAL CAREER OF NO. 134

by Rev. Philip Smith

In 1924, the Baldwin Locomotive Works in Philadelphia completed an order for five Reading G-lsa Pacifics (4-6-2), Nos. 130-134. Later that year, a full-sized replica of No. 134, constructed almost entirely of wood, was placed on the boardwalk at Atlantic City for a Miss America Pageant. It must have been built by railroad carpenters, for no casual crew could have matched the detail. Everything was fashioned according to blueprint specifications. In addition to obvious features like the Reading-style tender, cab, wide Wootten firebox, and round number plate, that replica sported classification lights, full Walschaerts valve gear with power reverse, a superheater damper control, tall spoked drivers in the "rods down" position, matching spoked pilot wheels, a front coupler, and air and signal hoses. A photograph of this replica appears on page 157 of **The Collector's Book of the Locomotive** by Edwin P. Alexander. The one clue to its origin is the air tank above the boiler-tube pilot. That was part of an automatic train-stop used only on the Reading's "Boardwalk Flyers" between Camden and Atlantic City. Since they roared along at 80 miles an hour, a collision would have been disastrous. To avoid that, an automatic brake system was installed on those seashore locomotives. If an engineer passed a red signal, the brakes would take hold automatically and stop the train. On the replica, that was a professional detail. It's likely that the Reading built the replica and put it on display to attract attention to its passenger trains. It's like the STP emblems that pit crews put on race cars, except on a grander scale. Furthermore, such a publicity coup would have also been intended to put Reading's arch rival for the seashore traffic - the Pennsylvania Railroad - in its place.

Eight years later, in 1932, a vast firebox dominated the cover of the Lionel catalogue. Its jutting, curving flank gleamed golden in the sun. Subtle streaks of color gave the impression of roaring speed, awesome power. The wire mesh running board in front of the cab was drawn on the upper flank of a wide Wootten firebox — a Reading characteristic. Numbers beneath the arm of the dauntless boy engineer are nearly invisible, but

they seem to be 134 in the Reading style.

Lionel published a photograph of No. 134 in two subsequent catalogues: 1936 (p. 20) and 1937 (p. 24). Thundering up from the lower right corner, black smoke billowing up the page, No. 134 thrusts her smokebox at Lionel's readers. Clearly visible is a new rectangular number plate beneath the headlight, plus a glimpse of the fireman's side of her boiler. To the right of her stack is Lionel's proclamation: POWERFUL/MASSIVE/ENGINES. In both catalogues, No. 134 shared the page with a freight set (No. 377W) and a passenger set (No. 366W) headed by Standard Gauge steamer No. 1835E.

After World War II, steam locomotives gradually gave way to diesels. On the Reading, a landmark date came about on May 6, 1952. On that cool Tuesday morning, steam was necessary to provide heat for the coaches on a local passenger train from Newtown to Reading Terminal, Philadelphia (28 miles). A diesel with a steam generator was not available, so a steam locomotive was called to duty. That turned out to be the Reading's last regularly scheduled steam passenger train. The locomotive? No. 134.

About that time, a full front view of No. 134 thundering around a curve with a Reading passenger train was used to illustrate the "Railroad" heading in the **World Book Encyclopedia**.

In 1976, Bruce Greenberg published with M. Klein an operator's guide to Lionel trains. The **World Book Encyclopedia** photo of No. 134 appeared again, expanded to a full page.

Most recently, that same picture gave an authentic touch to the cover of a Johnny Cash album, **Songs of Trains and Rivers**.

Appendix

10 And 100 Series Trucks

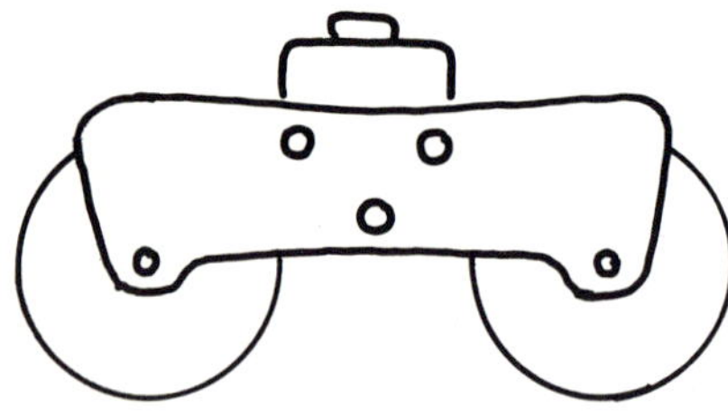

10 Series, Type I
200, 500 And Six Wheel Standard Trucks

10 Series, Type II
Has open side frame, three rivets, cutout bolster and embossed springs

10 Series, Type III, Large Hole Eyelet
Notice open side frame, cutout bolster and embossed spring

10 Series, Type IV
Type IV also has an open side frame, but has embossed rivets and springs and may have a hollow or large hole eyelet

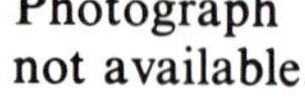
Photograph
not available.

100 Series Type I

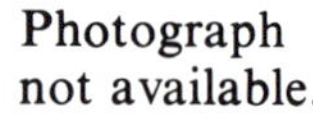
Photograph
not available.

100 Series Type II

100 Series, Type III
For Freight Cars: solid side frame, with embossed rivets and springs and a hollow rivet rounded end bolster

Photograph
not available.

100 Series Type IV
Same as Type V but nickel

100 Series, Type V
Same as Type IV, but black; used on 100 Series Freights

200, 500 & Six-Wheel Standard Trucks

200 Series Truck

Embossed side frame, rectangular cutouts, with journal boxes.

500 Series, Late, for Freight Cars

Embossed springs on side frame, with reinforcing (bolster) bar instead of cutout slots and bright journals (1927-40)

500 Series, Early, for Freight Cars

Embossed springs on side frames, cutout slots in frame, with black journals (1927-40)

Six-Wheel Truck

Used on 392 Tender

INDEX